# THE LAST GREAT MUSLIM EMPIRES

# The Last Great Muslim Empires

## History of the Muslim World

with contributions by
H. J. KISSLING • F. R.C. BAGLEY
N. BARBOUR • J.S. TRIMINGHAM
H. BRAUN • B. SPULER • H. HÄRTEL

translations and adaptations by
F. R.C. BAGLEY

introduction by
RICHARD M. EATON

**Markus Wiener Publishers**
**Princeton**

For information write to: Markus Wiener Publishers
114 Jefferson Road, Princeton, NJ 08540

**Library of Congress Cataloging-in-Publication Data**

Hans J. Kissling, et. al.
[Geschichte der islamischen Länder. English]
History of the Muslim world/Hans J. Kissling: with a new introduction by Richard M. Eaton.
Vol. [1] has new introduction by Jane Hathaway.
Vol. [2] has new introduction by Arthur Waldron.
Vol. [3] has new introduction by Richard M. Eaton.
Previously published:The Muslim World. Leiden: E.J. Brill, 1960-<1969 >
Includes bibliographical references and indexes.
ISBN 1-55876-095-4 (v.1)
ISBN 1-55876-079-2 (v. 2)
ISBN 1-55876-112-8 (v. 3)
1. Islamic Empire—History. I. Title.
DS35.63S68 1994 94-11585
909'.097671—dc20 CIP

Printed in the United States of America on acid-free paper.

CONTENTS

# TRANSLATOR'S PREFACE

*Neuzeit* ("Modern Times"), the third part of the *Geschichte der islamischen Länder* in the *Handbuch der Orientalistik* (Abteilung I, Band VI, Abschnitt 3), was published by Messrs. E. J. Brill in 1959. Six scholars contributed to the work, as follows:

H. J. KISSLING, The Ottoman Empire to 1774.

H. SCHEEL, Ottoman History from 1774 to 1918.

G. JÄSCHKE, Turkey since the Armistice of Mudros.

H. BRAUN, History of Iran since 1500.

E. KLINGMÜLLER, The Arab World in Modern Times; and Egypt since 1799.

H. HÄRTEL, History of India since 1525.

The range in time and space covered within the 292 pages of *Neuzeit* is thus very wide, though not inclusive of some important regions of the Muslim World.

An English translation of *Neuzeit* seemed likely to be even more useful if it could be accompanied by additional chapters on these regions. For Central Asia, Professor BERTOLD SPULER kindly agreed that I might translate part of his *Geschichte Mittelasiens seit dem Auftreten der Türken*, which is a component of K. JETTMAR, H. W. HAUSSIG, B. SPULER and L. PETECH, *Geschichte Mittelasiens*, Leiden 1966 (*Handbuch der Orientalistik*, Abteilung I, Band V, Abschnitt 5). Mr. NEVILL BARBOUR kindly wrote a chapter on North West Africa from the 16th century to the present day. The Rev. J. SPENCER TRIMINGHAM kindly lent me his drafts of two unpublished articles on Islam in Sub-Saharan Africa, and I reworked them into a chapter for this book. There also seemed to be a need for a chapter on Egypt and the Eastern Arab World in the first three centuries of the Ottoman period, and I have ventured despite lack of adequate knowledge to write it. Most unfortunately Professor G. W. J. DREWES, who had kindly offered to contribute a chapter on Indonesia and Malaysia, was obliged to withdraw.

The inclusion of these additional chapters made the work too long for one volume. I have therefore split it chronologically into two volumes, with the dividing line at the end of the 18th century or the commencement of European occupation, and have called the third part "The Last Great Muslim Empires". It is hoped that a contribution on Indonesia will be obtainable for the fourth part.

The split into two volumes has necessitated division and renaming of Dr. BRAUN's, Professor HÄRTEL's, and Mr. BARBOUR's chapters, and extraction of excerpts from Professor SPULER's work (pp. 226–265 and 288–289 in the *Geschichte Mittelasiens*). A small amount of textual adaptation has also been necessary. Furthermore, in translating the German contributions, I have on occasion slightly amplified the original texts, which on account of space limitations in *Neuzeit* were written in somewhat condensed form. All the contributors kindly read my typescripts and made corrections, which I have incorporated; but in so far as I have modified or added to what they originally wrote, I and not they bear responsibility for what now appears. I am also responsible for any clerical and proof-reading errors.

Transliteration has presented the usual problems, and while generally aiming to keep it consistent, I have often preferred that it should be natural. For Professor KISSLING's chapter I have used modern Turkish spelling with a few modifications; in this chapter only, *C* in Turkish words corresponds to the English *J*, *Ç* to *Ch*, and *Ş* to *Sh*, while *ɨ* represents the undotted Turkish *I*, and *D* sometimes stands for the Turkish *T* (e.g. *Murad* for *Murat*). For Dr. BRAUN's chapter I have used slightly modified Arabic-style transliteration rather than modern Persian transliteration. Mr. BARBOUR has frequently used current French transliteration, but has also given Arabic-style spellings of important names. Different spellings of many names, with cross-references in some cases, are given in the index. It is hoped that this may facilitate reference to other works, even though many of them, such as the *Encyclopaedia of Islam*, use an international system of transliteration which differs from English systems, notably in replacing *Ch* by *Č*, *J* by *Dj*, and *Q* by *Ḳ*.

The bibliographies at the end of every chapter for the most part include only Western and translated works. Guidance to source materials may be found in the bibliographies attached to many articles in the *Encyclopaedia of Islam* and the Turkish *İslâm Ansiklopedisi*, and in works such as C. A. STOREY's *Persian Literature*, C. BROCKELMANN's *Geschichte der arabischen Litteratur*, and F. BABINGER's *Die Geschichtschreiber der Osmanen*.

Mr. BARBOUR and Dr. BRAUN prepared the genealogical trees for their chapters, and I prepared those of the Ottomans and the Moghols. For trees and lists of other dynasties, reference may be made to C. E. BOSWORTH, *The Islamic Dynasties*, Edinburgh 1967; B. SPULER, *Regenten und Regierungen der Welt*, 2 vols., Würzburg 1962/64, with *Nachtrag* 1965; and E. DE ZAMBAUR, *Manuel de généalogie et de chronologie pour l'histoire de l'Islam*, Hanover 1927.

After some effort and expenditure of time, I gave up the attempt to provide maps for this part. A good modern atlas will be found useful, in addition to historical atlases, e.g. WESTERMANNS *Atlas zur Weltgeschichte,* Brunswick 1963 (especially for the Ottoman empire), and R. ROOLVINK, *Historical Atlas of the Muslim Peoples,* Amsterdam 1957 (for outlines of frontier changes).

F. R. C. BAGLEY

# INTRODUCTION
## BY RICHARD M. EATON

Several currents in recent Euro-American history-writing have inclined scholars to see Islamic history as a useful entry to world history. One of these has been the renaissance in writing about Islam itself, as historians have sought to free the study of Islam and Islamic civilization from the grip of the Orientalist school, which dominated the nineteenth and early twentieth centuries during Europe's imperial age. Whereas Orientalists tended to isolate Islam from history's "mainstream" or to treat it as Europe's long-term significant "Other," recent historians have sought instead to integrate Islamic history into ever larger frameworks of analysis. In the 1960s Marshall Hodgson argued that the only geographical framework large enough to comprehend the "venture of Islam," as he put it, was the entire Eurasian belt from Spain through China. Today, most Islamicists would expand that to include the entire globe.

In a separate current, the 1980s and 1990s witnessed the appearance—more accurately, a revival—of world history as a major subfield in the history profession. Students of world history naturally sought units of analysis that would move beyond the study of particular nations, continents, or cultures. The history of Islam and of Muslim peoples became especially suitable for this purpose, since historically, it was Muslims who had created the very first world civilization. From the seventh to the seventeenth century, all the major civilizations of the Old World—Greco-Roman, Irano-Semitic, Sanskritic, Malay-Javanese, and Chinese—were for the first time brought into contact with one another through the medium of, and within the framework of, this single overarching civilization that had evolved out of a relatively parochial Arab cult. What is more, Muslims synthesized elements from other civilizations (especially the Greek, Persian, and Indian) and added them to their Arabian heritage to evolve a distinctive civilization that proved one of the most vital and durable the world has ever seen. How did this happen, and why is it relevant to students of history today?

Very early in the Islamic venture, Arabs found themselves ruling over a plurality of autonomous and self-regulating religious communities—Greek Orthodox Christians, Monophysites, Nestorians, Copts, Zoroastrians, Manichaeans, Jews—as well as a plurality of linguistic and literary traditions that included Greek, Coptic, Syriac, Armenian, Middle Persian, and various dialects of Aramaic. In forging an independent "Islamic" identity amidst these older religious communities, Muslims faced a momentous choice: either they could constitute themselves as one more autonomous community on the model of those they found among their subjects, thereby preserving "Allah" as an Arab deity, "Islam" as an Arab cult, and Arabic as the language of the ruling class; or, they could try to bring all these diverse communities and traditions together into a new cultural synthesis. During the initial decades after their conquest of the Fertile Crescent and Egypt, Muslim rulers generally opted for the former alternative, and Islam briefly became the proud emblem of the Arab ruling élite. But by the eighth century, convinced of the political imprudence of a tiny ethnic minority ruling indefinitely over an enormous non-Muslim majority, the Caliphs openly encouraged their non-Arab subjects to convert. Henceforth the Arabic language and the Islamic religion would provide a sense of civilizational coherence by uniting hitherto separate religious and linguistic communities into a single ethno-religious identity, initially transcending and ultimately supplanting all other such identities. It was because Muslims chose this second option that Islam became a world civilization, and not just one more parochial, ethnic cult amidst a sea of other cults or sects. It is clear, moreover, that Muslims saw themselves as playing this unifying role, as we see from the Qur'an's passages (e.g. 4:170-71) exhorting Jews and Christians to set aside their differences and to return to the pure, unadulterated monotheism of Abraham, their common spiritual ancestor.

Islamic history feeds into world history in still other ways. Islamic civilization became a global phenomenon, for example, in its capacity to receive and absorb culture from one end of the world and then pass it on to other parts of the world. One sees this in thc rapid movement, within the Islamic world, of paper-making or irrigation technology, of herbs and agricultural crops, or of scientific knowledge, especially mathematics, astronomy, and medicine. Demographically, too, Islam became a global reality. Although the religion is stereotypically identified as peculiarly and especially Middle Eastern, the worldwide distribution of the world's one billion Muslims—more than two-thirds of whom live *outside* the Middle East—tells quite a different story. Furthermore, over four-fifths of the world's Muslims are non-Arabs, with the majority of the worldwide community living in monsoon Asia, not the Middle East (Indonesia is the largest Muslim country in the world, followed by Pakistan, Bangladesh, and India).

The study of Islam has also opened up to students of world history a good many themes and processes suitable for cross-cultural comparisons. One of these is religious conversion. Since no continent has remained uninfluenced by Islam, which is today the world's fastest growing religion, historians of Islam are in a unique position to compare Islamization with other kinds of culture change. Moreover, conversion to Islam is no longer understood, as it once was, exclusively in terms of the *expansion* of something, implying imposition, which in turn suggests the old European stereotype of Islamic militancy; but rather in terms of the *assimilation* of something. In other words, instead of adopting the perspective of one standing in Mecca, looking out upon an ever-widening, ever-expanding religious tide that is uniform and monolithic, one instead adopts the perspective of receivers who, standing in a remote and dusty village, incorporate into their existing religious system elements considered useful or meaningful that drift in from beyond the ocean, from over the mountains, or simply from the neighboring village. This shift in perspective has dramatically changed the way in which scholars think not only about Islam, but about the dynamics of religious change generally.

Islamic history is also relevant to world history with respect to "world systems theory." As conventionally understood, this theory concerns the expansion of economic networks, especially capitalist networks, that historically cut across political boundaries in efforts to incorporate peoples into expanding structures of production and consumption. But historians of Islam are beginning to realize that in the post-thirteenth century period Muslims also constructed a "world system," though one radically different from that modeled on *homo oeconomicus*. It was, rather, a world system linking men and women through informal networks of scholars and saints, and built upon shared understandings of how to see the world and structure one's relationship to it. Above all, it was a world system constructed around a book, the Qur'an, and consisting of humanity's attempt to respond to its message by fulfilling both its external project of building a righteous social order and its internal project of drawing humans nearer their Maker.

Nowhere is this Islamic "world system" more vividly captured than in the genre of travel literature that emerged after the thirteenth century. The Qur'an itself enjoins its community to "Journey in the land, then behold how He originated creation" (29:20). From the earliest days of Islam, pious Muslims followed this injunction quite literally; indeed the tradition of peripatetic scholars and saints is traceable in part to this verse. In the fourteenth and fifteenth centuries yet another purpose for "journeying in the land" appeared when increased European demand for spices and Mongol disruptions of overland routes triggered trade diasporas throughout the Indian Ocean and Sahara Desert. For both pious and commercial reasons, Muslims during these two centuries began moving through the known world in unprecedented numbers. They also recorded their experiences.

One of the most famous works in this genre is the memoir of Ibn Battuta (d. 1368-69), the fourteenth century cosmopolitan Moroccan who was at once pilgrim, judge, scholar, devotee of Sufism, and ambassador. Although he is often dubbed the "Marco Polo of the Muslim world," the comparison is badly misleading. Having for thirty years criss-crossed North and West Africa, the Middle East, the steppes of Central Asia, India, Southeast Asia and China, for an estimated total of 73,000 miles, Ibn Battuta traveled much further and visited many more places than did his Venetian counterpart. The two travelers differed most profoundly, however, in their relationship to the societies they visited. Marco Polo, who died the year before Ibn Battuta embarked from Morocco in 1325, had been a stranger everywhere he went, and he knew it. Indeed, his fame derives from his having introduced Europe, which in the thirteenth century was just emerging from being a global backwater, to a fabulous but utterly alien world of which it had only the haziest impressions. On the other hand Ibn Battuta, in his intercontinental wanderings, moved through a single cultural universe in which he was utterly at home. Most of his travels took place within the Islamic world, and everywhere he went he found the civilized company of merchants, scholars, Sufis, or princes. With them he would converse, in Arabic, on topics ranging from mysticism to jurisprudence, and especially on events taking place elsewhere in the Muslim world. Overall, his book conveys a self-assured tone in which the civilizational coherence of Islam, from Spain to China, was not even an issue. It was simply taken for granted. In short, if Ibn Battuta intuitively understood that the Muslim world of his day constituted a truly global civilization, even a "world system" of sorts, it has taken Western historians some considerable time to understand it as such.

It is here that we can appreciate the work of the German scholar Bertold Spuler (1911-1990), whose career bridged the twilight of the age of Orientalist scholarship and the rise of both world history and what one might call "the new Islamic social history." Like his near-contemporary Marshall Hodgson, Prof. Spuler understood Islamic history as embracing far more than the Middle East; indeed he saw it as a subset of world history. His trilogy of works on Islam, recently republished in paperback as *The Age of the Caliphs*, *The Mongol Period*, and the present volume, *The Last Great Muslim Empires*, constitutes something of a milestone in both world history and Islamic history, for it was Prof. Spuler who more than anyone else constantly forced us to stretch our conception of the Islamic World northward and eastward so as to include Central Asia. Whereas this comes through most vividly in his celebrated work on the Mongols (the subject of volume two), it is foreshadowed in his work on the later `Abbasids (in volume one), as well as in his contribution to the present volume, in which Prof. Spuler treats Central Asia from the later Timurids (sixteenth century) to the khanates of Bukhara, Khoqand and Khiva in the eighteenth and nineteenth centuries. For the period spanning the sixteenth to nineteenth century, which is the chronological focus of the present volume, other regions of the Islamic world are surveyed by F.R.C. Bagley, Hans Joachim Kissling, Nevill Barbour, J. Spencer Trimingham, Hellmut Braun, and Herbert Härtel. The contributions of these authors—covering Iran, India, North Africa, Sub-Saharan Africa, and the Ottoman Empire—amply illustrate the geographic expansion of Islamic studies, as well as the extrication of the field from "Near Eastern Studies," in which it had long been confined.

The present volume will also be of interest to students of comparative imperial systems. One of the common themes of all three volumes is how the Islamic religion was related to, or was articulated through, particular political structures. Thus in volume one, *The Age of the Caliphs*, Prof. Spuler explores the rise of the earliest Islamic empire, a sprawling multicultural and multiethnic entity that was run by Arabs through the medium of the Arabic language. Among the later Islamic empires, by contrast, not only were the subject populations mainly non-Arab, but so, too, were their ruling classes: the Ottomans were Turkish, the Safavids were Iranian, and the Mughals were Turko-Iranian-Rajput in point of culture and ethnicity. Moreover, these empires adopted extremely varied positions vis-à-vis the Islamic religion. For their part, the Mughals of India not only patronized Hindu institutions, but even punished their own officials for having converted non-Muslims to Islam. What, then, does this tell us about "Islamic" empires? A comparative analysis of the data presented in the three volumes suggests that, to say the least, the notion of the Islamic empire underwent very profound changes between the seventh and nineteenth centuries.

The later Islamic states surveyed in the present volume can also be compared to other empires of their own day, most prominently the Ming and Ch'ing of China, the Russian empire that emerged in the mid-sixteenth century, and the various Western European empires that followed on the "voyages of discovery" from the late fifteenth century. The European empires, whether of the Iberian royal type (Portugal, Spain) or of the north European capitalist type (Netherlands, England), differed fundamentally from any of the Islamic states surveyed in this volume in that the former were all based on sea power and the latter on land power. In this sense, the "Islamic empires" of the present volume may be most fruitfully compared with contemporary Chinese empires. Military, all were based on land power, relying especially on the expertise of mounted archers. And they all developed sophisticated bureaucracies whose function it was to channel surplus revenue from a large agrarian peasant society to rich and opulent courts that were, in turn, integrated into global commercial networks by long-distance traders. Yet these empires differed in the ethnic composition of their subject populations. Both the Safavid and the Ming empires ruled over populations that were, at least in principle, ethnically homogeneous (Iranian in the former case, Han Chinese in the latter), whereas the Ottoman, the Mughal, and the Ch'ing all ruled over enormously diverse populations. Thus, the information in this volume concerning the "Islamic empires" challenges our understanding both of "Islamic" and of "empire."

In the last analysis, students of comparative history and world history alike are dependent on the spade work of archival historians. And, although Bertold Spuler himself did not employ the comparative method in ways that many modern historians do, he did give us the information and the insights on the basis of which such analyses may be made. In this sense his scholarly achievements shall always remain fresh and useful.

Tuscon, AZ
September 1995

# THE OTTOMAN EMPIRE TO 1774

BY

HANS JOACHIM KISSLING

Translated from the German text in *Neuzeit*, with slight modifications

How did the Ottoman empire come into being? Despite much valuable research by German and other orientalists, this problem with its many detailed aspects has by no means yet been fully solved. The old Ottoman sources are semi-fabulous in character; their substratum of facts evidently cannot be isolated with any precision from the overlying mass of legends. Little or no understanding of the backgrounds of events can be gleaned from these early chronicles, which in form and content resemble biographies of Muslim saints.

Even the Turkish nomad chiefs named as ancestors of the future world-conquering Ottoman dynasty emerge as shadowy figures of fable scarcely having a claim to real historical identity. Foremost among them is *Süleyman*, who according to the traditional account migrated westwards at the head of his tribe of 50,000 souls after they had been forced by the onslaught of Jingiz Khān's hordes to quit their homeland in Khurāsān. They are said to have marched into the area between Erzincan and Ahlat in eastern Asia Minor, and to have lived as nomads in those parts for seven years; and then to have again marched forth, this time in an eastward direction, on account of changes in the political scene after Jingiz Khān had died and after the Khwārizmshāh had met defeat at the hands of the Selcuks (Saljūqs) of Rūm. During their passage of the upper Euphrates, in 1231, Süleyman was drowned. His sudden death was followed by the break-up of his tribe, one section of which migrated to Syria, while the other remained in Asia Minor living the nomad life. Süleyman's son *Ertuğrul* also figures as a nomad chief; he is reported to have been one of four brothers, but of them he alone gains prominence in Ottoman historiography. He first settled with a few hundred families in the area east of Erzurum, but later decided to seek a safer and more fruitful abode in the Rum Selcuk realm, then ruled from Konya by the Sultan Alaeddin II. A favourable opportunity arose when Alaeddin was threatened by powerful Mongol hordes, and Ertuğrul, by coming to his help, extricated him from a difficult situation. He thus became the Sultan's right hand man, and entered the Selcuk service as a feudal tenant. The fiefs conferred upon him are said to have been the Domaniç hill-pastures and Ermeni mountains for summer quarters and the plain of Söğüd for winter quarters. Such is the gist of the old Ottoman accounts. Amid all their fancy they may well contain some truth. This is not the place for an attempt to evaluate them, nor for a discussion of the related problems of the collapse of the Selcuk realm in Asia Minor and rise from its ruins of a large number of small Turkish states.

According to the tradition, the Ottoman dynasty was founded by a son of Ertuğrul, said to have been born in 1258, who bore the name *Osman*. Modern opinions differ on the question whether this name, which is spelt *ʿUthmān*, might be a subsequent arabicization of an originally pure Turkish name. After his father's death in 1289, Osman emerges as an old-style *gazi*, i.e. hero of the faith, active in frontier warfare and already established as ruler of part of Bithynia. Girt with the sword of Islam by a *derviş şeyh*, Edebali, who was his father-in-law, and inspired by a dream which foretold world dominion for his progeny, Osman had resumed the *cihad* ("holy war") against the Christian Byzantines and had been joined by numerous militant believers, whom he organized on the lines of a *derviş* fraternity. Also attracted to his banner were members of the artisans' and shopkeepers' guilds, known as *ahi* confederations, which were similarly organized and had earlier acquired an influential position in the Rum Selcuk polity. The recklessly aggressive spirit of these recruits must have been a significant factor in Osman's great victories; but their contribution to the upbuilding of the Ottoman state has probably been exaggerated. However that may be, Osman was able to equip his new realm in north west Asia Minor with an adequate social and administrative structure. The *gazis* were employed in warfare and the *ahis* in economic activities. Bureaucratic and in particular financial functions appear to have been even at this stage performed mainly by Christians and Jews. Educational and cultural tasks were as a matter of course entrusted to Islamic jurists, who at the same time fulfilled the social role of a clergy.

As early as 1288 Osman had been able to seize from the Byzantines a town called in Greek Melangeia and in Turkish Karaca Hisar; and here he established his first capital. The continuing influx of *gazis* from every district and tribe of Turkish Asia Minor relieved him of anxiety over his growing manpower needs. Karaca Hisar was fitted out with buildings requisite for Islamic observance, a Christian church being turned into a mosque; and the administration of justice, control of markets etc. were placed in the hands of competent officials. Osman himself is said to have been frequently invoked as an arbitrator and to have given proof of perfect impartiality.

Although in principle there was a state of permanent war on the frontier, in practice hostilities had to be suspended from time to time. During these calmer periods, peaceful traffic between the opposing sides was carried on; indeed Osman is reported to have maintained positively cordial relations with a number of Byzantine noblemen. Notable among them were the governor of Bilecik, and another dignitary who later went over to Islam, Köse Mihal. On the other hand, Osman did not lack ill-wishers on the Muslim side of the frontier. After the conquest of Karaca Hisar he is said to have enjoyed almost seven years of undisturbed peace; but he did not in these years of relaxation let go any of the old fire of his fighting spirit. One soon to feel it was the governor of Bilecik. Having become jealous of Osman, he joined with his prospective son-in-law, the governor of Yar Hisar, in a dastardly plot to murder their suzerain at the wedding feast to be held in celebration of the latter's marriage with his daughter Nilüfer. Thanks to the trusted Köse Mihal, warning of the plot reached Osman in time. In a bold attack, he took by surprise the castle of Bilecik, caught the unsuspecting bridegroom on the way from Yar Hisar, and carried off the beautiful Nilüfer, whom he later gave in marriage to his son Orhan. He also captured the castle of Yar Hisar and another castle named İnegöl. Osman's grip on his own domain was greatly strengthened by the acquisition in one stroke of these three important fortresses. His subordinate status as a vassal of the Selcuk Sultan Alaeddin II came to an end at some uncertain date after 1300, when the Mongols finally dismantled the Rum Selcuk state; since they made no attempt to extend their authority into north west Asia Minor, where Osman's realm lay, he was able to continue ruling and expanding his territory without interference from the Īlkhāns of Tabrīz. The real birthdate of the Ottoman empire may thus be placed a little after 1300, when Osman became effectively independent; more commonly it is given as 1288 or 1290, the year of the conquest of Karaca Hisar, where Osman asserted his independence by causing his own name to be pronounced in the Friday prayer.

Around the turn of the century, Osman reorganized his government. He granted Karaca Hisar as a fief to his son Orhan, made Yenişehir the capital in its place, and thereafter concentrated his energies on further expansion towards the Sea of Marmara and the city of Nicaea on its eastern gulf. The bad state of the Byzantine castles and poor morale of their garrisons, together with special difficulties created for them by a catastrophic flood of the Sakarya river, facilitated Osman's advance, against which the Byzantines and their Catalan mercenaries commanded by Roger de Flor put up no very serious opposition. In 1301 the Byzantines suffered a severe defeat at Koyun Hisar; six years later the combined resistance of the governors of Edrenos, Madenos, Kete and Kestel (Byzantine castles near Bursa) was smashed; and in 1308 Osman was able, with the help of his friend Köse Mihal, to outflank the Byzantine frontier strongholds on the Sakarya. On his southern frontier a threat from the Mongol forces was parried by his son Orhan, who thereby gave proof of fitness for the succession. Osman's next objective was the town and district afterwards called Kocaeli, west of the Sakarya; and he did not hesitate to entrust the task of conquering them to Orhan, who with the aid of veteran *gazis* achieved complete succes. This conquest placed Osman in a position to threaten Nicaea (İznîk), the most important Byzantine frontier stronghold, and also Prousa (Bursa). The castles surrounding Nicaea were captured one by one, and the city, thus hemmed in on all sides, was slowly but surely strangled. Much the same tactics were used at Bursa; Osman set up in the city's immediate environs a number of well defended forts whence his *gazis*, under their trusted commander Orhan and brave officers such as Köse Mihal and Kongur Alp, sallied forth in a protracted guerrilla campaign. Ten years passed before Orhan could report, in 1326, to his then dying father that Bursa had voluntarily opened its gates, its commander having decided, after the fall of Edrenos, to pay him 30,000 Byzantine gold pieces in return for a safe conduct. Bursa thus passed into Ottoman hands without bloodshed. Orhan, now ruler of the state founded by Osman, chose it for his capital, and there interred his father's mortal remains. This "Green City" and "Cradle of the Ottomans" was to be the last resting place of the dynasty's monarchs from Osman to Murad II; Mehmed II and the Sultans after him were buried at İstanbul.

Before the events of *Orhan's* reign (1326–1359) are recorded, note must be taken of the religious situation in the rising Ottoman state; for religious problems were to affect its development for long to come. The beliefs prevalent among the Muslim inhabitants were popular rather than orthodox in nature, with discernible Shīʿite features. Although the *sunnah* of the Prophet and his Companions was respected, sympathy was felt for the Shīʿite Imāms as Muḥammad's rightful successors; and there was also a widespread tendency to retain and assimilate cults and practices of earlier religions. In these circumstances, sects sprang into life and flourished. The rapidly expanding *derviş* orders were especially influential, in army units, in artisans' and shopkeepers' guilds, and also among the general populace. Not unnaturally the orthodox *ulema* (religious dignitaries) disliked and stood apart from all such movements; and as time passed this mutual aloofness grew into a bitter enmity, sometimes enhanced by economic considerations, which was to provoke many a bloody clash in the course of Ottoman history. In this early phase, however, the representatives of orthodoxy were not aggressive, with the result that *Ṣūfī* preachers and *derviş* orders could receive uninhibited patronage from the first Sultans, for the establishment of monasteries, endowment of kitchens for the poor, and other similar charities in their care.

Orhan strictly followed the example of rulership set by his departed father Osman, who is said to have particularly insisted that the royal authority should never be shared – perhaps because he knew from history how often such division had brought Muslim states to ruin. Orhan's brother Alaeddin remained obedient to their father's last wishes in this respect, but accepted the new ruler's request that he should serve the state as its highest functionary, i.e. as *vezir*. To him are attributed important reforms and certain peculiarly Ottoman institutions. Under Osman, who had been at least nominally the Selcuk Sultan's vassal, Rum Selcuk coins had remained in use; now, under Orhan, the time was ripe to issue an independent Ottoman currency. Alaeddin carried out the technical side of this operation. A silver coin, known as the *akçe* ("white piece") was minted on the model of the Byzantine *aspron* ("asper") and put into circulation from 1328 onward. This move had political as well as economic significance, issue of coinage and mention of the ruler in the Friday prayer being traditional symbols of a Muslim state's assertion of independent status. Another of Alaeddin's measures was the regulation of dress. The various nations and classes were required to wear distinctive clothes. This was a long-standing oriental custom, now applied by Alaeddin in the Ottoman social context. Even more than uniforms in modern society, costume and especially headgear possessed until quite recent times very great significance in the east, where whole communities, classes and nations were distinguished by the colour or shape of their garments or hats. Under Orhan and his successors the typical Turkish headgear was the white felt hat. White was also the royal colour; but the costumes of the courtiers were full of variety. Alaeddin's biggest task was to reorganize the army. Hitherto it had consisted mainly of cavalry, the arm most needed in the guerrilla fighting of Osman's days, when the surprise attack and equally sudden retreat were the usual tactic of the *gazis*. In later years the role of these horsemen, whose command is said to have remained hereditary in the house of Köse Mihal, became relatively less important. They were grouped into formidable spearhead units of storm-troops (*akîncîs*), with the general function of carrying out lightning raids on enemy territory to seize booty and spread havoc and terror; the name "raiders and burners" given to them in western chronicles was well deserved. Besides these mounted troops, an infantry corps was now brought into being. Since the infantrymen (*yaya* or *piyade*) received regular pay, the Ottoman state may be said to have acquired a standing army at this early date. Whether the Janissary corps dates from Orhan's time, as many writers declare, is uncertain; more probably it came into being, at any rate in its distinctive form, under Murad II, and will therefore be discussed when that reign is reached.

Rudiments of the feudal system on which the later Ottoman imperial structure was to be based can already be seen in the accounts of Orhan's reign. Newly conquered lands were assigned to deserving warriors who, in return for their use, undertook to supply the ruler with specified numbers of fully equipped horsemen in time of war. The assigned lands were classified by size into small fiefs (*tîmar*), large fiefs (*ziamet*), and later also into fiefs of the imperial household (*hass*). There was an inviolable rule that these grants should depend upon service and should not be heritable. Long afterwards, when the empire was in decline, all sorts of abuses crept into this system; indeed its vitiation was one of the main causes of the collapse of Ottoman power. Labour on the feudal estates was performed mainly by *râya*, i.e. Christian natives of the conquered territories. In accordance with traditional Islamic principles, these non-Muslim subjects of the realm were required to pay customary taxes and crop-shares, but were left entirely free to practise their own religion. With the later expansion of the empire, these principles were not always strictly observed; e.g. particular groups of *râya* were sometimes exempted from taxation in return for contractual services such as guarding important mountain passes or imperial forests and hunting grounds. The question arises whether the Christian peasants were materially worse off under their Muslim Turkish masters than under their previous Christian masters. While conditions doubtless varied in different places and at different times, it seems clear that much of what has been written about Turkish oppression of the Christian peasantry must be fictitious.

In the fourth decade of the 14th century important new conquests were registered. The defenders of Nicaea, tired at last of incessant guerrilla fighting, chose in 1330 to surrender without a struggle; and a force later sent from Constantinople failed to recover the city. Around 1333 Ottoman sovereignty was extended northwards through the conquest of Göynük, Tarakcî and Modrene by troops under the command of Orhan's son

Süleyman, who first rose into prominence as his father's deputy in this campaign. Orhan's attention was next drawn to the Türkmen principality of Karasî (in the ancient Mysia), where the deceased ruler's sons had begun to fight for power among themselves; gladly profiting from this situation, Orhan marched into the territory and in 1336 annexed it, thereby acquiring the important town of Bergama and the hinterland of the Dardanelles. Occasional attempts to set foot on European soil – i.e. in Thrace – are reported from this time, but were probably marauding raids rather than planned expeditions. Orhan knew how to make his name respected. The Byzantine emperor John Cantacuzenus took care to keep on good terms with him, and in 1346 the two rulers concluded a treaty of friendship; this was sealed by the gift of the emperor's daughter Theodora to Orhan, who thus became related by marriage to the Roman imperial house.

Orhan had two outstandingly able sons: Süleyman, who has already been mentioned, and Murad. Süleyman was to take charge of the Ottoman invasion of Europe, and Murad, who held in fief the province of Bursa (thereafter called Hudavendigâr – i.e. the "royal" province), was to be his father's successor. Some writers wrongly describe Süleyman as "Sultan" and make him the first of those bearing that name; but he died before his father, and during his lifetime was Crown Prince. He is said, however, to have issued his own coinage.

Much effort was expended by Orhan and Murad on the embellishment of their capital Bursa, which till the present day has retained the character of a typically Ottoman city, and on the encouragement of cultural life. Mosques, Qur'ān schools, baths, caravansarais and public kitchens were erected; and thanks to all this activity, architecture and craftmanship flourished in the city, while the *derviş* orders made further headway. In Bursa are buried, along with the early Sultans, famous statesmen such as Candarlî Halil, thought by many to have been the founder of the Janissary corps.

Orhan's treaty of friendship with the Byzantine emperor did not impede his son Süleyman from intervening in Byzantine internal disputes, nor from taking advantage of havoc caused by an earthquake to land a small party of dare-devil *gazis* on the Gallipoli peninsula. Probably in the year 1354, they crossed the strait from Asia Minor on rafts and captured first the coastal fort of Tzympe (later called Çimenlik), then the town of Callipolis (Gelibolu). More bands of *gazis* followed, and before long Süleyman was master of the whole peninsula, which he appears to have governed autonomously. Already his men's occasional long-distance raids were spreading panic in the interior of Thrace. The years 1354–1368 may be regarded as the dawn of a new historical epoch; for ever since then Muslim Turks have had a foothold in Europe. In 1358 this brave Crown Prince was struck down by a blow of fate; he died suddenly after a hunting accident at Bulayr in the northern part of the Gallipoli peninsula. On hearing the news of Süleyman's death, his brother Murad hastened to Gallipoli to take over the task of conquering the Balkans. Their father Orhan passed away in 1359.

*Murad I* (r. 1359–1389) was the first Ottoman ruler to assume the title *Sultan*, his predecessors having been called *Beg*, the Turkish equivalent of *Amīr*. His reign and that of his successor form a dramatic period filled with campaigns and conquests in south eastern Europe. These were the work of Turkish warriors, who flooded over from Asia Minor in ever increasing numbers. The old social order, outlined above but very imperfectly known in detail, could still produce great triumphs. The upper class continued to be of relatively pure Turkish origin; not until later times, beginning with the reign of Murad II, did foreign-born renegades acquire influence at the expense of the old feudal families. Strengthened and systematized by various reforms, the Ottoman feudal society formed a solid foundation for the new empire and stood the test of long centuries to come. Political conditions in the Balkan peninsula also favoured Murad I's policy of expansion. The Shishmanid kingdom of Bulgaria was just as feeble as the Byzantine remnant-state, while Serbia, which under its king Stephen Dushan had been a powerful state, fell after his death in 1355 into utter confusion. Divided by mutual distrust and weakened internally by feuds and disorders, the successive Balkan coalitions formed to resist the confident and well disciplined Ottoman armies were doomed to pitiable failure.

Before letting his forces become deeply involved in Balkan affairs, Murad I had to deal with troubles in Anatolia, especially at Ankara (Angora; the ancient Ancyra). This city, said to have been annexed to the Ottoman realm in 1354 by the Crown Prince Süleyman, attempted after Orhan's death to cast off the Ottoman yoke. With lightning speed, Murad descended upon Ankara and crushed the revolt, which had been started by the local *ahi* confederation with help from the neighbouring principality of Karaman. Having thus secured his rear, the Sultan was free to embark on his ambitious plan of Balkan conquest. The offensive began with an invasion of Thrace, launched from Gallipoli. Its success was due in large measure to the outstanding efficiency of Murad's senior officers, in particular Lala Şahin, Timurtaş, Haci İlbegi and Evrenos. The Byzantines now felt the full force of the conqueror's fist as their cities and fortresses fell one after another. In 1360 the strongly defended town of Didymoteichos (Dimetoka) was lost in consequence of a successful ruse by the Turks; for a few years it served as their seat of government. In 1362 Lala Şahin captured the key city of Adrianople (Edirne), which remains Turkish today and was to be the Ottoman empire's capital for almost a century (1365–1453). The Turkish advance continued along the Maritza (Meriç) valley and up to the foot of the Balkan range. Lala Şahin had the satisfaction of taking Philippopolis (Filibe; Plovdiv). His colleague Timurtaş was the conqueror of the lands further east, around Zağra (1363), Yanboli (1365) and the later Kizil Ağaç; and the Sultan himself victoriously entered the towns of Aytos and Karnobat (1366). Southern Thrace fell prey to Evrenos, who after capturing Keşan and advancing almost to Gümülcina (Komotini), administered the district from his headquarters at Ipsala near the Maritza mouth.

The Western Christian world reacted very mildly to these disquieting events in south eastern Europe. Pope Urban V did indeed try hard to foster the idea of a new crusade; but the fiery zeal of earlier centuries had now died away. In 1365 the Adriatic city state of Ragusa gladly concluded a commercial treaty with the Sultan Murad I. Only Count Amedeus VI of Savoy, known as the "Green Count" (Conte Verde), had enough courage to embark on a desperate mission for the relief of Christendom's threatened bulwark at Constantinople. After successfully landing his force at Gallipoli and advancing some way inland, he found the Byzantines unwilling to concert plans with him and had to withdraw (1366). Eastern Thrace also fell into Ottoman hands, at uncertain dates but probably between 1361 and 1370. These conquests by Murad I and his generals thus brought about the complete isolation of Constantinople from Western Europe and the virtual if not formal end of Byzantine independence.

In 1371, when the Sultan was again occupied in Anatolia, the Serbian prince Vukashin of the Niemanid house ventured to challenge the Ottoman forces; but at the hard-fought battle of Çirmen in 1371 the Serbs were thoroughly beaten by Haci İlbegi and had to abandon their Macedonian provinces. Haci İlbegi did not live long to enjoy the fruits of this victory, for he was perfidiously poisoned at the instigation of a rival general, probably Lala Şahin, who later conquered Sofia in 1382 and Nish in 1386.

In Asia Minor meanwhile, Murad I's affairs were not prospering so brilliantly as in Europe. In 1381 he had annexed the principality of Hamid in the western Taurus; but a minor war with the Egyptian Mamlūks on the Cilician border turned out unfavourably for him, and he temporarily lost the port of Antalya (Adalia) to the Frankish king of Cyprus. On the other hand, he acquired another Anatolian territory, Germiyan, through the marriage of one of his sons, Bayezid, to a princess of its former ruling house. His authority in these regions, however, was dangerously threatened when his elder son Savcî rebelled against him in league with the Turkish ruler of Karaman and a Byzantine prince. Murad had to undertake a campaign against the rebels, which ended in 1386 with a great victory for him near Konya. By this time the Ottoman empire's European provinces were again in turmoil. The Bulgarian Tsar Shishman III—incidentally one of Murad's brothers-in-law—had taken advantage of the Sultan's involvement in distant Anatolia to join with the Serbs and Bosniaks in a tripartite anti-Ottoman coalition; and at the battle of Plochnik in 1387 their united forces had been able to decimate the hitherto ever-victorious troops of Lala Şahin. The Turks were not slow in taking vengeance. Within a year, their general Ali Paşa, a scion of the well known Candarlî family, marched across the Balkan range to the gates of Tirnovo and Şumla (Shumen) and inflicted a sharp defeat on the Bulgars, whose Tsar Shishman III now had to accept the status of a tributary vassal of the Sultan and promise surrender of the fortress of Silistria on the Danube. Later he made one more attempt to throw off Ottoman suzerainty, and again was lucky to save, for the time being, his life and throne. In the following year came the trial of strength which was to seal the destiny of Balkan Europe for many centuries. The Serbs formed a new alliance with their Bosniak, Hungarian, Bulgarian and Albanian neighbours; and Murad I, being well aware what this challenge meant, marched against them in person, at the head of an army which he had specially reinforced with auxiliaries from Asia Minor. On St. Vitus's day, June 20, 1389, the Ottoman and combined Balkan armies met on the historic plain known as Kosovo Polye (the "Blackbird Field"). After many vicissitudes, the battle ended in a great Turkish victory over the Serbs, whose allies finally deserted them. Their king Lazar was captured and put to death. The Ottoman Sultan also met his death on this fateful day; before the fighting was over, a Serb named Milosh Obilich contrived to stab him. Murad I's reign of thirty years is remembered mainly because of the great Turkish conquests in Europe, but was also distinguished by constructive achievements, particularly at Bursa, where fine mosques and accessory buildings such as Qur'ān schools and kitchens were erected at his behest. His generals and high officials vied with one another in endowing pious foundations. Lala Şahin is credited with the introduction of rice growing into south eastern Europe; it was practised mainly in the

Maritza valley and was at first reserved to Muslims, but afterwards allowed to Christians.

The might of the early Ottoman empire, so largely forged by Murad I, remained intact and indeed gained further impetus under his son and successor *Bayezid I* (r. 1389–1402). He was a man of stern and martial temperament, already possessing wide experience of warfare; on the plain of Kosovo he had commanded the right wing with distinction. Since his favourite tactic was the lightning-swift surprise attack, his contemporaries nicknamed him *Yîldîrîm* ("Thunderbolt"). The task which lay before him, and which he himself seems to have clearly discerned, was to consolidate and extend his father's handiwork. He performed this task well, so much so that the empire could emerge unscathed from the disaster which was to befall it in 1402 and from ten subsequent years of disruption. Throughout this period the monarchs of the house of Palaeologus in Constantinople were to all intents and purposes Ottoman vassals; this was made evident in 1390, shortly after Bayezid's accession, when the emperor Manuel under pressure from the Sultan took part with him as an auxiliary in the Turkish conquest of Philadelphia (Alaşehir), the last Greek possession in Asia Minor. In Europe, the next Ottoman objective was to complete the subjugation of Bulgaria and eastern Thrace. The old city of Tirnovo, where Bulgaria's kings were crowned, fell to Bayezid on July 17, 1393. A protracted last stand, in which the brave patriarch Euthymius played a leading part, could not alter the fate of the Bulgar nation, for whom some six centuries of Turkish rule lay ahead. The Ottoman forces, in the course of their operations, captured important bridgeheads across the Danube. Bayezid was also, during the early years of his reign, involved in wars with Turkish princes who ruled parts of the former Selcuk domain in Anatolia. In 1391 and 1392, he annexed Alaşehir, Aydîn with Ayasoluk (Ephesus), Saruhan, Tekke, Menteşe, Beyşehir and Karahisar in the west and south, and not long afterwards Osmancîk, Kastamonu and Amasya in the north. He had to leave hastily for Europe when his territories south of the Danube were invaded by the Wallachian prince Mircea the Old, who was perhaps acting in concert with certain Anatolian Turkish princes, particularly the prince of Amasya. A hard fought battle at Argeş in the summer or autumn of 1393 ended unfavourably for the Wallachians, and Mircea had to accept vassal status and an obligation to pay tribute, thereby surrendering his country's independence. Another territorial increment in Asia Minor came when the cities of Tokat, Sivas and Kayseri sought the Sultan's protection against the designs of a local poet-prince, Burhaneddin, and acknowledged Ottoman suzerainty. In 1394 Bayezid could thus claim undisputed mastery of an immense empire stretching from Nish to eastern Anatolia and interrupted only by the small but vital enclave of Constantinople. Seeing himself, with good reason, as one of the orient's mightiest rulers, he thought fit to validate his position by obtaining from the contemporary ʿAbbāsid puppet Caliph in Cairo a diploma formally investing him with the title "Sultan of Rūm", i.e. of the (East) Romans. The controversial question of Bayezid's "seven year siege of Constantinople" (1394–1401) cannot be discussed here. Many scholars doubt whether such a siege ever took place. Most probably there was no regular military operation, but rather a state of affairs which today would be called "cold war" arising from resistance by the Palaeologi to conditions imposed on them as virtual Ottoman vassals. A covert blockade, bringing economic ruin to this city at the junction of two great Ottoman land masses, was the obvious policy in these circumstances.

Bayezid's military successes aroused great alarm in Christian Western Europe and for a time seemed likely to revive the old crusading spirit. King Sigismund of Hungary led an army of enthusiastic but militarily ill-prepared Christian warriors from Buda to Nicopolis, an Ottoman fortress on the Bulgarian side of the Danube, to which they laid siege; but largely as a result of dissensions and jealousies among their leaders, Bayezid was able to rout them on September 27, 1396, and Sigismund only got back to Hungary with great difficulty. A massacre of the prisoners of war was carried out on the Sultan's order. A Bavarian knight, Hans Schiltberger, escaped this fate, and after living through manifold adventures amidst the Turks, Mongols and Mamlūks and at Constantinople, returned home to write his memoirs in a book which won immediate popularity. Ottoman troops pursuing remnants of the crusader army are said to have penetrated as far west as Styria. The Frankish rulers who then held much of Greece were punished for their sympathy with the crusaders by a series of sanginary Turkish raids. Bayezid's triumphant career was not destined, however, to last much longer. He continued his policy of expansion in Asia Minor, defeating the prince of Karaman and other rulers; but this policy was to bring him into conflict with the mighty Central Asian conqueror Tīmūr the Lame (Tamerlane). Thc dispossessed Turkish princes hastened to Tīmūr's camp and aroused his feelings against the grasping Ottoman Sultan. An attack by Bayezid in 1400 on the ruler of Erzincan, a Muslim prince said to have been of Armenian origin who had acknowledged Tīmūr's suzerainty, was to provide a casus belli. At first Tīmūr retaliated only by sacking the town of Sivas and slaying its Ottoman garrison; he had still to secure his southern flank against danger from the Mamlūks in Syria. In 1402 he marched back into Asia Minor. The decisive battle of Ankara, or battle of Çubukabad, was fought near Ankara on July 20. From the outset Bayezid suffered a disadvantage because his army's morale was not good. His Muslim troops lacked fanaticism in this fratricidal war with fellow-believers, and most of those recruited from the annexed Anatolian territories remained inwardly loyal to their former princes; while his Christian auxiliaries were secretly pleased that the Sultan should be taught a lesson. Defeated and taken prisoner, Bayezid I "the Thunderbolt" was at first chivalrously treated by Tīmūr, but later after attempting to escape is said to have been locked up and carried around in an iron cage. While still in Tīmūr's custody he died on March 8, 1403, according to some sources by his own hand.

Despite Bayezid I's absorption in warfare, he had not neglected art and letters. In accordance with custom, he endowed pious foundations and erected buildings, among which the Great Mosque and a Qur'ān school at Bursa deserve special mention. He was friendly with religious scholars and patronized poets and learned men.

The Ottoman empire was shattered by the seemingly lethal blow dealt to it at Ankara. In the Anatolian provinces which Bayezid had annexed Tīmūr reinstated the former rulers; and from all the Muslim princes of Asia Minor he exacted recognition of his suzerainty. To rule the Ottoman realm in Europe as his vassal, he designated one of Bayezid I's sons, Süleyman. The entire Turkish domain of "Rūm" was thus formally incorporated into Tīmūr's enormous empire; but Tīmūr died at Otrār in Central Asia on January 19, 1405, and that empire soon fell apart.

For the Byzantines, this meant a respite from Ottoman encirclement. Constantinople was to remain Greek for another half century.

The defeat and dismemberment of 1402 closes the first phase of Ottoman history. The next period, lasting until the restoration and reunification of the empire by Mehmed I, is a ten-year interregnum, in which the main events were as follows. Bayezid I had five sons, four of whom—*Isa*, *Süleyman*, *Musa*, and the aforementioned *Mehmed*—escaped death at Ankara, while the fifth—*Mustafa*—disappeared and was probably killed in the battle. Mehmed secured a footing in the region of Amasya and Tokat; Isa seized control of Bursa; Süleyman had been placed by Tīmūr in charge of "Rumelia", as the European territories were collectively named; and Musa was for the time being a captive in the hands of the restored prince of Germiyan. Mehmed proposed to Isa that they should divide Anatolia between them, and when Isa refused, went to war with him; Isa was defeated at the battle of Ulubad and took refuge with the

Byzantines. Süleyman, not being content to rule only Rumelia, now sent troops to Anatolia under the command of Isa, who was again defeated by Mehmed and perished. In 1404 Süleyman himself crossed over to Asia Minor at the head of an army which expelled Mehmed from Bursa and a year later from Ankara. Meanwhile Musa had been set free by the prince of Germiyan and had joined with Mehmed, who put him in command of an expedition which was to attack Süleyman in Rumelia with support from the Serbs; but Süleyman was able to halt the invaders near Constantinople and force them to retire. In 1410, however, Musa successfully landed in Europe. Süleyman's troops now seized the opportunity to revolt against him, his vicious ways having rendered him thoroughly unpopular; he fled, and soon afterwards was murdered. Musa, having thus become master of Rumelia, was unwilling to recognize Mehmed as Sultan. His first step was to attack the Serbs, on whom he put the blame for his earlier defeat by Süleyman. He also invaded Thessaly. When he demanded tribute from the Byzantine emperor Manuel, the latter entered into an alliance with Mehmed against him. This at first harmed rather than helped the Byzantines, because Mehmed was fully occupied in Anatolia, his authority having been challenged by local potentates at Smyrna and Ankara. After subduing these trouble-makers, Mehmed was in a position to punish Musa. He invaded Rumelia in 1412 and finally defeated Musa's army at Çamurlu (near Sofia) in July 1413. Support from the Serbs, who rallied to Mehmed's side against Musa, and also from the Greeks, contributed much to this victory, which made Mehmed the undisputed Sultan of the now reunified empire; he showed his gratitude to them by retroceding certain lands.

*Mehmed I* during his short reign (1413–1421) came up against the backwash of these convulsions. His victory at Çamurlu had eliminated his last brother and rival but not the distress prevailing throughout the empire. The country had been bled dry by Tīmūr's invasion and the civil wars of the interregnum, and a mood of gloomy despair had spread among the Muslim masses. This had imparted a radical, indeed socialistic, trend to their religious feeling, which as already stated was very largely unorthodox and pro-ʿAlid and sometimes positively Shīʿite. Such a climate favoured the agitator proffering some new path to salvation. The thriving *derviş* orders with their intrinsically non-Sunnite cults now became nuclei of politico-sectarian movements, which attracted not only Turks but also "subjects" *(râya)* through ideologies capable of appealing to Christian sentiment. Mehmed I had to spend most of his reign in action to quell outbreaks expressing this general discontent. An adventurer named

Cüneyd, who had seized power and paraded independence in the Smyrna district during the troubles of the interregnum, was the first to learn that the new Sultan, despite his youth, was no weakling. In 1414 Mehmed dealt him a chastening blow, and also punished the contumacious prince of Karaman. Much graver was the threat posed by a movement associated with the name of a learned *şeyh* and former army judge *(kazasker)*, Bedreddin ibn Kazi Samavna. After gaining distinction in his early career as an orthodox legal scholar, he was converted around 1400 to Ṣūfism, became a *derviş*, and conceived ideas which were strongly socialistic in nature and also envisioned a union of the Islamic, Christian and Jewish faiths. He acquired a numerous following. Moreover, having served as *kazasker* to the prince Musa and having been banished to İznîk after Mehmed's victory, he was ill disposed towards the Sultan. The chroniclers ascribe to him, to certain socialistic peasant leaders among whom the most notable were Bürklüce Mustafa and Torlak Hu Kemal, and to the prince of Sinop and the voivode Mircea the Old of Wallachia, the responsibility for having set in motion a very serious rebellion in 1416, which they say was meant to overthrow the Ottoman dynasty. The rebellion certainly placed Mehmed in a critical position, because just at this juncture his birthright to the throne was challenged by an impostor, Düzme Mustafa, claiming to be the prince Mustafa who had disappeared at the battle of Ankara. After government troops detailed to subdue followers of Bedreddin troubling the Aydîn district had been cut to pieces in the headland of Karaburun (opposite Chios), where the desperate rebels led by Bürklüce Mustafa had their stronghold, it became necessary to despatch large, specially levied forces to this front. Eventually Bürklüce Mustafa and his zealots were captured and put to a cruel death. Bedreddin himself was later caught in a mountain pass in the Balkans and hanged at Serres in Macedonia on December 18, 1416. His movement did not wholly disappear, but maintained an underground existence for a century and a half; its adherents tended to join either the politically active Ṣafavid order or the Bektaṣi and other *derviş* orders. As for Düzme Mustafa, it was not until the next Sultan's reign that the pretender's adventurous career of trouble-making could be brought to an end. Mehmed I also came to blows with Venice, whose subjects in the Aegean islands rejected his demand for their allegiance; he had to abandon these pretensions when his sea-squadrons received a beating off Gallipoli on May 21, 1416, from the Venetian fleet of the future doge Loredano. On the other hand, Mehmed secured recognition as Sultan and suzerain from the great majority of the European and Anatolian tributaries; he is therefore rightly considered to be the restorer of the Ottoman empire. He died young in 1421 at his capital, Edirne. His reign being filled with continual wars was culturally unfruitful; but the "Green Mosque" built for him at Bursa deserves mention.

In Mehmed's son and successor, *Murad II* (r. 1421–1451), the empire acquired a capable and resolute Sultan who was at the same time respectful of legality and conciliatory in temper; for him war was an unavoidable evil rather than an integral part of life. His first task, however, was to defend his throne against the pretensions of Düzme Mustafa and also those of his own younger brother, who had a following in Anatolia. The Byzantine emperor Manuel is alleged to have secretly supported these dissidents. Düzme Mustafa was soon defeated and killed by Murad II's troops, and order was restored in Asia Minor. The refractory prince of Sinop was now brought to obedience and forced to cede parts of his territory to the Ottoman empire. By 1425 it was possible to free Smyrna from the stranglehold of the adventurer Cüneyd, who was finally defeated later in the year and put to death. The tolerably satisfactory vassal relationship which had existed between the Byzantine empire under Manuel Palaeologus and the Ottoman Sultanate was upset by the former's ambiguous role in the intrigues of the false Mustafa. Murad II held that reparation was due, and accordingly summoned the Byzantines to cede Salonica, which formed an enclave still under their rule. To prevent this, the Byzantine and Venetian governments hastily concluded a treaty by which the city was sold and handed over to Venice in 1427. Murad, feeling that he had been cheated but that he was not yet strong enough to settle the matter by force, agreed reluctantly to acknowledge the city's new status against payment of a tribute. He nevertheless remained intent upon conquering Salonica at the first opportunity. Before long skirmishing began between the now amplified Ottoman fleet and the Venetian outposts in the Aegean islands. Early in 1430 Murad judged the time ripe for an attack on Salonica; he was not mistaken, for at the end of March or beginning of April the city was captured by the besieging Ottoman forces, but with so much destruction of life and property that many years were to pass before it regained prosperity.

Foreseeing the probability of conflict between his empire and its northern and western neighbours, particularly Hungary, Murad II carefully built up adequate military strength. During his reign, the Janissaries *(yeni çeri*, i.e. "new troop") first rose into prominence as the Ottoman corps d'élite. The question when this corps came into being is obscured by legend and has not yet been answered by modern scholarship.

Even if it must be accepted that Murad II was not the actual founder, it is nevertheless clear that he was the Sultan who built up the Janissary corps into a powerful instrument of war, destined to play a major part in Ottoman affairs until its bloody liquidation in 1826. The Janissaries were not native Turks, but sons of Balkan Christian parents taken from them under a levy system which has been described as "diabolically ingenious." Selected for their superior physique and intelligence by recruiting commissions which toured the land every second year, these youths were removed from their homes, taught Islamic beliefs and customs, and subjected to rigorous drill and discipline. They were then employed as bodyguards of the Sultan and in a wide variety of other services required by the imperial household *(saray)*. Since certain regions—roughly speaking, Asia Minor, Greece, and later Constantinople and the conquered Hungarian territories—were exempted from the levy, the nations which suffered most from this fearful haemorrhage were the Balkan Slavs and the Albanians. On the other hand, capable Janissaries could look forward, notwithstanding their origin, to brilliant careers. From Murad II's time onwards, the "harvest of boys" *(devşirme)*, as the levy was called, provided a perennial reserve of manpower for staffing high offices of the Ottoman state. Ottoman history abounds in examples of the Christian-born conscript who climbed up the Janissary ladder to elevated rank in this Muslim empire. No doubt such cases attenuated some of the resentment of the deprived families and nations against the cruelty of the system. In later periods the Sultans were to find that the Janissaries could be dangerous; they constituted a distinct and powerful military group, and were also to become involved in a remarkable association with the notoriously heretical and demagogic Bektaşi *derviş* order, which despite official efforts to promote counteraction by rival orders was able to preserve a lasting influence among them. Not only the Janissary corps, but also other branches of the armed forces, benefited from Murad II's effort to build up Ottoman military strength; during his reign the first guns made their appearance. The artillery only acquired real importance, however, under his son Mehmed II.

The general character of the Ottoman state began to change significantly during Murad II's reign. The old Turkish social structure was now disintegrating, and the political power of the Turkish population-group entered upon a steady decline as the Sultan opened the highest military, bureaucratic and palace positions to non-Turkish "renegades", i.e. to men of the subject nations who had either been conscripted into the Janissary corps or had voluntarily embraced Islam, whether from opportunism or from conviction. The ruling class thus became increasingly non-Turkish, while the old Turkish noble families, who had once virtually monopolized high functions, gradually saw themselves reduced to a powerless, even if not unprosperous, role as landlords living on their estates. This process, which was not completed until Mehmed II's reign, appears to have met with some unsuccessful resistance; it may well have been the source of internal frictions which in all probability lay behind the curious incident (to be discussed later) of Murad II's temporary retirement from the throne. Nor was Murad's reign free from religious strife. Numerous reports which have come down indicate that the Ḥurūfīs, a heretical sect of Persian origin so called because they gave supernatural meanings to the letters *(ḥurūf)* of the Arabic alphabet, were then particularly active.

The Ottoman government, from Murad's time or perhaps earlier until long afterwards, operated an efficient secret service which supplied accurate intelligence of developments in Christian Europe. Agents of the Sultan contrived to infiltrate royal retinues, privy councils of Italian city-states, and the Roman Curia itself. In such activities help was often obtained from the commercial establishments of the Italian republics, who in their eagerness to hurt their competitors and to retain or extend their own Levantine possessions carried on a quite shameless game of intrigues, which in the end could only benefit their common Ottoman adversary; its intricate details lie beyond the scope of this book. One point which must be noted is the progressive "deturkification" of the Ottoman dynasty, or at least of the blood flowing in its veins, as the middle ages drew to their close. Peculiar royal marriage customs and relationships precluded Turkish women from becoming Sultan's wives. The majority of the dynasty's subsequent monarchs were sons of slave women of many different nationalities. Already in Murad II's time the royal princes and princesses were of mixed stocks in which the Turkish component was not large. This explains the remarkable variations of physical and psychological type to be found among the descendants of Osman.

A process of "deturkification" was also at work in the empire's intellectual life. In prose and poetry, Persian styles and themes came into increasing use, as models to be followed no less carefully when the language of composition was Turkish than when Persian itself was used. In theology and jurisprudence, Arabic naturally prevailed. Already literary Turkish showed symptoms of the Arabo-Persian turgidity which was to overwhelm it in the 16th and 17th centuries.

Another noteworthy feature of Ottoman life in Murad II's reign was the great and growing influence of the *derviş* orders. The Sultan himself favoured them; and he showed particular esteem for an order which was viewed by the orthodox Sunnite *ulema* with much suspicion, namely the Mevlevi or "dancing" *dervişes* who traced their spiritual ancestry to the great Persian mystic poet Mawlānā Jalāl al-Dīn Rūmī of Konya (d. 1273). The gradually widening rift between orthodoxy and Ṣūfism was to have political consequences in later times.

Murad II is also remembered for his building activity, especially at his capital Edirne, which owes to him a number of fine edifices such as the beautiful Üç Şerefeli mosque and various palaces on islands in the Tunca river.

In 1438 Murad II reckoned that his power was adequate for a campaign against Hungary; he was able to conquer the fortress of Semendria on the Danube. Two years later he unsuccessfully besieged Belgrad. The Catholic Christian world now realized that something must be done to check the westward Ottoman advance. An impassioned appeal by Pope Eugenius IV kindled a new crusading spirit, particularly in Hungary, Poland, Germany and France. In 1442 the Magyar national hero John Hunyadi (Hunyadi János) defeated an Ottoman army at Nagy Szeben (Hermannstadt; Sibiu) in Transylvania; and in 1443 George Castriota (Skanderbeg) began his 23-year struggle against the Turks for Albanian independence. Murad thus became involved in war on two fronts, to which was added, also in 1443, a third in Asia Minor against the Karamanlis, long-standing opponents of Ottoman supremacy who, perhaps in concert with Murad's western adversaries, now again took up arms. Later in the same year John Hunyadi marched with a large crusading army to attack the Turks, and beat them at the battle of Yalovatz (between Sofia and Plovdiv) but was unable to exploit his victory; the jubilation which it called forth in Europe turned out to be premature. Murad nevertheless felt obliged to open peace negotiations and accept the terms of a ten-year truce, arranged at Szeged (Szegedin) in 1444, whereby the Danube became the frontier and Wallachia passed under Hungarian suzerainty. The Ottoman empire was then shaken by an unexpected event; for reasons which have not yet been satisfactorily determined, Murad handed the Sultanate to his son Mehmed II, then still a minor, and retired to Manisa in Asia Minor. For a short time the government was carried on by the Crown Prince with the help, but not to the satisfaction, of the capable ministers then in office. In September 1444, however, the truce of Szegedin was repudiated by its Christian signatories. This step, taken against John Hunyadi's advice, has been much debated by Hungarian and Polish historians; it appears to have been prompted mainly by objections to any dealing with the

Muslim infidel, though frontier disputes had also arisen. The grand *vezir* then hastily recalled the ex-Sultan and sent the Crown Prince away to Manisa as governor. A large, mainly Magyar army, under the command of John Hunyadi and the young Hungarian king Ladislaus (László), marched through the Balkans towards the Black Sea coast, whence according to plan a Venetian fleet was to ship them to Constantinople; but the Venetian fleet failed to appear. Instead, Murad II and an Ottoman army arrived, to measure swords with the crusaders at Varna. The battle, which took place on November 9, 1444, went initially quite well for the crusaders, but ended in their total defeat, largely through folly on the part of King László, who lost his life. The Palaeologi were punished in 1446 when the Sultan attacked their possessions in the Peloponnese, destroying the Hexamilion Wall near Corinth; both Corinth and Patras were then annexed to the Ottoman empire. Two years later, in 1448, John Hunyadi, since László's death regent of Hungary, again invaded Ottoman territory in the hope of avenging the defeat at Varna; he met Murad II's army on the same Kosovo Polye which had been the scene of an earlier Turkish triumph, and was decisively beaten. After the battle Hunyadi was held captive for a while by Serbs hostile to the Magyars. Finally, however, he was able to arrange another Hungarian-Ottoman truce on terms very disadvantageous to Hungary. The struggle in Albania, meanwhile, had not been progressing favourably for the Turks, who were obliged in 1450 to abandon their siege of Skanderbeg's stronghold Kroya (Kruje).

Murad II's sudden death from an apoplectic stroke on February 3, 1451, led to the assumption of power by his son *Mehmed II*, now twenty years old, who grew to be one of the most formidable monarchs of Ottoman and indeed world history. In character he was an autocrat, cruel and uncompromising, altogether unlike his father. He was to be the conqueror of Constantinople and founder of a new empire lacking the predominantly Turkish quality of the early Ottoman state. He was to carry the Ottoman frontiers to the Adriatic Sea and to the edge of the Īrānian plateau, and poise his spearheads for a thrust to the heart of Christian West Europe.

Mehmed II's first action in his reign of thirty years (1451–1481) was to have his younger half-brother Ahmed strangled as a precaution against risk of civil war over the succession. The precedent thereby set became an unwritten law of the Ottoman dynasty, whose incoming Sultans until 1595 regularly ordered the liquidation of their brothers and half-brothers. There may also have been another reason for this barbarous, and distinctively Ottoman, practice. On Mehmed II's and every subsequent ruler's accession, the Janissaries received, or rather extorted, a bonus over and above their normal pay. So great was their power that no Sultan could afford to disregard their claim to an "accession gift". A danger thus arose that the Janissaries might contemplate multiplying these gifts by deposing a Sultan at any time and setting up another Ottoman prince in his place; but if no eligible princes remained alive, the danger would be averted. Whether or not the youthful Mehmed entertained such thoughts, his action gave evidence of his utter lack of sentimentality. He found himself forthwith at war, quelling a revolt in Asia Minor where the prince of Karaman had again challenged Ottoman supremacy in confident expectation that the change of rulership would be followed as in the past by internal disorder. This situation induced the last emperor of the house of Palaeologus, Constantine XI, to make an unwise move. Since Murad II's reign he had held in custody an Ottoman prince named Orhan, for whose maintenance he received a subvention from the Ottoman government. Constantine now asked Mehmed for a large increase in the subvention, failing which he threatened to let Orhan loose as a pretender to the Ottoman throne. This step by the rash Byzantine ruler sealed the fate of his realm and dynasty. Mehmed first asserted his power by instituting a sort of economic blockade of Constantinople; he built a mighty fortress, Rumeli Hisar, on the European side of the Bosphorus and required all ships bound for the city to pay burdensome tolls. When the emperor sent envoys to plead with him against the construction of the fortress, he had them beheaded, thereby formally declaring war. For this final struggle the Ottomans assembled a large army, which included an artillery contingent of remarkable strength for those days, with some huge guns founded by the Transylvanian master of the artillery Urban. Western Christian experts, most of them Italian, advised the Sultan as he besieged Eastern Christianity's metropolis, and through their suggestions greatly facilitated his success. Only the Genoese on the island of Chios lifted a hand to help the Byzantines. In Western Europe much concern was expressed, but little zeal was shown for action. Last-moment plans for a reunion of the Catholic and Orthodox churches, which the Pope regarded as a precondition for Western aid to the Byzantines, came to nothing on account of fanatical popular opposition instigated by Orthodox monks. With their city under fire from Mehmed's guns, the people were saying "Better the Turkish turban than the Latin mitre in our midst". After a siege lasting two months, the Ottomans took Constantinople by storm and with grim slaughter on May 29, 1453 – a date considered by many historians to be one of the turning points which mark the end of the middle ages and commencement of modern times. A relief force finally assembled by the Western Christian powers was still at sea in the Aegean when the city fell. The last Roman emperor, Constantine XI, died fighting bravely. The crescent replaced the cross on the great dome of St. Sophia, built by the emperor Justinian in 532; and Constantinople, known in Turkish as İstanbul, became the capital of the Ottoman empire, so to remain until 1922.

The new rulers took vigorous steps to repopulate Constantinople, with Turks, and with returning Greeks, Balkan Slavs and various elements from Asia Minor. They also endeavoured to reorganize the Ottoman system of government, and in so doing were influenced by the Byzantine prototype. Greek families who now settled in the Phanar quarter of the city were in later times to play an important role in the Ottoman state, notably as interpreters to the Sublime Porte (*Bāb-i ʿĀlī*, i.e. the imperial chancellery). The subject peoples, designated as *râya* (i.e. "flocks"), were not in any way restrained from practising their religions and customs, nor from using their own languages; in accordance with Islamic precedent, they were placed under the jurisdiction of their respective religious dignitaries. At the head of the Orthodox community stood the patriarch Gennadius, a Greek strongly antagonistic to Rome, who compiled for the Sultan a much appreciated treatise on Christian beliefs and practices. Mehmed's curiosity about the Christian religion was prompted solely by political considerations, but was sufficient to induce widespread rumour in Western Europe to the effect that he was at heart a Christian. The truth seems to be that privately he was a free-thinker, while publicly he sought and obtained the support of the Sunnite *ulema*. With the Western maritime states then represented at İstanbul, among which Genoa was still preeminent, relations were adjusted by means of commercial treaties authorizing continuance of their trade against payment of agreed imposts. On the other hand, not a few of the city's learned scholars fled before or after its fall to Italy, where they contributed to the revival of interest in classical antiquity associated with the Italian Renaissance.

Having plucked out the Byzantine thorn from the heart of his empire, Mehmed II, now surnamed *Fatih* ("the Conqueror"), was free to direct his ambitious gaze towards prospects of further conquest. He had good reason to assess them as favourable, considering the state of contemporary Western Europe. The insensate warring of the Catholic Christians, their obtuse disregard of danger, spiteful pleasure in one another's misfortunes, and suicidal propensity to treason, were Mehmed's strongest weapons against his Western adversaries; except for these, it is doubtful whether even he, with all his efficiency and ruthless drive, could ever have won such great victories. Never at a loss to find pretexts for his actions, he set out after 1455 to round off his Balkan holdings. Ainos (Enez), at the Maritza mouth, was taken from the Genoese in 1456, and a campaign was begun to subdue the Serbs. Their prince George Brankovich was forced to flee the country. He took refuge in Hungary with John Hunyadi, who now received reinforcement with the arrival of an enthusiastic but ill equipped army of Crusaders raised by an eloquent Franciscan friar, Giovanni di Capestrano. In a battle fought on June 22, 1456, they relieved Belgrad from its Ottoman besiegers and compelled Mehmed to retire. A few weeks later, however, first Hunyadi and then Capestrano died; and Brankovich followed them to the grave in 1458. The disappearance of the opposing leaders facilitated Mehmed's task in Serbia, which was reduced to obedience with much severity and in 1459 was declared to be an Ottoman province. In westward forays Ottoman troops penetrated into the northern Adriatic coastlands. Parts of the Peloponnese (Morea) still held by the Palaeologi were also harshly subjugated by Mehmed II, in 1460. In Albania, the irrepressible Skanderbeg had been receiving help from the Kingdom of Naples and the Papal State, and since 1458 also from Venice; Mehmed in 1460 granted him a ten-year truce conditional upon payment of tribute.

In Asia Minor, action was taken in 1461 against the Comneni of Trebizond, scions of an earlier Byzantine dynasty who had maintained their independence and were allied diplomatically and also conjugally with Uzun Ḥasan, chief of the Aq Qoyunlu ("White Sheep") Turkomāns and at the time ruler of Erzincan. After conquering and annexing the Turkish principality of Sinop (Sinope), Mehmed was able to liquidate the independence of Trebizond with little difficulty, because the Aq Qoyunlu, not yet feeling strong enough to challenge the Ottoman army, gave no effective help to their Greek allies. The breach between Uzun Ḥasan and Mehmed was temporarily patched through the diplomacy of Uzun Ḥasan's mother.

The kingdom of Bosnia, which in the past had acknowledged Ottoman suzerainty, was liquidated in 1463/4. From then on Ottoman rule was firmly established in most parts of Bosnia and Hercegovina, where the local nobility for the most part went over to Islam; but in the north it was frequently challenged by the Magyars as long as Hungary remained independent. The year 1463/4 also registered the commencement of a long war against the Venetians, who had already clashed with the Sultan on various occasions since his intervention in the Morea. In the early years of this war the Albanian chieftain Skanderbeg, who was induced to break his truce with the Ottomans, again played a prominent part. Northern Albania became the scene of a fierce though small-scale conflict, and Kroya again resisted an Ottoman siege; but after Skanderbeg's sudden death on January 17, 1467, the dream of Albanian independence faded. To assert their mastery, the Ottomans erected in thirty days a "land-subduing" fortress, Elbasan. The Albanians never lost their love of freedom; but in the course of time Islam spread widely among them, and many sons of this small nation achieved high rank in the Ottoman service as generals and *vezirs*.

The Ottoman onslaught against the scattered Venetian outposts in Albania and Greece sorely tried the Italian republic's strength. Hoping to involve Mehmed II in a war on two fronts, the Signoria of Venice had already entered into an alliance with Uzun Ḥasan, but the difficulty of arranging common action was to prove insuperable; while a league of Italian states formed ostensibly for mutual defence against the Turks turned out to be quite valueless. In fact Venice stood alone. In the summer of 1470 Ottoman troops landed on Euboea and stormed Negroponte (Chalcis), Venice's oldest and strongest Levantine base. Two years later, however, the Ottomans were threatened on their eastern flank by Uzun Ḥasan. Having taken over the sovereignty of western Īrān and of ʿIrāq and the Jazīrah between 1466 and 1469, the Turkomān ruler ventured upon an offensive against Tokat and Kayseri. Mehmed II personally took the field against him early in 1473. Uzun Ḥasan inflicted an initial defeat on the Ottoman vanguard, but suffered a severe reverse when he encountered Mehmed's main army in the late summer near Erzincan; he was nevertheless able to retire with the bulk of his forces, and Mehmed decided not to attempt a pursuit in such difficult country. The partial victory at Erzincan represented an important success for Mehmed, because the Aq Qoyunlu did not again dare, despite persistent Venetian urgings, to invade Ottoman territory; moreover, there were plenty of troubles inside their own empire to keep them otherwise occupied. After dealing with the Cilician and other buffer states in 1474, Mehmed could reckon that his eastern flank was secure and that further westward thrusts would be feasible. At this very juncture a new field for expansion was opened to him. He received an appeal for help from certain Tatar chiefs in the Crimea who were at odds with the local Genoese colonies. The Genoese had long possessed important trading establishments on the north shore of the Black Sea, with Kaffa (later Feodosia) as their chief centre, and they were on good terms with the Khān of the Crimea, Mengli

Girāy. When the Khān took the side of the Genoese in their disputes, Mehmed seized the opportunity to intervene. Kaffa surrendered to an Ottoman fleet on June 6, 1475, and the Crimean Khānate became a vassal state under Ottoman suzerainty, while the Genoese trade with the Black Sea was ruined. This event had great historical importance, not merely for the Tatars and the Genoese, but also because it marked the closure of the last remaining route from Western Europe to India and the Far East not already under Ottoman or Mamlūk control. The fall of Kaffa was one of the factors which gave urgency to the European quest for new routes to India in the Age of Discovery. Mehmed II's war with Venice finally came to an end in 1479 when the proud Republic felt obliged to accept an inglorious peace. The Venetians ceded the islands of Euboea and Lemnos, and various possessions in the Morea and on the Albanian coast; they purchased freedom for their trade in the Levant by agreeing to pay a war indemnity of 100,000 ducats and an annual rent of 10,000 ducats.

During the next two years, which were to be the last of Mehmed II's allotted span, his appetite for conquest remained insatiable. In 1480 Ottoman forces seized a foothold on Italian soil, at Otranto in Apulia; they held it until shortly after his death. On the other hand an expedition against the Knights of St. John on Rhodes was unsuccessful. According to Ottoman historians, Mehmed had set out on a second attempt against Christian Rhodes when he died suddenly at his camp near Gebze on the Sea of Marmara on May 3, 1481. In the light of modern research it can be taken as fairly certain that he was poisoned, at the behest of his son and successor Bayezid and through the instrumentality of a politically active *derviş* order, the Halvetiye. Prince Bayezid, who was serving as governor of Amasya, had grounds for belief that his father intended to do away with him and substitute a younger son, Prince Cem, as heir to the throne.

Mehmed II has been described by some historians as a typical Renaissance prince and as having an interest in classical Greco-Roman culture. In reality his curiosity about Italy arose from purely strategic considerations. As a patron of Muslim and especially Persian men of letters he did indeed show considerable munificence, though none of the poets whom he supported won any significant place in literary history. His architectural taste was not very distinguished and in no way comparable with that of his father Murad II or of his great-grandson Süleyman the Magnificent; his chief surviving monuments are the much reconstructed Fatih (Conqueror's) mosque in İstanbul, various appendages to palaces such as the Persian-style Çinili (Faience) Kiosk, the so-called "Ahter Medreses," and a large number of castles attesting his paramount interest in military affairs. As a freethinker he felt no religious objection to any kind of art, and in the last year of his life he even had his portrait painted by the Venetian artist Gentile Bellini. Mehmed II's place in history depends upon his conquests, not upon cultural achievements. He firmly established Ottoman rule in the regions which were to remain the empire's heartland for almost half a millennium.

Mehmed II's son *Bayezid II* (r. 1481–1512) has acquired an undeserved reputation as a weak and irresolute Sultan. Recent research, however, shows that this view must be revised. He was not temperamentally a conqueror, and knew that he was not; he preferred cautious calculation, and practised it with much skill. In the transition from the old Ottoman state to the future multinational Near Eastern empire, his reign gave a pause for consolidation. Though his piety bordered on bigotry, he had genuine spiritual leanings and a rooted aversion to war. He could strike hard, however, when it was a question of defending his own position or, as would several times be seen, of extirpating heretics. In his readiness to use underhand methods such as poisoning and assassination, he resembled other contemporary rulers in both the East and the West. He had first to fight a long civil war in defence of his throne against the claims of his younger half-brother Cem, who took up the sword when Bayezid refused to divide the empire with him. After the failure of his appeal to arms, Prince Cem fled to Egypt and then, after an unsuccessful raid into Asia Minor, to Rhodes. He afterwards met with extraordinary adventures. The Christian powers of the West were eager to use him as an instrument of pressure against the Sultan, since he had many supporters inside the Ottoman empire; but the Knights of St. John, who had made peace with Bayezid, would not join in such schemes. They sent him to France and kept him in custody at various places in that country. Plots to kidnap him were constantly being hatched, and his continued presence on the scene caused the Sultan many a sleepless night. After seven years he was transferred to Papal custody in Rome, where in 1495 he was captured by King Charles VIII of France; a month later he died, having allegedly been poisoned at Bayezid's request by Pope Alexander VI (formerly Cardinal Rodrigo Borgia). Apart from the usual forays into Christian territory, the Ottoman empire's first military involvement in Bayezid's reign was with Poland, whose expansion towards the Black Sea coast aroused concern at İstanbul; an Ottoman army had to be sent to Moldavia in the summer of 1484, and the important harbours of Kilia (Chilia) and Ak Kerman (Cetatea Alba, now Belgorod) at the mouths of the Danube and Dniestr were conquered. In the following year Bayezid found himself at war with another enemy, namely the Mamlūks of Egypt and Syria, who claimed to be the paramount power in the Muslim Near East and looked upon the Ottoman dynasty as upstarts. This war, which arose from trouble over the buffer states of Cilicia and Elbistan, lasted from 1485 to 1491 and did not turn out well for the Ottomans, who in consequence of a defeat at Ağa Çayiri in 1488 lost Adana and Tarsus. In Europe skirmishing continued as usual beyond the western and northern frontiers; the Austrian provinces of Carniola, Carinthia and Styria frequently suffered from destructive raids by Ottoman *akincis* (cavalry scouts). When the Venetians took over Cyprus in 1489 and occupied Naxos, Bayezid preferred not to make an issue of these matters; but in 1499 he decided to challenge a coalition formed by Venice, Hungary and the Pope. The war was fought with varying success until 1503, when Bayezid was content to make peace in return for the abandonment by Venice of her claims to Durazzo (Draç; Durrës) in Albania and Lepanto (Navpaktos) and Messinia in Greece. His empire's eastern borderlands now lay under the shadow of a great power which had newly arisen in Īrān and which represented a rival religious tendency, namely the Shīʿite state of the Ṣafavids. Bayezid himself, however, did not live to take part in the impending clash. His sons began disputing among themselves about the future succession, and in 1512 one of them, Selim, compelled him to abdicate and then had him poisoned.

Bayezid fostered art and literature in the best tradition of eastern royal patronage. Ottoman poetry was much influenced at this stage by the work of Jāmī (1414–1492), the Persian poet and Ṣūfī scholar of Harāt, with whom Bayezid corresponded. Among the many buildings which he caused to be put up, his mosque in İstanbul, called the Bayezid mosque or mosque of the doves, is the most notable, with its Persian-style architecture and lavish but tasteful ornamentation.

The short but eventful reign of *Selim I*, surnamed *Yavuz* ("the Grim"; 1512–1520) was almost wholly devoted to war against the Shīʿite Ṣafavid kingdom and the hitherto mighty Mamlūk sultanate. Internally its most important feature was a ruthless persecution of all Shīʿite movements, which must have appeared the more obnoxious to the Sultan in that they could look for support from the Ṣafavids. Already in the last year of his father's reign, south western Anatolia had been convulsed by a dangerous Shīʿite revolt, which was suppressed with much bloodshed. Shīʿite sects nevertheless maintained an underground existence, and the Sunnite-Shīʿite discord continued to smoulder through the centuries. Selim also had to sustain a long and bloody struggle against his elder half-brother

Ahmed before his position on the throne became secure. Not until two years had passed did he feel strong enough to undertake a campaign against the Ṣafavids. In 1514, at the battle of Çaldiran (Chāldirān; in Āẕarbāyjān) he defeated the Ṣafavid Shāh Ismāʿīl and temporarily occupied his capital Tabrīz. Freed thereby from further danger in the north, Selim was in a position to take steps, which he must assuredly have planned in advance, against the Mamlūk empire. He dealt first with the buffer state of the Dhū'l-Qadr Turkomāns in Elbistan and Marʿaş, defeating and killing their aged prince 'Alā' al-Dawlah who was his own grandfather. On August 24, 1516 he met the Mamlūk army at Marj Dābiq, north of Aleppo, and won an overwhelming victory, thanks partly to his artillery and partly to the desertion of a Mamlūk general. In the autumn he triumphantly entered Damascus; and after the Mamlūks had rejected his demand that they acknowledge Ottoman suzerainty, he resumed his victorious advance. In January 1517 Cairo fell, and in April the last Mamlūk Sultan, Tūmān Bāy, was captured and executed. All of Egypt and its dependencies thus passed into Ottoman hands. Selim thereby acquired for his dynasty the titular guardianship of the Muslim holy places in the Ḥijāz. He also assumed the title Caliph, hitherto used by an ʿAbbāsid dignitary resident in Cairo but long shorn of its once great importance; it was to be retained by his descendants until 1924. The former Mamlūk territories annexed by Selim were brought into a rather loose relationship with the Ottoman government. In Egypt the local Mamlūk aristocracy was able to retain a dominant position. The Venetians hastened to obtain confirmation of their trading rights from the new sovereign authorities; and arrangements were made concerning the Holy Sepulchre at Jerusalem. In consequence of Selim I's conquests, the Ottoman empire became the defender of Sunnite orthodoxy and incomparably the foremost Muslim power, and such it was to remain until the 20th century. With the Western Christians, Selim was involved only in unimportant skirmishes; but the alarm called forth by his eastern triumphs rekindled crusading zeal in Europe, and he evidently began planning campaigns in that direction. By 1519 preparations for an attack on Rhodes had reached an advanced stage. This was not to be led by Selim, however; for in 1520 he was suddenly snatched away by the plague.

Selim I's appellation "the Grim" was well deserved. His reign could not be a time for much cultural effort; but one achievement deserves mention. This is a geographical work, executed primarily for strategic purposes: namely the first world map of the Ottoman admiral Piri Reis, which is considered on strong grounds to incorporate a lost map prepared by

Christopher Columbus in illustration of his American discoveries. This map, and a second world map showing South America, were probably pickings of Ottoman espionnage, in which Italians as so often in those days must have played the leading part.

The struggle against the Shīʿah, which had begun under Bayezid I, was conducted with much cruelty and bloodshed. A notable feature of it was the transplantation of whole population groups from one part of the empire to another; this contributed to the ethnic variety still found in many regions once under Ottoman rule. Bayezid's amical policy towards the *derviş* orders was reversed, and an attempt was made to suppress them, but without success.

Selim I's reign left a lasting impact upon Ottoman history. Internally, Sunnite orthodoxy supplanted the pro-Shīʿite, or at least pro-ʿAlid, tendencies apparent in earlier times, and thenceforward maintained an unquestionable supremacy. Externally, the Ottoman state, which had hitherto fulfilled the role of successor to the old Byzantine empire of "Rūm" in Europe and Asia Minor, now assumed new commitments of world-wide importance as the dominant Muslim power in the entire Near East and Mediterranean basin.

After Selim I's unexpected death, the throne passed without contention to his son *Süleyman* (r. 1520–1566), the greatest of all the Ottoman Sultans. In Western Europe he became known as the "Magnificent" on account of his grandiose tastes, expressed above all in the assiduous building of splendid edifices. To the Turks he appears as the "Lawgiver" *(Kanunî)*, on account of his important legislation in fields such as reform of the bureaucracy and of the military feudal system, regulation of the status and land-tenure of non-Muslims, improvement of procedure etc. He had the good fortune and good sense to obtain first-rate advice from the grand *vezir* İbrahim Paşa, the *Şeyhülislâm* (i.e. grand *muftī*) Ebüssuud, the architect Sinan, and other outstandingly able men. In international affairs, the empire's position underwent further change. Hitherto the Ottoman Turks had been viewed in Europe as unwelcome intruders who ought to be pushed back into Central Asia; now they became an essential factor in the European balance of power. From Süleyman's reign dates the beginning of a centuries-long Franco-Ottoman collaboration prompted by common antagonism against the house of Habsburg. For the consolidation and eventual expansion of the immense territories under Ottoman rule, three immediate strategic objectives stood forth: to secure the north west frontier; to win naval command of the Mediterranean Sea; and to maintain a stable equilibrium with Shīʿite Īrān.

Süleyman's first campaign, in 1521, resulted in the capture of Belgrad from the Hungarians. He then mobilized all available forces to expel the Knights of St. John from their stronghold Rhodes, which lay like a pistol pointed at the heart of the empire. In this task, which both his father and his grandfather had planned, he succeeded; Rhodes fell to the Ottomans, after a long siege, in December 1522. Its defenders and its Greek inhabitants were well treated, in keeping with the Sultan's generous and humane disposition; the Knights received a safe-conduct and withdrew, first to Italy, and then in 1530 to Malta, whence the Ottoman navy was never able to dislodge them, while the inhabitants received guarantees of immunity from enslavement and confiscation and a five-year exemption from taxes. In 1526 Süleyman decided to invade Hungary, whose former strength had been eroded by internal strife. At the battle of Mohács in August 1526, the Magyar army was destroyed and the young King Louis (Lajos) II was drowned. Therewith the independent kingdom of Hungary came to an end. The reversion of the Hungarian crown now became a bone of contention between the Ottomans and the Habsburgs. Both King Ferdinand of Austria and Bohemia and the voivode John Zápolya (Szápolyai János) of Transylvania claimed the crown of St. Stephen, and the Sultan supported the Transylvanian claimant. In 1529 Süleyman conquered Buda and began the first Turkish siege of Vienna, but luckily for the defenders was obliged to withdraw on account of difficulty in supplying his troops. The result of the campaign was that the greater part of Hungary fell into the Ottoman sphere of influence under Zápolya's formal authority. In a second campaign, Süleyman attempted unsuccessfully in 1532 to conquer the rest of Hungary; tenacious resistance at Köszeg (Güns) delayed his advance towards Vienna, and when the besieged fortress ultimately fell his attention was drawn to new disputes with Īrān. In 1533 the various parties arranged a truce whereby the territorial status quo was restored and both Ferdinand and Zápolya undertook to pay tribute to İstanbul.

In the meantime, Christian and Ottoman naval forces had been at war in the Mediterranean since 1525. Ottoman sea power was greatly reinforced during these years through the collaboration of the famous corsair Hayreddin Barbarossa (d. 1546), who had given allegiance to the Sultan, then Selim I, in 1518. By birth a Greek, Hayreddin had been engaged since the first decade of the century in piracy and private warfare with the Spaniards on the North African coast, where he had captured a number of bases; in 1529 he finally drove the Spaniards out of Algiers. Thanks to arrangements with the French, he was able to operate in the north west Mediterranean also. In 1533 Süleyman appointed him admiral in chief of the Ottoman navy. Since Hayreddin and his successors placed their North African possessions—the so-called "Barbary States"—to all intents and purposes at the Sultan's disposal, the Ottoman empire became incomparably the strongest Mediterranean power. On the opposing side, a great reputation was won by the Genoese admiral Andrea Doria, to whom was due the credit for the Emperor Charles V's recapture of Tunis in 1535. The Turkish corsairs returned the blow by besieging the Venetians on Corfu and temporarily closing the Strait of Otranto.

Hostilities with Īrān were resumed in 1534, after Süleyman had extended his suzerainty over the Kurdish principality of Bitlis (Bidlīs) and laid claim to Baghdād, where a rebel had given allegiance to the Ottoman Sultan, though Ṣafavid authority had later been restored. The war turned out favourably for Süleyman, who took Tabrīz and Baghdād and occupied Āẕarbāyjān and ʿIrāq. Henceforward Baghdād was to remain Ottoman, except for an interval of restored Ṣafavid rule in 1623–1638, right up to 1917.

The policy of alliance with France was endorsed in a commercial treaty of 1536, which initiated two and a half centuries of close collaboration between the Sultan-Caliphs and the Most Christian Kings, and ensured the preeminence of France in Levantine trade. The treaty also sanctioned the so-called "capitulatory" rights of consular jurisdiction over French residents in Ottoman territory. In the following decades similar rights were obtained by various other European powers. In 1538 a naval expedition sent from Egypt established Ottoman hegemony in the south-western tip of Arabia, but failed to oust the Portuguese from their stronghold of Diu on the coast of Gujarāt in India. Another war now began in Western Europe, where the Pope, the Venetians and Charles V joined in 1538 to form a "Holy League". The emperor's fleet under Andrea Doria suffered a bad reverse off Preveza in 1540, and a tract of Italian soil near Otranto was again occupied by Ottoman troops. The Venetians, who had borne the brunt, then made peace; they had to surrender Nauplia (Navplion), their last foothold in the Morea. An attempt in 1541 by Charles V's ships to recapture Algiers failed miserably. In the same year nearly all of Hungary passed under Ottoman rule; John Zápolya had died, and in answer to King Ferdinand's renewed pretensions to the throne, Süleyman invaded the country and annexed it outright. Fighting continued until 1547, when a truce was made. A narrow strip of western and northern Hungary was left to the Habsburgs; over Budapest the Ottoman flag was to fly more than a century and a half. Not long afterwards came another war with Īrān, which was ended in 1555 by the peace treaty of Amasya; 'Irāq remained in Ottoman hands, and Georgia was divided into Ottoman and Īrānian spheres under native vassal princes. The war in Hungary was then resumed, and in 1562 King Ferdinand was forced to cede Temesvár and the districts south of the Maros (Mureş) river and to renounce his claim to Transylvania.

Fortune, which had thus far been extraordinarily favourable to Süleyman, ceased to smile upon him in his later years. Bloodstained family dissensions and vicious harem intrigues began to weaken the government and foreshadowed the dynasty's future decline. In 1565, after Ferdinand had died and John Zápolya's hitherto insignificant son had put forward claims to north west Hungary, a new war with the Austrians flared up and Süleyman once more led a a great army to the west. The fortress of Sziget, gallantly defended by Count Zrinyi, stood across the Ottoman path. During the siege Süleyman died in his tent on September 6, 1566; two days later Szigetvár fell and Zrinyi was slain. The war was brought to a close in 1568 by a truce whereby Ferdinand's successor, the Emperor Maximilian II, ceded certain small areas and undertook to pay tribute to the Ottoman Sultan.

The Ottoman empire rose during the reign of Süleyman the Magnificent to its zenith. Himself a talented statesman, he was served by brilliant advisers, such as the Albanian İbrahim Paşa, grand *vezir* from 1524 until his downfall and death in 1536. An equally high level was attained in artistic life, particularly in architecture. The genius of the great architect Sinan brought into being the superb Süleymaniye mosque in İstanbul and a vast number of other fine buildings. Even Süleyman's bitterest enemies looked upon him as an august and at the same time chivalrous and conciliatory monarch. At home and abroad he made an indelible impression on the minds of his contemporaries.

Süleyman's death in 1566 is reckoned by modern historians to mark the commencement of the Ottoman empire's long decline. Although its external expansion did not yet come to a halt, its internal condition began to show dangerous symptoms of decay. First and foremost these affected the ruling dynasty. From this time onwards, the house of Osman ceased, on the whole, to produce capable rulers; with few exceptions, the princes who thereafter ascended the throne were spineless weaklings, addicted to the pleasures of their harems and often pathologically degenerate. The dynasty and the government fell more and more under the influence of palace cliques carrying on intrigues for their own particular ends under the protection of influential harem ladies; a period of "petticoat rule" was beginning. Effective power passed from the titular Sultan to court parasites, and corruption spread in all quarters. The old strictness in the enforcement of laws which ensured the state's wellbeing gave way to laxity. The feudal system, which had been the mainstay of the military structure, became warped by grave abuses. The Janissary corps gradually lost its distinctive character and former efficiency, but was able to make and unmake Sultans like puppets. Cultural activity, on the other hand, remained at a fairly high level. In Turkish literature, however, the early simplicity was supplanted by a euphuistic style, overloaded with Persian and Arabic words, in which preciosity and jingle took precedence over thought and content.

Süleyman the Magnificent's incapable son and successor *Selim II* "the Drunkard" (r. 1566–1574) scarcely deserves mention save that his name is borne by the Selimiye mosque at Edirne, one of Sinan's finest architectural masterpieces. Effective power during his reign lay with the Serbian-born grand *vezir*, Sokollu Mehmed Paşa, who had already served Süleyman in that office since 1536, and with a Jew, Joseph Nasi, who controlled the finances. In distant South Arabia, where Ottoman troops had been stationed since 1538, a partly successful rebellion broke out under the leadership of the Zaydites of the High Yaman. With Austria, peace on the basis of the status quo was restored in 1568, and in the same year a treaty was signed for the restoration of peace with Īrān. Sokollu Mehmed Paşa is said to have planned an invasion of Spain with help from North Africa and from the Spanish Moriscos; since these plans were never translated into action, one can only speculate what might have been their outcome. Nor did success attend an expedition sent in 1569 with a view to conquering the Volga estuary from the Muscovites, with whom peace was restored in the following year. Attention was next given to the problem of Cyprus, which remained in the possession of Venice and seemed to constitute a permanent threat to the coasts of the Ottoman heartland. An ultimatum demanding cession of the island was despatched to the Signoria and underlined by the sequestration of all Venetian property and ships in Ottoman territory and ports. When the Venetians refused, the Ottoman fleet landed troops on Cyprus in May 1570. After heavy fighting, the island was conquered in August 1571. No help from the West reached the defenders, even though Pope Pius V had again brought Spain and Venice together in a Holy League, to which other Italian states adhered. The Ottomans sought to check the Pope's move by an alliance with France; but on this occasion their diplomacy proved ineffective, as the French were preoccupied with internal wars of religion. Off Lepanto

(Navpaktos; Aynabahtī) in October 1571, the Holy League's fleet under the command of Don John of Austria won a great victory over the Ottoman navy and effectively destroyed the legend of Ottoman invincibility. Don John, however, failed discreditably to follow up the victory, and the Christian allies soon fell apart. The Ottomans thus had time to rebuild their fleet. The Spaniards were content to maintain Spanish naval supremacy in the western Mediterranean. They temporarily reoccupied Tunis, whence Ottoman forces had in 1571 dislodged the last Spanish-protected Ḥafṣid prince, but in 1574 lost the city to the Ottomans for good. In March 1573 Venice had concluded a separate peace with the Ottomans, recognizing the cession of Cyprus and undertaking to pay a war indemnity of 300,000 ducats. The formal truce with Austria was renewed late in 1574, though on the borders informal guerrilla warfare continued; this led eventually to the institution of the "military frontier." Selim II, whose role in all these affairs was negligible, died in December 1574.

His son and successor *Murad III* (r. 1574–1595) was an almost equally insignificant ruler, being interested mainly in the pleasures of his harem. Affairs of state he left gladly to the care of his mother, Nur Banu, and of his favourite wife, who was Italian by birth. The Venetians, no longer expecting help from the Western powers, now sought an alliance with Shāh Tahmāsb of Īrān in the hope of embroiling the Ottomans on two fronts. Tahmāsb's death in 1576 and the subsequent weakness of the Ṣafavids provided an opportunity to frustrate the threatened Īrāno-Venetian coalition. The Sultan's troops invaded Caucasia, occupied Tiflis, and brought almost the entire region south of the Caucasus range under Ottoman hegemony. In 1579, however, the empire's internal stability suffered a severe blow when the grand *vezir* Sokollu Mehmed was murdered. Thereafter the high offices of state changed hands frequently. The protracted war against Īrān went on until the new Shāh ʿAbbās I assented in 1590 to an inglorious peace treaty, recognizing the annexation of Georgia, Shīrvān, Qarabāgh, Tabrīz and Luristān by the Ottomans, who thus extended their sovereignty to the Caucasus and the Caspian Sea and onto the Īrānian plateau. Besides accepting these losses, the Īrānians undertook to stop anti-Sunnite practices in the territory left to them. In 1593 a new war was undertaken in the west, where the governor of Bosnia had met with a bloody defeat in the guerrilla fighting in Hungary. Before military operations began in earnest, the incapable Murad III died, in January 1595. His son and successor *Mehmed III* (r. 1595–1603) thus had an opportunity to show that Sultans could still be warriors. He personally took part in the famous battle of Keresztes in October 1596, when the Ottomans won a brilliant victory over the Habsburg forces. Already before this success they had captured the nearby fortress of Eger (Erlau), thus opening the way towards Moravia. The war nevertheless dragged on indecisively and did not come to an end until 1606, in the next Sultan's reign. Meanwhile in the east disorders had broken out which enabled the mighty Ṣafavid ruler ʿAbbās I to resume hostilities in 1603 and recover Tabrīz. Fortune did not befriend Mehmed III during most of his reign; he died in December 1603.

His son *Ahmed I* (r. 1603–1617) was a relatively humane ruler and the first Sultan since Mehmed II to refrain from massacring the royal brothers and other potentially rival princes; the practice henceforward was to keep them in gilded imprisonment. Ahmed I was also responsible for the building of the beautiful "Blue Mosque" in İstanbul and for a plan to regularize the empire's administrative and commercial laws. He inherited the unfinished Austrian and Īrānian wars and in neither of them met with good fortune. After the defeat of his troops at Salmās near Lake Urumīyah in 1605, the Īrānians reoccupied Erivan, Kars and Shīrvān, and threatened Baghdād, Mosul and Diyarbakır. In the war with Austria, the situation was more favourable to the Ottomans. They had the satisfaction of seeing the election of Stephen Bocskay (Bocskai István), an opponent of the Habsburgs and protector of Protestants, to the voivodeship of Transylvania, which he governed as a loyal vassal of the Ottoman empire. By the truce of Zsitvatorok, concluded in November 1606, Austria also recognized him as voivode, besides ceding to the Ottomans Eger, Kanizsa and Esztergom (Gran); the question of suzerainty was left in suspense. Concurrently with the long war in the east, internal Shīʿite revolts broke out in eastern Anatolia and the province of Aleppo; it was not possible to suppress them until 1607/8. In 1612 the Ottoman and Ṣafavid empires made peace, only to resume fighting four years later and make peace again in 1618, when Āẕarbāyjān, Shīrvān and Georgia were retroceded to Īrān. Sultan Ahmed I had died in the previous year. His death was followed by a period of chaos resulting from the indiscipline of the Janissaries and from setbacks abroad. His brother and rightful successor *Mustafa I* turned out to be a weak-minded tool in the hands of a clique of courtiers, and was dethroned by a palace revolution after a reign of three months. In his place was set a prince still of minor age, *Osman II* (r. 1618–1622). Border clashes now gave rise to a war with Poland. At the battle of Jassy (Iasi) in September 1620 the Ottoman troops were victorious; but in the following year their siege of Hotin (Choczim), at which the young Sultan himself was present, failed ingloriously, and an unsatisfactory peace treaty had to be concluded with the Poles. There were good grounds for blaming this reverse upon the conduct of the Janissaries, and Osman II was persuaded to join in a scheme to get rid of them; but reports of his intentions leaked to the palace guard and a coup d'état was staged. This cost Osman II his throne and presently also his life. The half-witted Mustafa I was reinstated on the throne for almost a year. The real rulers, however, were the Janissaries, who soon made themselves universally unpopular and in some provinces provoked fairly serious disturbances. Not until the autumn of 1623 did wiser forces prevail. Mustafa I was then again deposed, and replaced by *Murad IV* (r. 1623–1640), a brother of Ahmed I and likewise only a boy. As he grew up, Murad IV was able to take the reins into his own hands and govern quite autocratically. Realizing that unless he faced the challenge of the Janissaries he too might become their pawn, he took peaceful steps to cut down the strength of the corps by suspending the levy of boys and by building up other army corps such as the *cebecis* ("armourers") and *bostancis* ("gardeners"; in fact a sort of police). He also sought to restore the government's finances, now crippled by corruption, through rigorous control of the accounts and systematic confiscation of all suspiciously swollen private fortunes. In 1634 the "capitulatory" rights of foreign residents were formally renewed. Murad IV personally supervised the execution of his decrees and savagely punished contraventions. He was particularly severe against two luxuries which had become fashionable in Ottoman society since the turn of the century, namely tobacco smoking and coffee drinking. In foreign affairs, the Ottoman cause did not prosper in the early years of Murad IV's reign, but made a remarkable recovery after he took over the reins of power. The worst blow fell in the east, where the Īrānians were able to regain Baghdād in 1623. Another ignominy was the appearance of seafaring Cossacks on plundering raids off the Bosphorus and along the Turkish Black Sea coast. At the same time trouble was brewing in the vassal Tatar state of the Crimea. In the Lebanon a very serious danger arose when the Druze prince Fakhr al-Dīn, who had already played a part in the Shīʿite disorders of 1607, joined with Tuscany, whose Duke hoped to open a new trade route to the east, in an anti-Ottoman league also including the Papal State and Spain. Taking advantage of the Ottoman-Īrānian wars, Fakhr al-Dīn succeeded in carving out an autonomous Syrian domain in defiance of Ottoman authority. In 1633, however, his open attacks on Ottoman troops compelled the Sultan to take drastic action, and a campaign was mounted by land and sea against the rebels, ending with the capitulation of the Druze leader, who was removed to İstanbul and beheaded in 1635. The following years were taken up with continual fighting in the Ottoman-Īrānian border zones. In 1638 Murad IV personally reconquered Baghdād, to the accompaniment of shocking massacres of the Shīʿite population. Peace with Īrān was restored in 1639 by a treaty which confirmed the Ottoman possession of Baghdād while leaving the fiercely contested Armenian city of Erivan in Īrānian hands. The Ottoman recovery came to an abrupt halt, however, with Murad's premature death early in 1640, and was not to be resumed until several years later. He was the last of the fighting Sultans, and the last who really governed.

In complete contrast, his brother and successor *İbrahim* (r. 1640–1648) was a politically incompetent weakling, though reputed to be a more than ordinarily ardent voluptuary in the harem. Indeed he showed symptoms of psychopathic derangement. Always ready to comply with any courtesan's whim, no matter how absurd or costly, he felt no concern whatever for the solvency of the Treasury. The strongest influence over him, however, was exercised by the notorious *softa* (religious student) Cinci Hoca, an Ottoman Rasputin who merely encouraged the erratic Sultan in his misguided passions. The empire thus fell back under "petticoat rule". The capable grand *vezir* Mustafa did what he could to check this evil and maintain the finances, but only brought down on himself the enmity of the palace cliques and other affected interests; in 1644 they instigated a pronunciamento of the Janissaries against the *vezir*, whom İbrahim readily sacrificed to the mutinous rabble. After this, the bold decision was taken to make war against the Venetians in the hope of conquering Crete, their last important Levantine possession. A casus belli had arisen when Maltese corsairs found shelter in Cretan waters after attacking an Ottoman convoy. Advocates of offensive action gained the upper hand at İstanbul, and in 1645 Ottoman troops were landed on Crete and sent into Dalmatia. The fighting, however, dragged on indecisively. Meanwhile the Sultan carried his extravagances to a degree suggestive of insanity. He was finally brought down by his own mother. A palace putsch which she set in motion swept the uxorious Sultan from the throne and ten days later to the gallows. The reign of his minor son and successor *Mehmed IV* (1648–1687) began with a disordered period of of incessant factional intrigues, which together with the continuing Venetian war and manifold other embarrassments seemed to be steering the Ottoman empire towards certain disaster. It was to be saved by the energy of an octogenarian official of Albanian origin, Mehmed Köprülü. Summoned to the vezirate in 1656, he assumed plenary powers and kept a firm hand at the helm. His success in bringing about a massive recovery of Ottoman strength was a feat of great historical importance. With iron will and unflinching severity, he curbed the pernicious influences of the Janissaries and the harem ladies, and made a clean sweep of incompetent and corrupt elements in the barracks and government offices. He had no inhibitions against utilizing pious foundations (*evkaf*), which came under the authority of the *ulema*, for secular governmental purposes, nor against curtailing the generally very ample incomes of the high religious dignitaries. Even the Sultan's private fortune was not exempt. Frequent death sentences showed that the aged *vezir* was no man to be trifled with. It was fortunate for the empire that when the elder Köprülü died in 1661, his office was made over to his equally competent son Ahmed, who while using milder methods persevered in the same policy.

The first neighbouring ruler to learn how the tide had changed at İstanbul was the Transylvanian prince George Rákóczy (Rákóczy György), who had taken advantage of the earlier Ottoman weakness to evade his feudal obligations to the Sublime Porte. The Ottoman government deposed him in 1657, sent troops into the country, and installed a pro-Turkish candidate, Michael Apaffy (Apaffy Mihály) in his place. This action, while restoring Ottoman hegemony in the Transdanubian region, caused a new international crisis because the Habsburg emperor, in deference to Magyar wishes, refused to recognize the new appointment; and when the Porte threatened war, all Western Europe seemed ready to join forces against the Turkish peril now reemerging in the east after a long quiescence. Even the Most Christian king of France saw fit to disregard the old Franco-Ottoman friendship; in response to a Papal appeal he agreed that his Rhenish allies might place their troops at the emperor's disposal. The government at Vienna nevertheless adopted a policy of procrastination, in the hope that the dispute might be settled peacefully. By 1663 the Porte was unwilling to be kept waiting longer and sent troops into the part of Hungary under Habsburg rule. The line of march of certain Ottoman columns suggested that their target might be Vienna. Urgent appeals for help went forth from the emperor to the Rhenish League and even to Sweden. The imperial forces commanded by the Count of Montecuccoli were able, however, to check the Ottoman invasion. Although Neuhäusl (Érsekújvár), north of the Danube, fell to the Turks, Montecuccoli won a brilliant victory over them at St. Gotthard on the Raab (Rába) river in 1664. This led the Ottoman government to sign in 1665 the peace treaty of Eisenburg, whereby the Austrians, who were more afraid of France, conceded favourable terms; they acknowledged the Ottoman suzerainty over Transylvania and possession of Neuhäusl. The Magyars, who had contributed much to the victory at St. Gotthard, looked upon this treaty as a betrayal. It had been negotiated by an impressive Ottoman mission, notable for having had among its members the indefatigable traveller Evliya Çelebi, whose perspicacious account of his journeys is one of the masterpieces of 17th century geography and of Turkish literature. Valuable geographical works in Turkish were also written by Mehmed Aşik and by the noted bibliographer Haci Halife (d. 1658).

Having made peace with Austria, the Ottomans were able to fix their attention on the long drawn out war in Crete. The conjuncture was propitious, because Venice now stood alone, while France could no longer pursue a tortuous diplomacy but was forced to make a painful choice. In an attempt to protect the Mediterranean sea-routes from depredations by the Barbary pirates, who were nominally Ottoman subjects, the French had gone so far as to bombard Algiers and Tunis. The Sublime Porte resented such violent action and was also incensed by the support which France had given, even if half-heartedly, for the crusading plans discussed in 1663. At the same time the Most Christian king Louis XIV needed the Turks as allies in his policy of encirclement directed against the Habsburg empire. He therefore wished to conciliate the Porte, and delayed sending the promised French help to the beleaguered Venetians until it was too late. Their last stronghold, Candia (Iraklion), fell in 1669, and in a peace treaty signed in 1670 they ceded Crete to the Ottoman empire while retaining a right to keep three small establishments on the island.

Meanwhile, in the north, menacing storm clouds had gathered. The Cossack *hetman* Peter Doroshenko, who was considered by the government of Poland to be a Polish subject, had placed himself in 1668 under the suzerainty of the Ottoman Sultan. Not surprisingly the Turks were eager to tighten this relationship and turn it to good advantage. After obtaining an assurance from the Most Christian king that there would be no French objection, the Sublime Porte sent an ultimatum to the Poles in 1672 demanding formal cession of the Ukraine to the Ottoman empire. The demand was followed by immediate war. The Ottoman troops captured Kamenets (Kamieniecz) in the autumn, but failed to take Hotin (Choczim), another important fortress in Podolia. Before the year was out, King Michael Wisniowiecki hastily signed the peace treaty of Buczacz, whereby he conceded the Ottoman demand for title to the Ukraine and even promised to cede Podolia; but such terms were unacceptable to the Polish army commander John Sobieski, who after Michael's death in 1674 was elected king. He resumed the struggle against the Turks, and won several victories before suffering a defeat at Zurawno in 1676, which wiped out his gains and obliged him to accept virtually the same peace terms in regard to Podolia and the Ukraine. Seen in retrospect, however, the Turkish victory may be said to have opened the way for a future conflict which was to endure through the centuries; for through it the Ottoman Turks (not just their Crimean vassals) first became next-door neighbours of Russia. In October of the same year 1676 Ahmed Köprülü died, and the grand vezirate passed to his brother Kara Mustafa.

War with Russia was not long delayed. The Sublime Porte intervened in hostilities which took place between the Cossacks and Russia in the years 1677–1681. Peace was restored in 1681 by the treaty of Radzin, which provided for Ottoman recognition of Russia's annexation of Kiev and adjacent districts, and for the grant of Black Sea trading rights to the Cossacks.

With the Austrians, a sudden crisis arose in 1682, when the Porte gave active help to the anti-Habsburg revolt of a section of the Magyar nobility led by Count Tököly. In the early summer of 1683 a powerful Turkish army marched forth from Belgrad under the grand *vezir* Kara Mustafa and laid siege to Vienna. The defenders under Prince Starhemberg fought bravely but were greatly outnumbered. The Most Christian king, who stood wholeheartedly on the side of France's Turkish ally, had adopted a threatening attitude towards the Habsburg monarchy. Vienna was nevertheless relieved by King John Sobieski's Polish troops together with German troops under Duke Charles of Lorraine. On September 12, 1683, the Ottoman army met with a memorable defeat on the heights of the Kahlenberg above the city, and took to a headlong flight, abandoning vast quantities of baggage. The grand *vezir* was condemned to death. The German and Polish allies, even though they were at cross purposes, did not rest content with the Ottoman retreat. They judged the time ripe to liberate Hungary from the Turks. Now that the worst was over and the Turks had been beaten, no difficulties arose over the formation of a "Holy Alliance" to take advantage of the situation. The partners were Austria, Poland, Venice and the Papal State. Not much success fell to the lot of the Poles, who strove in vain to recapture Kamieniecz. The Austrians, on the other hand, captured Buda on September 2, 1686, putting an end to Turkish rule which had lasted 145 years. The Venetians scored some transient successes in the Morea in 1687 and also temporarily occupied Athens; unfortunately the Parthenon, which was being used as an Ottoman powder-magazine, suffered extensive damage when hit by Venetian gunfire. The Russians joined the alliance in 1687, and by 1689 were at the walls of Azov. In midsummer 1687 the Austrians inflicted a crushing defeat on the Turks at the historic fields of Mohács, scene of the great Ottoman victory over the Magyars in 1526. The Hungarian diet at Pozsony (Pressburg; Bratislava) thereupon made the crown of St. Stephen hereditary in the male line of the Habsburg dynasty. Within the Ottoman realm, and especially at the capital, unprecedented panic prevailed. The Janissaries mutinied, and many people expected a total collapse. The grand *vezir* Süleyman was sacrificed to the clamour of the mob, and the Sultan himself was declared by an assembly of senior *ulema* to be unfit to rule because he preferred the pleasures of the chase to the duties of the monarchy. Mehmed IV's long reign was thus brought to an inglorious end, and the throne was given to his brother *Süleyman II* (r. 1687–1691). News from the war-fronts did not, however, become any less discouraging. Great alarm was caused when the Electoral Prince Maximilian Emmanuel of Bavaria, known to the Turks as the "Blue Prince", took Belgrad by storm in 1688, and when Prince Ludwig of Baden routed an Ottoman army at Nish in the autumn of 1689. The allies could now talk optimistically of driving the Turks out of Europe. Once again, however, the Ottoman empire found a saviour, and once again from the house of Köprülü. This was the new grand *vezir* Mustafa, who took vigorous action to restore order, stabilize the finances, and rehabilitate the demoralized armed forces. Already by 1690 he was able to bring in Tatar reinforcements and launch an offensive in the west. Nish, Semendria, Belgrad and parts of Transsylvania fell again into Turkish hands, and a Venetian invading force was driven out of Albania. Süleyman II died in 1691 and was followed by his incompetent brother *Ahmed II* (r. 1691–1695). Unfortunately for the Ottoman cause, the valiant Mustafa Köprülü lost his life at the battle of Szalánkemén, fought in August 1691 near the Danube-Tisza confluence against imperial troops under Prince Ludwig. Further blows were yet to come. The fortress of Peterwardein (Petrovaradin) on the Danube successfully resisted Ottoman besiegers in 1694, and the Aegean island of Chios fell for a year into Venetian hands. After Ahmed II's death, the throne passed to his nephew *Mustafa II* (r. 1695–1703), an energetic Sultan who personally took the field in Hungary and recaptured Temesvár (Timişoara). The opposing forces, however, were too strong for him, and as a strategist he was no match for the brilliant Austrian commander, Prince Eugene of Savoy; in September 1697 he was decisively beaten at Zenta on the Tisza river. Meanwhile, in August 1969, the Russian Tsar Peter the Great had conquered Azov. A new grand *vezir*, Amucazade Hüseyin, who was also a Köprülü, saw fit to enter with English and Dutch mediation into peace talks; and at the end of January 1699 a treaty was signed at Karlowitz (Karlovci) on the Danube. By it the Ottoman empire lost extensive territories: Hungary (except Temesvár), Transylvania, Slavonia and part of Croatia, to the Habsburg emperor; Kamieniecz and all Podolia with parts of the Ukraine to Poland; and the Morea (except Lepanto) and part of Dalmatia to Venice. With Russia a peace treaty was signed in 1700, when Azov was formally ceded to the Tsar. Deeply mortified by these events, the Sultan withdrew from public life and allowed the grand *vezir* Feyzullah, who had replaced Amucazade Hüseyin, to manage affairs as he chose; his corruption and nepotism made him thoroughly unpopular and in the summer of 1703 provoked a successful insurrection against him. The Sultan himself was then deposed, on account of his neglect of public business, and replaced by Ahmed III, a son of Mehmed IV.

*Ahmed III's* reign (1703–1730) is known in Ottoman history as the "Tulip Period". As in Western Europe, this was an age of elegance, and its characteristic feature among the Turks was a craze for tulip-growing. The last levy of Christian-born Janissary recruits took place in this reign, and the *bostancı* corps was abolished. One effect of the cessation of the *devşirme* was that the Balkan peoples formerly subjected to it henceforward became more conscious of their national identities. In foreign affairs the new Sultan favoured caution. When Francis Rákóczy (Rákóczy Ferenc) led a Magyar revolt against Habsburg rule, the Porte refrained from intervening, but finally granted asylum to him at Rodosto (Tekirdağ) on the Sea of Marmara. Asylum was also granted, at the Ottoman fortress of Bender on the Dniestr river, to King Charles XII of Sweden after he had been defeated by the Russians in 1709. Peter the Great then turned his attention southwards. He called for a revolt of the Ottoman empire's Christian subjects, but met with little response except from the Moldavian Hospodar, Demetrius Cantemir. At the battle of the Pruth river in 1711, the Tsar and his army came within a hair's breadth of total destruction; but thanks to the venality (so it was said) of the grand *vezir* Baltacı Mehmed Paşa, he got off lightly with a peace treaty which only required Russia to retrocede Azov and demolish Taganrog and other fortresses. It was nevertheless an important gain for Ottoman policy that Russia should no longer have access to the Black Sea. In 1714 incidents in Montenegro gave grounds for war with Venice, and the Ottoman army and navy launched large-scale offensives; during the next four years the Adriatic republic lost Corinth, Argos, Nauplia and the rest of the Morea, and its three remaining footholds on Crete. In 1716, however, the Austrians intervened, and their forces under Prince Eugene again beat the Turks in August near Peterwardein; they then occupied Temesvár and "Little" (i.e. western) Wallachia, and a year later succeeded in conquering Belgrad. They could not fully exploit this resounding victory because the emperor Charles VI was preoccupied with Spanish ambitions in Italy. He was glad to make peace in 1718 on rather meagre terms by the treaty of Passarowitz (Pozsarevac; south east of Belgrade). The Habsburg empire annexed Temesvár, Belgrad and northern Serbia, and Little Wallachia. The Morea and the Cretan ports remained in Ottoman possession.

During the next two decades, events in Īrān were to cause the Sublime Porte great anxiety. The breakdown of the Ṣafavid regime enabled Peter the Great to march into Dāghistān, whose native princes then called upon the Ottoman Sultan for help; but their appeal came too late, as the Russian troops had already seized Darband and Bākū on the Caspian coast and established themselves in Transcaucasia. Their Ottoman rivals were only able to take Tiflis. In 1724 Russia and the Porte concluded an agreement by virtue of which Ottoman troops occupied Tabrīz and Ḥamadān; and although the Afghān leader Ashraf Shāh defeated a superior Ottoman force south east of Hamadān in November 1726, he made peace in the following year and acknowledged the Ottoman annexation of western Īrān. These events stirred up great excitement at İstanbul, especially among the Janissaries. When the Sultan hesitated to prepare for war against the Ṣafavid Shāh Tahmāsb II, whose troops after defeating Ashraf had begun an anti-Ottoman offensive, a revolt broke out in the capital. Its leader was a Janissary, formerly a sailor, named Patrona Halil; besides objecting to "Frankish" manners and also to military reform schemes then in vogue at the court, he and his followers put forward socialistic demands and were able to force Ahmed III to abdicate in October 1730. His nephew *Mahmud I* (r. 1730–1754) was then made Sultan, and a virtual dictatorship was exercised by the Janissaries until they were bloodily brought to heel two years later. Meanwhile in Īrān, Tahmāsb had been supplanted by his victorious general Nādir, who later became Shāh. With tacit Russian support, he warred with varying but on the whole considerable success against the Ottomans, until in 1736 they were forced to make a truce and retrocede Georgia, Shīrvān and Armenia to Īrān.

The Russians in their policy towards the Turks had not lost sight of their great aim of reaching the Black Sea coast and if possible even further. For some time their attention was absorbed in Polish affairs; but in 1735 they resumed their southward pressure when the Porte called for

Tatar help in the Ottoman-Īrānian war. A new Russo-Ottoman war began, and in 1736 the Russians recaptured Azov. In 1736 the emperor Charles VI, who by his alliance with Russia was bound to come to her aid, joined in the war after various attempts at mediation; but fortune did not favour the Austrians, and in September 1739 they signed the inglorious peace treaty of Belgrad, whereby the Ottomans recovered that city and northern Serbia together with Little Wallachia. The Russians, who did not have much success either, accepted peace terms which left Azov in their hands but required them to demolish its fortifications; they also renounced their claim to navigation rights in the Black Sea. The Porte benefited in this war from the support of French diplomacy, and rewarded it in 1740 with a renewal of France's privilege of protecting Catholic Christians in the Ottoman realm.

War with Īrān was resumed when Nādir Shāh prepared to invade ʿIrāq after the Ottoman government's rejection of his demand for its recognition of the so-called Jaʿfarite (i.e. Twelver Shīʿite) school as a fifth orthodox school of Islamic jurisprudence. As in the previous war, Nādir failed to conquer Baghdād, and although he routed an Ottoman army near Erivan in 1746, internal troubles in Īrān prevented him from following up his success. Peace was therefore again concluded on the basis of the common frontier fixed under Murad IV in 1639; and after Nādir's death in 1747 nothing more was heard of the Jaʿfarite question. The Sultan Mahmud I died in the autumn of 1754.

The next ruler was Mahmud's somewhat unbalanced brother Osman II (r. 1754–1757). During his short reign the frontier regions seethed with unrest, while insubordination on the part of feudal magnates, especially in Anatolia, showed how creaky had become the whole structure of the empire. Himself a puritan eccentric, the Sultan decreed that wine shops should be closed, that women should not go out unveiled, and that non-Muslims should wear prescribed costumes. In the autumn of 1757 he died and was succeeded by *Mustafa III* (r. 1757–1774), a son of Ahmed III. Pleasure-loving but not incapable, the new Sultan had the good fortune to be served by a congenial and statesmanlike grand *vezir*, Rağib Paşa (d. 1763), who successfully restored the finances and put the army into quite good fighting order. A peaceful foreign policy was pursued. When the Seven Years war broke out in Europe, King Frederick the Great of Prussia sought an Ottoman alliance against Austria and made proposals for joint military action; but the only results were a treaty of friendship signed in 1761 and the despatch of an Ottoman mission to Berlin in 1764 under Ahmed Resmi Efendi.

During the years which followed the Tsarina Catharine the Great's intervention in Poland in 1764, Russian troops engaged in the pursuit of Polish fugitives frequently violated Ottoman territory and the lands of the Crimean Khānate. In 1769 the Sultan decided to declare war. The Crimean Tatars, who stood in the front line, were overwhelmed by Catharine's forces, which also captured Hotin, while others invaded Transcaucasia. Jassy and Bucarest fell later, and in 1770 the Russians reached the Danube and captured Kilia and Braila as well as Bender. In Greece, Christian corsairs known as Mainotes attempted with Russian encouragement to organize a rebellion, and later received help from a Russian fleet which had sailed from the Baltic into the Aegean sea; an Ottoman fleet which gave battle to the Russians off Çeşme (opposite Chios) in July 1770 was sent to the bottom. The same Russian fleet attempted to help the dissident troop commander ʿAlī Bey in Egypt and Syria, and in 1773 bombarded Beirut and briefly landed troops in that city. Meanwhile, in 1771, after a Russian army had crossed the isthmus of Perekop and conquered the Crimean peninsula, the Tatar Khān had acknowledged the suzerainty of Catharine II. On the Balkan front, Russian forces had crossed the Danube and were besieging Silistria and Varna; the Sultan Mustafa III intended to take personal command of a campaign to throw them back beyond the river. This plan was cut short by his death in January 1774. He was succeeded by his benevolent but feeble brother, *Abdülhamid I* (r. 1774–1789). In the event, Varna and Silistria were successfully defended by their Turkish garrisons. The decisive blow came in July 1774 when the main Ottoman force commanded by the grand *vezir* suffered a disastrous defeat at Şumla (Shumen) in Bulgaria. Negotiations were then commenced with the Russians. They ended on July 21, 1774, with the signature of a peace treaty at Küçük Kaynarci̇, a village south of Silistria. This treaty forms a turning point in Ottoman history. Russia annexed the fortresses of Kerch and Yeni Kale at the entrance to the Sea of Azov and Kinburn at the mouth of the Dniepr, together with the North Caucasian territories of Great and Little Kabardia; the Crimean Tatars became Russian instead of Ottoman vassals; and the inhabitants of Moldavia and Wallachia were assured of an amnesty and religious freedom. The right thus granted to Russia to protect Orthodox Christians in Ottoman territory was to have wide repercussions on the future development of Balkan affairs. The Russians also acquired unrestricted rights of navigation on the Black Sea and through the Straits, thus depriving the Ottoman empire of its long established sway over Levantine trade. In the following year Austria annexed Bukovina. The treaty of Küçük Kaynarcî made clear to all the world the Ottoman empire's internal and external weakness. From this time, on the Ottoman Turks were to be victims, not authors, of events. As their power declined, so too did their prestige. European statesmen began to speak confidently of driving the Turks out of Europe. The "Eastern Question" in its 19th century sense had come into being.

THE OTTOMAN DYNASTY FROM 1289 TO 1789

- Süleyman
  - Ertuğrul (d. 1289)
    - Osman (r. 1289–1326)
      - Orhan (r. 1326–1359)
        - Süleyman (d. 1359)
        - Murad I (b. 1326?) (r. 1359–20 June 1389)
          - Bayezid I "Yîldîrîm" (b. 1354) (r. 20 June 1389–20 July 1402) (d. 8 March 1403)
            - Isa (at Bursa, 1402–03)
            - Süleyman (at Edirne, 1402–10)
            - Musa (at Edirne, 1410–13)
            - Mehmed I "Çelebi" (at Amasya and Bursa, 1402–13; as sole ruler, July 1413–May 1421)
              - Murad II (b. 1403/04) (r. May 1421–3 Feb. 1451)
                - Mehmed II "Fatih" (b. 1429) (r. 3 Feb. 1451–3 May 1481)
                  - Bayezid II (b. 1447/48) (r. 3 May 1481–25 April 1512) (d. 26 May 1512)
                  - Cem (b. 1459) (d. 25 Feb. 1495)
                - Ahmed (d. 1451)

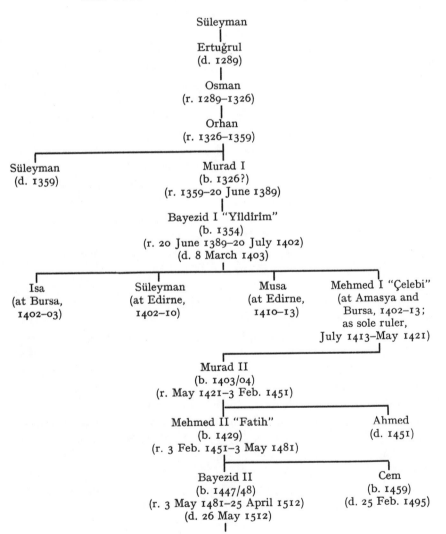

## THE OTTOMAN DYNASTY FROM 1289 TO 1689 (continued)

- Ahmed (d. 1513)
- Selim I "Yavuz" (b. 1467/68 or 1470/71) (r. 25 April 1512–20 Sept. 1520)
  - Süleyman I "Kanuni" (b. 1494/95) (r. 20 Sept. 1520–6 Sept. 1566)
    - Mehmed (d. 1547)
    - Mustafa (d. 1553)
    - Bayezid (d. 1561)
    - Selim II "Mest" (b. 1524) (r. 6 Sept. 1566–13 Dec. 1574)
      - Murad III (b. 1546) (r. 13 Dec. 1574–16 Jan. 1595)
        - Mehmed III (b. 1567) (r. 16 Jan. 1595–22 Dec. 1603)
          - Ahmed I (b. 1590) (r. 22 Dec. 1603–22 Nov. 1617)
            - Osman II (b. 1603) (r. 26 Feb. 1618–19 May 1622) (d. 30 May 1622)
            - Murad IV (b. 1612) (r. 10 Sept. 1623–9 Feb. 1640)
            - Ibrahim (b. 1615) (r. 9 Feb. 1640–8 Aug. 1648) (d. 18 Aug. 1648)
              - Mehmed IV (b. 1641) (r. 8 Aug. 1648–8 Nov. 1687) (d. 17 Dec. 1692)
                - Mustafa II (b. 1664) (r. 8 Feb. 1695–21 Aug. 1703) (d. 31 Dec. 1703)
                - Ahmed III (b. 1673) (r. 21 Aug. 1703–1 Oct. 1730) (d. 30 June 1736)
              - Süleyman II (b. 1642) (r. 8 Nov. 1687–23 June 1691)
              - Ahmed II (b. 1643) (r. 23 June 1691–8 Feb. 1695)
          - Mustafa (b. 1591) (first reign, 22 Nov. 1617–26 Feb. 1618; second reign, 19 May 1622–10 Sept. 1623) (d. 1638)

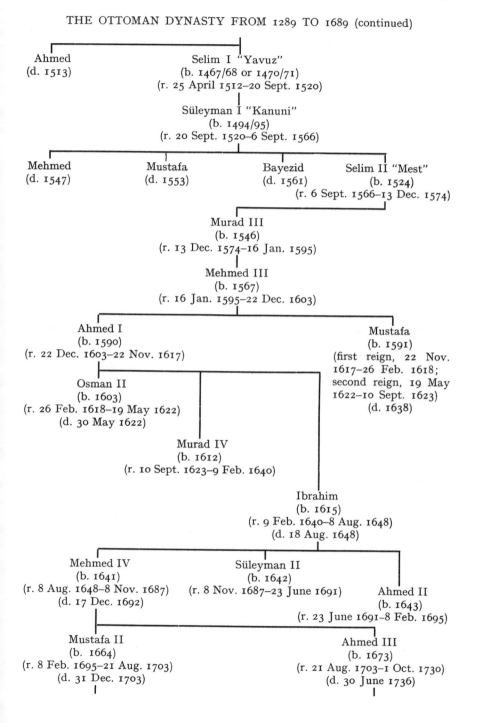

THE OTTOMAN DYNASTY FROM 1289 TO 1789 (continued)

Mahmud I
(b. 1696)
(r. 1 Oct. 1730–13 Dec. 1754)

Osman III
(b. 1699)
(r. 13 Dec. 1754–30 Oct. 1757)

Mustafa III
(b. 1717)
(r. 30 Oct. 1757–24 Dec. 1773)

Abdülhamid I
(b. 1725)
(r. 24 Dec. 1773–7 April 1789)

# BIBLIOGRAPHY

(by F. R. C. Bagley)


BIRGE, JOHN KINGSLEY, *A guide to Turkish area study*, Washington 1949.

BABINGER, FRANZ, *Die Geschichtsschreiber der Osmanen und ihre Werke*, Leipzig 1928.

MORAVCSIK, GYULA, *Die byzantinische Quellen der Geschichte der Türkvölker*, Budapest 1942.

VON HAMMER-PURGSTALL, JOSEPH, *Geschichte des osmanischen Reiches*, 10 vols., Pest 1827–1835; French tr. by B. HELLERT, 18 vols., Paris 1835–1846.

VON HAMMER-PURGSTALL, JOSEPH, *Des osmanischen Reichs Staatsverfassung und Staatsverwaltung*, 2 vols., Vienna 1815.

ZINKEISEN, JOHANN W., *Geschichte des oamnischen Reiches in Europa*, 8 vols., Hamburg 1840–1863.

IORGA, NICOLAE, *Geschichte des osmanischen Reichs*, 5 vols., Gotha 1908–1913.

CREASY, Sir EDWARD S., *History of the Ottoman Turks*, London 1878, reprinted Beirut 1966.

LANE-POOLE, S., GIBB, E. J. W., and GILMAN, A., *The story of Turkey*, London 1888.

EVERSLEY, Lord, and CHIROL, Sir VALENTINE, *The Turkish empire from 1288 to 1922*, London 1923.

ALDERSON, A. A., *The structure of the Ottoman dynasty*, Oxford 1956.

UZUNÇARŞILI, ISMAIL HAKKI, *Osmanlî Tarihi*. Vols. I (1961); II (1949); III, 1 (1951); III, 2 (1954); IV, 1 (1956); IV, 2 (1959). Ankara, Türk Tarih Kurumu Yayînlarî (Publications de la Société d'Histoire Turque). (From the Selcuks to the 18th century.)

INAN, AFET, *Aperçu général sur l'histoire économique de l'empire turc-ottoman*, Istanbul 1941.

WITTEK, PAUL, *The rise of the Ottoman empire*, London 1938 (Royal Asiatic Society Monographs, XXIII).

BABINGER, FRANZ, *Beiträge zur Frühgeschichte der Türkenherrschaft in Rumelien*, Brünn 1944 (Südosteuropäische Arbeiten 34).

GIBBONS, HERBERT A., *The foundation of the Ottoman empire; a history of the Osmanlis 1300–1402*, Oxford 1916.

VAUGHAN, DOROTHY M., *Europe and the Turk; a pattern of alliances* (1350–1700), Liverpool 1954.

BIRGE, JOHN KINGSLEY, *The Bektashi order of dervishes*, London 1937.
KISSLING, HANS JOACHIM, *The role of the dervish orders in the Ottoman empire*, in G. E. von GRUNEBAUM ed., *Studies in Islamic cultural history*, 1954 (American Sociologist, Memoir No. 76).
KÖPRÜLÜ, MEHMED FUAD, *Alcune osservazioni intorno all'influenza delle istituzioni bizantine sulle istituzioni ottomane*, Rome, Istituto per l'Oriente, 1953.
HASLUCK, FREDERICK W., *Christianity and Islam under the Sultans*, 2 vols., Oxford 1929.
BABINGER, FRANZ, *Mehmed der Eroberer und seine Zeit*, Munich 1953; French tr., Paris 1954; Italian tr., Milan 1957.
BABINGER, FRANZ, *Süleyman der Grosse*, 2 vols., Stuttgart 1922.
FISHER, SIDNEY NETTELTON, *The foreign relations of Turkey 1481–1522*, Urbana (Illinois) 1948.
STRIPLING, GEORGE W. F., *The Ottoman Turks and the Arabs*, Urbana (Illinois) 1942.
LYBYER, ALBERT HOWE, *The government of the Ottoman empire in the time of Suleiman the Magnificent*, Cambridge (Mass.) 1913.
DE BUSBECQ, OGIER GHISELIN, *Lettres*, tr. by E. S. FORSTER, *Turkish Letters*, Oxford 1927.
WEISSMANN, NAHOUM, *Les janissaires, étude de l'organisation militaire des Ottomans*, Paris 1938.
ANDERSON, R. C., *Naval wars in the Levant*, 1559–1853, Princeton 1952.
MILLER, BARNETTE, *The palace school of Muhammad the Conqueror*, Cambridge (Mass.), 1931.
MILLER, BARNETTE, *Beyond the Sublime Porte: the Grand Seraglio of Istanbul*, New Haven (Conn.), 1931.
PENZER, N. M., *The Harem ... ... as it existed in the palace of the Turkish Sultans*, London 1936.
ADIVAR, ABDÜLHAK ADNAN, *La science chez les Turcs ottomans*, Paris 1939.
VON RANKE, LEOPOLD, *Die Osmanen und die spanische Monarchie im 16. und 17. Jahrhundert*, Hamburg 1827, in *Sämtliche Werke*, 4th ed., Hamburg 1928.
EVLIYÂ ÇELEBI, *Narrative of travels in Europe, Asia and Africa by Ewliya Efendi*, tr. from Books I and II of the *Siyâhetnâme* by JOSEPH VON HAMMER (-PURGSTALL), London 1834–1850.
PALLIS, A. A., *In the days of the Janissaries*, London 1951. (Selections from the *Siyâhetnâme* of EVLIYA ÇELEBI).
LEWIS, BERNARD, *Istanbul and the civilization of the Ottoman empire*, Norman (Oklahoma), 1963.
VON SAX, C., *Geschichte des Machtverfalls der Türkei*, Vienna 1913.
D'OHSSON, IGNATIUS MOURADGEA, *Tableau général de l'empire Ottoman*, 7 vols., Paris 1788–1824.
GIBB, Sir HAMILTON A. R., and BOWEN, HAROLD, *Islamic society and the West*; Vol. 1, *Islamic society in the eighteenth century*, Parts 1 and 2, London 1950–1957.
GIBB, EDWARD J. W., *A history of Ottoman poetry*, 6 vols., London 1900–1909.
VON HAMMER-PURGSTALL, JOSEPH, *Geschichte der osmanischen Dichtkunst*, 4 vols., Pest, 1836–1838.
YÜCEL, HASAN ALI, *Ein Gesamtüberblick über die türkische Literatur*, tr. from the Turkish by O. RESCHER, Istanbul 1941.

# EGYPT AND THE EASTERN ARAB COUNTRIES IN THE FIRST THREE CENTURIES OF THE OTTOMAN PERIOD

BY

F. R. C. BAGLEY

## CHARACTERISTICS OF OTTOMAN RULE

During the first half of the 16th century, Egypt and all the eastern Arab countries, except some remote parts of Arabia, were annexed to the Ottoman empire. They were to stay within it three or four hundred years —a longer time than under any of the previous Muslim régimes in their histories; but until the 19th century they were seldom to play big parts in its affairs. They were annexed mainly for strategic reasons arising from the Ottoman-Ṣafavid conflict. The addition of their vast expanses and large Arabic-speaking populations did not shift the empire's geopolitical basis. The Ottoman Sultanate continued to be the "Sultanate of Rūm", the Muslim successor of the former Christian Byzantine empire; and its attention continued to be fixed mainly on offensive or defensive war and diplomacy in Europe.

At the same time, possession of the Arab provinces brought advantages to the Ottoman empire. The elimination of the former Mamlūk Sultanate of Egypt and Syria ensured the safety of the Ottoman southern flank until the late 18th century and greatly strengthened the Ottoman strategic position against Īrān. In the finances of the central government at Istanbul, annual remittances of tribute from the provinces, and above all from Egypt, formed a substantial item. The guardianship of Mecca, Madīnah and Jerusalem, and of the pilgrimage routes to Mecca from Damascus and Cairo, was an important factor in the legitimation of Ottoman rule, whereby the *'ulamā* and the whole population took the Sultan's title to sovereignty for granted and even the rebels who usurped local power in the 17th and 18th centuries thought fit to profess continuing loyalty.

The Ottoman government was interested primarily in keeping control of the main routes and great cities (Aleppo, Damascus, Cairo and Baghdād) and in securing the tribute payments. These tasks fell upon the governor (*wālī* or *pāshā*) sent from Istanbul and on the provincial bureaucracy and garrison, whose expenses together with the tribute had to be met from the provincial revenue. The bureaucracy, headed by the director of finance (*daftardār*), was generally staffed by local citizens; so too was the Muslim judiciary under the *muftī*. The garrison, nominally or actually under the *wālī*'s command, consisted of janissaries and other Turkish-speaking regiments, which in the early phase drew their recruits from outside the province. When the need arose, local levies also were raised, and sometimes in emergencies central government troops were sent in. The Ottoman feudal system, which had already begun to lose importance in Rumelia and Anatolia, was not introduced into the Arab provinces; the Arabic-speaking peoples were consequently not exposed to rural colonization by Turkish military feudatories (timariots) and their followers. In Egypt the self-perpetuating Mamlūk military oligarchy was left in being as part of the Ottoman garrison. In Syria and 'Irāq local princes and tribal chiefs who governed inaccessible areas were normally left in possession as long as they professed allegiance and paid some tribute; officially they were looked upon merely as tax-farmers (*multazims*) in the service of the provincial governors, not as vassals of the Sultan. Only the Sharīfs of Mecca held a more exalted status. Contingents from the Turkish garrisons were sent to battle-fronts in Īrān and sometimes also in Europe; but in general the Arab populations were not required to supply fighting men for the Ottoman empire's wars.

In Egypt and Syria under the Mamlūk Sultanate, military power had likewise lain in the hands of Turkish-speaking troops, while the civil and judicial administrations had been conducted in Arabic by Egyptian or Syrian scribes and *qāḍīs*. The change of régime must have made little difference to the inhabitants, except in so far as the Ottoman administration was at first more efficient. The long established social structures, and the traditional loyalties to religion, locality, profession, tribe and clan, were not significantly disturbed. The cultural decline of the Arab world, which had already become apparent in the 15th century, is attributed mainly to a drying of the springs of inspiration; but it became more marked in the next three centuries, and must have been accentuated by Ottoman rule. In Mamlūk times, historians and scholars writing in Arabic had been patronized by some of the Sultans and governors, while Cairo, Damascus and Aleppo had been adorned with fine mosques and buildings. The Ottoman Sultan Sulaymān I (1520-1566), and certain governors, particularly in the 18th century, also left some fine architectural monuments, at Damascus, Jerusalem, Aleppo, Hamā and Baghdād; but in general the arts were neglected. Civil business was conducted to a large extent in Turkish, and Arabic literature was seldom officially patronized. Although the Ottoman governors were sometimes men of distinction, their tenures were usually too short and insecure to permit much attention to culture. No Arabic poetry of any value was produced, and the belles lettres and Ṣūfī literature of this period, though large in quantity, is not rated highly in quality[1]. Numerous local chronicles were written, and some of them have considerable historical value[2]. Ḥājjī Khalīfah (d. 1658), a Turk of Istanbul who had served as an army clerk at Baghdād and Damascus, compiled in Arabic a most valuable encyclopaedia of Arabic, Persian and Turkish literature entitled *Kashf al-Ẓunūn*. Sayyid Murtaḍà al-Zabīdī (1732-1791), a Yamanī resident at Cairo, revived Arabic lexicography and Muslim theology by his dictionary and his commentary on Ghazālī. Arabic literature also advanced among the Maronite Christians of Syria, under the influence of scholars trained at the Vatican (see below, p. 72).

Economic decline had already befallen the Arab provinces before the Ottoman conquest. Misgovernment and disorder in the 15th and early 16th centuries, epidemics of plague and cholera, and the devastation left in 'Irāq and Syria by the Mongols and Tīmūr, had done lasting damage to the towns and countrysides. In 'Irāq, extensive rural areas had been depopulated, and the void was filled by immigrations of beduin, most of whom took to more or less sedentary agriculture while retaining their tribal organization. Beduin encroachment on settled areas also took place in Syria and in both Upper and Lower Egypt; but in those countries the village structure remained intact. Egypt had already begun to lose its lucrative position as an entrepôt for spices and textiles from the Far East and India. From 1503 onwards, Portuguese ships had challenged Muslim commerce in the Indian Ocean, and the Mamlūk government's countermeasures had not been successful. The stronger action of the Ottoman government partly repaired the position in the rest of the 16th century; but in the 17th and 18th centuries the European East India companies were able to divert most of the Indian Ocean trade to the Cape route. The loss to Egypt was only to a small extent offset by increasing trade with Nubia, Abyssinia and the Yaman, notably in coffee. The commercial prosperity of Aleppo and Baghdād depended in part on transit trade with Īrān, particularly in silk for export to Europe. In the 16th century, despite the Ottoman-Ṣafavid wars, this trade flourished;

---

[1] e.g. the Egyptian *qāḍī* and anthologist al-Khafajī (d. 1659); the Syrian *qāḍī* and biographer al-Muhibbī (d. 1699); the Egyptian Ṣūfī writer al-Sha'rānī (d. 1565); the Syrian Ṣūfī writer al-Nābulsī (d. 1731).

[2] e.g. the accounts of the Ottoman conquest of Egypt by Ibn Iyās (d. 1522) and of the French conquest of Egypt by al-Jabartī (d. 1825).

in the 17th century, much of it was diverted through the new Īrānian port of Bandar 'Abbās to the Cape route. The fortunes of Baghdād and Baṣrah revived in the 18th century, when Īrān lay in disorder while 'Irāq enjoyed relative stability under semi-independent Pāshās. Throughout the period, Aleppo was the Ottoman empire's second city and commercial centre. Its vast warehouses (*khāns*) and bazaars stored goods from all the eastern provinces and from Īrān and Europe. Its hospitality attracted merchants of many nationalities and creeds, including European merchants. Less important groups of foreign merchants were also to be found in the Mediterranean ports and at Cairo, but not at Damascus which had a reputation for xenophobia. Although attitudes to foreigners, and to indigenous Christians and Jews, varied from place to place, the religious minorities were not subjected to systematic vexations as they had been in Mamlūk times, and could usually count on respect for the rights of their *millets*. Shī'ite Muslims had no recognized status and were not admitted to official employment, but were not persecuted unless suspected of disloyalty (as they were in Asia Minor). When insecurity prevailed, as it often did in the 17th and 18th centuries, members of all religious communities suffered equally. Insecurity was the most important single cause of the economic decline of the Arab provinces under Ottoman rule.

During most of the 16th century, when Ottoman strength was at its zenith, the Arab provinces enjoyed remarkable stability and relatively good government, though there is evidence that in Egypt the burden of taxation was excessive. Even then, the Ottoman practice was to appoint provincial governors for one year at a time, with possibility of renewal. Although in Sulaymān I's reign two Wālīs of Egypt held office for 13 and 11 years respectively, such cases were rare, and terms of one or two years were usual. The practice was motivated by fear that a governor, if given time to gain local influence, might enrich himself at the central government's expense or defy its orders. During the period of Ottoman military and financial decline, appointments were often made in return for gifts, and quickly terminated in anticipation of further gifts, or of confiscations. Such methods, besides promoting corruption and oppression at all levels, undermined the authority of the Pāshās sent from Istanbul. From the last years of the 16th century onwards, regiments of the local garrisons began to evict Pāshās whom they disliked, and later also to set up their own leaders as de facto masters of the province. Often rival regiments intrigued or fought against each other, and made alliances with factions among the citizens. With the gradual cessation of the *devşirme*, the Janissaries tended to acquire the character of such a faction; they married local women, handed on their billets to their descendants, and engaged in trade and politics more than in military duties. The Pāshās sometimes maintained their positions by tactics of 'divide and rule', fanning dissensions and balancing rival regiments and factions; less frequently they kept or regained control with the help of loyal troops or reinforcements from Istanbul. When a refractory troop leader could not be restrained or dislodged, the Porte usually acquiesced in the fait accompli and appointed him Pāshā. Some of these semi-independent rulers founded dynasties of Pāshās. The weakening of authority also enabled mountain princes and tribal chiefs to expand their domains. In return for official recognition, the semi-independent Pāshās were usually willing to pay tribute and sometimes helpful in matters of high policy. The successful defence of Baghdād against Nādir Shāh, and that of 'Akkā against Napoleon, were undertaken by semi-independent Pāshās. The Porte did not gladly tolerate their presence, but could not take systematic action against them until the reign of Mahmud II (1808-1839).

Semi-independent régimes of varying duration and character, some beneficent, others oppressive, emerged in Egypt, 'Irāq and different parts of Syria. Their rise had nothing to do with nationalism, which did not then exist in any modern sense. The Rumelian and Anatolian provinces experienced a similar phenomenon in the rise of the *derebeys* towards the end of the 18th century. Although some of the semi-independent rulers entered on their own initiative into relations with foreign states, Ottoman prestige or power remained sufficient to deter secession. The only challenge to Ottoman suzerainty came from beduin of Najd stirred to rebellion by the revivalist preaching of Muḥammad ibn 'Abd al-Wahhāb (d. 1792). Until 1798, the Ottoman empire shielded its Arab provinces against attack. They thus escaped involvement in European war and diplomacy, but missed the intellectual stimulus which closer contact with Europe might have given.

## OTTOMAN RULE IN EGYPT IN THE 16TH CENTURY

The Ottoman Sultan Salīm I, after his partial victory over the Ṣafavid Shāh Ismā'īl at Chaldirān in 1514, intended to lead a second campaign against his Shī'ite adversary, but instead made war in 1516 against the Mamlūk Sultan of Egypt and Syria, Qānṣūh al-Ghūrī. Spies had reported a Mamlūk-Ṣafavid understanding, and Qānṣūh himself had left Cairo to take command of a large Mamlūk force at Aleppo. Salīm's decisive victory at Marj Dābiq, north of Aleppo, on August 24, 1516, was attributed to the defection of Khā'ir Bey, the Mamlūk governor of Aleppo, to the Ottoman use of fire-arms, and to Qānṣūh's death on the field from an apoplectic fit. The rest of Syria, and Palestine, fell to Salīm's army almost without resistance. Hesitating to advance further, Salīm offered to recognise the new Mamlūk Sultan, Tūmān Bāy, as ruler of Egypt under Ottoman suzerainty; when this offer was refused, he crossed the Sinai desert and entered Cairo on January 23, 1517, after defeating the main Mamlūk force at Raydānīyah outside the city. Tūmān Bāy escaped and assembled another Mamlūk force; he was again defeated, at Gīzah on April 2, and again escaped, but was betrayed by beduin Arabs with whom he had taken refuge; finally he was hanged at one of the gates of Cairo on April 14, 1517.

Salīm stayed in Egypt until September 1517, attending to its affairs; he was the only Ottoman Sultan who visited the country. Small groups of Mamlūks continued to resist, and Arab tribes profited from the collapse of the old administration to overrun most of Upper Egypt and parts of the Delta. Salīm's policy was to conciliate and utilize the Mamlūks. The governorship of Egypt, with very wide powers, was given to Khā'ir Bey in appreciation of his services. The task of garrisoning the country was given to detachments of Janissaries, cavalry and other Turkish troops from the victorious Ottoman army, and to Mamlūks taken into the Ottoman service. Salīm also established naval bases at Alexandria, Damietta and Suez, and sent troops to Aswān in Nubia. Among the vassals who sent messages of submission to him was the governor of Mecca, the Sharīf Barakāt; the Ottoman Sultans thereby acquired the title "Servitor of the two Sanctuaries" *(Khādim al-Ḥaramayn)*.

Khā'ir Bey held office until his death in October 1522; he remained loyal when the throne passed to Sulaymān I in October 1520. His successor, Muṣṭafà Pāshā, and all subsequent governors of Egypt in so far as they were chosen by the Ottoman government, were officials from Istanbul, not Mamlūks. Muṣṭafà successfully put down a rebellion of unreconciled Mamlūks; but the third govenor, Aḥmad Pāshā "the Traitor", himself rebelled in February 1524 and assumed the title Sultan of Egypt. He was supported by some of the Mamlūks and was alleged to be in communication with Shāh Ismā'īl Ṣafavī. Within a month he was defeated by the Janissaries, who were reinforced by sea, and by loyal Mamlūks.

This incident prompted Sulaymān I to send his grand *vezir*, Ibrāhīm Pāshā, on a mission to Egypt, and to embody Ibrāhīm Pāshā's recommendations in a decree of 1524/5, the *Qānūn-nāmah* of Egypt. The document conferred a unique viceregal status on the governor of Egypt (who may therefore be called 'viceroy'), and required him to act in consultation with a council *(dīwān)* modelled on the Sultan's *dīwān*. Not only the viceroy, but also the chief judge *(qāḍī 'l-ʿaskar)* and the director of finance *(daftardār)*, were to be sent to Cairo from Istanbul. From the revenues of Egypt were to be paid the expenses of the local garrison and bureaucracy, an annual tribute *(irsālīyah)* to the imperial treasury in Istanbul, and various imperial expenses. The revenue districts into which the country was divided were put in the charge of inspectors *(kāshifs)*, with collectors *(ʿāmils)* under them, who were responsible for the collection of taxes and maintenance of irrigation works; they were in principle salaried officials, and in practice usually of Mamlūk origin. In areas controlled by Arab tribes, the shaykh was regarded as the *kāshif*; thus, Asyūt and most of Upper Egypt were held by a clan of the Hawwārah tribe until they were ousted in 1576. The army of Egypt, numbering about 20,000 men, consisted of six regiments, to which a seventh was added in 1554/5.

Although the *Qānūn-nāmah* assigned no specific function to the leading Mamlūks, who were known as *beys*, they received official salaries and were evidently allowed to continue the practice of buying Caucasian and Bosniak boy slaves and training them to arms in their 'households'. While the Mamlūk caste was thereby perpetuated, its solidarity was impaired by factionalism. Besides supplying the regiments with many of their officers and some of their men, the Mamlūks obtained important appointments, e.g. those of commander of the annual pilgrimage caravan *(amīr al-ḥajj)* and commander of the annual caravan carrying the tribute to Istanbul *(amīr al-khaznah)*. They thereby dominated the viceroy's *diwān*, which acquired some importance on account of the short tenure of most viceroys, while the *diwān* in Istanbul became merely ceremonial. When a viceroy departed before the arrival of his successor, the *diwān* appointed an acting governor *(qāʾim maqām)*.

Events in Egypt, as in other provinces, were influenced from the late 16th century onwards by the weakening of the central government, and also by financial difficulties. Although more land was brought under cultivation, Egypt still suffered intermittent famines, and its once important foreign trade was stagnant. The tribute payments, averaging 500,000 gold pieces annually in the 16th century, were a very heavy burden, to which had to be added the imperial expenses such as food supplies for the Ḥijāz, pensions payable at Mecca, naval expeditions, garrisons in Red Sea dependencies, gunpowder for the naval arsenal in Istanbul, sugar for the

Sultan's kitchen, etc. Financial stringency probably explains why tax collecting functions were increasingly farmed out to *multazims* (concessionaires). Before the end of the 16th century, local government passed into the hands of *beys*, who were nearly always Mamlūks, and the *kāshifs* became their subordinates. Economic grievances also lay at the root of the first troop mutinies.

Ottoman Egypt in the 16th century passed through a singularly uneventful period of internal history, but played a part of some importance in the Red Sea and Indian Ocean.

## THE OTTOMAN TURKS AND THE PORTUGUESE

After Vasco da Gama's discovery of the Cape passage in 1497-99, the Portuguese had established themselves on the coasts of western India and East Africa, and had carried on warfare since 1503 against Muslim shipping. Under the leadership of Afonso de Albuquerque, they planned to seize strategic keypoints on Indian Ocean routes, and were able to capture Goa, which they made their headquarters, in 1510, and Malacca in 1511. They landed at the island port of Hurmuz in 1507, seized Masqaṭ in 1508 and finally won the upper hand in the Persian Gulf in 1515, when they conquered Hurmuz at the third attempt. They also attempted, but in vain, to acquire a base dominating the Red Sea. The island of Socotra, which then had a Christian population, was occupied by a Portuguese force from 1507 to 1511, but proved useless on account of its lack of safe anchorages. In 1513 Albuquerque appeared off Aden, which was successfully defended by its inhabitants, and then entered the Red Sea intending to make contact with the Christian Abyssinians and to attack Jiddah; he achieved neither purpose, but destroyed many Muslim ships including pilgrim ships.

The Mamlūk Sultan Qānṣūh al-Ghūrī had replied in 1505 to the Portuguese challenge by appointing a Kurdish admiral, Ḥusayn, to be governor of Jiddah, which he fortified and developed as a naval base. In 1508 Qānṣūh sent Ḥusayn with a strong fleet to the help of the Sultan Maḥmūd of Gujarāt, and the combined Egyptian and Gujarātī fleets won a victory over the Portuguese off Chaul (south of Bombay); but in 1509 they suffered a severe defeat off Diu. Another Egyptian fleet sailed to Gujarāt in 1515, and on the return journey landed a force of Mamlūk troops in the Yaman. In 1517 a Portuguese fleet under Lopo Soares sailed into the Red Sea hoping to destroy the Egyptian fleet (which by then had passed into Ottoman possession). After approaching Jiddah, which he found too strong to be attacked, Soares occupied Qamarān island and built a fort as a permanent base; but having lost most of his men through disease, he evacuated the island after three months. He later sacked Zaylaʿ and approached Aden, but was forced to withdraw. Another Portuguese fleet landed an embassy to the Negus (emperor) of Abyssinia at Maṣawwā in 1524. The Arabs of Aden, being reluctant to submit to Ottoman rule, were sometimes willing to collaborate with the Portuguese, and they together defeated an Ottoman fleet sent from Suez in 1529. After the Portuguese seizure of Diu in 1537, a powerful Ottoman fleet under the command of the viceroy of Egypt, Khādim Sulaymān Pāshā, sailed in 1538 from Suez and Jiddah to Gujarāt, and on the way out captured Aden; the Turks besieged Diu for three months, but had to depart empty-handed in 1539 when the Gujarātīs came to terms with the Portuguese. The last Portuguese expedition to the Red Sea set out from Goa in 1541 under Estevão da Gama, son of Vasco. He sailed first to Maṣawwā, where he landed 400 troops under the command of his brother Cristovão; they were to play a big part in the history of Abyssinia. He then prepared to attack Jiddah, but was driven off by the Sharīf of Mecca, Abū Numayy. In the hope of meeting the Ottoman fleet, he sailed as far as Ṭūr, at the mouth of the Gulf of Suez, but did not venture further. The naval struggle against the Portuguese was continued by the celebrated Turkish navigator and cartographer Piri Reis when he was appointed *qapūdān* (admiral) of Egypt. In 1547 he recaptured Aden, where an Arab chief had rebelled and had sought Portuguese help. In 1551 he set out with a strong fleet to dislodge the Portuguese from the Persian Gulf. He took Masqaṭ after an eighteen-day bombardment, laid siege unsuccessfully to Hurmuz, and having lost many of his ships, sailed on to Baṣrah. The Portuguese afterwards recovered Masqaṭ, and remained dominant in the Persian Gulf for seventy more years. Piri Reis was blamed for the failure of this expedition and executed at Cairo in 1554/5. Another Turkish admiral, Sidi ʿAlī Reis, was commissioned to sail the ships back from Baṣrah to Suez; but they were damaged by severe storms and driven onto the Indian coast. The Ottoman Turks, despite their possession of Baṣrah, made no further effort to win naval power in the Persian Gulf.

In the Red Sea, however, Ottoman supremacy was firmly established; and in spite of the Portuguese presence in the Indian Ocean, Muslim ships carrying pilgrims and goods were generally able to reach Jiddah and Suez without much difficulty. The Egyptian and Venetian transit trade in pepper and spices, which had fallen sharply in the last years of the Mamlūk régime, showed a certain revival in the mid-16th century. In 1554 Sidi

ʿAlī Reis compiled at Aḥmadābād in India a comprehensive nautical handbook of the Indian Ocean based on sailors' reports. The strength and pugnacity of the Portuguese now began to decline, especially after the union of the Spanish and Portuguese crowns in 1580. Attacks on their settlements at Masqaṭ and in East Africa were made in 1580, 1584 and 1589, by ships from Mokhā under the command of a Turkish corsair, Mīr ʿAlī Bey, whom they finally took prisoner. There was no longer any question, however, of large-scale Ottoman naval effort in the Indian Ocean. As the Portuguese threat receded, the Ottoman government, with its many other preoccupations, lost interest in the Indian Ocean and in the Yaman and Abyssinia.

## THE OTTOMAN TURKS IN THE YAMAN

The Ottoman and Mamlūk intervention in the Yaman, prompted initially by the Portuguese challenge, was not the first intervention by rulers of Egypt in this remote country with its commercially and strategically valuable ports at the approach to the Red Sea. Links between the ports and Egypt have been a factor in Yamanī history since ancient times. Another factor has been the country's geographical and social fragmentation. Attempts to impose a single government have been frustrated by conflicts between the seafaring communities of the ports, the agricultural communities of the highlands, and the nomadic tribes. Yamanī Muslim annals record the simultaneous existence of two or more states in the country from the 9th to the 12th centuries A.D. During the 9th century, Ismāʿīlite Shīʿism was introduced under the influence of Fāṭimid Egypt, and Zaydite Shīʿism took root in the northern highlands. The Zaydite Imāms established themselves at Saʿdah in 897 and were at times able to extend their authority to Ṣanʿā, the chief town of the central highlands. In 1173 the Sultan of Egypt, Salāḥ al-dīn al-Ayyūbī, sent his brother Tūrānshāh to the Yaman with a Turkish and Kurdish army which conquered most of the country. The Ayyūbid régime (1173–1228) and the subsequent Turco-Kurdish Rasūlid dynasty (1228-1456) controlled the coasts and the southern highlands, and promoted Sunnism of the Shāfiʿite school. Their strongholds were Zabīd, in the Tihāmah plain near the Red Sea coast, and Taʿizz in the southern highlands; they also at most times held Ṣanʿā. Yamanite seafaring and trade then reached their peak, and Aden was the leading port. The Rasūlids were superseded in 1456 by a dynasty of Arab descent, the Ṭāhirids, under whom conditions remained prosperous until internal disorders and the Portuguese offensive began to damage Yamanite seafaring and trade. Ṣanʿā was occupied in 1507 by troops of the Mamlūk governor of Jiddah, Ḥusayn al-Kurdī, but later fell to the Zaydites.

After Albuquerque's entry into the Red Sea, the Sultan Qānṣūh al-Ghūrī resolved to conquer the Yaman. A Mamlūk force travelling overland, together with men of the fleet returning from Gujarāt, took possession of Zabīd and Taʿizz, and put an end to the Ṭāhirid dynasty, in 1515. They advanced inland to Ṣanʿā, but were driven out in 1516 by the Zaydites. Aden and other places took the opportunity to make themselves independent. In 1517 the Mamlūk troops gave allegiance to the Ottoman conqueror of Egypt, Salīm I. The Yaman received the status of an Ottoman province in 1536, and Aden was conquered in 1538. The conquest of the highlands was accomplished by Özdemir Pāshā, a Mamlūk officer, who was sent out as governor with strong reinforcements. Ṣanʿā fell to the Turks in 1546. The Turkish régime was objectionable, mainly on religious grounds, to the Zaydites, who revolted in 1567 and within a year captured Ṣanʿā, Aden, and most of the country except Zabīd. The Ottoman government then sent out an expeditionary force under the viceroy of Egypt, Sinān Pāshā, who quelled the revolt and recaptured Ṣanʿā in 1570. The Zaydites again rebelled and temporarily took Ṣanʿā in 1576. Later, under their Imāms Qāsim (1597–1620) and Muḥammad (1620–1646), they waged an intermittent but tenacious and ultimately successful war against the Turks. Ṣanʿā fell in 1628, and Aden in 1630; another Ottoman expeditionary force was defeated in 1635. The Turks then gave up the struggle, and in agreement with the Imām evacuated Zabīd and Mokhā in 1636. The Zaydite régime remained strong under the Imām Ismāʿīl (1646–1676), but was afterwards weakened by internal dissensions, and small independent states then arose in various parts; one of these was the ʿAbdalī state of Laḥej, which took possession of Aden in 1735.

During the 17th century, when the spice trade was largely monopolized by the Dutch, the loss to the Red Sea ports and to Egypt was partly compensated by a growth of local trade, in ivory and slaves from Africa and above all in coffee grown in the highlands of the Yaman. A shaykh of the Shādhilī darvīsh order, ʿAlī ibn ʿUmar, who died in 1418 at Mokhā on the Red Sea near the Strait of Bāb al-Mandab, is said to have first discovered the use of this beverage for sustaining wakefulness in religious vigils. Notwithstanding prohibitions by theologians, and by rulers such as Qānṣūh al-Ghūrī, Sulaymān the Lawgiver, and the Sultan Murād IV

(1623–1640),[1] coffee drinking spread gradually from Ṣūfī circles to all classes in the Arab countries and Turkey, and thence to Europe. Mokhā, as the centre of the coffee trade and as the Ottoman naval base in the Yaman, rose from the mid-16th century onwards to be the principal port, taking the place of Aden, which sank to the level of a poor fishing village. From 1636 to 1849 the Zaydite Imāms kept control of Mokhā, whose prosperity culminated in the early 18th century, when ships of many nations came to load coffee, and Dutch and French "factories" were established in the town. This prosperity vanished before the mid-18th century under the pressure of competition from coffee plantations established by the Dutch in Ceylon and Java. Mokhā finally fell into insignificance when the British occupied Aden in 1839, and when the Ottoman Turks, on returning to the Yaman, founded Ḥudaydah in 1849.

Ḥaḍramawt, lying east of the Yaman and beyond the range of Ottoman or Zaydite influence, deserves mention for its role in the spread of Islam in the 18th and 19th centuries. This narrow inland valley, irrigated by ancient dams and very deep wells, has long supported a dense population. Its history is a record of conflict with tribes of the coast and of the intervening plateau. *Sayyids* (descendants of ʿAlī)[2] came to form a large proportion of the population because they enjoyed immunity in the fighting; they also developed a tradition of Islamic learning of the Shāfiʿite school. The local Kathīrī dynasty came to power in the 15th century, and many *madrasahs* arose in its capital Say'ūn and at Tarīm. At Shiḥr, the chief port, which the Portuguese held for a while in the 16th century, Kathīrī influence was tenuous. To quell the coastal tribes, mercenaries were recruited in the 19th century from the Yāfiʿī tribe behind Aden. Their leader, who had prospered through supplying mercenaries to the Niẓām of Hyderabad in India, took over Shiḥr and Mukallah (afterwards the chief port) in 1867 and founded the Quʿaytī dynasty. The Quʿaytīs then acquired most of the valley, but the Kathīrīs kept Say'ūn and Tarīm. Shortage of land forced the Ḥaḍramīs to emigrate, and also to evolve a unique multi-storey style of architecture. They went mainly to Indonesia and East Africa, where they prospered as merchants and married native women. The Sultanate of Pontaniak in Borneo (dating from 1772) and the Sultanate of Perlis in Malaya were founded by Ḥaḍramī immigrants. They also used their religious prestige to inculcate stricter Islamic belief and

---

[1] The word *qahwah* occurs in early Arabic poetry with the meaning "wine" and was later used to mean "coffee". *Encyclopaedia of Islam* (1st ed.), article *Ḳahwah*.

[2] The Ḥaḍramī *sayyids* claim to stem from a descendant of the Sixth Imām Jaʿfar al-Ṣādiq, named Aḥmad ibn ʿĪsà, who came to Ḥaḍramawt from Baṣrah in the 10th century.

practice. The rooting of the Shāfiʿite school in both Indonesia and East Africa was mainly due to Ḥaḍramī influence.

## THE STRUGGLE FOR ABYSSINIA IN THE 16TH CENTURY

The emergence of Muslim states in Abyssinia, and their relations with the long established Christian Ethiopian empire, are discussed in chapter IV, pp. 170-1. The Mamlūk and Ottoman governments feared a potential Portuguese-Ethiopian alliance, and Mamlūk troops landed in 1516 at Zaylaʿ on the Gulf of Aden, then the chief Muslim port in the region; in the following year the Portuguese drove them out and burnt the town. Zaylaʿ afterwards passed into the hands of Aḥmad Grañ, the Muslim military leader whose Ṣōmālī and Danqalī troops conquered almost the entire territory of the Christian empire between 1529 and 1537. His success arose largely from the use of fire-arms supplied by the Turks in the Yaman, to whom he paid tribute. Christian Ethiopian resistance only gathered strength in the reign of the emperor Galāwdewos (Claudius; r. 1540–1559), who owed much to the presence of the four hundred Portuguese troops landed at Maṣṣawā (then a Christian town) in 1541. They marched inland, and together with the Ethiopians won two victories over Aḥmad Grañ, who appealed to the Ottoman governor of the Yaman, Özdemir Pāshā, and obtained from him a force of musketeers. With their help Aḥmad Grañ won a victory in which the Portuguese lost half their number, including their leader Cristovão da Gama, who was captured and put to death. The remaining two hundred made their way to the Negus Galāwdewos, whose troops together with the Portuguese defeated and killed Aḥmad Grañ in a decisive battle at Zāntera near Lake Tana in 1543. The Muslim empire which he had founded then fell rapidly to pieces.

Özdemir Pāshā later obtained permission from the Sultan Sulaymān I to attempt an Ottoman conquest of Abyssinia. In 1555, with an army recruited in Egypt, he marched into Nubia hoping to reach his goal by way of the Nile; but the obstacles were too great, and he withdrew. (Nubia was then Muslim; see chapter IV, pp. 166-7). In 1557 he sailed with his troops to Sawākin on the Red Sea, which had been annexed by the Mamlūks in the early 15th century and had passed to the Ottomans. From there he occupied Maṣṣawā, Zaylaʿ and other points on the coast, and began advancing inland. In 1559, however, he died, and his plans to conquer Abyssinia were dropped. The occupation of the ports prevented the Portuguese from making further contact with the Christian Ethiopians, except in so far as they travelled in disguise on Muslim ships; and the

Ethiopians, in reaction against a Jesuit attempt to convert them from Monophysitism to Catholicism, expelled the Portuguese in 1632. Özdemir's conquests were constituted as the Ottoman province of Ḥabash (i.e. "Abyssinia") and administered from Jiddah. In the 17th and 18th centuries Ottoman control weakened, while Zaylaʿ passed into the hands of the Zaydite governors of Mokhā. The Ottoman possessions or claims in "Ḥabash" (other than Jiddah) were transferred in 1830 to Muḥammad ʿAlī Pāshā of Egypt.

## EGYPT IN THE 17TH AND 18TH CENTURIES

Five mutinies took place in the army of Egypt between 1586 and 1605, under the impulsion of grievances over pay and presents, or resentment of vice-regal attempts to stop abuses. Egypt like other Ottoman territories was suffering at that time from inflation, caused by an influx of silver from Spanish America and consequent fall in the value of the silver currency; and the troops were probably suffering real hardships. In 1605 mutinous cavalrymen murdered the viceroy. The next viceroy, Muḥammad Pāshā, crushed the revolt with the help of loyal troops and Mamlūks, and attempted in his four-year term of office to reform the administration. His successors, who usually stayed only one or two years, relied more and more on the Mamlūk beys, who were thus able to tighten their grip. In 1631 the Mamlūks deposed a viceroy who had treacherously murdered one of their leaders, and installed a *qāʾim maqām* (acting viceroy) in his place; and the Sultan in Istanbul endorsed their action. The office of *qāʾim maqām* had often to be filled in later years, and always went to a Mamlūk bey; so too did the office of *daftardār* (director of finance), which had formerly been reserved for functionaries from Istanbul. The annual tribute payments, and the contributions for imperial expenses, continued to be made, and troops were sometimes supplied for service outside Egypt; but the amounts paid as tribute declined, apparently because of a decline in the revenues reserved for this purpose.

For a quarter of a century until his death in 1656, the most powerful man in Egypt was Riḍwān Bey, who held the post of *amīr al-ḥajj* and in an adventurous career frustrated all viceregal and factional attempts to oust him. His supporters among the Mamlūks were known as the Dhūʾl-Faqārī or Faqārī faction, and his opponents as the Qāsimī faction. For a century to come the Mamlūks were split into these two factions, each of which made alliances in the Cairo bazaar and with beduin tribes. In 1660 the Qāsimī beys in concert with the viceroy defeated and put to death the leading Faqārī beys, but in 1662 the next viceroy treacherously murdered the Qāsimī leader, Aḥmad Bey, who was a Bosniak. A period of greater viceregal ascendancy followed; but the influential posts remained in the hands of Mamlūk beys.

Towards the end of the 16th century, the Janissaries, who by then were to a large extent local-born, became increasingly undisciplined and politically active. A former sergeant-major *(başodabaşi)*, Kücük Muḥammad, who probably represented the local-born Janissaries, conducted an adventurous struggle against the senior officers, and in 1692 carried out a coup d'état with the help of some Faqārī beys. He was assassinated in 1694 at the instigation of the senior officers. During his brief tenure of de facto power he tried to suppress abuses and to prevent prices from rising after a crop failure. The Janissaries remained influential after his death, but their privileges and arrogance made them odious to the other regiments, especially the *ʿazabs* (armourers). A seventy-day civil war in 1711 between the Janissaries, supported by some Faqārī beys, and their opponents, led by Qāsimī beys, ended in the defeat of the Janissaries and death of their leader, another *başodabaşi* named Afranj Aḥmad. The viceroy, who had been a virtual prisoner of the Janissaries, was deposed and replaced by a *qā'im maqām*.

After this event, the Mamlūk beys were the sole masters of Egypt. Their number was usually 24, and the most powerful bey came to be known as the *ra'īs* (leader). The *rī'āsah* (leadership) was sometimes shared between two or three beys. The Ottoman viceroys adopted a policy of supporting any *ra'īs* who showed ability to provide stable government and willingness to remit some tribute to the Porte. In these circumstances, rivalry between the "households" of leading beys became more important than the strife between the two factions. The Qāsimī faction remained in the ascendant under Ismāʿīl Bey, who was *ra'īs* from 1714 until his assassination in 1724. Another civil war in 1730 led to a victory of the Faqārī faction, whose beys contended for the *ri'āsah* until one of them, Ibrāhīm Kāhyā (Kadkhudā) prevailed in 1744. He ruled despotically but benevolently until his death in 1754 and gave Egypt a much needed respite from disorder. Although he held the *ri'āsah* jointly from 1748 to 1754 with the head of another Mamlūk "household", he was the effective master; and from his time, or perhaps a little later, the dominant Mamlūk bey in Egypt came to be known by the title *shaykh al-balad*. Ibrāhīm Kāhyā diverted a large part of the Egyptian revenues to the upbuilding of his own Mamlūk "household", which soon outclassed the others and was to monopolize important appointments until the French conquest.

At the same time he paid the imperial expenses and sent useful even if diminished sums of tribute to the Porte, which consequently viewed his rule with favour.

In the frequent fighting among the "powers" of Egypt before and after the *ri'āsah* of Ibrāhīm Kāhyā, not only Mamlūks and regimental troops, but also beduin Arabs, and armed *sayyids* and guildsmen, were roped in. The Hawwārah tribe regained control of Asyūt and Upper Egypt under the leadership of Shaykh Humām (d. 1769), who won a reputation for chivalry but practised extortion on the inhabitants; he habitually sheltered fugitive Mamlūks of defeated factions. The outbreaks of fighting did great economic harm. The victors, in order to pay for their expenses, used to impose levies and confiscations called *avanias* on the artisans and merchants, including the few foreign (mainly French) merchants. Insecurity and extortion, together with the decay of traditional industries such as linen and sugar, and the loss of Indian Ocean trade in the 17th and 18th centuries, progressively impoverished Egypt.

Ibrāhīm Kāhyā's death was followed by struggles for power among the beys of his "household", until the post of *shaykh al-balad* was given in 1760 to a young officer of Caucasian origin, ʿAlī Bey, whom Ibrāhīm Kāhyā had bought, trained and promoted. ʿAlī Bey soon showed despotic inclinations. He tried to build up a personal following with the help of his own Mamlūk and right-hand man, Muḥammad Bey "Abū al-Dhahab."[1] At the same time he tried to eliminate the other leading beys, who in March 1766 turned against him and forced him to flee to Palestine, where he contacted the de facto ruler of ʿAkkā, Shaykh Ẓāhir al-ʿUmar, and the Ottoman governor of Gaza. With the latter's help he returned to Egypt, and although he was again forced to leave Cairo, he and Abū al-Dhahab were able to gather a force of Mamlūk supporters in Upper Egypt. With this force, and with military help from Shaykh Humām, ʿAlī Bey re-entered Cairo in October 1767; and in the following year he crushed all Mamlūk opposition, and turned against Shaykh Humām, who was defeated and later died. The Arab tribes ceased from then onwards to be an important force in Egyptian politics, and gradually became assimilated with the peasants (*fallāḥīn*).

ʿAlī Bey had come to an agreement with the Ottoman authorities whereby they recognised his right to take possession of revenues previously assigned to defeated Mamlūk rivals, and he in return undertook to make payments to the Porte called *ḥulwān* ("douceur", i.e. ex gratia),

[1] So called because he scattered gold *(dhahab)*, instead of the usual silver, to the crowd at the ceremony of his promotion to the rank of bey.

besides fulfilling Egypt's obligations in respect of imperial expenses. In the event, after deposing two successive viceroys in 1768 and 1769 and appointing himself *qā'im maqām*, he cut off payments to the Porte and spent the money thus saved on building up his own armed forces on modern lines. The Russo-Turkish war of 1769-1774, which was to prove so disastrous for the Ottoman empire, had by then broken out, and the Sultan had called upon 'Alī Bey, as upon other provincial governors, to mobilize troops for the war. He used them instead for the advancement of his own ambitions, which presaged those of Muḥammad 'Alī Pāshā in the next century. In 1769 he issued coins bearing both his own and the Sultan's names, thereby showing that he intended to recognize only a nominal Ottoman suzerainty. In 1770 he intervened in the Ḥijāz, on behalf of a Sharīfian claimant to the governorship of Mecca who was also backed by the Porte; a sea-borne force under the command of Abū al-Dhahab installed the claimant at Mecca and for the time being replaced Ottoman by Egyptian influence in the Holy Places. 'Ali Bey then, like many other rulers of Egypt, turned his attention to Syria. He also sent messages to the European powers offering increased trade and asking for help, and received emissaries from the Russian fleet which had entered the Mediterranean by way of Gibraltar and had annihilated the Ottoman fleet at Çeşme in July 1770. At the end of 1770 'Alī Bey sent a force into Syria under Ismā'īl Bey, who joined up with Shaykh Ẓāhir but hesitated to attack Damascus. He then sent a second force, 30,000 strong, under Abū al-Dhahab, who captured the city except the citadel in the summer of 1771; but the Porte, which had earlier condemned 'Alī Bey as a traitor, persuaded Abū al-Dhahab of the wrongness of rebellion in wartime and offered him the prospect of future mastery in Egypt. After a brief occupation Abū al-Dhahab withdrew from Damascus and marched back to Cairo. He was finally able, in April 1772, to oust his father-in-law 'Alī Bey, who fled to Shaykh Ẓāhir at 'Akkā. A year later, after obtaining some arms from the Russian fleet, 'Alī Bey rashly returned to Egypt, where he was wounded in an encounter and taken prisoner; he died a week afterwards. Abū al-Dhahab ruled Egypt with complete autonomy, but remained loyal to the Ottoman government and made regular *ḥulwān* payments to it. When the Porte, after the end of the Russo-Turkish war, resolved to get rid of Shaykh Ẓāhir, Abū al-Dhahab led the Mamlūk contingent, probably hoping to receive Palestine as a reward; but he died suddenly at 'Akkā in the spring of 1775, and his troops hastened back to Egypt.

In the ensuing struggles among the Mamlūk beys, the protagonists were the already mentioned Ismā'īl Bey, and two former protégés of Abū al-Dhahab, Ibrāhīm Bey and Murād Bey. Rivals at first, these two dominated the scene from 1779 onwards, and from 1784 maintained a duumvirate in which they alternated as *shaykh al-balad*. By withholding and pocketing sums due as *ḥulwān*, they incurred the wrath of the Porte, which had already begun to feel misgivings about Mamlūk misrule. In 1786 an expeditionary force under the Qapūdān Pāshā (Admiral of the Fleet) Ḥasan sailed to Alexandria and Rosetta. After defeating a Mamlūk force, Ḥasan Pāshā entered Cairo in August 1786. He made a serious attempt to stop abuses and introduce reforms, on the basis of the *Qānūn-nāmah* of Sulaymān I. He offered an amnesty to the Mamlūk beys, some of whom rallied to him; but Ibrāhīm and Murād held out in Upper Egypt, and when Turkish troops were sent in pursuit of them to Aswān, withdrew into Nubia. The Ottoman empire being then at war with Russia and Austria, Ḥasan Pāshā and his force were recalled in the following year for service in Europe. The subsequent Ottoman viceroys were again powerless. Ismā'īl Bey, whom Ḥasan Pāshā had made *shaykh al-balad*, held Cairo until his death in a plague in 1791, when Ibrāhīm and Murād again made themselves masters of the city and of all Egypt. They scrapped Ḥasan Pāshā's reforms, but were now willing to pay sums of *ḥulwan* at least sufficient to win the Porte's reluctant acquiescence in their rule, which lasted until the French invasion in 1798.

The self-appointed Mamlūk rulers of Egypt were thus able in the course of the 18th century to win virtual independence. They appropriated most of the revenues formerly sent to Istanbul, and also revenues formerly spent in Egypt for Ottoman imperial purposes – e.g. on the now neglected naval bases and Red Sea fleet, and on irrigation works. They did not, however, reduce the burden of taxes. Contemporary reports indicate that the peasants and townsfolk were ground down to an unprecedented extent, by taxation and by looting and *avanias*; and that lands ceased to be cultivated and the population declined. Complaints from the French merchants about Mamlūk misrule, and the manifest weakening of Ottoman authority, prompted King Louis XV's minister the Duc de Choiseul in 1759 to consider a French conquest of Egypt in compensation for the loss of France's Indian and Canadian colonies; but the French monarchy remained loyal to its long-standing alliance with the Ottoman sultanate. Another sign of European interest in Egypt was an agreement reached in 1775 between Abū al-Dhahab and the British Governor-General in India, Warren Hastings, whereby British ships were to be admitted to Suez. The agreement was negotiated by the Scottish traveller and explorer of

Abyssinia, James Bruce. Nothing came of it, because the Cairo-Suez caravan route was too often insecure, and because the Ottoman government, as guardian of the Holy Places, disapproved of the entry of foreign ships into the Red Sea. During the 18th century, the British East India Company, besides trading with Mokhā, was in fact able to send a few ships to Jiddah; and a few British travellers made their way between India and Europe through the Red Sea and Egypt. Further unsuccessful efforts to open this route for trade were made in the time of Ibrāhīm and Murād by George Baldwin, a British merchant who became consul at Cairo (1786-1793), and by Carlo Rossetti, an Italian merchant who was consul for Venice and Austria. Egypt's potential importance was becoming apparent. It was soon to be recognised by a very powerful visionary, Napoléon Bonaparte.

## OTTOMAN SYRIA, 1516–1831

After his departure from Egypt in September 1517, Salīm I spent nearly six months attending to the affairs of Syria. He entrusted the whole territory south of the province of Aleppo to Jānbirdī al-Ghazālī, the last governor of Damascus under the Mamlūk sultānate, who had gone over to the Ottoman side. Small Ottoman detachments were left in Damascus and other cities; there were also local troops raised by the governor. Most of the tribal and mountain chiefs had already submitted, and were now confirmed in their positions and financial obligations. Among them were 'Assāf the Turkomān, who held the Kisrāwan district in the Northern Lebanon, and the Druze chief Fakhr al-Dīn of the Ma'nid clan, who held the Shūf district in the southern Lebanon; the Buḥturids, formerly masters of the Gharb district in the central Lebanon and paramount chiefs of the Druzes, were stripped of authority because they had remained loyal to the Mamlūk sultanate during and after the battle of Marj Dābiq. Ottoman troops had to be employed against Ibn al-Ḥanash, a Sunnite chief, and Ibn al-Ḥarfūsh, a Shī'ite chief, who rebelled in the Biqā' and Tyre districts; both were eventually defeated and killed. The 'Alawites (Nuṣayrīs) of the district of al-Lādhiqīyah, who had fought hard against the Ottomans, were subdued with much bloodshed. The province of Aleppo, with its mixed population of Arabs, Turks, Kurds and Christians, and its great city, was placed under the authority of an Ottoman Turkish governor.

On learning of Salīm I's death, Jānbirdī al-Ghazālī rebelled at Damascus and overpowered the Ottoman garrison. He appealed in vain to Khā'ir

Bey in Egypt and also (according to a Persian source[1]) to Shāh Ismāʿīl Ṣafavī. After laying siege to Aleppo, he was forced to retire to Damascus, where he proclaimed himself an independent Sultan; but he was soon defeated and killed, in February 1521, by a force of Janissaries, who punished the citizens with undue severity. From this time until 1660, Syria was divided into three provinces: Damascus (including Palestine, the present Transjordan, and Beirut); Tripoli (including Ḥimṣ, Ḥamā and al-Ladhīqīyah); and Aleppo. The *wālīs* of these provinces, and often also subordinate district governors, were henceforward sent from Istanbul. Their power tended increasingly to be limited by the shortness and insecurity of their tenures. By the end of the 16th century, both Damascus and Aleppo were under the sway of Janissaries, now no longer recruited through the *devşirme*; the dominant Janissaries at Aleppo came from Damascus. Tripoli was dominated by a clan of Kurdish origin, the Banū Sayfā, lords of the nearby plain of ʿAkkār; their chief Yūsuf obtained the governorship of Tripoli for himself in 1579 and on several subsequent occasions.

During most of the 16th century, however, Syria enjoyed stability and prosperity. The growth of Aleppo as a commercial centre has already been mentioned. Reports speak of the flourishing state of the northern Lebanon under ʿAssāf the Turkomān (d. 1522) and his successors Manṣūr (d. 1580) and Muḥammad (d. 1590); and of the southern Lebanon under Fakhr al-Dīn I al-Maʿnī (murdered in 1544, at the instigation of a *wālī* of Damascus) and his son Qurqumāz (d. 1585). The Maronite Christians then lived mainly in the north of the mountain, but were already migrating to the centre and south; they were governed by their own feudal chiefs (*muqaddams*) acting as stewards for the Turkomān and Druze overlords, who in turn acted as tax-collectors for the Ottoman *wālīs*.

This harmony was upset in 1584, when brigands at Jūn ʿAkkār near Tripoli looted the caravan carrying the tribute of Egypt to Istanbul. The crime was blamed on the Druzes. An Ottoman force ravaged their territory and overthrew their chief Qurqumāz, who died in hiding a year later. Yūsuf al-Sayfā took the opportunity to extend his influence, and in 1590 eliminated the last ʿAssāfid. His rule was not liked by the Maronites.

A serious revolt at Aleppo threatened Ottoman authority in 1605–1607, while a war with Īrān was in progress. The Janissary dominance had been

---

[1] *Tārīkh-i Jahāngushā-yi Khāqān*, tr. by A. D. Muztar "*The foundation of Shīʿa Rule in Persia*" (thesis, Manchester University, 1967), pp. 721–722. This anonymous history of Shāh Ismāʿīl Ṣafavī calls Jānbirdī al-Ghazālī "Jahānvardī Ghazāloghlī" and says that after his death his son with a large number of "Ghazālī, Jabal ʿĀmilī and Kar **kī** Arabs and Ṣūfīs" migrated to Ṣafavid territory.

temporarily ended with the help of Ḥusayn Jānbulāt (Jānpūlād), chief of the Kurds and governor of Killis in the north of the province. Afterwards, with the Porte's approval, he forcibly took over the governorship of Aleppo; but in 1605 he was arrested and executed at Vān for alleged failure to supply troops punctually for the war. His nephew ʿAlī then rebelled, and with 30,000 troops made himself master of a territory stretching from Ḥamā to Adana. He fought against Yūsuf al-Sayfā in alliance with the Druze leader Fakhr al-Dīn II al-Maʿnī. After two years an Ottoman expeditionary force overpowered him. The Jānbulāt clan maintained their friendly relations with Fakhr al-Dīn, and in 1630 some of them migrated to the Lebanon, where they became converts to the Druze religion (an offshoot of Ismāʿīlite Shīʿism) and important figures in the Druze community.

The rise of Fakhr al-Dīn II (b. 1572, d. 1635), who was a 12-year old fugitive when his father Qurqumāz died, stemmed from his own skill in leadership and diplomacy, and from the weakening of Ottoman ascendancy. After winning to his side the Druze and Maronite chiefs, and also neighbouring Sunnite and Shīʿite chiefs, he warred with some success against Yūsuf al-Sayfā for possession of Beirut and the northern Lebanon. The *wālīs* in Damascus and authorities in Istanbul, while generally supporting Yūsuf, did not want him to become too powerful and at first welcomed Fakhr al-Dīn's influence as a counterbalance. Fakhr al-Dīn was thus able to obtain recognition as *amīr* of the Lebanon, and later also the governorships of Sidon and Ṣafad. He maintained order and religious toleration in his domains, and worked for their economic uplift by fostering agriculture and overseas trade through Sidon and Beirut. The resultant prosperity attracted immigrants, mainly Maronite farmers from the northern Lebanon who settled in the Druze districts, and Orthodox Christian townsfolk from other parts of Syria and Palestine. Foreign merchants—Tuscans from Livorno, Venetians and Frenchmen—were encouraged to settle at the ports. The Lebanese silk industry, and the rise of Beirut, date from this time.

Fakhr al-Dīn's economic policy was inspired mainly by fiscal considerations. He raised enough revenue to provide for a standing infantry force as well as feudal levies, and to pay large bribes at Damascus and also Istanbul in addition to tribute obligations. He first gave offence to the Ottoman authorities by his alliance with ʿAlī Jānbulāṭ. Later they became alarmed over his private army and his diplomatic negotiations in 1611 with the Grand Duke of Tuscany and the Pope. Moreover, he extended his authority to Nāblus in Palestine and to the Ḥawrān and

ʿAjlūn districts east of the Jordan through understandings with local Arab chiefs, who acknowledged his overlordship and paid tribute to him; he thereby usurped revenues due to the *wālī* of Damascus, and dominated the Damascus-Mecca and Damascus-Jerusalem roads which it was the *wālī*'s duty to protect. The *wālī*, Ḥāfiẓ Aḥmad Pāshā, who held the office from 1609 to 1615 and was influential at Istanbul, obtained strong reinforcements and invaded the Lebanon in 1613, while an Ottoman fleet blockaded the coast. Fakhr al-Dīn chose to escape by sea, and spent five years in exile, at Livorno and Florence in Tuscany, and at Messina in Sicily which then belonged to Spain. In his absence his son ʿAlī was recognized as *amīr* with his brother Yūnus as regent. In 1618, however, he obtained the Porte's permission to return to the Lebanon. He was again recognized as *amīr*, and quickly resumed his expansionist policies. He warred with Yūsuf al-Sayfā, who died in 1624, and with the *wālī* of Damascus, Muṣṭafā Pāshā, whom he defeated and took prisoner in 1625. His influence and bribes induced the Porte to grant him Nāblus and ʿAjlūn officially in 1622; and in 1624 he obtained an imperial title to the lands "from the borders of Aleppo to the borders of Jerusalem." Now at the zenith of his power, he continued to build up his private army and his finances, and to foster trade and intercourse with Italy. His resources, however, were insufficient. He had to deal with troubles in outlying parts of his enlarged domain, and in 1633 with an insurrection of certain Druze clans at its centre.

In 1630 the Sultan Murād IV started a new war with Īrān, which was to last until 1638. He looked upon Fakhr al-Dīn's growing power and foreign connections as a potential strategic threat, and in 1633 ordered the *wālīs* of Damascus, Aleppo and Cairo to overthrow him. An expeditionary force was also sent by sea. Fakhr al-Dīn's resistance was soon overwhelmed. His son ʿAlī was defeated and killed, and he himself finally took refuge in a cave. In 1635 he was caught and sent to Istanbul, where a few weeks later he was strangled.

The Ottoman authorities cut back the area of the Druze amīrate, but did not abolish it. They supported one of the clan chiefs who had revolted against Fakhr al-Dīn, while most of the clans supported Fakhr al-Dīn's nephew Mulḥim. In the end Mulḥim prevailed and won official recognition. To keep the Lebanon under closer supervision, the Porte in 1660 carved out a new province of Sidon, stretching from Beirut into northern Palestine. With the death of Aḥmad (r. 1657–1697), the Maʿnid male line became extinct. The clans wanted his wife's nephew Bashīr al-Shihābī to be the new *amir*; finally the Ottoman authorities appointed another relative Ḥaydar, then aged 12, with Bashīr as regent. The Shihābid family had long been allied with the Maʿnids, but did not profess the Druze religion. At least outwardly they professed Sunnism; but it is not unlikely that they kept their inward feelings hidden in accordance with the Druze and Shīʿite practice of *taqīyah* (protective dissimulation). Some of their descendants intermarried with Maronite families and professed, or appeared to profess, Christianity, while others professed Sunnism, and others Druzism. The amīrate remained with Ḥaydar al-Shihābī's heirs until its extinction in 1842. The murder of Bashīr at Ḥaydar's instigation in 1707 gave rise to four years of factional strife among the Druzes ending in victory for Ḥaydar; many of the vanquished then migrated to the Ḥawrān mountains on the desert fringe, which came to be known as the Jabal al-Durūz. Under Ḥaydar (d. 1732) and his two sons Mulḥim (abdicated 1754) and Manṣūr (deposed 1770), the Lebanon and its Druze and Maronite clans were generally peaceful, though Manṣūr's title was disputed. The *amīrs* kept on good terms with the *wālīs* at Sidon, Tripoli and Damascus, and extended their sway to Beirut and the Biqāʿ. Renewed prosperity attracted further, mainly Christian, immigration. A cultural revival also began. The Maronites had by now generally abandoned Syriac for Arabic, except in their liturgy. Their relations with the Vatican had become increasingly close since the foundation of a Maronite College at Rome in 1584; their church finally acquired Uniat status in 1741. Two of their clergy were outstanding Arabic scholars: Germanus Farḥāt (1670–1732), who was Maronite archbishop of Aleppo, and Yūsuf al-Samʿāni (Assemani), who laboured at Rome.

While the Maʿnid-Shihābid amīrate secured a substantial and beneficial degree of autonomy for the Druzes and Maronites in the Lebanon, other Syrian minority groups stagnated or decayed. The Twelver Shīʿites of Baʿlbak and the Tyre district (Jabal ʿĀmil) had in the 16th century supplied leading theologians to Ṣafavid Īrān, but did not afterwards play any significant part; their chiefs of the Ḥarfūsh family were usually allies and sometimes adversaries of the Lebanese *amīrs*. The extreme Shīʿite ʿAlawites maintained their obscure existence, despite frequent conflicts with the Sunnite dignitaries of Ḥamā, with the Ismāʿīlites of Miṣyāf, and among themselves. In the late 17th and early 18th centuries, beduin of the ʿAnazah confederation migrated in large numbers from Najd to the Syrian desert, where they became the most powerful tribe; they made their influence felt as far as Aleppo. Most parts of Syria and Palestine nevertheless remained under direct Ottoman administration. Although northern Palestine could not always be controlled, the Pāshās of Damascus normally kept a firm grip on Jerusalem and Jaffa. Christian pilgrims continued to arrive, but in diminishing numbers, mainly, it seems, because the Christian world was losing interest in pilgrimage to Jerusalem. Within the fine city walls built by Sulaymān I in 1542, the city, according to travellers' accounts, presented an increasingly decrepit appearance, with a population of less than 10,000. There were resident Christian clergy of various churches and nations at Jerusalem, Bethlehem and Nazareth. Small communities of learned Jews lived at Jerusalem, Hebron, Tiberias and Ṣafad. Palestine experienced a general decline of trade and agriculture, caused *inter alia* by beduin incursions, a spread of malaria, and misgovernment, particularly in the late 18th century.

At Damascus and Aleppo, few events of more than petty local importance occurred. In 1657 the *wālī* of Aleppo, Ābāzah Ḥasan Pāshā, called for dismissal of the reforming grand vezir Muṣtafā Köprülü and rebelled with support from Damascus; two years later he was lured into surrender and executed. Forces of "new" Janissaries from Istanbul were then quartered in Damascus, where they came to form an additional faction, usually at loggerheads with the "old" Janissaries. Other contestants in the struggles for local influence were non-Janissary regiments, artisan guilds, *aʿyān* ("notables") and *ashrāf* (i.e. *sayyids*; descendants of ʿAlī). The *aʿyān*, who were often of military or official origin, were influential landowners; the *ashrāf*, who had the advantage of being tax-exempt, were mostly merchants and were grouped in corporations under a hereditary head *(naqīb)*. At Aleppo the Janissaries predominated until the mid-18th century, and again in the early 19th century, after an interval in which the upper hand lay with the *ashrāf*. In both cities forceful Pāshās, who kept the factions in order, occasionally appeared, but seldom lasted long; a few are remembered for mosques and buildings which they have left. The *wālīs* of Damascus, from the late 17th century onwards, assumed the title *amīr al-ḥajj* and often personally took command of the annual pilgrim caravan, instead of entrusting it to subordinates; the reason for this may have been that increased beduin raiding was making the route to Mecca more insecure.

For some 30 years in the mid-18th century, the Porte allowed Damascus and much of Syria to be governed by Syrian officials, of the al-ʿAẓm family from Maʿarrat al-Nuʿmān. Ismāʿīl Pāshā al-ʿAẓm became *wālī* of Tripoli, and was transferred in 1725 to Damascus, at the request of the *muftī*, after fighting between "old" and "new" Janissaries had prevented the departure of the pilgrim caravan. A brother then became *wālī* of Tripoli, and a son *wālī* of Sidon. In 1730, after the deposition of Aḥmad

III, they were all dismissed; but not long passed before members of the family were again governing at Tripoli, Sidon, Damascus and further afield. Sulaymān Pāshā, brother of Ismāʿīl, was *wālī* of Damascus from 1733 to 1738 and again from 1741 to his death in 1743, when he was succeeded by his nephew Asʿad (1743–1757), the greatest governor of Damascus in Ottoman times. Ismāʿīl, Sulaymān and Asʿad alike had to face great difficulties from the warring factions and from hostile intrigues, both at Damascus and in Istanbul. After three years of struggle, Asʿad Pāshā overcame all his local adversaries, and governed justly and benignly. He is remembered for this and for the beautiful palaces built by him at Damascus and at Ḥamā, which he added together with Ḥims to the province of Damascus. Intrigues at Istanbul led to his transfer to Aleppo in 1757, and to his dismissal and liquidation in 1758. The family was to supply many more governors, at Damascus and elsewhere; but its great days were over.

During this time, Galilee and other parts of northern Palestine belonging to the province of Sidon had fallen into the hands of Shaykh Ẓāhir al-ʿUmar, chief of a settled Arab tribe, the Zaydānīs. After occupying Ṣafad with the connivance of the *amīr* of the Lebanon, he seized Tiberias and Nazareth in 1737 and ʿAkkā in 1750. With the help of an able Christian treasurer, Ibrahīm al-Ṣabbāgh, he restored the harbour of ʿAkkā, attracted foreign ships and merchants, and raised revenue by means of tolls and monopolies. Sulaymān Pāshā al-ʿAẓm died on a campaign against him, but Asʿad Pāshā left him in peace. He maintained order and justice, and paid regular tribute. Later he hired Maghribī mercenaries, and angered the neighbouring Pāshās by seizing more places. He obtained a confirmatory decree from the Porte in 1768, before the start of the Russo-Turkish war of 1769–74. This did not stop the *wālī* of Damascus from threatening him; so he made an alliance with the rebel master of Egypt, ʿAlī Bey, whom he had earlier sheltered as a fugitive. In 1770 and again in 1771 his troops fought alongside the two invading forces sent into Syria by ʿAlī Bey. In the second invasion, the Egyptians occupied Damascus except the citadel, but withdrew soon afterwards when their commander, Muḥammad Abū al-Dhahab, was induced to turn against his patron. Shaykh Ẓāhir's troops then single-handedly defeated the forces of the *wālī* of Damascus and captured Sidon. Among the defeated forces were Lebanese troops supplied by the young *amīr* Yūsuf al-Shihābī, who was in alliance with the *wālī* even though many of the Druze clans sympathized with Shaykh Ẓāhir. Meanwhile, in Egypt, ʿAlī Bey had appealed for help and arms to the Russian fleet; but having been driven out of Egypt by Muḥammad Abū al-Dhahab, he again fled to Shaykh Ẓāhir in 1772. The Russian fleet then landed the arms at ʿAkkā. Shaykh Ẓāhir's troops proceeded to besiege Beirut, and the *amīr* Yūsuf appealed to the *wālī* of Damascus, who sent reinforcements; they were commanded by Aḥmad al-Jazzār, a Bosniak Mamlūk who had once been in the service of ʿAlī Bey in Egypt, where he had earned his nickname "*al-Jazzār*" ("the Butcher"). The Russians bombarded Beirut in support of the besiegers, who were nevertheless driven back by al-Jazzār. ʿAlī Bey marched back to Egypt, where he was defeated and died in 1773. At Beirut, friction arose between the *amīr* Yūsuf and al-Jazzār, who refused to recognize the *amīr*'s authority. The Russians were persuaded to intervene on Yūsuf's behalf; they again bombarded Beirut, and landed troops who stayed in the town from October 1773 to February 1774 and forced al-Jazzār to withdraw. After the end of the war with Russia, the Porte ordered Muḥammad Abū al-Dhahab and the *wālī* of Damascus to march against Shaykh Ẓāhir. Betrayed by his son and his mercenaries, who succumbed to bribery, Shaykh Ẓāhir fled and was murdered, at an age of well over 80, in 1775.

The Porte rewarded al-Jazzār by appointing him *wālī* of Sidon. He resided at ʿAkkā, which replaced Sidon as capital of the province, and while duly fulfilling his obligations to the Porte, made himself semi-independent and irremovable. He twice also held the governorship of Damascus, from 1785 to 1787 and from 1800 to his natural death in 1804. He built up a large army of Bosniaks, Albanians and Maghribīs, and a private navy. To pay for them, he overtaxed the people and (like Shaykh Ẓāhir before him) set up monopolies, which became more and more extortionate and did great harm to economic life. Although he kept order, his brutality was notorious. With the aim of weakening the Lebanese amīrate, he stirred up strife among the Druze clans; and after quelling a revolt of his own troops, he found a pretext to attack the *amīr* Yūsuf, who had given some help to the mutineers. Yūsuf surrendered after a defeat in 1788, and was hanged in prison. The Druze chiefs had already agreed that the succession should go to his distant cousin Bashīr II al-Shihābī; and al-Jazzār consented in the belief that the 21-year old Bashīr would be a tool in his hands. Although Bashīr overtaxed his people to pay the sums demanded by al-Jazzār, he soon showed that he was no puppet. In 1797 he did to death some Druze chiefs whom al-Jazzār had incited to revolt in favour of a son of Yūsuf.

When Napoleon invaded Palestine, al-Jazzār won a place in world history. With help from a British naval squadron under Sir Sidney Smith, he withstood a siege from March to May 1799 and repulsed the French from ʿAkkā.

Although the Shīʿites and other victims of al-Jazzār's tyranny rallied to the French, Bashīr II did not commit himself. Afterwards he helped the grand *vezir*'s army on its march to Egypt, and was rewarded with a decree placing the Lebanon under the direct jurisdiction of the Porte. In the face of new threats from al-Jazzār, he departed in 1800 on board a British warship to Cyprus, but was able to return later in the same year. He was to rule the Lebanon until 1840. The death of al-Jazzār in 1804 greatly strengthened his position. The chief aim of his policy was to replace the feudal system with a stronger and more centralized system of government. As a result he clashed on several occasions with various Druze clans. He overcame their resistance by virtue of an efficient army of 15,000 local levies which he built up. Another result was that he tended for political reasons to favour the Maronites. On the other hand, he settled persecuted Druzes from Aleppo in the Lebanon, and encouraged immigration of Orthodox Christians from Aleppo and Damascus. His own religious faith cannot be known, but most probably was Druzism. His kindness to Christians led the Vatican and the French consuls to suppose that he was a Catholic and assured him of French support. In the very beautiful palace which he built at Bayt al-Dīn, in the mountains not far from Beirut, he installed both a mosque and a chapel. After his death at Istanbul in 1851, he was buried in an Armenian Catholic cemetery.

With the Pāshās who succeeded al-Jazzār at ʿAkkā, Bashīr II was generally able to maintain good relations; but having made himself master of the Biqāʿ, he clashed with one of the *wālīs* of Damascus and routed him in a battle in 1810. He then joined with the next *wālī*, who was his nominee, and repulsed a Wahhābite invasion of the Ḥawrān, thereby earning the goodwill of the Porte. His policies cost a great deal of money and necessitated severe taxation, which provoked a peasant rebellion *(ʿāmmīyah)* in 1820 in the mainly Maronite northern districts. Having failed to subdue the rebels, who were encouraged by two of his cousins, Bashīr abdicated and retired to the Ḥawrān. After a short period of disorder, the clan-chiefs recalled him and reinstated him in 1821. Shortly afterwards, he fought and defeated the *wālī* of Damascus, who during his absence had attempted to seize the Biqāʿ. On this occasion the Porte supported the *wālī*'s claims and offered him the governorship of ʿAkkā in addition to Damascus. Rather than submit, Bashīr again went into exile, in Egypt. The Pāshā at ʿAkkā refused to leave his post, and resisted a siege. Both he and Bashīr were pardoned and reinstated in 1822, thanks to the intercession of Muḥammad ʿAlī Pāshā of Egypt, on whose help the Porte was dependent in the struggle against the rebellious Greeks. Bashīr's return was resented by the Jānbulaṭ clan, who organized a formidable revolt against him in 1825. This was crushed, and the old feudal system was partly eliminated through confiscation of the estates of the rebels. From then on many Druzes harboured grievances against their autocratic *amīr* and against their traditional allies the Maronites, who to a large extent took over the confiscated lands. Bashīr II is nevertheless favourably remembered for the roads and bridges which he built, for the impetus which he gave to trade through Beirut, and for his encouragement of efforts to introduce modern education. His relative Ḥaydar al-Shihābī wrote at this time a notable history of the Lebanon under the Shihābid *amīrs*.

During his exile in Egypt, Bashīr II had entered into an alliance with Muḥammad ʿAlī Pāshā; and when the latter's son Ibrāhīm Pāshā invaded Syria in 1831, he duly fulfilled it, though not without reluctance, because most of the Druze leaders favoured the Ottoman cause. The Maronites, on the other hand, at first welcomed the Egyptians. Bashīr II's troops made a significant contribution to Ibrāhīm Pāshā's great victories, and to his rule in Syria. The downfall of the Egyptian régime was to put an end to Bashīr II's long reign in 1840, and to the Lebanese amīrate in 1842.

## ʿIRĀQ AND KURDISTĀN 1508–1831

During most of its history from the time of Cyrus, the Land of the Two Rivers had been politically linked with Īrān; but its population, while always mixed, had stayed predominantly Semitic. The Muslim conquest and accompanying Arab immigration resulted in the dominance of Islām and Arabic, although the ʿIrāqī peasants, whom the Arabs called "Nabaṭaeans", continued for a long time to speak Syriac, which remains the language of the small Christian and Mandaean (Ṣubbī) minorities. There was also a large and long established community of Jews. Shīʿism took root at an early date, and was fostered by the Īrānian Būyid dynasty (945–1055) and by the Banū Mazyad, an Arab tribe on the lower Euphrates who made themselves semi-independent in the 11th–12th centuries and built the town of Ḥillah. The shrines of the Imāms at Najaf, Karbalā, Kaẓimayn, and Sāmarrā were centres of pilgrimage, and Najaf and Ḥillah became seats of Shīʿite learning. The Saljūq and Mongol conquests left a residue of "Turkomān" settlers, around Khanaqīn, Kirkuk, Irbīl, Mosul and Diyār Bakr (then called Āmid). Hūlāgū Khān's invasion in 1258 caused great loss of life at Baghdād and reduced it to the rank of an Īrānian provincial capital. The trade of Baṣrah moved to Kīsh and later Hurmuz at the mouth of the Persian Gulf. In 1401 Tīmūr sacked Baghdād and massacred its inhabitants, doing greater damage than Hūlāgū had done. Floods and epidemics, such as the "Black Death" in 1357, also caused devastation. The breakdown of the elaborate irrigation system which had sustained 'Irāq's prosperity in Sāsānid and 'Abbāsid times probably took place in the two centuries after 1258, and above all after 1401. Large areas became depopulated, and the empty places were filled by beduin tribes, particularly in the 15th and 16th centuries. In the course of time, these tribes took wholly or partly to agriculture; and under the influence of the *'ulamā'* of Najaf, those in the south adopted the Shī'ite faith. 'Irāq sank to its lowest ebb under the turbulent Qara Qoyunlu dynasty (1410–1467), and did not significantly revive under the Aq Qoyunlu (1467–1508); the stable rule of Uzun Ḥasan (d. 1478) and Ya'qūb (d. 1490), who resided at Tabrīz and called themselves Shāhs of Īrān, was followed by disorder under their successors.

North-east and north of the Mespotamian plain, the mountains were inhabited by Kurdish tribes speaking an Īrānian language considerably different from Persian. Turkomāns occupied the foothills and the upper Tigris valley; they also then roamed in the Jazīrah and the northern Syrian desert. The Jacobite and Nestorian Christians had been reduced to small communities mainly around Mārdīn and north of Mosul. Further north Armenians were numerous, forming the majority around Lake Vān. In the 15th century the Turkomāns were the dominant element, under the leadership of the Qara Qoyunlu and Aq Qoyunlu federations, both of which first arose in the Erzurūm-Erzinjān region. The Turkomāns and the Kurds were always competitors for land, and the Aq Qoyunlu rulers tried systematically to weaken the Kurdish princes and chiefs. The Qara Qoyunlu had been extreme Shī'ites, and although the Aq Qoyunlu were Sunnites, Ṣafavid propaganda during their time won a great many of the Turkomāns to Twelver Shī'ism. The Kurds in general remained faithful to Sunnism.

After the Ṣafavid conquest of western Īrān in 1501–1503, Aq Qoyunlu princes and governors held out in 'Irāq and Diyār Bakr. Shah Ismā'īl quelled the Kurds of Āẕarbāījān in 1505/6, when the Kurdish prince of Ardalān (now Iranian Kurdistān) submitted to him, and added the Diyār Bakr region to his empire after hard-fought campaigns in 1507/8 and 1508/09. Some of the Kurds continued to resist, while others, such as the prince of Bitlis (Bidlīs) near Lake Vān submitted. In 1508 Shāh Ismā'īl entered Baghdād without resistance, the last Aq Qoyunlu governor having fled. Mosul and Baṣrah were also annexed. At Baghdād, Shāh Ismāʿīl put a number of leading Sunnites to death, destroyed the Sunnite shrines of Abū Ḥanīfah and ʿAbd al-Qādir al-Gīlānī, and ordered the building of a splendid shrine at the tomb of the Seventh Imām Mūsà al-Kāẓim. A start was made on a new Euphrates-Tigris canal, and an immigration of Īrānian merchants revived trade. The Shāh also visited Karbalā, Najaf and Sāmarrā, bestowing lavish gifts. He then marched to quell the Mushaʿshaʿ Arabs, extreme Shīʿite "heretics" who held the Khūzistān bank of the Shaṭṭ al-ʿArab. On the other side of the river, Baṣrah was left in the hands of an Arab shaykh who acknowledged Ṣafavid suzerainty.

After Shāh Ismāʿīl's defeat at Chāldirān in 1514, Ottoman troops with Kurdish assistance conquered Diyār Bakr in 1515 and Mosul in 1516. Many of the Turkomāns then migrated to Ṣafavid territory, continuing a process which had begun with the formation of the Mawṣillū, Dhū'l-Qadr and Shāmlū "tribes" of the Qizilbāsh (Ṣafavid) army; their departure improved the position of the Kurds and enabled Arab nomads to advance into the Jazīrah. The province of Diyār Bakr was considered one of the more important in the Ottoman empire, and the city was always strongly garrisoned. The Kurdish princes and chiefs *(āghās)* willingly accepted Ottoman sovereignty, and were rewarded accordingly. Five hereditary vassal principalities were recognized, of which the most important and durable was Bitlis, and governorships of districts *(sanjaqs)* and castles were given to the chiefs, who often also made their positions hereditary. In the ensuing centuries, Kurdish potentates fought among themselves and against the Ottoman provincial governors, and some of them changed sides in the frequent Ottoman-Īrānian wars; but in general the Kurds remained loyal to the Ottoman Sultans.

Meanwhile Ṣafavid viceroys continued to govern at Baghdād. Their authority was temporarily shaken in 1530 when a Kurdish officer named Dhū'l-Faqār seized the city in the name of the Ottoman Sultan. In 1534 Sulaymān I began the first of his three wars against Shāh Tahmāsb, and after conquering Tabrīz, Hamadān and Kirmānshāh entered Baghdād without resistance. He restored the shrines of Abū Ḥanīfah and ʿAbd al-Qādir al-Gīlānī, ordered the completion of the shrine of Mūsà al-Kāẓim, and visited Karbalā and Najaf. Baghdād became the centre of a new Ottoman province, with a strong garrison of Janissaries and *ʿazabs* (armourers). Except in the Kurdish district of Shahrazūr, which was put under the jurisdiction of the *wālī* of Baghdād, Ottoman authority was not threatened by the Īrānians until 1623. Baghdād regained some prosperity as a centre of trade with Īrān and Arabia. Baṣrah was at first left under Arab tribal rule; but as a precaution against possible danger from the Portuguese, Ottoman troops occupied the town in 1547. A separate province of Baṣrah was constituted, with jurisdiction stretching to the oasis of al-Aḥsā'[1] and the adjacent coast opposite Baḥrayn, the local shaykhs having acknowledge Ottoman suzerainty. Communications between Baghdād and Baṣrah were continually threatened by the Arab tribes of the desert and of the lower Euphrates and Tigris. The Ottoman authorities were thus in no position to develop the trade of Baṣrah or to build up a navy in the Persian Gulf.

Except in the near vicinity of Baghdād and Baṣrah, Ottoman control was very loose. The Arab tribes occupied whatever lands they could get with no official title. Towards the Shīʿites, the Ottoman policy was tolerant. Sulaymān I had promised that the Shīʿite pilgrimages might continue, and the routes to Karbalā and Najaf were kept open. The merchants were mostly Shīʿites of Īrānian origin and Jews. Military and official employments, however, were reserved for Sunnites. As in other provinces, the garrison troops tended to become hereditary classes, with grievances and ambitions of their own. The Janissaries and *ʿazabs* were usually at loggerheads. In the frequent expeditions against Arab and Kurdish tribes, local levies were often employed. A mutinous officer, Muḥammad al-Ṭawil, seized Baghdad in 1603/04, and Ottoman troops did not regain the city until 1608. At Baṣrah, an officer, Afrasiyāb, who had purchased the governorship in or about 1612, made himself semi-independent, and the Ottoman authorities acquiesced. At Baghdād, a Janissary commander, Bakr the Ṣūbāshī,[2] defeated and killed the *wālī*, who was in league with his rivals, and then usurped the governorship. The Porte sent troops from Diyār Bakr against him. While they were besieging the city, he appealed to Shāh ʿAbbās of Īrān. The Porte then recognized him as *wālī*, and the siege ended. The Shāh, however, did not accept this *volte-face*. His troops advanced and in their turn besieged Baghdād, which was treacherously surrendered to them by Bakr's own son, in 1623. Bakr himself was then put to death.

The Ṣafavid troops massacred a large number of Sunnites and sold others as slaves. The shrines of Abū Ḥanīfah and ʿAbd al-Qādir al-Gīlānī were again destroyed. The Sarāi of Baghdād, still in use as the seat of government, was built by the Ṣafavid governor. Kirkuk and Mosul also

[1] The date growers of this remarkably large oasis were and are Shīʿites. In the 10th and 11th centuries it had been the stronghold of the extreme Shīʿite Carmathians (Qarmaṭīs).

[2] i.e. "police chief". He had apparently been the police chief earlier in his career.

fell to the Īrānians, but only for a few months. At Baṣrah, Afrasiyāb (d. 1624) and his son and successor ʿAlī warded off Īrānian attacks in 1624/5 and 1629, but did not otherwise participate in the war. The Arab and Kurdish tribes, in so far as they were affected, changed sides according to the fortunes of the fighting. The Ottoman government was determined to recover Baghdād, and after unsuccessful attempts in 1625 and 1630, found the time ripe when Īrān was weakened by Shāh ʿAbbās's death. The Sultan Murād IV set out at the head of a large force including Janissaries from Istanbul, and in 1638 obtained the surrender of Baghdād from the outnumbered Ṣafavid governor. Some ardent Shīʿite soldiers of the garrison went on fighting, and the Ottoman troops massacred a number of the city's Shīʿite inhabitants. The Sultan caused the destroyed shrines to be repaired, and authorized continuance of the Shīʿite pilgrimages. He also left behind a large garrison of Janissaries. Although peace was restored in 1639 and lasted until the fall of the Ṣafavids, Baghdād for long after this war was less populous and prosperous than it had been earlier. Its history in the rest of the 17th century was uneventful, apart from a few clashes between the dominant Janissaries and the large local army which had to be maintained for action against the tribes.

At Baṣrah, Afrasiyāb and ʿAlī maintained good relations with the tribes, and revived trade by admitting European ships. The Portuguese, having lost Baḥrayn and Hurmuz, made most use of the port. Family dissensions after ʿAli's death (c. 1652) enabled the *wālī* of Baghdād to seize Baṣrah, but a popular rising reinstated ʿAlī's son Ḥusayn in 1654. He was finally ousted by troops sent from Baghdād in 1668. The Afrasiyāb dynasty then came to an end, and the province of Baṣrah became a dependency of the Pāshās at Baghdād.

In the late 17th century, while the provincial administrations under transient *wālīs* grew weaker, important developments took place among the tribes. On the lower Euphrates, a number of small tribes including the Marsh Arabs joined in the Muntafiq confederation. They briefly seized Baṣrah in 1694, and together with the Ḥawīzah Arabs, who were Īrānian subjects, long controlled its approaches. The northward migration of the ʿAnazah beduin drove a section of their enemies, the Shammar, across the Euphrates into the Jazīrah; the resultant disorder sometimes endangered the routes from Baghdād and Mosul to Aleppo. In 1716 a group of ʿAnazah tribesmen founded the town of Kuwayt on a waterless bay between Baṣrah and al-Aḥsāʾ. Under their *amīrs* of the Āl Ṣabāḥ family, they made it a shipbuilding and shipping centre, using imported water and timber. They recognised the authority of the *wālīs* of Baṣrah.

The Ottoman-Īrānian frontier was not clearly delimited, and Shahrazūr, which extended to Kirkūk, was claimed by the Kurdish prince of Ardalān, who was an Īrānian vassal. Later a new Kurdish principality arose in this region under the Bābān family. The founder, Aḥmad al-Faqīh, was a religious leader—a phenomenon often seen in Kurdistān. Around 1677 his grandson Sulaymān Bey established himself in the village of Qal'ah Chōlān and obtained recognition from the Porte as a district governor. He and his successors encroached southwards beyond Khānaqīn and eastwards into Īrān. In the early 18th century Ottoman authority was re-established by the *wālī* of Baghdād Ḥasan Pāshā, and for a short time Shahrazūr became a *vilayet* with Kirkūk as capital. The Bābān princes helped the Ottoman forces in the Īrānian wars of 1723–1746, and regained official recognition with the title Pāshā. Their rule was unstable on account of internal struggles, in which rival claimants obtained help from the *wālīs* at Baghdād and the Īrānian governors at Kirmānshāh, while their continuing encroachments troubled both authorities. In 1783/4 Ibrāhīm Pāshā Bābān founded Sulaymānī[1] as their capital. None of the other Kurdish principalities had more than minor local importance, except Bitlis, where the Kurds and Armenians lived in concord and prospered. One of the princes of Bitlis was the historian of the Kurds, Sharaf al-Din Bidlīsī.[2]

The tribal problem may explain why the Porte let Ḥasan Pāshā, who was of Georgian origin, govern Baghdād from 1704 to 1723 and build up a local force of purchased Georgian youths (Ar. *Mamlūk*; T. *Kölemen*). He took vigorous action against the Muntafiq Arabs and Bābān Kurds, and ruled justly. In the Ottoman invasion of Īrān in 1723, he and his son Aḥmad, who was *wālī* of Baṣrah, captured Kirmānshāh, where he died. The troops put Aḥmad in his place, and the Porte approved. Aḥmad Pāshā led subsequent campaigns in Īrān and successfully defended Baghdād when it was besieged by Nādir Shāh in 1733. Later in that year, after the rout of the main Ottoman force near Kirkūk, he made peace with Nādir on terms unacceptable to the Porte, and was transferred to Aleppo; but when war broke out again in 1736, he was sent back to Baghdād, which he again defended against Nādir in 1743. He continued to recruit Georgian Mamlūks and put them in the principal administrative posts. On his death in 1747, the Porte appointed a *wālī* from

[1] In Arabic, Sulaymānīyah; said to have been named after the viceroy of Baghdād, Sulaymān Pāshā "the Great".

[2] He began his career in the Ṣafavid service, and was placed on the throne of his ancestors by the Ottoman Sultan. In 1596 he abdicated in order to write his history (in Persian), the *Sharafnāmeh*.

outside. Two years later, Aḥmad Pāshā's Mamlūk son-in-law, Sulaymān Pāshā "Abū Laylah,"[1] who was then in charge at Baṣrah, marched on Baghdād and took over the governorship. The Porte acquiesced. Baghdād and Baṣrah remained under Mamlūk rule, with short intermissions, from 1749 to 1831.

Mosul also resisted Nādir's attacks, under its *wālī* Ḥājjī Ḥusayn Pāshā of the Jalīlī family. Members of this family held the governorship on a semi-hereditary basis during most of the period 1726–1834.

While northern ʿIrāq suffered much from the Ottoman-Īrānian fighting, Baṣrah after the repulse of Īrānian attacks in 1735 and 1743 enjoyed relative security at a time when Īrān was in disorder. Dutch, English and Masqaṭī ships made increasing use of the port. The English East India Company opened a factory at Baṣrah in 1727 and posted a resident there in 1764. A substantial amount of Īrānian trade was diverted from Bushire to Baghdād and Baṣrah. This was the main reason why the Īrānian ruler, Karīm Khān Zand, went to war and captured Baṣrah in 1775. There had also been troubles involving the Bābān principality, and molestations of Shīʿite pilgrims by tribesmen. The defeat moved the Porte to act against the Mamlūks of Baghdād. ʿUmar Pāshā (1764–1776) was replaced by an outsider, who proved incapable of keeping order. In 1779, partly as a result of British representations, the governorship was again given to a Mamlūk, Sulaymān Pāshā "the Great."[2] Formerly in command at Baṣrah, he had been a prisoner at Shirāz until the war ended with the Īrānian evacuation of Baṣrah in 1779. His rule (1780–1802) was efficient at first, but weakened as he grew older. He was at most times able to control the tribes, by diplomatic and military means. For his troops he bought arms from the English East India Company, who appointed a resident at Baghdād in 1798. Despite floods and plagues, the revival of Baghdād and Baṣrah continued.

The Wahhābites, in their northward advance, began to attack ʿIrāq in 1792. They had already seized al-Aḥsāʾ, whose shaykh was an Ottoman vassal, and obtained the submission of Kuwayt. Raiding from the desert was no new phenomenon, but had hitherto been conducted with a measure of chivalry *(murūwah)*. The Wahhābites were fanatical and ruthless. They were at first beaten back by local levies under Shaykh Thuwaynī, the capable head of the Muntafiq. In 1797 Sulaymān Pāshā sent a force of levies under Thuwaynī's command to recover al-Aḥsāʾ. The shaykh was assassinated, and the force melted away. In the following year, a

[1] So called because he led night patrols against burglars.

[2] Büyük Süleyman Paşa.

stronger expedition with Janissary reinforcements under a Mamlūk officer, ʿAlī Pāshā, reached al-Aḥsāʾ but soon withdrew; and a truce was then arranged. In 1802, however, the Wahhābite crown prince Saʿūd suddenly bore down upon Karbalā, which being a sanctuary had never been garrisoned. His pretext was that some ʿIrāqī Shīʿites had molested a pilgrim caravan guided by Wahhābites. The shrine was desecrated, and its treasures were carried away; at least 5,000 men, women and children were slaughtered. The outrage horrified the Sunnites as well as the Shīʿites, who rebuilt the shrine with help from Fatḥ ʿAlī Shāh of Īrān. Meanwhile Sulaymān Pāshā had died and been succeeded after a struggle in 1802 by ʿAlī Pāshā, who repulsed further Wahhābite attacks against Najaf and Ḥillah in 1803 and 1806 but was in no position to break the Wahhābite domination of the desert. He was assassinated in 1807 and succeeded by his nephew Sulaymān Pāshā "the Little."[1]

The Sultan Maḥmūd II, who hoped to strengthen the empire by a policy of centralization, made his first attempt to oust the Mamlūks from Baghdād in 1810. Imperial troops overthrew and killed Sulaymān Pāshā, but again failed to keep order; and the Porte again had to recognise the local Mamlūk authority. After a series of factional struggles, the choice fell upon Dāʾūd Pāshā (1817–1831), the last Mamlūk governor of Baghdād. Born to a Christian family in Georgia, he had been sold at the age of 13, and although unscrupulous had won a reputation for Islāmic learning and piety; he maintained elaborate pomp and circumstance at his court.

Besides the usual troubles with Arab tribes and internal dissensions among the Mamlūks, Dāʾūd Pāshā was involved in more serious fighting with the Kurds and a war with Īrān. The Īrānians had revived their claim to Shahrazūr in 1808, when ʿAbd al-Raḥmān Pāshā Bābān, having been worsted by a rival who enjoyed Mamlūk support, fled to Tehrān and pledged allegiance to Fatḥ ʿAlī Shāh; and although the Porte afterwards reinstated ʿAbd al-Raḥmān Pāshā, the Qājār government regarded the Bābāns as Īrānian vassals. In 1818, when rival Bābān pretenders obtained the support of Dāʾūd Pāshā and of the Qājār prince-governor of Kirmānshāh Muḥammad ʿAlī Mīrzā, the latter invaded ʿIrāq and defeated a strong Mamlūk force. Thereafter Īrānian troops remained at Sulaymānī. Although Fatḥ ʿAlī Shāh did not plan to reconquer ʿIrāq, the Īrānians felt bitterly about the sack of Karbalā, and knew that disaffection was spreading among the Ottoman Kurdish princes and chiefs as Maḥmūd II pursued his campaign against the semi-independent *derebeys* of Anatolia.

[1] Küçük Süleyman Paşa.

Raids by two Ottoman Kurdish tribes on Mākū in Īrānian Āẕarbāyjān gave a *casus belli* in 1821, and the Russians urged the Īrānians to war. Troops sent by the crown prince ʿAbbās Mīrzā from Āẕarbāyjān penetrated to Vān and Bitlis. From Kirmānshāh Muḥammad ʿAlī Mīrzā, after defeating a Mamlūk force, reached Baʿqūbah not far from Baghdād, where his troops were decimated by cholera from which he himself afterwards died. In the following year the Īrānians reached Shahrabān, south of Khānaqīn, but failed to take Kirkūk. Although the peace treaty signed at Erzurūm in 1823 stipulated a return to the *status quo*, the frontier was not defined, and the Īrānians maintained their claim to Sulaymānī and kept troops there until 1834. The Bābān principality survived, and its dissensions continued.

For some time, more important matters deflected Maḥmūd II's attention from ʿIrāq and Kurdistān. After the destruction of the Janissaries at Istanbul in 1826, Dā'ūd Pāshā on orders from the Porte dissolved the local Janissaries and then attempted to modernize his forces, with training by a French officer and British arms. The existence of the autonomous régime in ʿIrāq caused increasing anxiety at Istanbul when Muḥammad ʿAlī Pāshā of Egypt began to claim Syria. In 1830 the Sultan decreed Dā'ūd Pāshā's dismissal. The emissary carrying the decree was arrested at Baghdād and strangled. In 1831 an army under the new governor ʿAlī Riḍā Pāshā marched from Aleppo to Baghdād, where little resistance was offered, the city and garrison having been devastated by a Tigris flood and an epidemic of bubonic plague. Dā'ūd Pāshā himself was treated with favour, and ended his life in 1851 as custodian of the shrine at Madīnah; the remaining Mamlūks were exterminated. Baṣrah also was smitten by the plague and surrendered. The Porte thus recovered ʿIrāq a year before Muḥammad ʿAlī Pāshā's son Ibrāhīm conquered Syria.

While Syria was under Egyptian occupation, revolts against the Sultan's policy flared up in Ottoman Kurdistān. Although these have been described as a "Kurdish struggle for liberation," they were not synchronized or coordinated. Tribal and dynastic motives were uppermost in the minds of the leaders, and difficulties of communication largely precluded common effort. The Sultan's government, despite its weakness, had reimposed direct rule at Mosul without difficulty in 1834, and was able to send a punitive expedition from Sīvās in 1835 under Rashīd Pāshā, a former grand *vezir*. The leading rebels were Muḥammad Pāshā of Rawanduz, Saʿīd Bey of ʿAmadīyah, and Badr Khān of Bohtān, one of the old Kurdish principalities. The country between Irbīl and the outskirts of Diyār Bakr was in the hands of the rebels until Rashīd Pāshā and the governor of Mosul defeated them one by one. After Rashīd Pāshā's death in 1836, Badr Khān formed a confederation of tribes in the north and held sway over a wide area; he was not defeated until 1845. The Ottoman authorities used diplomacy as well as force, and never gained effective control of some remote parts. The dynasty of Bitlis was finally brought to an end in 1847. To some extent, these troubles disturbed the symbiosis of the Kurds and the Christian minorities. Nūr Allāh Beg, the rebel chief of the Hakkārī district, which then contained the seat of the Nestorian patriarchate (at Qōchannis), massacred a large number of Assyrians (Nestorians) in 1843 and again in 1847/8. In the Russo-Turkish war of 1877–78, the Russians tried to rouse both the Armenians and the Kurds, and encouraged a revolt by the sons of Badr Khān, whose 20th-century descendants became prominent in Kurdish nationalistic and cultural movements. Kurdish affairs gave rise to new Ottoman-Īrānian friction when the Īrānians again sent troops to Sulaymānī in 1840. The two governments, under British and Russian pressure, agreed in 1842 to negotiate, and finally in 1847 signed the second treaty of Erzurūm, whereby the Īrānians abandoned their claim to Sulaymānī and received most of the disputed Zuhāb district. Ottoman troops then moved into Sulaymānī and defeated the Bābāns, whose last Pāshā was removed in 1851.

## THE WAHHĀBITES

Central Arabia in the 16th and 17th centuries led an isolated life, except in so far as routes through it were used by pilgrims. The beduin tribes were ruled by their *shaykhs*; the oases, with their sedentary populations and market towns which the beduin frequented, were ruled by *amīrs* of beduin origin. Some of the towns were also religious centres built around tombs of locally popular saints. The customary desert warfare cannot have been very bloodthirsty, because population increase must have been a factor in the contemporary tribal migrations to ʿIrāq and Syria. The only external authority which the shaykhs and amīrs sometimes acknowledged was that of the Sharīfs of Mecca, who used to mediate between them in order to keep the pilgrimage routes open. These led to Madīnah from Najaf through Ḥā'il in the Jabal Shammar district, and to Mecca from Baṣrah through ʿUnayzah (later Buraydah) in the al-Qaṣīm district, or from al-Aḥsā' (where the Banū Khālid amīrs recognized Ottoman suzerainty) through ʿUyaynah in the Najd district.

The Sharīfs of Mecca in the 16th century enjoyed considerable prestige. Barakāt (1497–1525), Muḥammad Abū Numayy (1525–1566) and Ḥasan

(1566–1601) were secure in their position and capable. They were moreover able to obtain funds, not only from Ottoman Sultans and Pāshās, but also from Muslim rulers in India, Indonesia, the Sūdān and West Africa; and they used part of the money for payments to the tribes. The number of pilgrims from these countries increased, and some of them stayed permanently at Mecca, which thereby acquired a more cosmopolitan character and grew in importance as a centre of diffusion of Islāmic ideas in distant lands. While generally loyal to their Ottoman suzerain, the Sharīfs welcomed Shīʿite pilgrims from Īrān, the Yaman and India, and defied occasional orders from the Sultan to exclude them. The mob, however, could be excited by local Ottoman officials to rob and kill Shīʿites; the worst instance occurred in 1639, after Murād IV had gone to war against Īrān. The Sharīfs sometimes also clashed with Turkish *qāḍīs* sent to Mecca from Istanbul, and with the more rapacious Turkish officers at Jiddah. In the 17th and 18th centuries, the prestige of the Sharīfs was impaired by recurrent struggles between branches of their exceedingly numerous clan. At times rival Sharīfs held different parts of the sacred territory and fought with one another. Moreover, in the 18th century the Indian and Indonesian Muslim states fell into decay, and their gifts dwindled or ceased.

At that time the Ṣūfī movement, once the inspiration of great Muslim poetry and art, had largely degenerated into a vehicle of popular superstition and even magic. Only the Ḥanbalite school of Sunnism strongly resisted the popular beliefs and practices; and it did not have official support or much following in any important Muslim country. Its founder Aḥmad ibn Ḥanbal of Baghdād (786–855) and chief exponent Ibn Taymīyah of Damascus (1263–1328) had called for acceptance of the Qur'ānic word "without asking how" and for strict adherence to the *sunnah* (custom) of the Prophet and his Companions. They had vehemently condemned Shīʿite beliefs and Ṣūfī "innovations," such as the cult of saints. The Syrian Druzes, Mutawālīs and Nuṣayrīs had been targets of Ibn Taymīyah's bitter denunciation. The Ḥanbalite teachings implied a direct threat to Shīʿite communities and *darvīsh* fraternities, and a potential threat to the established religious, legal and political order.

Muḥammad ibn ʿAbd al-Wahhāb (1703–1792), the reviver of Ḥanbalism, was the son of the *qāḍī* of ʿUyaynah, then the biggest town in Najd. He spent many years studying at Madīnah, Baṣrah, Baghdād, and according to one account, also in Īrān during Nādir Shāh's reign. Among other subjects, he studied Ṣūfism; and presumably he became acquainted with Shīʿism. He finally embraced Ḥanbalism, and having returned to ʿUyaynah, began preaching it there after his father's death. His rigorism and vehemence aroused opposition. He forbade tobacco and (with less success) coffee, stoned an adulteress to death, and called Muslims who disagreed with him "infidels". In 1745 the amīr of ʿUyaynah was induced by neighbouring amīrs to expel him. He took refuge with the amīr of the small oasis of Dirʿīyah, Muḥammad ibn Saʿūd. Together they embarked on a career of conquest and conversion, which made slow progress. After ʿUyaynah had fallen to them in 1750, Riyāḍ became the chief town of Najd; their war with its amīr Dahhām ibn Dawwās went on from 1746 to 1773. Meanwhile Muḥammad ibn Saʿūd had died in 1765; his son and successor ʿAbd al-ʿAzīz retained Muḥammad ibn ʿAbd al-Wahhāb, who died in 1792, as *qāḍī* and chief preacher. The conquest of Riyāḍ made the Saʿūdī state dominant in Najd and al-Qaṣīm. Dirʿīyah remained the capital. Jabal Shammar was finally subdued in 1786/7. Amīrs and shaykhs who submitted were required to supply fighting men, and to enforce Wahhābite teachings and destroy shrines, while preachers were sent to inspire the men with faith and zeal for holy war *(jihād)* against non-Ḥanbalites. In the next 20 years Wahhābite attacks ranged from the fringes of ʿOmān and the Yaman to the Euphrates in ʿIrāq and the Jabal al-Durūz in Syria. The conquest of al-Aḥsāʾ (where the peasants preserved their Shīʿite faith through dissimulation) posed the first challenge to Ottoman authority. The fighting in ʿIrāq and the sack of Karbalā in 1802 have been described above (pp. 83-4).

The Ḥijāz was another target of Wahhābite raids, and the Sharīf Ghālib (1788–1812) organized a number of counterattacks. He also barred Mecca to Wahhābite pilgrims, for fear that they might seize the city and in reprisal for their closure of the routes to non-Ḥanbalite pilgrims. At the same time he kept up diplomatic relations with the ageing Saʿūdī ruler ʿAbd al-ʿAzīz; and in 1799 they concluded a treaty, whereby the frontiers of the Ḥijāz were to be respected and Wahhābite pilgrims, as followers of the recognised Ḥanbalite school, were to be readmitted. In 1800 ʿAbd al-ʿAzīz's heir apparent and commander in chief Saʿūd entered Mecca as a pilgrim. The Wahhābites did not long observe the truce. In the pilgrimage season of 1803, Saʿūd and his father returned to Mecca as conquerors. They destroyed the shrines of saints, and caused musical instruments and tobacco pipes to be burnt. The Sharīf Ghālib kept up resistance from Jiddah, and three months later recovered Mecca. Later in the year, while Saʿūdi reinburcements were besieging the holy city, a Shīʿite avenger of the desecration of Karbalā assassinated ʿAbd al-ʿAzīz in the mosque at

Dirʿīyah. In 1804, after six months siege, the Sharīf Ghālib again came to terms. He made a profession of Wahhābism, and was allowed to remain in office at Mecca under the eye of a Saʿūdī garrison. Jiddah then surrendered, and Madīnah was conquered in 1805. The Wahhābite troops prevented visits to the Prophet Muḥammad's and other tombs, and seized all their treasures, but could not find means to destroy the dome of the Prophet's tomb. They also put a stop to the annual pilgrim caravans from Cairo and Damascus, because they objected to the practice of carrying an elaborately decorated *maḥmal* (portable sanctuary) at the head of the caravan. The Ottoman government, which had earlier paid little heed to the Wahhābite threat, could not overlook this challenge to the Sultan's standing as protector of the Holy Places and of the pilgrimage. While pilgrims from Ottoman territory were excluded, pilgrims from India, Indonesia and West Africa still came by sea to Jiddah. The Wahhābite ideas which they absorbed stimulated militant fundamentalist movements in those countries in the following decades: Mujāhids in the Panjāb, Farā'iḍīs in Bengal, "Padres" in Sumatra, and the conqueror-theologian ʿUthmān dan-Fodio of Sokoto in what is now Northern Nigeria.

Although the French had been expelled from Egypt, Ottoman authority there was so weak that naval action to recover the Ḥijāz could not at first be considered. The Pāshā at Damascus was ordered to attack the Wahhābites, but only beat them off with Druze help when Saʿūd raided Transjordan and the Ḥawrān in 1810. Meanwhile Muḥammad ʿAlī Pāshā had obtained recognition as governor of Egypt and had begun to build up effective military and naval strength. He accepted the Sultan's order to expel the Wahhābites from the Ḥijāz, and in 1811 sent an expedition under his son Ṭūsūn to the port of Yanbuʿ and a cavalry force overland. The two forces joined, and were then severely defeated near Madīnah; but with the aid of reinforcements, Ṭūsūn captured Madīnah in 1812 and Mecca in 1813, and then invaded al-Qaṣīm. Saʿūd (d. 1814) and his son and successor ʿAbd Allāh fought back vigorously, until Ṭūsūn made a truce with ʿAbd Allāh in 1815, leaving Central Arabia and parts of the Ḥijaz in Saʿūdī hands. Muḥammad ʿAlī Pāshā repudiated the truce, and dispatched reinforcements under his elder son Ibrāhīm, who in 1818 forced ʿAbd Allāh to surrender at Dirʿīyah. ʿAbd Allāh was sent to Istanbul and beheaded, and Dirʿīyah was destroyed. Egyptian troops then occupied the principal forts as far as al-Aḥsā' and the Persian Gulf shore. The Wahhābites were by no means crushed. Turkī, a cousin of Saʿūd, seized Riyāḍ in 1821 and reestablished the Saʿūdī state, but was assassinated by one of his relatives in 1834. His son Fayṣal then gained the throne with the help of a Shammar shaykh, ʿAbd Allāh ibn Rashīd. The Egyptians, who had retired after Turkī's rise, afterwards recaptured Riyāḍ and deported Fayṣal. ʿAbd Allāh ibn Rashīd then established himself as amīr of Jabal Shammar with his capital at Ḥā'il, and maintained good relations with the Egyptians.

After Muḥammad ʿAlī Pāshā had been obliged to recall the Egyptian troops in 1840, the Ḥijāz continued to be governed by Sharīfs under the supervision of a Turkish *wālī* at Jiddah, and the Saʿūdī state continued to exist under Fayṣal, who was allowed to return to Riyāḍ in 1843. It was gradually outstripped in importance by the Rashīdī state of Ḥā'il. The Rashīdīs professed Wahhābism, but were not zealots. In 1891 their amīr conquered Riyāḍ, and the Sa'ūdī state ceased to exist until 1902, when Riyāḍ was seized by forty men under the leadership of the fugitive prince ʿAbd al-ʿAzīz, known as Ibn Saʿūd.

The Wahhābite movement was an important factor in the political history of the Near East, and in the development of Islām in distant countries. There is no evidence that it influenced the "Salafīyah" reform movement begun in Egypt by Afghānī (d. 1897) and ʿAbduh (d. 1905); they called likewise for a return to the pure original Islām, but had formed their ideas independently.

## MASQAṬ AND THE PERSIAN GULF

Another Arabian state beyond the Ottoman sphere played a part of some importance, namely Masqaṭ. The region east of the Empty Quarter contains a narrow coastal strip, the Bāṭinah, where irrigation permits date-growing, and a highland pastoral area, ʿOmān "proper". In common usage the whole region is called ʿOmān. Since ancient times its harbours such as Ṣūr, Masqaṭ and Ṣuḥār have been used by ships sailing with the monsoons to India, Aden and East Africa. Before Islām, the region was under Īrānian rule or influence,[1] but the Persian Gulf coast with its pearl fisheries and at least ʿOmān "proper" had already been occupied by Arab tribes. In the Umayyad period, when the viceroy al-Ḥajjāj (d. 714) sought to impose Caliphal authority, ʿOmān became a stronghold of Khārijism, and has so remained ever since. The Khārijites condemn hereditary rulership and stand for the elective imāmate, so that the worthiest man ("even if a negro slave") may be made Imām. In ʿOmān the school of Khārijism which prevailed was that of the relatively moderate Ibāḍites,[2] who reject

[1] There are still a few Persian-speaking villages. The Bāṭinah is irrigated by ancient subterranean water-channels like those of Īrān.

[2] The school was founded by ʿAbd Allāh ibn Ibāḍ of Baṣrah in the late 7th century.

the doctrine of war against non-Khārijites and admit that for the sake of stability Imāms may be elected from single tribes or clans. Refusing to acknowledge ʿAbbāsid sovereignty, they set up the first independent Khārijite state[1] in 750 under their elected Imām Julandā ibn Masʿūd, a tribal chief, who was defeated and killed two years later by ʿAbbāsid troops. Despite this and two subsequent ʿAbbāsid invasions, the Ibāḍites remained independent until the end of the 9th century at Nazwah, their stronghold in ʿOmān "proper", and further afield. Notwithstanding a spell of Carmathian (Qarmaṭī) Shīʿite dominance, the interior tribes clung to Ibāḍism. Later, for nearly three centuries until c. 1435, a hereditary dynasty, the Banū Nabhān, ruled much of the country. Most of the coastal places were in the hands of local potentates generally under the ultimate overlordship of the rulers of Fārs and Kirmān. The great commercial ports lay on or near the Īrānian shore: first Sīrāf in Fārs (destroyed by an earthquake in 977), then Kīsh (Ar. Qays; an island near the mouth of the Persian Gulf), and then its rival Hurmuz, situated originally on the mainland (where Marco Polo disembarked in 1294) but transferred in 1302 to an island further east. Hurmuz was founded and governed by an Arab dynasty, who recognized the suzerainty of the mainland rulers and in turn exercised suzerainty over the lesser ports from Baḥrayn to ʿOmān. Its trade, stretching from China and the Moluccas to East Africa, flourished. The seafarers were Arabs from ʿOmān and the Persian Gulf and also Īrānians[2].

When the Portuguese under Albuquerque attacked in 1507-08, Hurmuz was weak under a boy king and its vassals were disunited. The interior tribes of ʿOmān had already revived the Ībāḍite imāmate, but were then of no importance. Albuquerque with his better ships and tactics conquered the ports of ʿOmān one by one and forced Hurmuz to submit. Although he had to withdraw from Hurmuz, the ʿOmānī ports including Masqaṭ remained in Portuguese hands. Hurmuz fell under Ṣafavid suzerainty, which the Sunnites disliked, and in 1515 surrendered to another Portuguese fleet. Despite their ruthlessness and Christian militancy, the Portuguese were able to rule indirectly through the kings of Hurmuz and other Muslim vassals, and to carry on business with Muslim merchants. They also employed many Muslim seamen on their ships. They dominated

---

[1] Another Khārijite (Ibāḍite) state was set up by Ābd Allāh ibn Rustam in 761 at Tāhert in what is now Algeria and lasted a century and a half. The Algerian oasis of Mzāb and the Tunisian island of Jerbah are still inhabited by Ibāḍites.

[2] Arabic seafaring terminology contains many Persian words.

Hurmuz and Masqaṭ from their castles, and tried to control but not to wipe out Muslim shipping, their object being to monopolize the trade with Europe. The Ṣafavid Shāhs for a long time tolerated their presence while resenting their monopoly. The Ottoman fleet of Piri Reis only dislodged them temporarily from Masqaṭ in 1551 and failed to take Hurmuz (see above, p. 58). At its height their power must have extended to the head of the Persian Gulf, because a ruined Portuguese fort can be seen in Kuwayt. Baḥrayn (which had been a dependency of Hurmuz until a mainland Arab tribe conquered it in the mid-15th century) was held by the Portuguese for about 80 years until 1602, when sailors from Fārs drove them out. In 1620 a fleet sent by the English East India Company defeated a Portuguese fleet off Jāsk, and the English then made an alliance with Shāh ʿAbbās I of Īrān. With help from the English fleet, Īrānian forces captured Hurmuz in 1622. Its place as a trade emporium was taken by Bandar ʿAbbās, at that time commonly known as Gombroon (Gamrū). The Portuguese then made their headquarters at Masqaṭ, where the fine castles which they built still rise above the harbour. They remained strong enough to launch unsuccessful counterattacks until they made peace with the English in 1635. They kept a "factory" in Īrān at Kong near Lingah, and developed trade with Baṣrah.

In 1624 the Ībāḍites had elected an Imām, Nāṣir ibn Murshid of the Yaʿrūbī clan, who began to unify ʿOmān and to make war against the Portuguese. The next Imām, Sulṭān ibn Sayf, who was also a Yaʿrūbī, succeeded in expelling them. He took Ṣūr in 1643, Ṣuḥār in 1648 and Masqaṭ in 1650. With help from men who had worked for the Portuguese, and with imported timber, he built up a strong fleet of European-type ships and carried on the war against their settlements in India and East Africa. When he died, the imāmate passed after a struggle to one of his sons, Sayf ibn Sulṭān (1668-1711), who in turn was succeeded by his son Sulṭān II ibn Sayf. The latter died in 1718 leaving a minor heir, Sayf II, who grew up to be a drunkard and should not according to Ibāḍite principles have been Imām. Internal strife between two tribal factions called Ghāfirī and Hināwī greatly weakened ʿOmān at this time.

The ʿOmānīs gained nothing except booty from their attacks on Portuguese settlements in India, but won decisive victories in East Africa, where the local Arabs had appealed for their help in 1660. They captured the Portuguese stronghold Mombasa in 1698 (chapter IV, p. 177). Besides war, the ʿOmānis pursued commerce, and did much business with the Dutch. When the Ṣafavid regime weakened, they began to harass the Īrānian coast and to practise piracy in the Persian Gulf. In 1717 Sulṭān II seized Baḥrayn (which the ʿOmānīs did not hold for long) and Qishm island, and laid siege to Hurmuz. The Shāh's advisers were planning a major war against ʿOmān, and hoping for French naval help by virtue of a treaty with France, when the Ghalzā'ī Afghān rebels began their march which ended in the fall of Iṣfahān and of the Ṣafavids.

Nādir Shāh was determined to restore the Īrānian position in the Persian Gulf no less than elsewhere. After taking Baḥrayn in 1736, his forces entered ʿOmān in 1737 in response to an appeal from Sayf II for help against rebels. They marched from Julfar (now Ra's al-Khaymah) on the west coast through Nazwah to Masqaṭ, but withdrew to Julfar when Sayf II turned against them and their Arab seamen mutinied. In 1742 Sayf II was deposed in favour of his cousin Sulṭān ibn Murshid and again appealed for help; in the following year he died and his cousin was killed. The reinforced Īrānian troops again won no lasting success, and had to withdraw in 1744 to Julfar, whence they departed after Nādir's deatn. The campaigns in ʿOmān cost at least 20,000 Īrānian lives. The new Imām, chosen probably in 1744, was Aḥmad ibn Saʿīd, formerly governor of Ṣuḥār, who had resisted a siege and then adroitly brought about the Īrānian withdrawal. From him are descended the Āl Bū Saʿīd dynasties of Masqaṭ and Zanzibar.

Aḥmad ibn Saʿīd (d. 1783) revived the shipping and trade of Masqaṭ, and maintained friendly relations with the Turks at Baṣrah. Mombasa refused to recognize his authority, but Zanzibar remained in his hands. Some of the ʿOmānī tribes also rebelled against him. His son Saʿīd became the next Imām, but was indolent and unpopular. In or about 1786 Saʿīd, while keeping the title Imām, transferred the rulership to his son Ḥāmid (d. 1792). Thereafter the rulers ceased to be elective, and while professing Ibāḍism used the titles Sayyid and Sultan. During the disorders in Īrān following the collapse of the Zand régime, the Masqaṭīs under Ḥāmid's uncle and successor Sulṭān ibn Aḥmad seized points on the coast from Gwādar in Makrān to Bandar ʿAbbās, which had lost importance since the departure of the English and Dutch after Nādir Shāh's fall, its place being taken by Bushire. In 1798 the Qājār government leased Bandar ʿAbbās to the rulers of Masqaṭ, who kept it until 1868. Gwādar remained in their hands until 1958, when it was voluntarily ceded to Pākistān. The long connection with Makrān and employment of Balūchī troops account for the large Balūchī element in the population. Sulṭān ibn Aḥmad signed the first treaty with the British in 1798, promising not to admit the French or Dutch while they were at war with Britain. He resisted Wahhābite attacks by land and sea, and was killed while fighting Wahhābite pirates in 1804. In the ensuing struggle for the throne, a claimant with Wahhābite backing, Badr, at first prevailed. He was killed in 1806 by Sa'īd ibn Sulṭān, who reigned until 1856 (until 1821 jointly with his brother Sālim). He spent most of his time at Zanzibar and restored Masqaṭī influence on the coast, recovering Mombasa in 1837. In 'Omān he had to face revolts and Wahhābite attacks, which were gradually overcome with British support. In return the British pressed him to act against slave-trading, piracy and gun-running; and the treaties which he signed with them (in 1822, 1838 and 1847) did not enhance his popularity. He also made treaties with the U.S.A. in 1839 and with France in 1844. During his reign Masqaṭī shipping continued to flourish. When he died, the Viceroy of India intervened to prevent a struggle between his sons Thuwaynī, who held Masqaṭ, and Mājid who held Zanzibar. From 1856 Masqaṭ and Zanzibar went their different ways as separate states. Dissident 'Omānī tribes elected their own Ibāḍite Imām at Nazwah in 1913, and obtained in 1920 the then Sultan's recognition of their local autonomy, which lasted until 1955, when the Sultan's authority was restored with British help in order to permit oil exploration.

The British also took steps to stop piracy and slave trading in the Persian Gulf, which Īrānian weakness and the rise of Wahhābism had rendered increasingly insecure. Fleets sent by the East India Company punished the pirates in 1809 and 1819. Another source of British anxiety was the penetration of Ibrāhīm Pāshā's Egyptian troops to the Gulf shore. In 1820 the British signed their first treaties with the ruler of Baḥrayn, who was nominally an Īrānian vassal, and with the chiefs on the west coast of 'Omān, where the Sultans of Masqaṭ has ceased to exercise authority. Baḥrayn, with its oasis and pearl fisheries and mainly Shī'ite population, had been seized in 1783 by Sunnite Arabs from the mainland led by Aḥmad ibn Khalīfah, whose descendants despite an 'Omānī invasion in 1801 and a Wahhābite occupation maintained their hold and developed the islands' commerce. In 1853 the west 'Omān chiefs made a perpetual maritime "truce" with the British in return for British protection; the area then came to be known as the "Trucial Coast". The ruler of Baḥrayn placed himself under British protection in 1861 after the Īrānians had reasserted their claim to sovereignty. British influence in the Gulf was to remain predominant more than a century to come.

The historical importance of the Persian Gulf and 'Omān lay in the exploits of their sailors in the Indian Ocean and in the contribution which they made to the spread of Islām in distant lands. Their maritime prosperity was soon to be ruined by the advent of the steamship.

# BIBLIOGRAPHY

(by F. R. C. Bagley)

HOLT, P. M., *Egypt and the Fertile Crescent 1516–1922*, London 1966 (with bibliography).
STRIPLING, GEORGE W. F., *The Ottoman Turks and the Arabs*, 1511–1574, Urbana (Illinois), 1942.
DEHÉRAIN, HENRI, *L'Égypte turque*, vol. V of *Histoire de la nation égyptienne*, ed. by GABRIEL HANOTAUX, 7 vols., Paris 1935–1940.
COMBE, ETIENNE, *L'Égypte ottomane, de la conquête par Sélim a l'arrivée de Bonaparte*, vol. III of *Précis de l'histoire d'Égypte*, Cairo 1933.
IBN IYĀS, *Badā'i' al-zuhūr fī waqā'i' al-duhūr*, 2nd ed., Cairo 1380/1961; partial tr. by GASTON WIET, *Journal d'un bourgeois du Caire*, Paris 1960; partial tr. by W. H. SALMON, *An account of the Ottoman conquest of Egypt*, London 1921.
SHAW, STANFORD J., *The financial and administrative organization and development of Ottoman Egypt*, 1517–1798, Princeton 1962 (Princeton Oriental Studies, 19).
SHAW, STANFORD J., *Ottoman Egypt in the eighteenth century*, the *Nizâmnâme-e Misir* of CEZZAR AHMET PÂŞÂ, tr. from the Turkish, Cambridge (Mass.) 1962.
SHAW, STANFORD J., *Ottoman Egypt in the age of the French revolution*, tr. from the Arabic of HUSAIN EFFENDI, Cambridge (Mass.) 1964.
JABARTĪ, 'ABD AL-RAḤMĀN, *'Ajā'ib al-āthār fī'l-tarājim wa'l-akhbār*, Cairo (Būlāq) 1297/1879–80; tr. by CHEFIK MANSOUR et al., *Merveilles biographiques et historiques*, Cairo 1888–1896.
VOLNEY (pseudonym) = CHASSEBOEUF, CONSTANTIN FRANÇOIS, *Voyage en Égypte et en Syrie*, 1783–1785, ed. J. GAULMIER, Paris 1959.
CHARLES-ROUX, F., *Autour d'une route: l'Angleterre, l'Isthme de Suez et l'Égypte au XVIIIe. siecle*, Paris 1922.
BALDWIN, GEORGE, *Political recollections relative to Egypt*, London 1801.
HITTI, PHILIP KHOURY, *History of Syria, including Lebanon and Palestine*, London 1951.
HITTI, PHILIP KHOURY, *Lebanon in history*, London 1957.
LAMMENS, HENRI, *La Syrie, précis historique*, 2 vols., Beirut 1921.
ISMAIL, ADEL, *Le Liban au temps de Fakhr-ed-Din II*, Paris 1955 (vol. 1 of projected *Histoire du Liban du XVIIe. siècle à nos jours*).
SALIBI, KAMAL S., *The modern history of Lebanon*, London 1965.
IBN ṬŪLŪN, SHAMS AL-DĪN MUḤAMMAD, *Mufākahat al-khillān fī ḥawādith al-zamān*, ed. by MUḤAMMAD MUṢṬAFĀ, 2 vols., Cairo 1381/1962 and 1384/1964; partial tr. by RICHARD HARTMANN, *Das Tübinger Fragment der Chronik des Ibn Ṭūlūn*, Berlin 1926.
LAOUST, HENRI, *Les gouverneurs de Damas sous les Mamlouks et les premiers Ottomans*, Damascus 1952.
BODMAN, HERBERT L., *Political factions in Aleppo, 1760–1826*, Chapel Hill (North Carolina), 1963.
MASSON, PAUL, *Histoire du commerce français dans le Levant au XVIIe. siècle*, Paris 1896.
MASSON, PAUL, *Histoire du commerce français dans le Levant au XVIIIe. siècle*, Paris 1911.
CHARLES-ROUX, F., *Les échelles de Syrie et de Palestine au XVIIIe. siècle*, Paris 1928.
WOOD, ALFRED C., *A history of the Levant Company*, London 1933.
GIBB, Sir HAMILTON A. R., and BOWEN, HAROLD, *Islamic society and the West*: Vol. 1, *Islamic society in the eighteenth century*, Parts 1 and 2, London 1950–1957.
LONGRIGG, STEPHEN H., *Four centuries of modern Iraq*, Oxford 1925.

HUART, CLÉMENT, *Histoire de Baghdad dans les temps modernes*, Paris 1901.
NIKITINE, B., *Les Kurdes: étude sociologique et historique*, Paris 1956.
SHARAF AL-DĪN BIDLĪSĪ, *Cherefnameh, ou les fastes de la nation kurde, par Cheref ou'ddine*, tr. from the Persian by F. B. CHARMOY, 2 vols., St. Petersburg 1868–1875.
U.K., ADMIRALTY, *Western Arabia and the Red Sea*, London 1946.
KAMMERER, A., *La Mer Rouge*, 2 vols., Cairo 1929–1951.
HOGARTH, DAVID G., *Arabia*, Oxford 1922.
SNOUCK-HURGRONJE, C., *Mekka*, 3 vols., The Hague 1888–1889, vol. 1 (In German).
NALLINO, CARLO ALFONSO, *al-Yemen*, in *Enciclopedia Italiana*, vol. XXXV, Rome 1937.
TRITTON, ARTHUT S., *The rise of the Imams of San'a*, London 1925.
HUZAYYIN, S. A., *Arabia and the Far East*, Cairo 1942.
SAUVAGET, JEAN, *Instructions nautiques et routières arabes et portugaises des XVe. et XVIe. siècles*, 3 vols., Paris 1921–1928.
SERJEANT, R. B., *The Portuguese off the South Arabian coast*, Oxford 1963.
DANVERS, F. C., *The Portuguese in India*, 2 vols., London 1894.
PHILBY, H. ST. JOHN, *Saudi Arabia*, London 1955.
PHILBY, H. ST. JOHN, *Arabia*, New York 1930.
NIEBUHR, CARSTEN, *Beschreibung von Arabien*, Copenhagen 1772; *Description de l'Arabie*, Amsterdam 1774.
NIEBUHR, CARSTEN, *Voyage en Arabie et d'autres pays circonvoisins*, 2 vols., Amsterdam 1776–1780.
CORANCEZ, L. A., *Histoire des Wahabis depuis leur origine jusqu'à la fin de 1809*, Paris 1810.
BURCKHARDT, JOHN LEWIS, *Notes on the Bedouins and Wahabys*, London 1830.
BRYDGES, Sir HARFORD JONES, *An account of the transactions of His Majesty's mission to the court of Persia in the years 1810–1811, to which is appended a brief history of the Wahauby*, 2 vols., London 1834.
WINDER, R. BAYLY, *Sa'udi Arabia in the nineteenth century*, London and New York, 1965.
U.K., ADMIRALTY, *Iraq and the Persian Gulf*, London 1944.
WILSON, Sir ARNOLD T., *The Persian Gulf, an historical sketch ...*, Oxford 1928, 2nd ed. 1954.
SALIL IBN RAZIK, *History of the Imams and Seyyids of Oman, from A.D. 666 to 1856, translated from the original Arabic and edited with notes, appendices and introduction continuing the history down to 1870*, London 1871 (Hakluyt Society, Series 1, No . 43).
FAROUGHY, ABBAS, *Histoire du royaume de Hormuz*, Brussels 1949.
FAROUGHY, ABBAS, *The Bahrein islands*, New York, 1951.
FAROUGHY, ABBAS, *Introducing Yemen*, New York 1947.
HADI HASAN, *Persian navigation*, London 1928.
LOCKHART, LAWRENCE, *Nadir Shah: a critical study based mainly on contemporary sources*, London 1938.
SAID-RUETE, R., *Said bin Sultan (1791–1856), ruler of Oman and Zanzibar*, London 1929.
SAID-RUETE, R., *Die Āl Bū Sa'īd Dynastie in Arabien und Ostafrika*, in Der Islam, XX, 1932.
ABU HAKIMA, AHMAD MUSTAFA, *History of Eastern Arabia 1750–1800; the rise and development of Bahrain and Kuwait*, Beirut 1965.
ADAMIYAT, FERIDUN, *Bahrein islands*, New York 1955.

# NORTH WEST AFRICA FROM THE 15TH TO 19TH CENTURIES

BY

NEVILL BARBOUR

## INTRODUCTION

The XVIth century witnessed a fundamental change in the circumstances of the Maghrib. By 1500, the reigning dynasties, the Waṭṭāsids in Morocco, the Zayyānids (or ʿAbd al-Wādids) in Tlemsen, and the Ḥafṣids in Tunis, no longer exercised more than a titular headship beyond the walls of their capital cities. The result was an anarchic decentralization in which the various towns, the peoples of the Aurès, Kabyle, Rif, and Atlas mountains, and the tribes of the plains, led a more or less autonomous existence. Meanwhile on their north, the Christian Kingdoms of Portugal and Spain, now strongly centralized, had embarked on a course of imperial expansion. Selfish motives on the part of the two Iberian powers were reinforced and justified to themselves by crusading impulses which made Muslim North Africa an obvious target for their attacks. Portugal had been free from any Muslim menace for over two centuries, and no motive of self-defence justified the surprise assault on Ceuta which was delivered as early as 1415. Indeed King John warned his sons at the time that such an attack might provoke Muslim reprisals on Portuguese commerce through the Straits. In 1471 the operation was extended by the capture of Arzila and Tangier[1], and marked by the assumption by the Portuguese monarch of the title of King of the Two Algarves[2], meaning the southern province of Portugal, acquired from the Muslims in the 13th century, and the further Muslim territory now acquired in Morocco. With the annexation of Agadir, Safi, and Azemmour, in the first 20 years of the XVIth century, Portugal gained control of most of the Moroccan

[1] In the following pages, geographical names are given in forms likely to be found in available maps. Conventional English forms (such as Tangier, Algiers) are used where they exist. Otherwise the forms used are mostly French, and less frequently Spanish and Italian; in a few cases they have been slightly modified to conform with English spelling. In the Index, systematic transliterations of the written Arabic forms of some of these geographical names are given in brackets.

Arabic names of persons are transcribed in accordance with the system followed in other sections of this book.

[2] The Portugese form of the Arabic "al-Gharb", originally applied to the western portion of "al-Andalus" or Muslim Spain.

ports from Ceuta on the Straits to Massa on the Atlantic south of Agadir, and exercised a veritable protectorate over the Doukkala plain between Safi (Asfi), Azemmour, and Marrakesh.

In the Spanish case, the last Muslim kingdom on European soil was eliminated by the capture of Granada in 1492. The consummation of the Christian reconquest of Spain filled the coastal area of North Africa with a fresh wave of Spanish Muslim refugees; and these new arrivals intensified raids already being made by earlier refugees on Spanish coastal areas and shipping. The hope of eliminating this menace added a solid practical motive to the desire of Isabella the Catholic and Cardinal Cisneros to carry on the war for religious reasons against the Muslims on the south of the Straits. This attempt was inaugurated by the capture of Melilla in 1497 and of the Peñon de Velez in 1508. At this date the domains of Spain (or rather of Aragon) included Sardinia, Naples, and Sicily; and the next Spanish assault covered the Mediterranean coast of the Maghrib from Mersa al-Kabir (captured in 1505) and Oran (1509) to Bougie and Tripoli (1510).

This development brought into the picture an eastern Muslim power, the Ottoman Turks, who like the Spanish, were in full imperial expansion. The result was that the history of the eastern Maghrib was for the next three quarters of a century a function of a Spanish-Turkish struggle rather than of any local initiative.

With the definitive capture of Tunis by the Turks in 1574 and the defeat of the Portuguese at Alcazarquivir in Morocco in 1578, the struggle between Christian Iberia and Muslim North Africa reached a stalemate, though intermittent hostilities continued for another two centuries. The upshot was that the Maghrib remained Muslim, though the Spanish and the Portuguese retained a few footholds, the former in Oran and Melilla, the latter in Ceuta, Tangier, Arzila, and Mazagan. On the other hand Muslim expansion in the Mediterranean was arrested east of Malta, and the prospect of the restoration of Muslim rule in southern Spain, still a possibility at the time of the Morisco rising of 1569, had been definitely eliminated. But while Morocco under a new dynasty resumed its traditional system of government in a barely modified form, Tunis had lost its supremacy in the eastern and central Maghrib and took only second place among three Turkish military dominions, known as the Ojāqs or Regencies of Algiers, Tunis, and Tripoli, into which the whole area was now divided. These acquired frontiers which are substantially those of the modern states of Algeria, Tunisia, and Libya today.

The seventy years struggle between Spaniards and Turks had been carried on entirely at sea or in the form of what we may describe as combined land-sea operations. The nature of this warfare exercised a decisive influence on the character of the three Turkish Regencies to which it gave birth. As states, they acquired an organization which is very unfamiliar to us, and their history cannot be understood without a preliminary study of the naval operations which caused them to come into being.

The state budgets of the 16th century were not designed to sustain the expense of the continuous upkeep of large professional navies. Use was therefore made of the private profit motive. Individual adventurers, known as privateers or corsairs, were authorised to equip and man armed vessels. These might then attack the shipping of states with which the government of their owners was at war and make a profit from disposing of the booty taken. The proceeds were divided in legally fixed proportions between the owner, the government, the officers, and the crew; in this way war was made to pay for itself. In national emergencies this shipping and the crews formed a reserve for enlarging such regular forces as the state might possess. Captured privateers enjoyed the rights of prisoners of war. The finance might be provided by the monarch himself, by individuals, or by a syndicate. Officially such activities could only be carried on with previous permission of some national authority, against shipping belonging to enemies of the state and in accordance with internationally recognised conventions, modified or amplified by bilateral treaties between the states concerned. Such activities were, however, open to endless abuse, quite apart from the numerous doubtful cases as when ships were alleged to have been seized in neutral territorial waters, or where neutral subjects or goods were being carried in enemy ships, or enemy goods or subjects in neutral ships, or where ships fraudulently produced neutral passports. Privateers moreover used every kind of trick to catch their prey, such as approaching them under false colours. Very often the operations of privateers or corsairs were difficult to distinguish from those of pirates properly so-called; thus while privateers were regarded as heroes by their compatriots, they were generally abused as pirates by the citizens of the state on whose shipping they were preying. When privateers were caught in flagrant violations of the accepted conventions, complaints from the aggrieved nation sometimes forced their own government to inflict the death penalty on them, as happened with Sir Walter Raleigh. In the 16th and early 17th centuries privateers abounded off the coasts of Europe; English, French, Dutch and Spanish were all conspicuous among the Christian practitioners of the art. It was moreover legitimate to operate under the flag of a country other than that of the country of origin. Thus the English captain Easton took service with the Duke of Savoy, and the Dutch captain Dansa first with the Regency of Algiers and then with the French. In addition there were numerous pirates properly so-called. Some of these would devote themselves to outright piracy and then later make their peace with the authorities, like Sir Henry Mainwaring who became a member of the Admiralty Board after commanding a pirate fleet off Morocco. Piracy, as a naval historian has said, was then the school of seamanship.

In relations between Christian and Muslim states, the mutual tradition of Crusade and Holy War offered a ready pretext for actions of doubtful legality, as did similar pretexts in the case of wars between Catholic, Orthodox, and Protestant Christians. Thus at one extreme, privateering bordered on piracy; at the other it was an element of national expansion and empire building sanctioned by religion, as in the case of some of the Spanish conquistadores, of English seamen like Drake and Raleigh, and of Turkish seamen such as Khayr al-Dīn, ʿAlī Pāshā (Uluj Ali) and Dragut.

Privateers dealt not only in inanimate but also in animate goods. The risks of sea travel, great enough already from the elements, were thus increased by the danger of capture and enslavement. No Christian could sail the Mediterranean without the risk of finding himself a slave in a Muslim country. Nor could any Muslim do so without the risk of finding himself a slave in a Christian country, since Muslim slavery existed in the countries bordering on the Adriatic and the Mediterranean, including France at least for galley slaves. In the Kingdom of the Two Sicilies such slavery was not abolished until 1815. Privateers who could not dispose of Muslim slaves in their own country would ship them to a country where their sale was legal. Certain ports were clearing centres for the sale or ransom of slaves and for the disposal of booty: notably Salé, Tetuan, Algiers, Tunis, and Tripoli on the southern shores of the Mediterranean; Valetta, Messina and Leghorn on Christian territory. About 1650 there are said to have been as many as 35,000 Christian slaves in Algiers out of a total population of perhaps 150,000. In the Malaga area of Spain there were 5000–7000 Muslim slaves in 1610; in Malta 10,000 in 1720. In that island the last 2,000 were freed by Napoleon in 1798, while in Algiers the last 1200 Christians were freed by Lord Exmouth in 1816. State slaves in Europe as well as in Africa were housed in unsanitary underground prisons known as *bagni*, while domestic slaves (whose lot was much preferable) lived in their owners' houses. In both Muslim and Christian states, slaves were forced to row in the galleys in conditions of which very painful descriptions exist. On shore some were allowed to work for themselves, paying a percentage to their owners, and thus sometimes accumulated quite considerable sums. In the Muslim countries they were allowed to run taverns, officially for the use of their fellow Christians but frequented also by Muslims. They were allowed to practise their religion; numerous chapels existed in the north African states, and the existence of a mosque is recorded in Malta. Largely employed on public works in Algiers in the 16th and early 17th centuries, slaves were later principally an object of commerce in ransoms. Governments, local merchants, local Jews with international connexions, and Christian clergy of the Redemptorist order, handled the negotiations for ransom just as (with the exception of the Redemptorists) they negotiated disposal of the inanimate booty. In the Regencies, these operations became a national industry and a motive for declaring war.

From the latter half of the 18th century, the development of civilization in the European states caused the practice of privateering for personal gain to be considered as objectionable in principle and led to steps being taken for its abolition. At the same time the increasing European dominance in world affairs caused slavery of Europeans in North Africa to be regarded as an unmitigated scandal. The Regencies were not entirely without the same feeling with regard to privateering, and some modifications were introduced, privateering and the holding by individuals of other than black slaves being abolished at the end of the 18th century. Their traditions, however, made it difficult for them, and especially for Algiers and Tripoli, to adapt their constitutions to the changed circumstances of the times.

In placing this summary before the narrative of the events which it analyses, it may seem that the proper order of things has been reversed. Such treatment is, however, made necessary by the fact that almost all accounts of the Barbary Regencies until the very recent past have failed to put sufficient emphasis on the distinction between privateering and piracy and have presented the case as if no similar practices had existed among the European powers.[1] This has inevitably given rise to preconceptions which must be corrected if the history of the events concerned is to be presented in the appropriate light.

[1] The summary given in the *Enciclopedia Italiana* in its article on Algeria can serve as an example. "Its history till the French occupation of 1830 is one long sequence of piratical undertakings which sowed slaughter and lamentation over the Mediterranean; of struggles with the other Barbary state of Tunis, and with the Moroccan Sultan; of vain attempts by Christian powers to destroy these nests of brigands, and of internal revolts based on massacres and horrible crimes." Such a picture ignores many relevant factors which require to be taken into consideration.

## MOROCCO

The 16th century in Morocco was marked by the displacement of the Banū Waṭṭās rulers by a new dynasty, the Banū Saʿd. Under the latter the country recovered its unity, reduced the menace of Portuguese and Spanish encroachments, kept out the Turks, established a protectorate over the former empire of Songhay, and acquired a certain standing in international relations.

The encroachments of the Portuguese reached their climax in the first 20 years of the century, by which time they had occupied nearly all the ports, with the exception of Salé, from Ceuta in the north to Massa south of Agadir, and exercised a veritable protectorate over the Doukkala plain. While the Waṭṭāsid rulers struggled ineffectively against them in the north, leadership in the south was assumed by members of the Sharīfian family[1] of the Banū Saʿd, who were established at Zagora in the far south. Between 1511 and 1517 two brothers belonging to the family, *al-Aʿraj* and *Muḥammad al-Shaykh,* distinguished themselves in the fighting, half holy-war and half national reaction, against the Portuguese at Agadir. They had the approval of the Waṭṭāsid sovereign in Fez, whose authority, in spite of the increasing weakness of the dynasty, was still recognised in the south.

Confined at first to the area south of the Atlas around Tarudant, the Saʿdian leaders ed ed north between Marrakesh and Mogador. From 1518 when the important pro-Portuguese Moroccan leader Ibn Taʿfūft was killed, their influence was greatly increased and the elder, al-Aʿraj, overthrew and took the place of the local Waṭṭāsid ruler of Marrakesh, without breaking completely with the Waṭṭāsid Sultan in Fez. His brother, Muḥammad al-Shaykh, remained as ruler in Tarudant. By 1528 their growing power, and the connexions which they were making with influential religious leaders *(murābiṭs)* in various parts of the country, led the Waṭṭāsid to attack them. After indecisive fighting, a truce was arranged through the intervention of religious leaders; but Morocco was now divided into separate kingdoms, Marrakesh (Morocco) and Fez. An ensuing twelve years truce was utilized by Muḥammad al-Shaykh and his brother to prosecute the fighting against the Portuguese. In 1541 Muḥammad captured Agadir, with the result that the Portuguese abandoned their protectorate, giving up Safi and Azemmour. In the south they now retained only Mazagan, for prestige reasons and as a base for a possible return. Rivalry between the two brothers led to the flight of al-Aʿraj to Tafilalet,

---

[1] Families which claim the Prophet Muḥammad as ancestor.

while Muḥammad al-Shaykh resumed the struggle against the Waṭṭāsid. The latter thereupon sought aid from the Turks, who were by now firmly established in Algiers, and declared himself a vassal of the Ottoman Sultan. The Ottoman response was to send an ambassador to Muḥammad al-Shaykh instructing him to do likewise. This he flatly refused to do, and later he advanced on Fez. After an abortive attempt in 1548, he occupied the city in 1549, and then sent an army east under his son, who occupied Tlemsen, expelling the Zayyānid ruler. Though the Zayyānid had been a protégé of the Spaniards in Oran, the latter did not intervene on his behalf but allowed the Moroccan prince, acting against his father's instructions, to advance into Algeria and attack the Turks. This produced a Turkish counter-attack, which resulted in their recapture of Tlemsen (1552) and then of Fez (1554), where the Waṭṭāsid Abū Ḥasūn was replaced on the throne. This restoration, however, lasted only the few months until the latter had paid off the Turkish troops and handed over to them the Rif port of Peñon de Velez (Bādis), which the Moroccans had recaptured from the Spanish in 1522. In September 1554 Abū Ḥasūn was defeated and killed at a battle in the Tadla, and Muḥammad al-Shaykh became undisputed ruler of Morocco. Though the latter was himself assassinated by a Turkish emissary three years later, he was duly succeeded by his son *Mawlāy ʿAbd Allāh (al-Ghālib biʾllāh)*. The accession was, however, followed by the flight of the two brothers and potential rivals of the new ruler, ʿAbd al-Malik and Aḥmad, to Constantinople, where they acquired a Turkish training and outlook during seventeen years of exile. Mawlāy ʿAbd Allāh (1557–1574) consolidated his hold on the country and inaugurated a period of relative peace and prosperity, while successfully resisting Turkish attempts at infiltration from Algiers. In this he looked for aid to the Spanish, who were debarred from themselves occupying Moroccan territory east of Velez by an agreement made with Portugal in 1496 and were at the same time bitter enemies of the Turks. As a pious Muslim, the Sultan was embarrassed by the Morisco rising of 1569; it was impossible for him to give it serious support for lack of sea power, while if he sought this by cooperation with the Turks, he would certainly involve Morocco in the same subjection to them as the rest of the Maghrib, besides antagonizing the Spanish. All that he could do was to turn a blind eye to the smuggling of arms and volunteers and to employ refugees as recruits for his armed forces. The refugee Moriscos were in fact to become one of the principal military assets of the régime. But this element of compromise with the persecutors of the Muslims provoked the indignation of many religious leaders and strengthened their influence in the

Middle Atlas, where the effects were to be great half a century later.

On Mawlāy ʿAbd Allāh's death, he was succeeded by his son *Muḥammad al-Mutawakkil* (1574–1576). The change of ruler was seized on by his exiled uncles in Constantinople to reestablish themselves by means of their Turkish connexions. In 1576 ʿAbd al-Malik, who had served with the Turkish forces in the capture of Tunis from the Spaniards two years before, drove al-Mutawakkil from Fez with the aid of Turkish troops. These he promptly paid off, since his Turkish background did not imply any sympathy with Turkish claims on Morocco. His brief two years reign terminated with the decisive victory over the Portuguese at the Battle of Alcazarquivir or Wadi Makhāzin on August 1578. The battle took place after the deposed Sultan had persuaded King Sebastian of Portugal to replace him on the throne in return for a promise to make himself his vassal. Sebastian, at the time only 24 years old, was filled with romantic notions of crusading glory and the revival of the Portuguese position in Morocco. He landed his force of Portuguese soldiers, and German mercenaries with some Papal troops under the Englishman Thomas Stukely, at Arzila (Aṣīlah), which had been returned to the Moroccans in 1550 but was now in the control of the exiled Sultan's supporters. He then marched on Larache, in blazing summer weather, out of touch with his fleet, and burdened with camp followers and unnecessary equipment. In the battle, the entire Portuguese force was captured or destroyed, the Moroccans acquiring a vast booty in the field and later an enormous ransom for the prisoners. ʿAbd al-Malik, who was already suffering from a mortal illness as he organized the battle, died a natural death during the fighting, while King Sebastian and the deposed Muḥammad al-Mutawakkil were both killed, for which reason the engagement is also known as the Battle of the Three Kings. This war, disastrous to Portugal where the result was to be the passing of the crown to Philip II of Spain, inaugurated a period of splendour for Morocco, where ʿAbd al-Malik was succeeded on the field of battle by his brother *Aḥmad*, who received the honorific name *al-Manṣūr*, the Victorious (1578–1603).

By now the struggle between Spain and Turkey had resulted in a stalemate, and neither possessed the expansive vitality of the previous years. Morocco thus not only did not suffer from Spain's liberation from the agreement with Portugal which had debarred her from occupying Moroccan territory, but was even able to secure from her the return of the port of Larache by playing on Philip's fears of a Moroccan alliance with Spain's enemies, England and the Netherlands. Prevented from expansion eastward by Turkish strength, Aḥmad al-Manṣūr had indeed hopes of utilizing the Protestant Christian powers to help him restore Muslim rule in Spain. In his relations with them, he had considerable success in the commercial field, as England bought great quantities of Moroccan sugar, cultivated in the Sus valley. England's need of saltpetre, which Morocco could supply, enabled him to secure in return large quantities of wood for shipbuilding, though such exchanges had to be kept secret in view of the "cold war" relations between the Islāmic world and Christendom which made trade in potential war materials objectionable to public opinion on both sides. But though the English Queen Elizabeth was anxious for Moroccan financial and material aid in weakening Spain by replacing Philip with another claimant on the throne of Portugal, she was not interested in facilitating a Moroccan landing in southern Spain which was what Aḥmad al-Manṣūr desired. In the year before the Spanish Armada, she rejected his suggestion that he should be loaned 100 English ships to carry him with an army to southern Spain, for which he would pay 150,000 ducats as soon as they reached a Moroccan port. Checked in the north and east, the Moroccan ruler turned south. After a successful expedition to Gourara and Touat in the central Sahara in 1581, he sent an ultimatum to the Askia (king) of Songhay on the Niger (p. 157) demanding that the latter should pay a tribute on the Saharan salt trade to enable Morocco to carry on Holy War. When this was refused, he despatched an expedition across the Sahara to the Niger. The Moroccan force consisted of 2,500 arquebusiers who were mainly Morisco refugees from Spain, of whom 500 were mounted, with 1500 Arab lancers, and a pioneer corps with 8,000 camels and 1,000 pack horses. The commander, known as Jawdhar Pāshā, had come as a child from the neighbourhood of Granada. The journey across the desert, through Tinduf and Taoudeni, took five months during which half the force became casualties. On March 13, 1591, the forces of the Askia were completely defeated, thanks to the firearms of the Moroccan army. This victory, which resulted in the establishment of a Moroccan protectorate on the Niger for the best part of a century, further increased Aḥmad al-Manṣūr's reputation, bringing him not only booty and slaves but also control of the gold traffic from West Africa, on account of which he received the further honorific of *al-Dhahabī* ("the Golden").

Being themselves of southern origin, the Saʿdians made their capital in Marrakesh, to which they restored something of the splendour of Almohade days, enriching it architecturally with the *madrasah* (college) of Ibn Yūsuf and the Saʿdian tombs, both of which are still to be seen, as well as the famous palace al-Badiʿah ("the Peerless") which was destroyed by a ruler of the succeeding dynasty.

Fortified by his Saharan success, Aḥmad al-Manṣūr in 1601 again approached Queen Elizabeth with a proposal for an invasion of Spain. This time the Queen suggested instead assistance in English attacks on the Spanish possessions in America. Aḥmad al-Manṣūr's imagination was fired by the prospect of establishing new Muslim kingdoms across the Atlantic, but he required first a clear agreement as to the benefits which Morocco was to receive. Two years later, before any conclusion was reached, the reigns of both the Golden Sultan and the Virgin Queen were terminated by death.

In Morocco, the disappearance of Aḥmad al-Manṣūr was followed by a period of anarchy while his sons fought one another for the succession and various religious personages took advantage of the disorder to promote their particular tenets and their personal ambitions. During the half century in which this lasted, Morocco was once again divided into a kingdom of Fez and a kingdom of Marrakesh, while various princelets established themselves in the Sus and Tafilalet. Of three sons of Aḥmad al-Manṣūr, one, Zaydān, was proclaimed in Fez, a second, Abū'l-Fāris, in Marrakesh, while a third Muḥammad al-Shaykh al-Ma'mūn, who had at one time been designated as heir but later disgraced and imprisoned for scandalous conduct, was released and sent by Abu'l-Fāris to expel Zaydān from Fez. This he successfully did, but then had himself proclaimed as Sultan. Zaydān, after first taking refuge with the Turks, returned to Morocco and captured Marrakesh, whence he was expelled by his nephew ʿAbd Allāh, the son of al-Ma'mūn. Later he recovered the city and finally captured Fez also, while al-Ma'mūn took refuge in Spain. In 1610 al-Ma'mūn returned, having secured Spanish aid by promising to cede Larache to the Spanish king; he thus was able to reestablish himself in the north until he was assassinated in 1613, probably on account of his surrender of Larache. He was succeeded in Fez by his descendants until the occupation of the city by the *murābiṭs* of Dila in 1641. From 1610 *Zaydān,* who was generally regarded abroad as the legitimate ruler, reigned until his death in 1628, apart from the usurpation of power by the *murābiṭ* Abū Maḥallī from 1611 to 1614. Zaydān's heirs continued to reign in Marrakesh until the death of his grandson *al-ʿAbbās* in 1659. There followed a period of anarchy, which lasted until the capture of the city by Mawlāy al-Rashīd in 1669 marked the final collapse of the Saʿdian dynasty.

During these civil wars Captain John Smith, later famous as Governor of Virginia, had offered his services to Mawlāy Zaydān in Marrakesh, but left again in disgust, exclaiming that it was a matter of "perfidious, treacherous and bloody murders rather than war." The period was indeed one of much shame and no glory. Amid the confusion a number of new aspirants to power appeared, principally religious (militant Ṣūfī) leaders, known as *murābiṭs*. Chief among them were those of the *zāwiyah* (monastery) of Dila, near Khenifra in the Middle Atlas, who controlled Fez and the country as far as Rabat from about 1641 till their suppression by Mawlāy Rashīd in 1688. Another *murābiṭ*, al-ʿAyyāshī, for some years dominated the plain north of Rabat, attacking the Spanish in Larache and al-Mamura. In the south three other *murābiṭs* struggled against the last Saʿdians or with one another. A different element which achieved a temporary independence was the little republic of the river Bu Regreg at Rabat. This was constituted by Moriscos from Spain who arrived in 1610; they tried to maintain themselves by maritime trading and by privateering, achieving notoriety as the "Sallee Rovers." They came to terms with the governments of King James I and King Charles I of England between 1626 and 1628, but the arrangement at once broke down, not apparently through their fault. Their brief independence ended in 1641.

## THE ʿALAWITE DYNASTY

The ʿAlawites or Ḥasanī Sharīfs had come from the Ḥijāz and settled south of the Atlas in Tafilalet at the end of the 13th century, not long after the rise of the Marīnid dynasty; for this reason they are sometimes known as the Fīlālī Sharīfs. The founder of the family fortunes, *Mawlāy al-Sharīf* (1631–1636), was succeeded by his son *Muḥammad (Mahamad)* (1636–1663), who was displaced by another son *Mawlāy al-Rashīd*, who by 1669 was ruler of all Morocco. His successor *Mawlāy Ismāʿīl* (1672–1727) is the best-known member of the dynasty in its first century. He is held by his compatriots to have been a great ruler, a title which is due to one who reigned over a turbulent, largely medieval, empire for fifty-five years, during the latter part of which time it was said that a woman or Jew could walk safely and unaccompanied from one end of the kingdom to another. He corresponded with Louis XIV, whose illegitimate daughter, the Princess of Conti, he would have liked to have added to his ḥarem, and with James II, whom he urged to adopt Islām or at least to return to Protestantism which he regarded as less idolatrous than Catholicism. Though Mawlāy Ismaʿīl failed to extend Moroccan rule over Tlemsen or to recapture Ceuta and Melilla from the Spanish, he regained Larache and al-Mamura from them; while Tangier, which had been English since handed over as part of the dowry of Catherine of Bragança in 1662, was abandoned to him in 1684 after repeated Moroccan attacks had made its retention difficult. Of Mawlāy Isma'īl's vast building projects at Meknes, where he made his capital, there remain today little more than some magnificent gateways, of which the finest was designed by an English convert, and the walls of vast storehouses. It is due to the experiences of some hundreds of Christian prisoners among the thousands of forced labourers employed on these buildings that the ruler acquired the reputation for cruelty by which he is known in Europe. The Sultan's undertakings cost much effort as well as money, and it is said by the 19th century Moroccan historian al-Nāṣirī that his people had to work and pay taxes every day of every month in every year. His supremacy was due to an indomitable will and immense physical energy, aided by his austerity in the matter of food and drink and the strict observance of his religion. The security established by the constant campaigns of the first half of his reign was maintained by the building of forts on the main lines of communication. These were garrisoned mainly by black troops whom he formed out of the slaves remaining from Aḥmad al-Manṣūr's days (of whom he took a census) and of others whom he acquired by purchase or by expeditions through the Sahara. Young negroes were systematically mated with young negresses and the children carefully trained, the boys in military exercises and the girls in domestic arts. On the other hand, Mawlāy Isma'īl showed no awareness of the tremendous intellectual developments in the west, of which 'Abd al-Malik and Aḥmad al-Manṣūr had shown some consciousness; so that his reign did more to confirm Morocco in its medievalism than to prepare it to take its place in the modern world. His last years were marred by the bad conduct of his sons, and his death was the signal for another outbreak of civil war. This lasted for thirty of the most miserable years of Moroccan history, during which seven rulers succeeded or alternated with one another, while all competed for the favours of the black guard and of the Arab troops formed from the Oudaia tribe. One, Aḥmad, known sarcastically as *Aḥmad al-Dhahabī* on account of his lavish largess, reigned twice, while another, *'Abd Allāh,* was deposed and reinstalled no less than three times. Only the accession of the latter's son Muḥammad ibn 'Abd Allāh in 1757 broke the spell and began a century of five long reigns, which were interrupted only by two disastrous years from 1790 to 1792.

Sultan *Muḥammad ibn 'Abd Allāh* (1757–1790) was a devout Muslim who wished to restore the original simplicity of Islām and looked with favour on the Wahhābī régime in Arabia. Far less forceful than Mawlāy Ismā'īl, he relied on diplomacy as much as on military power in his dealings with the tribes and abandoned the effort to guard the direct route from Fez to Marrakesh along the edge of the Middle Atlas, fortifying instead the longer coastal route via Rabat and Casablanca. The remnants of the black troops were kept in check by the use of Arab and Berber tribes. An effort was made to fortify the coast against possible European attacks and to create a Moroccan fleet; this, however, failed for lack of competent seamen and never served any purpose beyond a tentative revival of privateering, which provoked reprisals. With Spain he established friendly relations, broken at one moment by a fruitless attack on Ceuta. On the other hand attacks on Mazagan secured the withdrawal of the Portuguese in 1769. Treaties were made with several European powers. Muḥammad ibn ʿAbd Allāh was also a considerable builder; apart from coastal fortifications, he erected new palaces in Marrakesh and Meknes and built new mosques and *madrasahs* as well as restoring others. His most original work was the building of Mogador, for which the principal architects were of French and English origin. Intended as the principal centre for foreign trade with the south, it was built in an Andalusian style with straight streets.[1] Taken as a whole, Muhammad ibn ʿAbd Allāh's régime may be said to have established a precedent for succeeding reigns until the occupation. A sincere Muslim, the ruler sought to preserve the traditional framework of Islāmic life, but could not inspire it with the vitality which made the greatness of the Almoravide and Almohade periods. While utilizing Europeans and their technical skills, he would at the same time have been willing to renew the *jihād* against Christendom if this had been possible.

The Sultan's later days, like those of so many of his predecessors, were darkened by the misconduct of his son and successor designate, *Mawlāy Yazīd*. The two years reign of this prince (1790–1792) were disastrous. Having initiated it with the pillage of the *mallāḥ* or Jewish quarter of Tetuan, Mawlāy Yazīd immediately antagonized his subjects at home by his cruelty, while breaking the peace which his father had established with Spain and thus provoking a bombardment of Tangier. Within two years he was killed while fighting a rebellion near Marrakesh. After his death, his brother *Mawlāy Sulaymān (Sliman)* (1792–1822) established himself as undisputed ruler during a four years struggle with two other surviving brothers. In character and policy he carried on the tradition of his father, and until 1810 he had many successes, notably in installing a Moroccan governor at Figuig on the Algerian border and in sending an

[1] Poised on what is almost an island, the tiny city with its dazzling white ramparts set against the sea and the sky has a romantic fairy-like appearance.

expedition to Gourara and Touat in the central Sahara. Later he had great difficulties with the Middle Atlas Berbers; during operations against them in 1818 he was himself taken prisoner, but then treated with respect and released, an episode which had little effect on the general situation. His foreign policy was generally peaceful, and he established good relations with the Regencies of Tunis and of Tripoli, supplying them with grain in a time of famine. In 1817 he agreed to put an end to privateering. During the Peninsular wars he rejected French threats, remaining on friendly relations with both Spain and England.

As successor Mawlāy Sulaymān named his nephew *Mawlāy ʿAbd al-Raḥmān ibn Hishām* (1822-1859) in preference to his own son, an unusual piece of altruism which made a considerable impression. After following his uncle's pacific policy for some years, Mawlāy ʿAbd al-Raḥmān was ill-advised enough in 1829 to authorize a privateering sortie which brought some Austrian sailing vessels into Larache and Rabat as prizes. This at once produced reprisals in the form of a bombardment of Larache and the destruction of the privateering vessels. The most important foreign event of the reign, however, was the French invasion of Algeria in 1830. The strength of Islāmic feeling made it impossible for Morocco to avoid involvement. Invited by the people of Tlemsen to take them under his protection, the Sultan acceded to their request, thus at the same time furthering a traditional Moroccan ambition. Then, however, faced with French displeasure and with local complaints concerning the indiscipline of his troops, he withdrew again. Later when ʿAbd al-Qādir, having organized resistance in western Algeria, offered allegiance to the Sultan, and then invoked his aid, the army which he sent under the command of his own son was ignominiously defeated by General Bougeaud in the battle of Isly near Oujda on August 13, 1844, while the French fleet bombarded Tangier on the 6th and Mogador on the 15th. Forced to yield, the Sultan agreed to expel or intern ʿAbd al-Qādir if he should later enter Moroccan territory. When the latter did so in 1845, he was attacked by Moroccan troops in accordance with this agreement and finally in 1847 forced to surrender to the French. In 1851 a minor incident at Salé led to a French bombardment of that port before a settlement was reached. It was now clear to European statesmen that Morocco was no longer in any position to resist specific European demands which were backed by armed force. The only possible policy for Moroccan rulers was to temporize and take advantage of the jealousy and rivalry between the various powers. It had in fact been partly fear of British reaction which had deterred the French government from allowing General Bougeaud to march on Fez, as he had wished to do after the victory at Isly. Britain now held a dominating position in Morocco and had constituted herself champion of the country's independence. In 1856 she secured a treaty granting certain trade privileges and the right of according 'protection' to a number of Moroccan subjects. This treaty was followed by similar arrangements with other Western powers, all of which had the effect of furthering European penetration.

The weakness of the still medieval empire, without roads or wheeled traffic, still using barbarous punishments such as cutting off the hands of thieves and sticking the heads of rebels on the city walls, was again made apparent in the first years of Mawlāy ʿAbd al-Raḥmān's successor *Sīdī Muḥammad* (1859-1873), the fourth of that name in the ʿAlawite dynasty. At the moment of his accession a dispute about the limits of Spanish Ceuta led to a Spanish invasion and the capture of Tetuan. A further advance on Tangier was only averted by British intervention. The restoration of peace was bought with an indemnity of 20 million dollars and the cession of the enclave of Ifni on the Atlantic coast; the latter was however not taken over by Spain until 1934. Sīdī Muḥammad then endeavoured to form an army on the European model, but with little success. His reign was another example of the effort to patch up a medieval type of administration which had become a complete anachronism in the modern world.

The same applies to the heroic efforts of his son and successor *Mawlāy al-Ḥasan* I (1873-1894). As man and ruler he commanded the respect of those Europeans who knew him, but his energies had to be devoted to continual expeditions around the country to enforce order and collect taxes. He never spared himself and won the reputation of an energetic and honourable ruler. But the state which he governed lacked every element which would have enabled it to renew and modernize itself by its own efforts. The machinery of government was rudimentary; tentative efforts to train an army with European instructors and to educate Moroccan students abroad failed because the background simply did not permit such projects to bear fruit. In 1893 Mawlāy al-Ḥasan led a great expedition across the Atlas to Tafilalet. On the return journey it was caught in blizzards in the High Atlas and the remnants arrived in Marrakesh with the Sultan a sick man, suddenly aged. He had to set off at once for the north to punish tribes whose unauthorized attacks on the Spanish had cost the country an indemnity of £650,000. On the way he died; his death was concealed by the Chamberlain, Abū Aḥmad, until the army reached Rabat where his young son ʿAbd al-ʿAzīz was proclaimed Sultan.

*Mawlāy ʿAbd al-ʿAzīz* (1894-1908), intelligent and filled with good intentions, readily absorbed ideas of reform from the Europeans with whom he liked to surround himself. But through lack of trained administrators, the attempt to introduce a modern form of land taxation and a new administrative system resulted merely in confusion, while the young Sultan's love of childish amusements antagonized the traditional supporters of the monarchy. The tribes escaped from control, and a pretender set up a rival court near Melilla. In these circumstances European governments constantly found new pretexts for interference. In 1904 the protection afforded by British opposition to the intervention of another European power was removed by an Anglo-French agreement which gave France a free hand in Morocco in return for her acquiescence in British actions in Egypt. The French made sure of Spanish consent by the promise of a Spanish zone of influence in the north. Italy was won over by an undertaking not to interfere with her own designs on Libya. The Congress of Algeciras (1906), whose meeting the Sultan secured by utilizing the German desire not to be left out when commercial advantages were to be gained in Morocco, gave international sanction to the principle of the integrity of the Sultan's domain and to that of equality of economic opportunity in trading with it, but at the same time prepared the way for Franco-Spanish interference in the policing of the ports, in the collection of the customs, and in other fields. In 1908 the Sultan's brother, *Mawlāy ʿAbd al-Ḥafīz*, at that time viceroy in Marrakesh, denounced his brother for subservience to the infidel and declared him deposed. After an almost bloodless civil war and an abortive attack by Mawlāy ʿAbd al-Ḥafīẓ's troops on the French, now installed at Casablanca (al-Dār al-Bayḍā), the insurgent prince was proclaimed Sultan in Fez while his brother took refuge with the French. Once on the throne, Mawlāy ʿAbd al-Ḥāfiẓ's only success was the capture of the pretender; but the exhibition of the latter in a cage and the barbarous punishments inflicted on his followers further antagonized European feeling while doing nothing to win him popular support. Soon the new Sultan was himself besieged by insurgent tribes in the capital, Fez, and was compelled to ask the French to relieve the beleaguered city. When they had done so, he had no choice but to sign the treaty which they presented to him. This document, known as the Treaty of Fez (March 30, 1912), made Morocco a French protectorate and authorized the French government to introduce such reforms as they thought fit, in return for which they undertook to defend the status of the Sultan and his successors. The right of the Spanish to a special position in the north of the country was recognised, while Tangier, long the seat of the diplomatic missions, was to retain its distinctive characteristics. The thousand year old independence of the Moroccan state was abruptly ended, and an entirely new era began.

## ALGERIA

Until the 16th century, the area known today as Algeria did not form a political unit, but was subject to the influence or control of Morocco, and later of Tlemsen, in the western half, and of Tunisia in the eastern half. By 1500, the decay of these powers resulted in the virtual independence of the various tribes and cities. The arrival of thousands of Muslim and Morisco (officially converted) refugees from Spain led to a certain development of agriculture, arts and crafts in the coastal regions, but also to a great extension of privateering directed primarily against Spanish possessions. This intensified the Spanish determination to attack the Muslim governments of North Africa. The ensuing Spanish invasion was countered by the intervention of the equally expanding Turkish empire, and the final outcome was the transformation of the central and eastern Maghrib into three Ottoman military dominions, known as the Regencies of Algiers, Tunis and Tripoli; among these Algiers, which became the centre of Turkish activity, took the place of Tunis as the predominant power. On both the Christian and the Muslim sides, the fighting was regarded by the mass of the population as a Holy War or Crusade, while for the rulers it was rather an issue of rapid national expansion, which was followed later by slow decay. In 1494 discussions between the Spaniards, the Portuguese and the Pope had led to the recognition of the right of the former to treat the kingdom of Tlemsen as an area which they were entitled to occupy; and in 1496 they seized Melilla, in an area which was in fact disputed between Tlemsen and Morocco. In 1505 they occupied Mersa al-Kabir, in 1509 Oran, and in 1510 Bougie and Tripoli. The alarm caused by these conquests was sufficient to lead smaller places, such as Tenes, Tedlys (Dellys) and Mostaghanem, to submit to Spanish overlordship. Among these was the little port of Algiers, whose inhabitants agreed to accept Spanish sovereignty and to hand over any Christian captives in their possession, for whose loss they were told they would be indemnified from the property of their Jewish fellow-citizens. The population was largely Spanish Muslim, and they were under the protection of the shaykh of the neighbouring Thaʿālibī tribe, by name Salīm al-Tūmī. For greater security, the Spaniards installed a garrison on the Peñon, the largest of the islets – *al-Jazā'ir*, the islands of the Banū

Mazghannā – lying just off shore, which had given the place its name.

Unlike the Spanish invasion, the Ottoman intervention was not due to planning by the central government but was the work of Ottoman subjects who began as privateers and became empire builders. The leading part was played by two brothers, *'Arūj* and *Khayr al-Dīn*, from the Aegean island of Mytilene. Their father was a former Muslim soldier, probably from a recently converted family of the European provinces. Their mother is said to have been the widow of a Greek priest. The Turks had by now been established in Europe for a century, and conversion to Islām, for one reason or another, was exceedingly common. The brothers became known to Europeans by the name *Barbarossa*, probably because they had red beards. The elder brother, 'Arūj, began his career by raiding the shipping of the Christian enemies of Turkey in the Aegean, with the sanction of the Ottoman prince Qorqud, governor in Asia Minor. On the latter's flight from his brother, the future Salīm I, and the banning of his shipping from the Aegean, 'Arūj transferred himself, probably about 1509, first to Alexandria where he was authorized by the Mamlūk Sultan Qānṣūh al-Ghūrī to continue privateering, provided that he observed the accepted international conventions and maintained strict discipline among the crews. A year or two later he transferred his services to the Ḥafṣid Sultan of Tunis, *Abū 'Abd Allāh Muḥammad*.

The latter was no doubt aware that King Ferdinand of Aragon was intending to capture Tunis, as he already had Bougie and Tripoli, though in fact he was diverted from the attempt. He was therefore glad to accept 'Arūj as a privateer, on condition that his actions gave no cause of complaint to his subjects and that 'Arūj paid him one fifth of the value of the prizes taken. In the following months 'Arūj and his brother Khayr al-Dīn, who had now joined him, seriously harassed Spanish shipping and rescued many hundreds of Moriscos from Spain. As their base they used Goletta, the port of Tunis, and apparently also the island of Jerba where the Spanish had been defeated in 1510. As well as the payments to the Ḥafṣid, the brothers took care periodically to send large gifts to Sultan Salīm in Constantinople with a view to a future reconciliation. In 1512 'Arūj made an unsuccessful attempt to recapture Bougie from the Spaniards, losing an arm in the attempt. Two years later he established himself at Jijelli. In 1516 he was invited by the people of Algiers to help them dislodge the Spaniards from the Peñon, this 'thorn aimed at our heart' as they described it. After first driving from Cherchell a rival Turkish corsair whom he mistrusted, 'Arūj attacked the Peñon but without success. This failure, combined with the demands and arrogance of his men, led the people of Algiers to make fresh approaches to the Spanish, whereupon ʿArūj put Salīm al-Tūmī and other leaders to death and made himself ruler. In September of the same year he repelled a Spanish attack under Diego de Vera, inflicting severe losses on the attackers. He then moved against the Shaykh of Tenes further west, who had also been negotiating with the Spanish, dispossessed him, and took the area over. His help was then requested by a Zayyānid pretender to the throne of Tlemsen, whose ruler had submitted to Spanish overlordship in 1511. Having driven the ruler out, ʿArūj did not place the pretender on the throne but imposed his own authority. A Spanish force, coming to the relief of their protégé, compelled Arūj to evacuate the town; during the retreat he was routed and beheaded by a Spanish ensign (1518), who as a reward for this exploit was later authorised to show ʿArūj's head on his coat of arms.

On leaving Algiers for these expeditions, ʿArūj had summoned his brother Khayr al-Dīn from Djidjelli and appointed him his deputy in Algiers. On receiving the news of the disaster, Khayr al-Dīn informed the people that he proposed to offer Algiers and its environs to the Ottoman Sultan. Only thus, he said, could their safety be guaranteed against Spanish attacks, which were regularly facilitated by the hesitating attitude of the local rulers. Salīm accepted the proposition, appointed Khayr al-Dīn a *Sanjaq Bey* (district governor), and sent him 2,000 regular troops and 4,000 Ottoman volunteers. The imposition of Turkish sovereignty seems to have provoked local opposition, which was suppressed by Khayr al-Dīn as earlier opposition had been by ʿArūj.

By now the Ḥafṣid ruler in Tunis had become aware of what was happening. The Spanish menace had been reduced, but it was clear that it had been replaced, as far as he was concerned, by a Turkish menace. He therefore made approaches to the ruler of Tlemsen for a joint front and endeavoured to suborn Khayr al-Dīn's allies in the Kabyle country east of Algiers. Meanwhile the latter in 1519 successfully repelled a second Spanish attack led by Hugo de Moncada. Shortly afterwards, however, Kabyle forces backed by the Ḥafṣid forced him to withdraw to Jijelli, leaving Algiers to the Kabyles and the Spanish garrison still in the Pẽnon. During the next five years, he succeeded in greatly strengthening his position around this more easterly base, capturing Bône and Constantine from their Ḥafṣid governors, driving the Kabyles from Algiers and occupying the Mitija plain behind the city. Finally in 1529 he captured the Pẽnon itself. Using captive labour, he then joined this to the mainland, forming the harbour of Algiers and constructing the fortifications by which it became the chief base of Ottoman sea-power in the west. In the following year the Emperor Charles V, now ruler of Spain, countered these measures by giving Malta as their new headquarters to the Knights of St. John, who had been driven from Rhodes eight years earlier.[1]

In 1533 Khayr al-Dīn's reputation was such that the new Sultan, Sulaymān, appointed him *Qapudān Pāshā* (Lord High Admiral), a very exalted post which carried with it the rank of *Beylerbey* (Governor General) and the general supervision of Ottoman maritime and overseas affairs. His first major operation in this capacity was the capture of Tunis in 1534. Though undertaken nominally on behalf of a Ḥafṣid pretender, the capture was followed by a declaration of the deposition of the dynasty. Khayr al-Dīn, who had frequented the *'ulamā'* of Tunis during his early stay there, was well received and had no difficulty in occupying the numerous ports of the east coast and the city of Qayrawān in the interior. These areas remained in Turkish possession when in the following year the Spaniards succeeded in driving the Turks from Tunis city. Charles V then restored the Ḥafṣid prince as a satellite ruler, supervising his actions from a fortress at Goletta which was built and garrisoned for the purpose. Khayr al-Dīn made his escape to Bône, where he had left some of his fleet. This he at once led on a raiding expedition, in the course of which over 4,000 prisoners were carried off from Minorca. Henceforth his duties as Qapudān Pāshā were to keep him away from Algiers. His actions as founder of the arsenal at Istanbul and his conduct of naval operations against the Spaniards belong to Ottoman history in general rather than to that of Algiers. It was, however, under his command that the Algerian fleet, now the western division of the Turkish navy, was in 1534 allotted the town and harbour of Toulon as winter quarters, in implementation of the alliance between Sultan Sulaymān and King Francis I of France; in accordance with this, Turkish naval forces cooperated with those of France in harrying Spanish possessions in Italy and elsewhere. Khayr al-Dīn's death occurred in 1547, and he was buried in a mausoleum which he had had constructed at Beşiktaş on the Bosphorus. His reputation was such that his tomb became a place of pilgrimage for Turkish naval commanders before setting out for operations.

In the words of the Spanish abbot Haedo, who was no admirer of

[1] As naval outposts of Islām and Christendom respectively, there was to be a close parallel between the privateering activities of Turkish Algiers and Malta of the Knights. This included government by a foreign minority from which the people of the country were excluded, the great number of prizes and slaves which they took, and their disappearance as states when they failed to adapt themselves to conditions in which privateering became an anachronism. The organization of the Knights was, however, distinguished by its specifically religious character, its charitable aspect as the Order of the Hospitallers, and the far greater stability and respectability of its internal régime.

Muslims, Khayr al-Dīn "was a man of great spirit, bold and ready to take risks, magnanimous, very liberal, in no way cruel except in war or when disobeyed. He was much loved, feared, and obeyed by his soldiers and very bitterly wept by them when dead."

During Khayr al-Dīn's absence as Qapūdān Pāshā, Algiers was administered by a deputy, first *Ḥasan Āghā*, who had been captured as a child in Sardinia, and then by Khayr al-Dīn's own son, also named *Ḥasan*, who was appointed governor in his own right after his father's death (1547–1551 and 1555–1567). The period of office of Ḥasan Āghā the Sardinian (1536–1543) was marked by the attack on Algiers by Charles V in person (1541), with a fleet of 500 ships and 24,000 soldiers. This resulted in a Spanish catastrophe, the Muslims being aided by heavy rain storms and tempests which destroyed much of the fleet. A subsequent attempt by the Spaniards in Oran to depose the Zayyānid prince of Tlemsen, who had taken the opportunity to disown them, had only a temporary success. Later a successful Turkish counter-attack against an invasion by a Moroccan prince, who sought to profit from the Turco-Spanish conflict and had advanced as far as Mostaghanem, brought Tlemsen under Algerian rule in 1552.[1] At this moment, however, Ḥasan ibn Khayr al-Dīn was replaced as governor by *Ṣalāḥ Ra'īs*, apparently at the request of the Sultan's French allies with whom Ḥasan (unlike his father) was little disposed to cooperate. Ṣalāḥ Ra'īs, a commander with much experience both on land and at sea, first moving south forced the oases of Wargla and Touggourt to pay tribute and then intervened in the civil wars in Morocco, where it was he who replaced the Waṭṭāsid Abū Ḥasūn on the throne of Fez (1554), receiving in part-payment for his services the Peñon of Velez Gomara, which for ten years became an advanced base for raiding the Spanish coast and shipping. Moving east, Ṣalāḥ Ra'īs then recaptured Bougie, thus ending 45 years of Spanish occupation. On his sudden death from plague in the following year, the Porte appointed as Governor General a certain Tekelerli. The Algiers garrison, however, were not willing to accept him; and soon after his arrival from Constantinople, he was killed during a rising, whereupon the Porte reappointed Ḥasan ibn Khayr al-Dīn.

Having resumed office, Ḥasan defeated a Moroccan force which was again besieging Tlemsen, and advanced on Fez, outside which the Turkish forces were defeated (1557) and forced to retreat, being harrassed at the same time by the Spaniards from Oran. The latter now made an attempt on Mostaghanem; this ended in a complete disaster for them (1558) and

[1] See under Morocco, p. 103.

marked the end of their efforts to expand their influence outside Oran city. In 1561 plans by Ḥasan for further operations in the west were interrupted by a plot on the part of the Turkish soldiery, who resented his use of local troops, Berber and Arab, and accused him of seeking to make himself independent. Sent to Constantinople in chains, he was cleared of the charge and returned to Algiers in the following year (1562). While preparing to attack Oran, he was summoned to take part in the siege of Malta (1565), at the end of which he received a naval command (1567). In the following year he was replaced as Governor General by *'Alī Pāshā*[1] (1568–1587), a Calabrian who had been captured as a young man and had adopted Islām when a galley slave. Immediately after his assumption of office, there occurred the rising of the Moriscos in Granada. 'Alī Pāshā seems to have favoured a major effort to help them, but was diverted by the Sultan's order to attack Tunis, where the Spanish were still installed in Goletta whence they dominated the puppet Ḥafṣid in Tunis. In 1569, having captured the city (but not Goletta), he installed a Turkish governor. Two years later the Turkish naval forces suffered the great defeat of Lepanto at Spanish hands (1571). 'Alī Pāshā, who had fought with great distinction on the Turkish side, was rewarded after the battle with the appointment of Qapudān Pāshā. Encouraged by the victory of Lepanto, the Spaniards commanded by Don John of Austria captured Tunis in a surprise attack (1573). The success was fleeting, for in the following year (1574) 'Alī Pāshā, organizing an attack both from Algiers and from Tripoli (which had been Turkish since 1551), captured not only Tunis city but also the fort at Goletta in which the Spanish had been established since 1534. This marked the virtual end of the long Spanish-Turkish struggle for supremacy in the central and eastern Maghrib, the only Spanish foothold left there now being the city of Oran. For most of the remainder of 'Alī Pāshā's period of office as Qapudān Pāshā, Algiers was entrusted to deputies, first *'Arab Aḥmad*; then *Ramaḍān* (1574–1577), son of a Sardinian goat herd, captured in his childhood, who in 1576 won Fez for the Sa'dian 'Abd al-Malik; and then *Ḥasan Veneziano*, of Venetian origin as his name shows. The latter was Pāshā at the time of the captivity of Cervantes, who speaks of his pride, his cruelty, and his energy. After a revolt against him, he was replaced by *Ja'far*, a eunuch of Hungarian origin, captured in childhood, in whose time 'Alī Pāshā prepared to lead in person an expedition against the Sa'dian Sultan of Morocco, Aḥmad

[1] Like other former Christians, he was sometimes called by the Arabs "al-Ilj" ("the Convert"), whence the European forms Uluj Ali, Euldj Ali, Ucciali, Occhiali, Lucciali. Later he was called honorifically by the Turks "Kïlïc ("Sabre") Ali".

al-Manṣūr; this was however prevented by his recall to Constantinople on more urgent affairs. After further disturbances, which brought *Mami Arnaut* into office, Ḥasan Veneziano returned for the years 1582 to 1588. After ʿAlī Pāshā died in 1587, he was succeeded by Veneziano as Qapudān Pāshā (1588), but without the governorship of Algiers. In view of the relatively stable position which Turkish rule had now acquired, Algiers and the two sister Regencies Tunis and Tripoli were for the future governed by Beylerbeys who held the title of Pāshā and were appointed for a period of three years, which was however renewable. All three Regencies had by now acquired the organization which was to determine their character for the next two hundred years.

The guarantee of Turkish influence consisted in the *ojāq (ocak)* or corps of militia who provided the backbone of the military forces on land. These were not properly speaking janissaries, though they enjoyed similar privileges. Janissaries were recruited from Christian children, captured in war or delivered as tribute, while the *ioldash* (*yoldaş*, literally "companions") of North Africa were recruited as adults, principally though not exclusively in Asia Minor, by sanction of the Sultan. No conditions of birth or education were involved. Once enrolled, these Turkish-speaking volunteers were promoted strictly by seniority. All members of the *ojāq* (properly "the hearth", where the rice for the communal meal was prepared) were maintained by the state, and they formed a highly privileged body whose pay was the first charge on the state finances. Unmarried men were lodged in handsome barracks; married men lived out. In the field, discipline was strict, and there was never any doubt about their military value, but they expected a great measure of licence after victory and were often overbearing when off parade; in some ways they resembled the later French Foreign Legion. The authority of the Porte was represented by the Pāshā, who was assisted by the *Diwān* (Council) of the Militia. State documents were headed, "We, Pāshā and Diwān of the Invincible Corps of Janissaries." Their authority was, however, tempered by the importance of the corsair captains, who came to be known as *Ṭāʾifat al-Raʾīs*, the Faction of the Qapudān Raʾīs, or Admiral, who appears to have been appointed by the Sultan. Their importance came from the size of the contribution which their prizes made to the public finances and to the wealth of individuals. With the dying down of the great struggle between Spain and Turkey and the decay of authority in Constantinople, the Regencies rapidly moved towards what may be called "dominion status," in which the Pāshā sent by the Porte, like the Governor General in the former British dominions, held a position of more dignity than power.

The traditions of their origin and their constitutions led the Regencies to make an industry of privateering, and they were soon arrogating to themselves the right to continue operations against the shipping of powers with which the Ottoman empire had made peace. Here again the development was parallel to that of the Maltese state of the Knights. In 1741, for example, the French government brought pressure on the Knights to give up their privateering activities in the Levant because these were provoking reprisals against French shipping. In the case of the Regencies, the enfeebled Porte was frequently unable to make its view prevail.

In these circumstances, the history of Algiers in the 17th century has often been presented as a series of piratical outrages followed by well-merited reprisals. There were in fact British naval demonstrations against Algiers in 1622, 1652 and 1672, and French in 1661, 1665, 1682, 1683 and 1688, as well as a French incursion at Jijelli in 1664 which proved disastrous for the invaders. Recent studies, however, show that the subject requires much further investigation before final judgement can be passed. Thus the demonstration under Sir Robert Mansel in 1622 was probably inspired as much by reasons of European policy as by Algerian privateering. It was followed in 1623 by a peace-treaty with Algiers, which the latter observed scrupulously for five years in spite of English breaches of it. It was presumably this fact which led King Charles I in 1628 to issue a proclamation forbidding attacks on Algerian (and also on Tunisian, Tetuani or Salé) shipping; this, like the peace-treaty, seems to have been ignored by English captains. In 1629 the Algerines gave 12 months notice of termination. It was during the ensuing war that there occurred the Algerine raid on the little Irish port of Baltimore (1631), in which 89 or more inhabitants were carried off into slavery in Algiers. Meanwhile, in 1621, the instructions given to Sir Thomas Roe, on proceeding to Constantinople as ambassador, chiefly concerned European affairs, but also referred to measures to be taken against the "insolencies of the pirates of Tunis and Algiers." In 1628, however, in the light of his experience abroad, we find the ambassador urging the reasonableness of seeking to make terms with the Algerines and informing the home government in plain terms that the "great licence given or taken by our ships will leave us no friend, nor place to relieve with a drop of water... Briefly," he concluded, "if in England better order be not taken and a bridle putt in these sea-horse mouthes, his majesties honor will be offended and all our trades forfeyted."[1]

[1] His experiences also taught him that Muslims were not the only offenders. On his

From this and similar evidence, it is clear that the offences were not all on one side. Religious prejudice played a great part; but at the same time both Christian and Muslim states, while periodically proposing a common front against those of the opposite faith, were always ready to make tactical alliances across this frontier. Rather later, in 1654, Cromwell's attempt to deal with the Regencies (as also with Tuscan and Maltese depredations) by ultimatums backed by naval force, seems to have had little success at the time, though ultimately the regular presence of British naval forces in the Mediterranean ensured better relations. The peace arranged with Algiers in 1682 finally produced a fairly satisfactory state of affairs which lasted for more than a century.

The last quarter century of the 16th and the first half of the 17th centuries had seen the maximum development of North African privateering. It is a remarkable fact that throughout this period the ship captains, the craftsmen in the arsenals, the secretaries in the administration, and the staff in charge of the interior economy of the palaces of the rulers, and other great personages, were largely of European origin; some were converts, who were known to contemporary Europeans as "renegades", others actual Christian slaves. Algiers was in fact an intensely cosmopolitan city. According to the Spanish Benedictine abbot, Haedo, who gives a lucid account of the city, the Turkish-speaking Muslim population consisted of "Turks (that is, Muslims) by birth and of Turks by profession." Among the former, he gives a rather better character to those from the European provinces than to those from Asia Minor. Those who were Muslims by profession, that is those of Christian (or Jewish) parentage who had become Muslims, far outnumbered those who were Muslims by origin. They included, he says, Spaniards and Italians from every province of Spain and Italy, and in addition, Russians, Rumanians, Bulgarians, Poles, Hungarians, Bohemians, Scandinavians, Irish, English, Scots, Portuguese, Slavs, Albanians, Bosniaks, Greeks, Cretans, Syrians, Copts, and even "Abyssinians of Prester John," Brazilians, and (Spanish) South Americans. While some of these had chosen Islām to better their position as slaves and others had been captured as children and brought up as Muslims, a very large number seem to have come of their free choice. The explanation is perhaps that life in Algiers offered a

---

way home the ship in which he was travelling was attacked by a Maltese galley, which was only driven off after a sharp fight, in spite (as he said) of the fact that "the Maltese have no quarrel of state against us, except they picke one for their nations being all French and Spaniards." On his way out, too, he had found at Messina that the Spaniards, having captured a Muslim galley with 13 English galley slaves and two English renegades, were using the 15 Englishmen as galley slaves for their own shipping.

far greater scope for advancement to people of humble origin than contemporary Europe did.[1]

In a period favourable to privateering, Algiers became a very rich and prosperous city, as can be seen from the comments of English travellers whose ships put in at its harbour for provisions. Many of the captains lived in great state, in oriental-style palaces, with courtyards adorned with fountains made of Italian marble. The country round the town was thickly spread with charming country houses and gardens, and its needs promoted a considerable agricultural development in the nearby Mitija plain.

Apart from the ruling Turks, the other inhabitants of the city towards the end of the 16th century included some 25,000 Christian slaves, many of whom were put to row in the galleys in the summer months. The original citizens, who amounted perhaps to some 12,000, were largely of Muslim Spanish origin, and earned their living as merchants, shopkeepers, craftsmen or market gardeners. As still today, there were also Berbers from the Kabyle country; many of these engaged in menial tasks. A special group among them was formed by members of the Zawāwah tribe (the later "Zouaves"), who were freely used as soldiers. There were Arabs from the surrounding countryside who drifted into the city, picking up what work they could find, or begging. Among the recently arrived refugees from Spain, two groups were distinguished: one composed of Moriscos from Andalusia and Granada known as Mudejars[2] and the other of Moriscos from north-eastern Spain, Valencia, Aragon, and Catalonia, known as Tagarins.[3] They included the best craftsmen, builders, gunsmiths, tailors and shoemakers, while many bred silkworms for the manufacture of silk. Having recently escaped from the activities of the Inquisition in Spain, they fanned a flame of hate against the Christian Spanish government.

Another important element in the population was the Jews, very largely also refugees from Spain. Though treated with scorn and subjected to much abuse and frequent monetary levies, they were, like the other communities, free to manage their own affairs in their own way. They were thankful to have escaped from Spain, it seems, since for generations they held a striking annual celebration to commemorate the defeat of

[1] A Turkish song current in Anatolia until recently called Algiers the city where the streets were paved in marble and where the Āghās and the Beys lived in tall houses but forgot Turkish and talked Arabic. Certainly men of the humblest origin such as the Barbarossas or ʿAlī Pāshā found scope there for developing their talents. ʿAlī Pāshā initiated a project for a Suez Canal, three hundred years before de Lesseps.

[2] From the Arabic *mudajjan*, "domesticated" or subject Muslims.

[3] From the Arabic *thaghr*, frontier or border.

Charles V's attack on the city in 1541. They played a great part in commercial activity, being assisted in this by their close relations with Jewish communities in Leghorn and elsewhere. Their rôle became increasingly important in the finances of the state, and in the disposal of the booty and of the slaves brought in by the privateers.

Among the 20,000 to 30,000 Turkish-speaking people who completely dominated policy and such political life as existed, there prevailed a sort of anarchic egalitarianism, which led to incessant upheavals as the control of the Pāshās weakened. As far as those who lived outside this magic circle were concerned, the state was more in the nature of a loose confederation, subject to a despotically minded minority, than of a unitary state. Kabyles, Arab tribes, smaller cities, and urban communities like the Jews, ran their internal affairs as they chose, their own communal authorities being responsible for the distribution within the community of the taxes due. In these circumstances, the members of the *ojāq*, generally of humble origin and little education, but with great esprit de corps and much arrogance towards the rest of the population, tended to encroach on the authority of the Pāshā. In 1659, when there are said to have been 22,000 of them, they succeeded in transferring all executive authority from the Pāshā to an *Āghā* selected by themselves. This régime greatly increased the instability of power, and all four Āghās elected during the 12 years which the system lasted were assassinated in the course of tumults raised by the same body which had chosen them. The resort to assassination thus initiated was somewhat reduced under the subsequent régime of the Deys, but it remained painfully frequent. In 1671 a reaction organized by the already mentioned "Admiral's Faction" *(Ṭā'ifat al-Ra'īs)* brought to power rulers known by the name *Dey*,[1] of whom the first four were selected not from the *ojāq* but from the members of the *Ṭā'īfah*. The new organization persisted till the fall of the Algerian state in 1830, though the later Deys were elected by a *Diwān* or Council of Ministers. In 1711 the tenth of these Deys, *'Alī Shāwush*, succeeded in persuading the Porte, to whose approval the appointment of the Dey was theoretically subject, to combine with it the imperial appointment of Pāshā. Deys were elected for life, which only too often meant until they fell a victim to assassination. Meanwhile the Dey exercised absolute power in internal affairs and practically speaking in foreign affairs also. Nominally, however, Algiers remained under Turkish suzerainty and in

[1] This Turkish word originally signified a maternal uncle; it was then applied to someone who distinguished himself in land or sea fighting. Later it signified a military officer of captain's rank, and finally the Head of State in Algiers, as it did earlier in Tunis.

fact continued to give naval or military help to the Porte when the latter required it, though financial or other reimbursement came to be increasingly expected. The Dey was advised by a Diwān or Council of Ministers, distinct from the Diwān of the Janissaries and from the Great Diwān; the latter included the members of the Ṭā 'ifah and decided all questions of peace and war. The Ministers forming the Diwān were known as the "Powers". They included the *Khaznajī* or Finance Minister: the *Wakīl al-Kharj* or Minister of Marine; the *Āghā* or Commander-in-Chief of the land forces; the *Bayt al-Māljī* or Intendant of Domains and Inheritances, and the *Khōjat al-Khayl* or Receiver of Taxes. Beneath these there were four State Secretaries; 200 Junior Secretaries; two Protocol Interpreters; and other lesser officials. The Dey had a special treasurer for his privy purse, which was kept strictly separate from the State Treasury.

The various sections of the non-Turkish population continued their existence as distinct units, except that from the time of the Āghās certain tribes, called as in Morocco *Makhzan* tribes, were exempted from state taxation in return for rendering military service. Their duties included taking part in the six monthly armed expeditions which collected taxes and tribute. For administrative purposes the country was divided into four areas. The first was the Dar al-Sulṭān around Algiers, which was directly under the Dey and administered by four *Qā'ids*; the others were the three provinces, Constantine in the east, Titteri, with capital at Medea, in the centre, and a western province with capital first at Mazuna, then at Mascara, and then at Oran when that city had been finally recovered from the Spanish in 1792, after first being temporarily recovered for the period of 29 years from 1708 to 1732. The provinces were governed by Governors having the title of Bey; sub-divisions known as *waṭans* were headed by Qā'ids.

In this form, the Regency acquired most of the attributes of an independent state, though, as has been said, Turkish sovereignty was recognised by military aid in wartime, as during the Greek War of Independence. As time passed and the conditions for privateering became less favourable, profits diminished, the population of the city lessened, and the state became progressively weaker. The demands of the *Ṭā'ifah* for opportunities to attack shipping made it impossible for the Dey to make peace with all countries at the same time, while the need for money to pay the militia compelled him to impose heavier contributions on the tribes. The Deys were never able to substitute a national army for the militia, though Algerian rulers periodically attempted to do so from the time of Ḥasan b. Khayr al-Dīn, nor to absorb the privateer fleet into a national navy as the European powers did. Though trade was far from negligible and Algiers helped to provision such British bases as Gibraltar and Minorca and supplied large quantities of wheat to France during the Napoleonic Wars, there was no great development of commerce to help Algiers in the way that the increasing European trade helped Malta. In 1668 the Dutch Admiral de Ruyter had estimated that one third of Algerian shipping was serving with the Turkish fleets, one third was engaged in privateering, and one third in commerce. In the following century Maltese privateering effectively prevented the carrying of goods in Muslim shipping, except in a very limited coastal traffic. In these circumstances the population of Algiers fell from perhaps 150,000 to 50,000; the number of the militia from 22,000 to 4,000, and of the European captives from several tens of thousands to a few hundred. In these circumstances, a large Spanish naval and military force in 1775 attempted a landing but was promptly forced to re-embark. At the end of the 18th century, the holding of slaves and the practice of privateering were forbidden to individuals, though still permitted to the state. In the last decades of the Regency the profits from privateering were nil, though a number of lesser European states continued to pay annual sums to ensure that their shipping should not be molested. The attempt to extort more taxation from the population, in order to make up for the reduced receipts, provoked discontent and abortive risings.

By the beginning of the 19th century it became clear that Turkish Algiers had become an anachronism which was bound to collapse by one means or another. If it were to be by foreign occupation, Spain had by now ceased to be a candidate. The possible occupiers were either Britain whose Consul, Broughton, was a warm advocate of this about 1808, or France, which had held important trading concessions at the Bastion and La Calle in the Bône area for over two centuries, and had long shown expansive tendencies in North Africa. Since Britain favoured the maintenance of Muslim independence rather than her own intervention, and had assured the suppression of European slavery and the security of her shipping by Lord Exmouth's bombardment of Algiers, in cooperation with the Dutch, in 1816, the attempt was more likely to be made by France. This was the position when the failure of the French government to satisfy an Algerian claim for payment for wheat, delivered to the government of the Directory in Paris more than a quarter of a century earlier, provoked an incident which in 1830 afforded the desired pretext for intervention.

## TUNISIA

We have already seen how a Spanish force (under Conde Pedro Navarro) captured Bougie and Tripoli in 1510, and how King Ferdinand only broke off preparations to capture Tunis itself because of Spanish difficulties in Italy. A thousand English archers whom he had borrowed from Henry VIII to assist in the expedition returned from Cadiz to England. We have seen too how the Ḥafṣid ruler, Abū ʿAbd Allāh Muḥammad, welcomed the coming of the Turkish corsairs ʿAruj and Khayr al-Dīn, probably in 1511 or 1512, and authorized them to operate from Tunis, seeing in them valuable allies against the Spaniards, but also how he soon realized that they were going to prove as great a threat to Ḥafṣid rule as the Spaniards themselves. This was due in part to the fact that their uncompromising opposition to the invading infidels made a much stronger appeal to Muslim opinion than did the temporizing attitude of the local rulers. We have seen how Khayr al-Dīn captured Tunis from Abū ʿAbd Allāh's successor Mawlāy Ḥasan in 1534, only to lose it again to the Spaniards in the following year, and how Mawlāy Ḥasan, having sought Spanish aid, was replaced by them on the throne as a satellite ruler. Thirty-four years later similar vicissitudes resulted in the end of Ḥafṣid rule, after ʿAlī Pāshā had first captured the city in 1569 and then lost it again in 1573, and had finally established Turkish rule by a joint attack with other Turkish forces from Tripoli in 1574.

We now have to examine these events from a more specifically Tunisian point of view.

*Abū ʿAbd Allāh Muḥammad* (1494-1526), the last Ḥafṣid sultan to live out his reign in independence, was a cultured and benevolent but weak ruler; during his reign the Arabs of the interior largely escaped control. His prestige further suffered a shattering blow from the Spanish capture of Bougie and Tripoli in 1510. This was hardly mitigated by a Spanish disaster in the same year at Jerba, since this was due to the failure of the Spanish to find water for their troops rather than to the fighting qualities of their adversaries. A force which Abū ʿAbd Allāh sent to Tripoli to help in regaining that city had no success at all. At this point, the arrival of ʿArūj and Khayr al-Dīn brought some momentary optimism, as can be seen from the account given by a Muslim biographer of the scene of triumph when Khayr al-Dīn returned from an expedition in which a great Spanish ship had been captured[1].

[1] "When Khayr al-Dīn's ship was seen approaching, the entire population hurried down

This scene of euphoria was quickly overshadowed by the realization that these Turks were not likely to remain subordinates of the weak and inefficient local rulers. Only four years later Abū ʿAbd Allāh was refusing help to ʿArūj in his second attempt to recover Bougie from the Spaniards, and soon he was trying to organize an alliance of Arab rulers of North Africa against the Turkish newcomers. Meanwhile, in 1520, he lost Jerba also to the Spanish. On Abū ʿAbd Allāh's death in 1526, he was succeeded by a son, *Mawlāy Ḥasan*, whose accession was challenged by three of his brothers. Two were executed, but a third, Rashīd, took refuge with Khayr al-Dīn in Constantinople, and his claims served as the pretext for the attack on the city in 1534; though once it was captured, the dynasty was declared deposed and a Turkish governor was appointed. Mawlāy Ḥasan thereupon invoked Spanish aid and consented to be replaced on the throne as a protected sovereign, even after his attempts to prevent an appalling massacre of the citizens of his capital by the Spaniards had proved unavailing. His actions were moreover to be overseen from a fortress which the Spaniards built and occupied at Goletta, the port of Tunis, while the Turks were still installed in the seaports of the eastern coast and in the holy city of Qayrawān in the interior. When the Spaniards in these circumstances asked him in 1537 to send troops to assist them in the defence of Tripoli, it is not surprising that he should have replied that the thorns in his eyes were a more urgent problem for him than those in his feet. Five years later when Admiral Doria had cleared the Turks out of the ports, taking possession of them for Spain, he replied to a new request to send troops to Tripoli by saying that he must first take Qayrawān. The latter city had now been evacuated by the Turks, only to become the capital

to the shore, uttering cries of triumph. The hero's first thought on landing was to prepare a suitable gift for the Sultan. Following a long-established Tunisian custom, he dressed the captives in splendid costumes. Thirty mastiffs and twenty greyhounds which had been found on board were distributed to the fifty finest looking slaves, each of whom led one on a leash. Eighty trained falcons which had also been found on board were given one each to Khayr al-Dīn's valiant companions, each of whom carried one on his wrist. In this ingenious way, Christians and Muslims each came forward with the emblem appropriate to him. Four very beautiful Christian girls among the captives were also elegantly dressed and mounted on mules. One of the two Spanish nobles who had been taken had with him two daughters of incomparable charm. These were dressed to match their rank and given splendidly caparisoned horses to ride. The remaining gifts were borne by the Muslim crew. The procession moved forward with the Christians in front and the Muslims following, with their banners flying and their military music playing. The Sultan received them surrounded by his courtiers. After repeatedly congratulating Khayr al-Dīn, and declaring that such success was the reward of valour, he distributed monetary and other rewards to officers and men. Khayr al-Dīn received a robe of honour and a diamond aigrette such as royalty wear, but what pleased him more was the authorization to choose for himself whichever vessel he preferred in the royal arsenal". From *Ghazawāt ʿArūj wa Khayr al-Dīn*, tr. as *Fondation de la Régence d'Alger* by Sander-Rang and Denis, Paris 1837.

of a religious personage, Sīdī ʿArafah, who had organized the Shabbīyah and other nearby Arabs into a militant religious community which seems to have been of similar type to the Sanūsīyah organisation in Libya in recent times. When in 1542 Mawlāy Ḥasan attacked Sīdī ʿArafah's forces with Spanish help, his troops were routed, and he then crossed the sea to Naples to recruit Christian mercenaries as reinforcements. Informed while there that his son, *Aḥmad Sultan* (known as *Ḥamīdah*), the governor of Bône, had rebelled against him, on the grounds of his subservience to the infidels, he hurried back, only to be captured by his son and, after a period of imprisonment, blinded. In this condition he seems to have been allowed considerable liberty and to have become reconciled with the Arabs in Qayrawān, now themselves threatened by a new Turkish leader, *Dragut*, (in Turkish, *Torğud*) in Mahdīyah. In 1548, after visiting the Pope in Rome, he succeeded in obtaining an interview with the Emperor Charles V in Augsburg, appearing before him in Arab dress with a white bandage across his eyes. Having been promised aid, he died in 1549 while accompanying a Spanish expedition off Mahdīyah which in fact captured the city in the following year.

Dragut, who was thus expelled from Mahdīyah, was like ʿArūj an Anatolian corsair who began his career in the Aegean, and later took service under Khayr al-Dīn when the latter became Qapudān Pāshā in 1533. Captured off Corsica in 1540, he was purchased by the Lomellini, bankers of Genoa (then under the Spanish). As soon as he could, Khayr al-Dīn ransomed him for 3,500 ducats, apparently granting the Lomellini at the same time a concession for the valuable coral fishing at Tabarca on the Algerian frontier, which they were to hold for some two hundred years. Restored to liberty, Dragut established himself in Mahdīyah, whence he raided Spanish shipping and possessions. Driven out in 1551, he attempted to make himself a new headquarters in the Tunisian south but was blockaded with his ships in the Jerba channel. From this trap he escaped just in time to join the Turkish fleet coming from Constantinople under Sinān Pāshā and to assist in the capture of Tripoli in 1551. After a period of service in Greece and the Adriatic he was appointed Governor General (*Beylerbey*) of Tripoli in 1556. Thence he moved westwards, occupying Qayrawān and finally displacing the Shabbīyah in 1557. Meanwhile in 1555 ʿAlī Pāshā from Algiers had taken Bougie from the Spaniards. This had made their position in Goletta, now half way between two major Turkish bases, begin to look as hopeless as did that of Aḥmad Sulṭān, himself perilously poised in Tunis where he was receiving specious offers of help from Spanish and Turks alternately. In 1559 Philip II, in an attempt to restore the situation, instructed the Viceroy of Sicily to occupy Jerba as a base for an attack on Tripoli. Jerba was in fact occupied that autumn without difficulty; but in the spring of 1560 the Turks totally defeated the Spanish fleet off the island, sinking 30 ships and taking 5,000 prisoners, after which the garrison were also taken prisoner or killed. It was probably from the remains of these dead that a curious monument of skulls and bones was erected in Jerba and remained a local curiosity, until 1848 when the Tunisian Bey Aḥmad had it destroyed[1].

Though the wheel of fortune now turned in Spain's favour with the successful defence of Malta against the Turkish onslaught of 1565, in which Dragut was killed, Tunis (though not Goletta) was captured by ʿAlī Pāshā in 1569, while Aḥmad Sultan took refuge with the Spanish as his father had done before him. There followed another Spanish counter-triumph in the great naval victory of Lepanto. Encouraged by this success, Philip II sent his half-brother Don John of Austria with an expedition which once more drove the Turks from Tunis. On Philip's express instructions another Ḥafṣid puppet was installed, not however Aḥmad, who refused the terms proposed as too humiliating, but another prince, *Muḥammad*. Once again the city was sacked, during which the Ḥafṣid library was destroyed and the manuscripts scattered in the streets. After this a régime was established which seems to have been modelled on that set up by the Cid in Valencia, during the reconquest of Spain several centuries earlier. The Muslims occupied half the town, while the Christians occupied the other half, in spite of the protests of Muḥammad who wished to re-house there the thousands of refugees sheltering in the environs. For the administration of justice, the Muslim ruler and the Spanish governor Serbelloni sat side by side. This experiment, however, was to last for no more than ten months, after which a joint attack by Sinān Pāshā from Tripoli and by ʿAlī Pāshā from Algiers converged on Tunis, capturing first the city and then Goletta, by this time (1574) a fortress around which a Christian township had grown up. Therewith the Turco-Spanish struggle for control of Tunisia was at last decided in favour of the Muslim power, and the territory became a third Regency *(Ojāq)* like those already created at Algiers and Tripoli.

The events of the preceding 64 years, involving the occupation of

[1] These repeated disasters at Jerba made a deep impression on Spanish memories, which is reflected in the persistence of the refrain "Los Gelves, madre, malos son de ganar" ("Jerba is a bad place to take, mother"), and in a famous line of the poet Garcilaso, who fought at Tunis in 1534, concerning the earlier disaster, "O patria lagrimosa y como vuelves los ojos a los Gelves, sospirando" ("O weeping land and sighing, as you turn your eyes to Jerba").

Tunisian territory by Turks and Spaniards alternatively, and the fivefold capture and recapture of the capital, had dealt the country a terrible blow. In its new capacity as a Turkish dependency Tunis took second place in the area where it had been predominant for some 2,000 years. It was now Algiers, the original and principal Turkish base, which was established as the dominant power in an area including not only the former Kingdom of Tlemsen but also the western provinces of the former Ḥafṣid state, while Tripoli became an independent unit. Moreover the appointment of Khayr al-Dīn from 1533-1546 and of ʿAlī Pāshā from 1571-1589 as Qapudān Pāshā while they were at the same time governors of Algiers helped to create a tradition of Algerian primacy, since the post of Qapudān Pāshā, throughout the period of Turkish domination, seems to have included the general supervision of the North African dependencies, regarded as overseas possessions. This sense of primacy continued even when the post of governor of Algiers was withdrawn from Ḥasan Veneziano on his appointment as Qapudān Pāshā in 1589. The ensuing Algerian pretensions provoked a certain irritation in the minds not only of Tunisian rulers, who remembered the former extension of Tunisian influence in eastern Algeria, but also in those of Moroccans, who cherished the memory of Moroccan supremacy in western Algeria. Theoretically, however, the three Regencies appear to have been regarded as of equal status, at least from the time of ʿAlī Pāshā's death in 1589. Thereafter, in all three Regencies, Turkish authority was represented by Governors General appointed for three years; though officially Beylerbeys, they were henceforth generally referred to as Pāshās.

The change was no doubt inspired by the relative security of Turkish rule in North Africa, now that the great struggle with Spain had reached a stalemate, so that there was no longer the same necessity for a supreme commander on the spot. The result, however, was in fact a gradual decrease in control from Constantinople, and the assumption of power by local officials who tended to set local objectives before the interests of the Ottoman empire as a whole.

The organization of the *Ojāq* of Tunis after 1574 was very similar to that of Algiers. As in the latter, authority was to be exercised by a Pāshā, appointed for three years; he depended on a corps of 4,000 militia recruited from the Levant. As in Algiers, these formed a privileged body, and their pay was a first charge on the finances. As in Algiers, subsidiary troops were raised from the Zawāwah Berbers from the Kabyle country. As in Algiers, too, the power of the militia was balanced by that of the Admiral's faction. In Tunisia likewise the sea-captains were in the main of European origin, and here too Europeans, whether as converts or slaves, played a highly important part in shipbuilding, in administrative posts, and as confidential secretaries and servants. Here too privateering became an industry and a motive for declaring war, which would be fought only in this manner. On the other hand, indigenous elements soon made themselves felt rather more than in Algiers, though at first the Diwān of the Militia tended to arrogate power to themselves, as they did elsewhere. In 1590, however, the forty company-commanders of the militia, known as Deys, massacred the higher officers and appointed one of themselves to share authority with the Āghā or commanding officer, while retaining the designation of *Dey*. The power of this new official tended to increase at the expense of that of the Pāshā, and for about half a century two Deys, *ʿUthmān* (1590-1610) and his son-in-law *Yūsuf* (1610-1637), in practice acted as the Heads of State. In 1606, for the first time, a French envoy dealt directly with the Tunisian authorities as well as through the Porte. Both Deys gave much attention to restoring some degree of discipline among the Arab tribes, never fully reestablished since the collapse of Ḥafṣid rule. The former issued a code of laws, known as the *mīzān;* the latter gave a great extension to privateering, some of the proceeds of which he employed in new constructions. During this period the Deys welcomed a great influx of Morisco refugees from Spain. They settled mainly in the Mejerda valley and on the Cape Bon peninsula, notably at Mejez al-Bab, Krombalia, Zaghouan, Tebourba and Testour—in all in some twenty towns. In the words of a Tunisian chronicler "they planted vines everywhere, made gardens, and for the convenience of travellers opened roads suitable for carriages." They also introduced arts and crafts and promoted the *shāshīyah* (ṭarbūsh) and silk industries. In Yūsuf's time we first hear of fighting between the Regencies of Tunis and Algiers, in spite of abortive efforts by the Porte to prevent this. The underlying cause both then and later was the Tunisian desire to restore the former Tunisian influence in the region of Constantine. Fighting continued intermittently for four years or more; on the whole the Algerians had the best of it, but in the end Yūsuf secured a fairly satisfactory delimitation of the frontier. Meanwhile a new development was taking place within the country. This was the increasing influence of an official, known as the *Bey*, whose functions were the collection of the taxes from the tribes. The second of these Beys, *Murād* (1612–1631), succeeded in obtaining the right to transmit his office to his son, and in securing the title of Pāshā from the Porte. His heir, *Ḥamūdah Bey* (1631–1659), increased the prestige of the post by his handling of the tribes, and succeeded in transferring sovereignty over Jerba back to Tunis from Tripoli, to which it had been subordinate since the time of Dragut.

After the death of the Dey Yūsuf in 1637, Ḥamūdah Bey achieved a completely dominant position, in spite of a succession of over twenty more Deys, and it was he who dealt with a Maltese attack on Goletta in 1640, and refused to yield to Admiral Blake's ultimatum in 1655 when the latter, after destroying nine Tunisian or Turkish ships at Porto Farina, threatened Tunis itself. "We have our subsistence from the land" was Ḥamūdah's reply, "without needing anything from the sea; therefore he that will negotiate with us, let him come ashore...." His successor, *Murād II* (1659–1671), went further and actually imprisoned a Dey, ʿAlī Laz, in 1671, and established himself in semi-sovereign state in the Bardo palace of the Ḥafṣids outside Tunis. His death was followed by civil strife between his brother and his two sons; but the Dey failed to take the opportunity to restore his supremacy. The strife resulted, however, in one party inviting Algerian intervention, and in consequence of this an Algerian force took a principal part in a ten months siege of Tunis. Thus began an Algerian interference in Tunisian affairs which continued intermittently till almost the end of the Turkish period; and this accentuated the vague claim to Algerian supremacy which was always resented and usually successfully resisted by the sister Regency. Although the Algerian Dey Shaʿbān twice succeeded in imposing a Bey of his choice in Tunis between 1688 and 1695, the latter was speedily expelled on both occasions. War broke out again in 1700 when Tunisian troops led by Bey *Murād III* killed the Turkish Bey of Constantine and marched on Sétif, where they were defeated and driven back into Tunisia. There now followed another internal revolution, during which the Āghā or cavalry *(sipāhī)* commander, *Ibrāhīm,* slaughtered the surviving members of the Murādid house, who had attempted to establish themselves as hereditary rulers, and secured his own nomination as Bey (1702). Two years later he secured the rank of Dey also, and then his appointment by the Porte as Pāshā, thus uniting the three leading offices in his own person. In the following year, 1705, he was however killed at Kef while resisting a further Algerian attack. His cavalry commander, *Ḥusayn ibn ʿAlī al-Turkī,* rallied the defeated troops, retired on Tunis where he was himself acclaimed as Bey (1705–1735), and beat off the Algerians. Having abolished the office of Dey, he became de facto ruler, and when in 1710 a meeting of all the leading bodies declared that his son should succeed him as hereditary ruler, he thus founded the dynasty, known as the *Ḥusaynid,* which was to reign over Tunisia for 250 years. Ḥusayn ibn ʿAlī himself ruled for 30 years, of which the first twenty were years of prosperity and tranquillity. The Tunisian writer Muḥammad Ṣaghīr, author of *al-Mashraʿ al-Malikī*, writing some years after Ḥusayn's death, describes the refound security, the repopulation of the countryside, the building of houses, the restoration and fortification of Qayrawān and the construction of aqueducts and other works of public utility. As his presumptive successor, Ḥusayn long recognised his nephew ʿAlī who acted as what was later called the Bey of the Camp, i.e. the official in charge of the annual tax-collecting and order-enforcing tours around the tribes. When, however, his own son by a captive Genoese Christian girl reached the age of 15, Ḥusayn transferred the office of Bey to him, while trying to appease ʿAlī by securing for him the honorific position of Pāshā. ʿAlī first sulked, then rebelled, and finally fled to Algiers. The Dey of Algiers, after giving him hospitality, remained neutral, but later decided to support his claims; and in 1735, an Algerian force captured Tunis, placing ʿAlī on the throne, while the Bey Ḥusayn still maintained himself for a further five years in Qayrawān and its surroundings. In 1740, when the city fell, Ḥusayn was beheaded by his captor, ʿAli's son. The new ruler, known as the *Pāshā ʿAlī* (1735–1756), was an able but ruthless tyrant, who never hesitated to extort by torture the fortunes of any rich man who had the misfortune to arouse his suspicions. Nor was he any more merciful in dealing with the Arab tribes or other opponents. In 1737, he learned from intercepted correspondence that the managers of the French trading establishment near Bône in Algeria, who had a coral-fishing subsidiary at Cap Nègre in Tunisia, were plotting to seize the Genoese post at Tabarca,[1] with a view not only to increasing French trade but also to gaining a site from which they could "dominate Tunisia and all Barbary." The Pāshā therefore anticipated them by himself seizing the Genoese establishment and then that of the French, though later allowing trading to be resumed. Towards the end of his reign, he was faced with the rebellion of his own son, Yūnus. This was defeated, but was followed by an Algerian invasion on behalf of Beys Muḥammad and ʿAlī, the two sons of the uncle whom he had deposed. The expedition was led by the Bey of Constantine, and the capture of the city was marked by an atrocious sack, which the two princes were unable to prevent. After the capture it was only with difficulty that the Algerian Bey of Constantine, who had hoped himself to become ruler, was induced to depart. *Muḥammad* then became Bey, consenting to pay an annual token tribute to Algiers; after a temporary withdrawal, caused by an insurrection of the local Turkish militia in conjunction with some of the

[1] See p. 128 above.

invaders, he reigned for three years (1756–1759). On his untimely death he was succeeded by his brother *'Alī Bey* (1759–1782). Under the rule of the latter, Tunisia achieved a measure of prosperity as it recovered from the effects of the civil strife. 'Alī allowed the French to open new trading settlements at Bizerta and on the island of Galite (1770), and later in the Cape Bon area. This was in spite of a dispute arising from the French annexation of Corsica in 1768 and their demand for the return by Tunis of Corsican shipping seized by the latter when Corsica was still Genoese and as such at war with Tunis.

The next Bey, *Ḥamūdah* (1782–1814), was an active and successful prince. He did not submit to Venetian demands, which were supported by some of the last naval operations undertaken by the Most Serene Republic when they bombarded Sousse in 1784 and destroyed Goletta in 1785. In 1790 he secured favourable terms of peace from Spain, and in 1795 he brought about the restoration of the Pāshā of Tripoli by the despatch of Tunisian forces after the latter had been dispossessed by 'Alī Burghul in 1793[1]. In 1807 and 1813 he successfully resisted Algerian efforts to enforce the token symbols of Algerian supremacy dating from the restoration of 1756, and in 1811 he defeated an insurrection of the Janissaries and greatly reduced their number. It was he who built the handsome Dār al-Bey at the top of the town which serves today as the presidential offices. After the three months' reign of *'Uthmān*, he was succeeded by *Maḥmūd* (1814–1824), in whose reign European slavery was abolished under the pressure of the European powers at the end of the Napoleonic wars, four years after slavery of North African Muslims had been suppressed in the Kingdom of the Two Sicilies. In 1821 the old standing Tunisian-Algerian disagreements were at last settled by a peace arranged by the intervention of the Ottoman Qapudān Pāshā, who sent his secretary as mediator. During the same reign Tunisia despatched a squadron of four vessels under an admiral to assist the Turks during the Greek War of Independence. This was present at the Battle of Navarino in 1827, when three of the vessels were sunk by the French fleet during or after the fighting.

During the reign of the next Bey, *Ḥusayn ibn Maḥmud* (1824–1835), there occurred the French assault on Algiers. The Beys had too often suffered from the Algerian claim to primacy to feel regret at the prospect that the Turkish régime in Algiers might be ended. Supposing that this was the sole object of the French expedition, the Bey's government gave them some assistance and had hopes that Tunisian princes would be established as rulers in Constantine and Oran, as the French commander-

[1] See p. 145 below.

in-chief, Marshal Clauzel, had suggested. Disillusion followed when the French showed their intention of annexing the country, and the next Bey, *Muṣṭafà* (1835–1837), would have been glad to satisfy public opinion by taking direct action to assist the Bey Aḥmad of Constantine in his struggle against the French. The Turks also, whose apprehensions led them in 1835 to resume direct control in Tripoli, would have been glad to intervene in Tunis. This, however, was prevented by the French government, which was already cherishing dreams of extending its rule over Tunisia and had no intention of allowing Turkish sovereignty to achieve a greater reality. The French therefore despatched a naval force to Tunis to forestall any disembarcation of Turkish troops which might be attempted.

As was to occur again during the Algerian liberation struggle, 130 years later, Tunisian intervention had to be confined to the smuggling of arms and supplies to Constantine.

In 1837 a further Turkish project for a disembarcation was again foiled by a French counter-threat.

By this time Tunisia had done what Algeria had never succeeded in doing—forming a national state, modernized to the same extent as oriental states such as Turkey and Egypt. During the next few decades its history is indeed remarkably similar to that of Egypt. *Aḥmad Bey* (1837–1855) was a modernizing and westernizing sovereign in the style of Muḥammad ʿAlī's successors. He suppressed negro slavery, freed the Jews from humiliating restrictions, permitted and encouraged the opening of European schools, and endeavoured (at great expense but with very little success) to create a modern-style army and navy by the employment of European instructors. Meanwhile the increasing strength of the European powers, combined with the financial and administrative inability of the Muslim states to adapt themselves to the conditions of the modern world, caused Tunisia to become the scene of political manoeuvring between the consuls of Great Britain and France for the controlling interest in the country. As early as 1837 a French consul, in connexion with the fixing of the frontier between Tunisia and Algeria, had not only claimed areas which had been Tunisian for over a century, but even suggested that Tunisia ought to pay to France the tribute which the Regency of Algiers had often claimed but rarely received in the past. British policy on the other hand was directed to preserving the independence of the north African states, in order to prevent their occupation by a rival European power.

Towards the end of Aḥmad's reign, the cost of his reforming projects combined with his personal extravagances led to increased taxation which provoked revolts. In the reign of his successor *Muḥammad* (1855–1859), the condemnation to death of a Jew for blasphemy against the Muḥammadan faith led to such pressure being applied by the British consul Sir Thomas Reade and the French consul Léon Roches as to bring about the issue of a Fundamental Pact or Declaration of Rights to which the Bey swore adherence. The utility of such a measure, urged also by the reforming Tunisian statesman, Khayr al-Dīn, was not appreciated by the masses; they merely saw in it the increasing influence of the foreigners, their securing of concessions, and the constantly increasing taxation. In spite of the difficulties, however, the Russo-Turkish war, of which the Crimean campaign was part, led to the despatch first of transport animals and later of 10,000 men from Tunis to Constantinople. This force was employed against the Russians at Batum on the Black Sea, where some 5,000 became casualties.

The final crisis was reached in the reign of *Muḥammad al-Ṣādiq* (French: *Sadok*) (1859–1882). He sought to continue modernization and to disarm European critics by issuing a Constitution based on the Fundamental Pact. In fact, however, reliance on manipulating the dissensions of the foreign powers instead of on self-help had reduced the capability and will to resistance of the authorities to zero. Expenditure mounted and with it taxation, at which the people grumbled as they did at the innovations, of which they did not see the need but only that they were the result of foreign influence. Foreign loans on ruinous terms were negotiated by the Khaznadār (Treasurer) Muṣṭafà, who had been the power behind the throne since 1837 and who made an outrageous personal profit from these transactions. Meanwhile the unification of Italy produced a new candidate for intervention and a dramatic rivalry between the French and the Italian consuls. In 1864 a rising led the Bey to reduce the personal tax, known as *majbā*, which had been imposed by the Khaznadār Muṣṭafà in the preceding reign, and to abolish the Constitution. Popular feeling moved strongly in favour of Turkish intervention, but this was again defeated by French measures. Finally in 1868 an international commission was set up, formed by two Italians and by two British subjects from Malta representing local creditors, two Tunisians, and a French financial expert representing the French bankers who had granted the loans. Tunisia undertook to devote half the state revenue to repayments, these being guaranteed by the customs receipts. In 1873 the Khaznadār Muṣṭafà was at last dismissed and condemned to pay back 35 million francs, which however he managed to avoid doing. Great hopes were put in the assumption of office by Khayr al-Dīn, who was of Circassian origin, originally a slave, and had been prominent in urging liberal measures during the two preceding reigns. In 1871 he had already secured the agreed issue of an imperial *firmān*, which reaffirmed Turkish sovereignty while renouncing any claim to tribute. For four years he now endeavoured to bring the Tunisian administration into reasonable order, only to be dismissed by the Bey in 1877, after which he left for Constantinople where he was for a brief period to hold the post of Grand Vezir. By then the only solid guarantee of Tunisian independence left was the attitude of the British government. In 1878 this too disappeared, when Lord Salisbury withdrew his objections to French plans in Tunisia in return for French acquiescence in British administration of Cyprus. Three years later, in 1881, the French took the pretext of Tunisian tribesmen having advanced into Algerian territory to land one military force at Bizerta, while another crossed into Tunisia from Algeria. They then advanced on the Bey's residence (the Bardo palace) at Kassar Said, and imposed a treaty which authorized French military occupation, withdrew all authority in international relations and finance from the Bey, and provided for the naming of a French Resident Minister to act as intermediary between the French and Tunisian governments in all matters of common interest. The news of the Bey's capitulation provoked a rising in south Tunisia, during which Sfax was bombarded and captured after ten days fighting (July 1881). Qayrawān was occupied in October, Gafsa and Gabes in November. In 1883 the protectorate was made total by the Convention of Marsa, in which the Bey resigned control over internal policy by undertaking to introduce such administrative, judicial, and financial reforms as the French government might consider fit.

## LIBYA

Under the name of the Regency of Tripoli, Libya, like Algeria, became a political unit, with frontiers resembling those of today, as a result of Turkish intervention in the 16th century. Previously the more westerly portion, Tripolitania, had normally been subject, at least nominally, to whatever power ruled in Tunisia. Cyrenaica on the other hand, separated from Tripolitania by 300 miles of desert but relatively accessible from Egypt, generally had closer connexions with the eastern Arab world than with the Maghrib. As a result of immigration by the Arab tribe Banū Hilāl in the 11th century, the easterly province had gradually become a land sparsely inhabited by some 250,000 nomads or semi-nomads, where urban life was confined to two little cities, Benghazi and Derna. The third Libyan province, the Fezzan, consists of oases lying south of Tripoli, containing three little towns and five villages.

The change began with the Spanish capture of Tripoli in 1510. At that time, the city appears to have had some 15,000 to 20,000 inhabitants and to have been the rival of Tunis as a centre of trade. It was the terminus of one major caravan route from the Chad area and of another from West Africa. Its people are said to have been pacific. At the time of the Spanish attack it was administered by a Shaykh, named Ibn Sharaf, apparently a religious personage, who had made himself virtually independent of the Ḥafṣid ruler in Tunis.

The Spanish capture of the city cost them some 300 men, while the inhabitants are said to have lost between 3,000 and 5,000 killed and another 5,000–6,000 carried off as slaves—figures which suggest that they were in fact a normally pacific population. The 15,000 attackers, who included 3,000 Sicilian troops, had sailed from Sicily, and it was under the administration of the Spanish viceroy of that island that the conquered city was placed. An attack on Jerba, made in the heat of August a month later, resulted in the loss of 3,000 men, chiefly due to the failure of the invaders to find water. A similar expedition to the Kerkenna Islands also ended disastrously, with the loss of 400 men.

After the conquest, King Ferdinand the Catholic accepted the view of the Spanish commander, Pedro Navarro, that Tripoli, like Oran and Bougie, should be repopulated with Christians and that the conquest of Tunis should also be at once undertaken. He began himself to make preparations for this enterprise, but was forced to abandon them by more pressing commitments elsewhere. In order to encourage Europeans to settle in the city, offers were made of suitable houses, free land, customs exemptions, and other advantages, but the response was very small. As the Muslim population had fled and were not replaced by Europeans, trade was in fact very limited, and the chief revenue was derived from a poll tax of one ducat on every slave imported or exported. The former Venetian trade with the interior was diverted to Misurata. The authority of the Spanish garrison, which was lodged in the castle, was limited to an area of ten miles around the city and even there was very intermittent. Though a force sent from Tunis by the Ḥafṣid in support of an attempt of the inhabitants to recapture the city had no success, Turkish ships were already appearing threateningly off Tripoli by 1512, and Tajura, only a few miles east of the city, became a headquarters of Muslim resistance. In view of the lack of Christian settlers, encouragement was given to Muslims to return; and the Shaykh Ibn Sharaf, who had originally been exiled to Sicily, was allowed to return to encourage this movement. It does not appear, however, that any considerable number ever came, and in 1526 the Shaykh himself joined his compatriots in Tajura. Meanwhile Algiers had become a Turkish dependency under Khayr al-Dīn, and by 1530 the latter was represented in Tajura by a Turk, bearing the same name as himself, who acted as the Muslim leader against the Christian invaders. In the same year Charles V, in handing over Malta to the Knights of St. John, who had been expelled from Rhodes in 1523, made it a condition that they should take over responsibility for garrisoning Tripoli. This condition they accepted only with great reluctance. Their fears were in fact justified, and the 21 years of their occupation (1530–1551) were a prolonged period of dangerous and unrewarding garrison duty for them, as the 20 preceding years of occupation had been for the Spanish. In 1532 the Turkish presence in Tajura led the Ḥafṣid ruler in Tunis to send another expedition, this time against Khayr al-Dīn's supporters. It received no encouragement from the local Muslims, who made it clear that "they had given themselves to the Grand Turk and would sooner be cut in pieces than return under the crown of Tunis." Three years later, when the Ḥafṣid Mawlāy Ḥasan had become a Spanish satellite, the hopes which the Knights placed in him were shown to be vain, since he was now unable to drive the Turks from the ports in the immediate vicinity of his own capital. The position became desperate with the arrival in the area of the Turkish corsair Dragut.[1] In 1551 the garrison surrendered to Sinān Pāshā who commanded a Turkish fleet which had been sent from Constantinople to attack the city; he had been joined by Dragut when the latter escaped the Spanish blockade in the Jerba channel. Of the defenders, the 100 knights and a hundred of the 500 soldiers went free; the rest were enslaved, while the Muslim auxiliaries were put to death.

As governor of Tripoli Sinān Pāshā installed *Murād Āghā*, a eunuch of Ragusan origin, who had been the Turkish commander at Tajura since 1539. Five years later (1556) he was succeeded by *Dragut*, who received the rank of Beylerbey. Under Dragut's leadership the territory dependent on Tripoli was extended to include the Tunisian south and Jerba, and the latter island did not revert to Tunis until some eighty years later. As a naval commander, Dragut's activities were directed far afield, and we know little concerning the internal affairs of Tripoli during the remainder of his governorship which terminated with his death at the siege of Malta

[1] See under Tunis, p. 128 above.

in 1565. Nine years later, in 1574, the governor of Tripoli, now generally referred to by the title Pāshā, participated in the combined attack from east and west which put a final end to the Spanish intervention and established Turkish rule in Tunis and in the rest of the Maghrib east of Oran. In 1577 the authority of Tripoli was extended to the Fezzan.

The organization of the *Ojāq* or Regency of Tripoli closely resembled that of Tunis and Algiers. Under a *Pāshā (Beylerbey)* appointed from Constantinople, Turkish supremacy was maintained by a force of militia recruited in Turkey. In Tripoli, however, there was this difference that from an early date both renegades and *quloghlus*, that is the sons of Turkish fathers by local women, seem to have been admitted as members. The Pāshā was assisted by a Diwān or Council, administration being in charge of an official known as a *Dey*, while the army was commanded by a *Bey*. In Tripoli too a very important rôle was played by the *Ṭa'ifat al-Ra'īs*, the faction of the Admiral or *Qapudān Ra'īs*.

Having much more limited natural resources than the other two Regencies (a fact concealed from Europeans who knew only the fertile coastal strip), Tripoli was dependent on privateering for its prosperity and for the degree of importance which it managed to attain in the eyes of the European states. Such wealth as was accumulated as the result of the trans-Saharan caravan trade can only have played a secondary role.

Once the Spanish menace was definitely removed, the domination of the Turks soon came to be resented, and Tajura now became a centre of Arab opposition to Turkish rule as it had earlier been of Turco-Arab opposition to Spanish rule. In 1589 a *murābiṭ* from Morocco, who claimed to be the Mahdī, headed a revolt; while in 1614 complaints to the Sulṭān concerning the conduct of the Dey Sulaymān led to his arrest and execution. In the 17th century, the two most successful rulers were converted Greeks, both originally from the island of Chios and therefore known as Saqizly, which has that meaning in Turkish. The first, *Muḥammad* (1632–1649), had lived in Algiers as a Christian for some years and then adopted Islām and the profession of privateer. Coming to Tripoli he took service under the Pāshā *Ramaḍān*, whose daughter he married. Considerable influence was exercised in Tripoli at this time by a remarkable Arab woman, Maryam al-Shiblīyah,[1] whose husband was a member of the militia and in whose house the Diwān took to meeting. It is said to have been through her favour that Muḥammad was elected Dey, after which Ramaḍān

[1] Rossi in his translation of Ibn Ghalbūn's history suggests that she came from the Awlād Shibl tribe south west of Gharian. Féraud in his *Annales Tripolitaines* assumes her to be of Spanish Arab origin, connecting her name with Ishbīlīyah (Seville); this might accord better with her unusual position.

gladly handed over to him the exercise of power. Once in possession of executive authority, he reorganized the system of taxation and appointed his compatriot ʿUthmān, also a former Christian, to high military command. Trouble with the Fezzan was settled by an agreement under which Turkish troops were withdrawn, in return for the acknowledgement that an annual tribute should be paid. Tripolitanian authority was also asserted in Cyrenaica, where it became the custom for it to be exercised by an official with the title Bey, normally a son or brother of the ruler. In external relations, Muḥammad reduced privateering, making peace with Great Britain. Though he had achieved power with Arab aid, he then took steps to reduce Arab influence, and is accused of having done away with Maryam al-Shiblīyah after having first disposed of her husband and then married her himself. In 1649 he died (according to the rumour, by poison), and his compatriot *ʿUthmān* (1649–1672) was chosen as successor by the leading officials. ʿUthmān began his 23 years rule by remitting some of the taxes imposed by his predecessor and by securing the Porte's approval of his appointment. By degrees he filled most of the leading posts with men of Christian origin like himself. He also monopolized commerce in his own hands, imposed fresh taxes on the ownership of land, and gave a renewed extension to privateering. Accused by the ship's officers and crews of persistent meanness in his treatment of them, he was finally faced with a conspiracy and, considering that his position was hopeless, committed suicide.

His death was followed by a period of anarchy, which lasted for forty years as 22 Deys succeeded one another in rapid succession. The abuse of privateering led to bombardments by the British in 1676 and the French in 1685.

This epoch was ended in 1711 by the assumption of power by *Aḥmad Qaramānly*, who was to reign for 34 years (1711–1745) and establish a dynasty which lasted for a century and a quarter. In the first half of this period, Tripoli acquired a reputation for prosperity and power which was quite out of proportion to its man-power and its natural resources.

The Qaramānly family had come to Tripoli from Anatolia some generations earlier, and by 1700 had become naturalized by residence and by intermarriage with Arabs. In 1711 Aḥmad was a prepossessing young man of 25 years of age. He came to power by popular acclaim after the murder of a Dey called *Muḥammad*, nicknamed *Ibn al-Jinn*, which was followed by the suicide of the assassin who had tried to establish himself in the murdered man's place.

At the moment of Aḥmad's accession to power, the spirit of disorder and the wretched state of the country were such that the European consuls present in Tripoli saw little prospect of success for the new ruler. In fact he had to deal immediately not only with the internal anarchy but with the arrival from Constantinople of a dispossessed former Pāshā, Khalīl, bearing a *firmān* authorizing his reestablishment. Without ever directly rejecting the Sultan's authority, Aḥmad managed to dispose both of this attempt and of the efforts of two subsequent envoys. By 1714 signs of a reconciliation were evident when the Sultan, to whom he had sent valuable gifts, presented him with two fully armed ships. Like many of those used by the Muslim privateers, these were prizes, one of which had been taken from the Knights of Malta, the other from the Venetians. Aḥmad had, however, still to deal with risings in both Cyrenaica and the Fezzan and to bring to a successful issue difficult diplomatic discussions with the French, whom he played off successfully against the English, before it became apparent that his régime had come to stay. So far he had acted simply in the capacity of Bey, leaving the position of Dey to the stepfather who had brought him up and to whom his devotion was one of his most pleasing characteristics. After the latter's death the post of Dey was allowed to lapse, and when in 1719 Aḥmad was appointed by the Porte Beylerbey or Governor General, a post which carried with it the title of Pāshā, he passed the appointment of Bey to his step-brother to whom he was equally devoted. Subsequently all sons of the ruler were known as Beys.

According to an English resident in Tripoli sixty years after these events, Aḥmad at some early period of his rule reduced the power of the Janissaries by a large scale massacre. There are a number of parallels for such action, but in this case no confirmation exists.

Aḥmad was now able to establish a definite government organization and to devote attention to the improvement of agriculture and the establishment of some minor industries. He was an absolute ruler, advised by a Diwān. The senior Bey was responsible for the army and security; this post was normally held, as in Tunis, by a brother or son of the ruler. The fleet and arsenal were the responsibility of the Qapūdān Ra'īs, who was also in charge of the customs. Civil administration was the affair of the *Kāhyā*; finance that of the *Khaznadār*. The Governor of Tripoli city was known as the *Shaykh*; district governors as *Qā'ids*. A number of Secretaries of State formed a body from which ambassadors were chosen when required for foreign missions. Justice was frequently rendered by the Pāshā in person. Revenue was derived from customs, from tribal, personal, and agricultural taxes, and from the annual payments made by

Venice for a concession for the extraction of salt at Bū Kamash, near the Tunisian border. Some revenue was also derived from the trans-Saharan traffic which debouched in Tripoli and from the annual arrival of the Moroccan and Algerian pilgrim caravans on their way to and from Mecca. The limited foreign trade was for the most part carried in European ships, partly because European privateering, especially Maltese, Sicilian, and that of the Tuscan Knights of St. Stephen, was at least as prejudicial to Muslim shipping as Muslim privateering was to Christian. In favourable times much profit was derived from privateering, though like other commercial undertakings this could also result in heavy losses, apart from the destruction periodically caused by bombardments by European fleets. The deposition of Pasha Khalīl, mentioned above, had in fact been due in part to the discredit which he had incurred from the destruction in the Adriatic of two Tripolitanian ships at the hands of Maltese galleys, with the loss of 300 men killed and 400 captured and enslaved – the best part of the Tripolitan crews of the time.

In naval attacks on Tripoli, however, as on the other Regencies, the European powers were to some extent restrained by their fear that a break with Turkey might result if they made demands which went beyond enforcement of the internationally observed conventions concerning privateers. Difficulties were caused for them by the fact that the Porte was by no means always able to enforce its orders upon the Regencies. One unfortunate result of alleged violations of the accepted rules by either party, or of rumours of ill-treatment of captives, was the probability that reprisals would be taken against the unfortunate captives in the possession of the party which felt itself aggrieved.

While never entirely free from conspiracies and rebellions or from occasional reprisals from foreign powers, the second half of Aḥmad Qaramānly's reign was the golden age of the Regency of Tripoli. The economic position was favourable; the city's fortifications were strengthened, and the city itself embellished by a number of handsome monuments, of which the still existing Qaramānly mosque is a fine example. As the years passed, however, Aḥmad began to lose his sight. At the age of 59 his condition had become such that he committed suicide by shooting himself, preferring to end his life thus rather than to live on in sightless impotence.

His successor was his second son *Muḥammad* (1745-1754), who had been designated in his father's lifetime and had already proved his merit by his conduct of affairs. His elder brother, whom he appointed Bey of Benghazi, accepted the subordinate position without a struggle, even when some of his intimates were accused of treachery and executed. An attempt at invasion from Tunis by the sons of the executed men was defeated. A more serious problem was caused by the rebellion of corsair captains who objected to the ruler's determination to keep their activities within legitimate bounds. After this had been suppressed, a rising in eastern Cyrenaica led Muḥammad to increase the number of Turkish militia by recruiting some hundreds from the Smyrna area. Order was restored, but the Pāshā himself died at the early age of 45.

There followed the long reign of his son *ʿAlī* (1754-1794). A generally amiable but undecided character, timid but sometimes cruel, he placed his confidence mainly in converted Christians, whom he made his principal advisers and officials. As so frequently with despotic dynasties, the prosperity created by a vigorous founder was dissipated by his less energetic successor. Twenty five years of weak government produced neither the profits of successful privateering nor of peace. There followed several years of drought which caused a famine, from which large numbers died in the streets of Tripoli in spite of supplies of wheat sent by the Sultan of Morocco.

The famine was succeeded by an outbreak of plague (1785), which is said to have carried off two fifths of the Muslim population. In 1786 the French consul reported that the Pāshā now reigned only over rebellious subjects, sterile lands, and heaps of ruined masonry. Such trade as survived was almost entirely with Leghorn and in the hands of Jews, who dealt with their coreligionists in the Tuscan port. The situation was made worse by the dislike of the two younger sons, Aḥmad and Yūsuf, for their elder brother Ḥasan, who was energetic, gave evidence of competence, and was regarded as the heir. The most aggressive of the two was Yūsuf, for whom his father the Pāshā seemed to have a preference and whom his tolerant eldest brother described as 'that beautiful, rash youth'. Each brother had his armed retainers, and there was general apprehension that a catastrophe would occur. This was a constant cause of anxiety to their mother, the Pāshā's wife, so that she was delighted when Yūsuf came to her one day and told her that he wished to be reconciled with his eldest brother in her presence. Having invited her eldest son, unarmed, to the meeting, she witnessed the scene when Yūsuf, having thus lured his brother away from his guards, shot him in her presence and then ordered his guard to kill the wounded prince (1790). The only action taken by the Pāshā, whose indecision had been worsened by a stroke three years earlier, was to transfer Yūsuf to Misurata as governor. Here his insubordination increased; in the following year he was actually besieging Tripoli. In these circumstances, the city's inhabitants sent a message to the Sultan in Constantinople requesting his intervention.

This request was not unwelcome to the Sultan, who was anxious to display his authority. His choice of a personality to carry out the major operation of deposing the Qaramānlys fell on a Georgian renegade, known as ʿAlī al-Jazā'irī. After serving as Qapudān Ra'īs in Algiers, he had been dismissed and had taken up residence in Constantinople with his brother who was vice-admiral of the Turkish fleet. With the assent of the Sultan and the assistance of his brother, he undertook to raise a force, occupy the Regency, restore order, and pay a regular annual tribute to the Porte. In July 1793 he appeared off Tripoli, with a small armament flying the Ottoman flag, and sent ashore an official with 400 armed men, who read a document alleged to be a *firmān* of the Sultan declaring ʿAlī Qaramānly deposed and himself appointed in his stead, adding that in case of opposition the Qapudān Pāshā would arrive in person with a large force. ʿAlī Qaramānly wished to resist, but received little support, and at midnight fled in the direction of Tunis, with his eldest son Aḥmad and a small escort. ʿAlī al-Jazā'irī, or ʿAlī Burghul, as he came to be known locally, proceeded to instal himself in the Castle. After seeing his father to safety, Aḥmad returned, and when his brother Yūsuf joined him, they endeavoured to retake the city. When the attempt failed, they both followed the Pāshā to Tunis. ʿAlī Burghul then instituted a reign of terror. He not only tyrannized over the people of Tripoli, but also seized a Tunisian ship in Tripoli harbour, sent a force to occupy Jerba, and threatened to attack the seaports on the Tunisian east coast. This provoked the Bey of Tunis, and in November 1794 a Tunisian force recaptured Jerba and advanced on Tripoli, accompanied by Aḥmad and Yūsuf. Seeing that his position was hopeless, the usurper, after massacring his prisoners and some hostages, fled with the booty which he had collected. The Pāshā, thus restored, abdicated in favour of the elder son, who succeeded with the title of *Aḥmad II* (1795). In applying to the Porte for investiture, Aḥmad emphasized the misgovernment of ʿAlī Burghul and the tradition of Tripoli's submission to the Qaramānlys 'from father to son'. Meanwhile he gave himself up to easy living and excessive drinking, with the result that within six months Yūsuf had declared 'the drunkard' deposed and had himself been acclaimed by popular consent as head of state, with the acquiescence of his father, the former Pāshā. The deposed Aḥmad was offered and accepted the post of Bey in Cyrenaica, but having been driven into Malta by a storm changed his mind and retired to Tunis.

It is a remarkable fact that *Yūsuf Qaramānly* (1795-1834), who had murdered his eldest brother, rebelled against his father, and deposed his other elder brother, proved to be an able ruler, who made a favourable impression on well-informed European observers. "A just, pacific and liberal prince", was the description given of him by the Danish consul in Tripoli. "A fine looking man", was the comment of the Spaniard Badía y Leblich; "he is not without spirit, speaks good Italian, likes display and magnificence, and conducts himself with dignity without any lapse in manners or courtesy. After ten and a half years reign his people are contented with him".

Under Yūsuf's rule, the Regency recovered much of its former prosperity; to a considerable extent this was due to the Napoleonic wars, which offered a last chance to old-time privateering. Yūsuf profited from his constant support of Bonaparte. On the other hand he came into conflict with the United States, with whom he was at war from 1801 to 1805. During the attempted American blockade, the frigate Philadelphia was lost to the Tripolitanians and its 300 crew were captured. When the European wars came to an end, the decisions of the powers against North African privateering, together with the circumstances which were everywhere bringing about the disappearance of small city sea-powers, gave rise to an entirely new situation. Tripoli's natural resources were more limited than those of its neighbours. The French invasion of Algeria was the final blow. In 1834 Yūsuf abdicated and was succeeded by his son *ʿAlī II*. The succession was disputed, and this gave the Turks a pretext for intervention which they regarded, no doubt correctly, as the only hope of preventing a European occupation and preserving their own sovereignty. In 1835 a Turkish fleet deported all the leading Qaramānlys, and the Porte resumed direct control. For three quarters of a century Tripoli, and with it the Fezzan and Cyrenaica, became Turkish provinces, sharing the same sort of limited modernization as was the lot of the rest of the Ottoman Empire.

The most notable event of this period was the establishment in Cyrenaica of the Sanūsī fraternity or order. This was the work of a Muslim man of religion, *Muḥammad ibn ʿAlī al-Sanūsī*, who had come from Mazuna, once the capital of the western *beylik* of Algeria, and had spent in all some twenty years in religious studies in Arabia. In 1843 he established a *zāwiyah* or lodge at al-Bayḍā', some miles from the ruins of Cyrene in eastern Cyrenaica. From this original centre, the fraternity developed a missionary activity which spread into central Africa and to some extent into inland Tripolitania, Egypt, and beyond; this resulted in the creation of a network of lodges which preached a simple, rather puritanical Islām, giving the beduin a knowledge of their religion and a sense of unity within the fraternity. Its activities have been described as the promotion of justice, peace, trade, and education. In order to be freer from the disturbing influences of the coastal area, the Grand Sanūsī, as the founder was called, moved his headquarters to the oasis of Jaghbūb near the Egyptian frontier; in 1895 it was moved by his son *Muḥammad al-Mahdī* to the much more remote southern oasis of Kufra. In the Islāmic world such movements rarely fail to acquire political significance, particularly when the leadership of the order, as in this case, becomes hereditary in the family of the founder. For this reason the Sanūsī organization was regarded by the Turkish authorities with considerable suspicion, though they sympathized with and supported it in its resistance to the steady French infiltration from Chad and Tibesti in the south.

In 1908 the Turkish revolution gave a fresh impulse to Turkish reforming efforts in Tripolitania and Cyrenaica. Before these could bear fruit, however, an entirely new situation was created by the Italian invasion of 1911. The Italians had long had commercial and banking interests in the country, and having seen the French forestall them in Tunisia had finally decided to seize for themselves the only portion of north Africa not already occupied, or ear-marked for occupation, by another European power.

## THE SA'DIAN DYNASTY

- Muḥammad al-Qā'im bi Amrillāh
  - Aḥmad al-A'raj, 1525-1541 (Marrakesh)
  - Muḥammad al-Shaykh al-Mahdī, 1554-1557 (1541-1554 in Marrakesh)
    - 'Abd Allāh al-Ghālib billāh, 1557-1574
      - Muḥammad al-Mutawakkil, 1574-1576
    - 'Abd al-Malik, 1576-1578
    - Aḥmad al-Manṣūr, 1578-1603
      - Muḥammad al-Shaykh al-Ma'mūn, 1603-1613 (Fez)
        - 'Abd Allāh, 1613-1623 (Fez)
        - 'Abd al-Malik ibn al-Shaykh, 1623-1626 (Fez)
      - Zaydān, 1603-1627, Claimant till 1608 (Mainly in Marrakesh)
        - Abū Marwan 'Abd al-Malik, 1627-1631 (Marrakesh)
        - al-Walīd, 1631-1636 (Marrakesh)
        - Muḥammad al-Shaykh al-Aṣghar, 1636-1654 (Marrakesh)
          - Aḥmad al-'Abbās, 1654-1659 (Marrakesh)
      - Abū'l-Fāris Abd Allāh al-Wāthiq, Pretender in Marrakesh, 1603
      - Aḥmad, Pretender in Fez, 1627

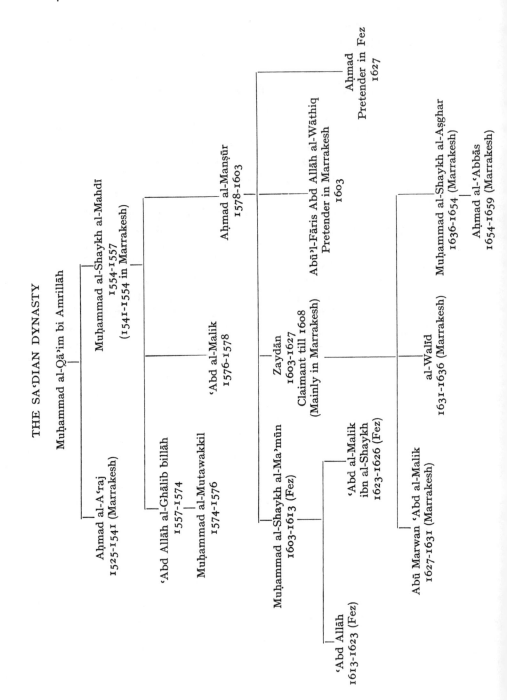

THE 'ALAWITE DYNASTY

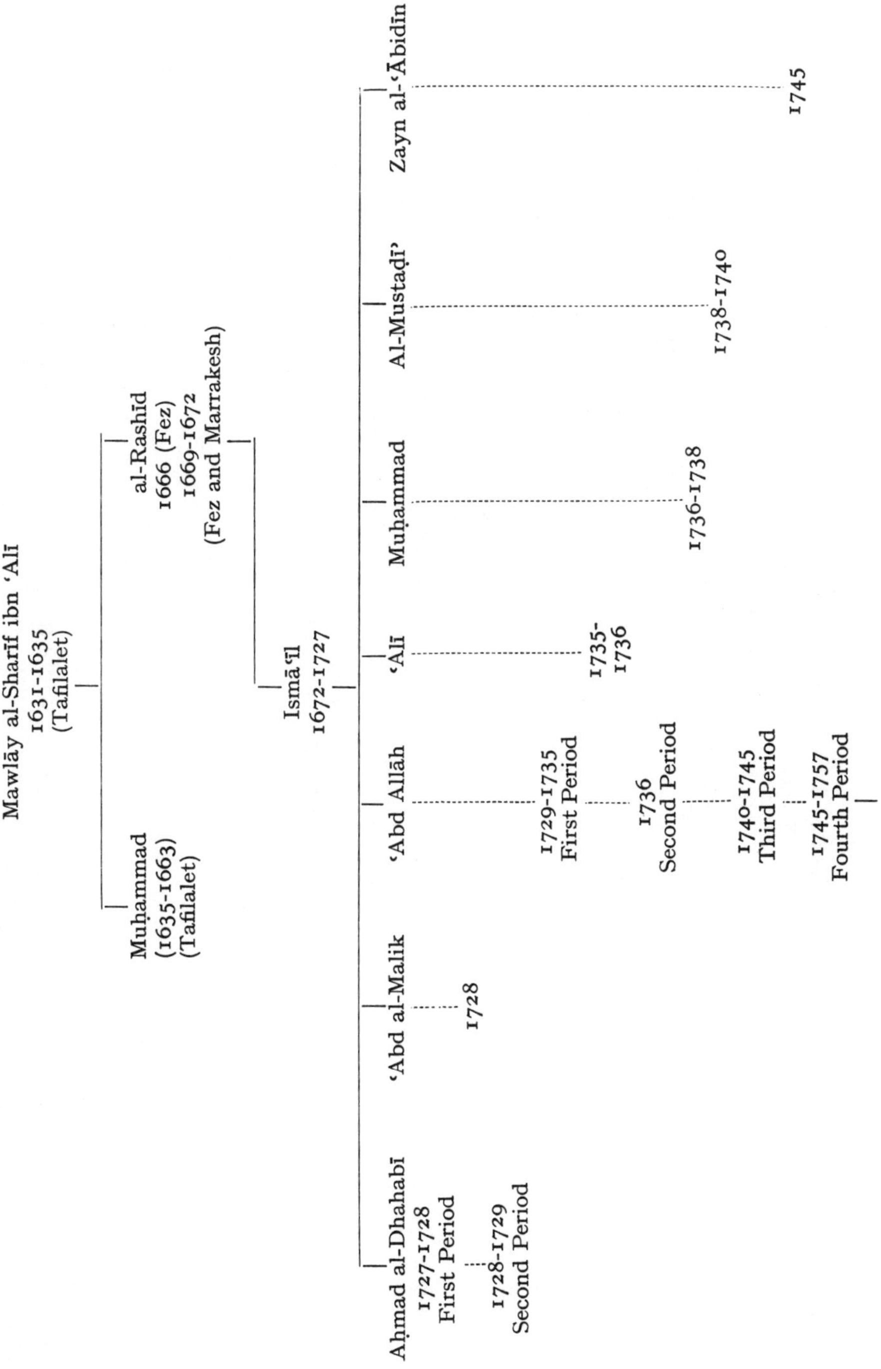
Mawlāy al-Sharīf ibn 'Alī
1631-1635
(Tafilalet)
Muḥammad
(1635-1663)
(Tafilalet)
al-Rashīd
1666 (Fez)
1669-1672
(Fez and Marrakesh)
Ismā'īl
1672-1727
Aḥmad al-Dhahabī
1727-1728
First Period
1728-1729
Second Period
'Abd al-Malik
1728
'Abd Allāh
1729-1735
First Period
1736
Second Period
1740-1745
Third Period
1745-1757
Fourth Period
'Alī
1735-
1736
Muḥammad
1736-1738
Al-Mustaḍī'
1738-1740
Zayn al-'Ābidīn
1745

Muḥammad b. ʿAbd Allāh
1757-1790

al-Yazīd
1790-1792

Sulaymān
1792-1822

Hishām
1791-1796
(Claimant in Marrakesh)

ʿAbd al-Raḥmān
1822-1859

Muḥammad
1859-1873

al-Ḥasan I
1873-1894

ʿAbd al-ʿAzīz
1894-1908

ʿAbd al-Ḥafīẓ
1908-1912

Yūsuf
1912-1927

Muḥammad V*
1927-1961

al-Ḥasan II
1961-

(Arafah)

(Muḥammad
ibn ʿArafah)

* During the two years 1953-1955 while Muḥammad V was exiled the throne was occupied by Muḥammad ibn ʿArafah.

The above tables are based on E. DE ZAMBAUR, *Manuel de Généalogie* (Hanover 1927); H. TERRASSE, *Histoire du Maroc*, Vol. II (Casablanca 1950); Coloured sheet of ʿAlawite sovereigns issued with sanction of the Palace in Rabat (Ed. Mars; Casablanca, undated); DE CASTRIES, *Doc. Inédits*, 1st series, France, Bibliography, Index.

## BIBLIOGRAPHICAL NOTES

The period 1500–1930 is covered in CHARLES-ANDRÉ JULIEN, *Histoire de l'Afrique du Nord*, Paris 1931, pp. 548–743. A 2nd ed., including only the section from the Arab invasion to 1830, was edited by ROGER LE TOURNEAU, Paris 1961. Both contain full bibliographies or bibliographical references. The following notes are explanatory or supplementary to them and to the bibliographical references in the *Encyclopaedia of Islam* (1st and 2nd eds.)

### GENERAL

N. BARBOUR ed., *A Survey of North West Africa (The Maghrib)*, 2nd ed., Oxford 1961, covers the whole area. It contains a brief list of Spanish works referring to Morocco. Since 1962, the CENTRE D'ÉTUDES NORDAFRICAINES at Aix-en-Provence publishes an *Annuaire*, treating historical, geographical, sociological and legal subjects; these include Libya.

### PRIVATEERING

SALVATORE BONO, *I corsari barbareschi*, Turin, E.R.I., 1964, with 63 pages of annotated bibliography, particularly detailed on Italian sources. JEAN MONLAÜ, *Les états barbaresques*, Paris 1964, a brief but useful survey in the *Que sais-je?* series. Three articles on privateering, slavery and redemption by H. DE GRAMMONT in *Revue Historique*, XXV, XXVI and XXVII, Paris 1884–85. R. COINDREAU, *Les corsaires de Salé*, Paris 1948, a valuable study.

### SLAVERY

No comprehensive study exists. There is a useful brief account of slavery in Tunisia 1590–1620 by J. PIGNON, *L'esclavage en Tunisie*, in *Revue Tunisienne*, 1930, pp. 18–37. Valuable accounts by Christian captives are, for Morocco: M. TER MEETELEN, *L'Annotation ponctuelle*, tr. from the Dutch, Paris 1956; T. PELLOW, *The Adventures of T. Pellow*, ed. R. BROWN, London 1890; G. MOUETTE, *Relation de la captivité du Sieur Mouette*, Paris 1653, tr. as *Travels* in STEVENS, *New Collection of Voyages*, vol. II, London 1711; for Algeria: F. KNIGHT, *Relation of Seven Years Slavery in Algiers*, in T. OSBORNE, *Collection of Voyages*, London 1748; THÉDENAT, *Une cour africaine au 18ième siècle* in *Revue Africaine*, 1848; E. D'ARANDA, *Relations de la Captivité*, Amsterdam 1651; F. PANANTI, *Narrative of a Residence in Algiers*, tr. from the Italian by E. BLANQUIÈRE, London 1818; and a number of references in the works of MIGUEL DE CERVANTES.

References to Muslim slavery in Europe are found in R. CAVALIERO, *The Last Crusader*, London 1961, which gives references to Maltese archives; JOHN EVELYN, *Diaries*, ed. AUSTIN DOBSON, London 1906, vol. I, p. 139; VICENTA CORTÉS, *La esclavitud en Valencia durante el reinado de los Reyes Católicos 1479–1516*, Valencia, Exmo. Ayuntamiento, 1964 (gives detailed statistics of sales, lists of names, and much information on conditions at the beginning of the 16th cent.); P. MOLMENTI, *La vie privée à Venise*, French ed., Venice 1896, vol. II, pp. 165–169; A. TENENTI in *Rivista Storica Italiana*, LXV 2, 1955; A. TRIA, *La schiavitù in Liguria*, Genoa 1947; H. LAPEYRE, *Géographie de l'Espagne mauresque*, Paris 1959, p. 182; J. VERNET GINÉS, *El Rescate del Arraez Argeli Bibi*, Tetuan 1952; R. CAPOT REY in *Revue Africaine*, 1934, p. 464; P. GRANDCHAMP, *La France en Tunisie*, 3 vols., Paris 1920, passim; T. ZAMMIT, *History of Malta*, Valletta 1929, p. 248; P. BORONAT Y BARRACHINA, *Los moriscos espanoles y su expuslión*, Valencia 1901, pp. 311–312. OSMAN AGHA, *Der Gefangene der Giauren*, German tr. with introd. and notes by R. F. KREUTEL and OTTO SPIES, Graz, Wien, Köln, Verlag Styria, 1962 (*Osmanische Geschichtsschreiber*, hrsgb. v. DR. R. F. KREUTEL, IV). ISMET PARMAKSIZOGLU, *Bir Türk kadisinin esaret hatiralari*, Istanbul, *Tarih Dergisi V.*, 1953, p. 71.

### MOROCCO

Vol. 2 of HENRI TERRASSE's scholarly and detailed *Histoire du Maroc* covers the years 1500–1912. Arabic sources are listed and analysed in E. LÉVI-PROVENÇAL, *Les historiens du Chorfa*, Paris 1927. The volumes of *Hesperis* (organ of the former École des Hautes Etudes Marocaines at Rabat), Paris 1921–1959, contain many important articles; this publication is now amalgamated with the former corresponding Spanish publication in

Tetuan as *Hesperis-Tamuda*, Rabat 1960. HENRI DE CASTRIES, *Les sources inédites de l'histoire du Maroc*, 21 vols., Paris 1905—, contains a wealth of documents, with summaries and notes in French, from French, English, Dutch, Portuguese and Spanish archives, dealing with the Saʿdian and early ʿAlawite periods. F. R. FLEURNOY, *British, policy towards Morocco 1830–1865*, Baltimore 1935, is excellent. J. L. MIÈGE, *Le Maroc et l'Europe*, 3 vols., Paris 1961–1964, gives detailed documentation of economic relations before the Protectorate.

## ALGERIA

There is no complete scholarly history. DIEGO DE HAEDO, *Topografía y historia general de Argel*, Valladolid 1612, reprinted Madrid 1906, French tr. in *Revue Africaine* 1870, 1871, is the best contemporary European source for the early Turkish period; the best Muslim sources are *Ghazawāt ʿArūj wa Khayr al-Dīn*, tr. SANDER RANG et DENIS, 2 vols., Paris 1837, and MUṢṬAFA IBN ʿABD ALLĀH KĀTIB CHELEBĪ (ḤĀJJĪ KHALĪFAH), *Tuḥfat al-Kibār fī Asfār al-Biḥār*, Constantinople 1728, partial tr. by J. MITCHELL as *History of the Maritime Wars of the Turks*, London, Oriental Translation Fund, 1833. H. DE GRAMMONT, *Histoire de la domination turque en Algerie*, Paris 1887, is valuable, but prejudiced and chiefly concerned with relations with France. The volumes of the *Revue Africaine*, Alger 1856—, are valuable. Consular life in Algiers from 1806 to 1812 is described in E. BROUGHTON, *Six Years Residence in Algiers*, London 1839, pp. 1–258. Useful studies of the closing period have been made by PIERRE BOYER, *La vie quotidienne à Alger à la veille de intervention française*, Paris 1966, and by H. G. BARNBY, *The prisoners of Algiers: an account of the forgotten American-Algerian war 1785–1797*, London 1966. PLAYFAIR, *The scourge of Christendom*, London 1884, must be used with great caution.

## TUNISIA

There is no complete history. A. ROUSSEAU, *Annales tunisiennes*, Alger 1864, and A. PELLEGRIN, *Histoire de la Tunisie*, Tunis 1944, must be used with caution. Valuable articles in *Revue Tunisienne*, Tunis 1894—. Among Arabic sources, ṢAGHĪR IBN YŪSUF, *K. al Mashāriʿ al-malikī*, tr. SERRÈS et LADGHAM, Paris 1900, illuminates the beginning of Ḥusaynid rule; IBN ABĪ DĪNĀR AL-QAYRAWĀNĪ, *Kitāb al-Mu'nis*, Tunis 1286 A.H., French tr. in *Exploration scientifique de l'Algérie*, vol. VII, Paris 1845, is useful for the second half of the 17th cent.

## LIBYA

There is no complete history. ENRICO ROSSI, *Il dominio degli Spagnoli e dei Cavalieri di Malta a Tripoli*, Rome 1937, covers 1510–1551. R. MICACCHI, *La Tripolitania e i Caramanli*, Rome 1936, covers 1706–1835. Both have bibliographical notes. C. BERGNA, *Tripoli dal 1510–1850*, Tripoli 1925, was not accessible to the author. The most substantial Arabic source is IBN GHALBŪN, *Kitāb al-tidhkār fī man malaka Tarābulus*, Cairo 1349 A.H., annotated Italian tr. by E. ROSSI, Bologna 1936. An interesting consular view at the end of the 18th cent. in R. TULLY, *Letters during a ten years Residence at the Court of Tripoli*, London 1857, new ed. London 1957. On the rise of the Sanūsīs, NICOLA A. ZIADEH, *Sanūsīyah, a study of a revivalist movement in Islam*, Leiden 1958. C. FÉRAUD, *Annales Tripolitaines*, ed. A. BERNARD, Paris and Tunis 1927, must be regarded with caution.

# ISLAM IN SUB-SAHARAN AFRICA, TILL THE 19TH CENTURY

BY

J. SPENCER TRIMINGHAM

abbreviated & adapted

BY

F. R. C. BAGLEY

Islam was carried into sub-Saharan Africa over land and by sea. The principal land routes led from Morocco into the Upper Niger and Senegal regions (Western Sudan); from Tripolitania and Tunisia into the Lake Chad region (Central Sudan); and from Egypt into the Nilotic Sudan. The sea routes led from the Yaman, the Ḥijāz and Egypt, and from the Persian Gulf, to the Red Sea, Gulf of Aden and Indian Ocean coasts. In general the African peoples who were won to Islam fell into three categories: nomadic peoples whose way of life bore some resemblance to that of beduin Arabs; peoples who had already developed a basis of urban mercantile culture and large-scale state organization; and detribalized inhabitants of towns and ports and their environs. Among the agricultural and cattle-breeding peoples, with their generally isolated and self-sufficient economies and their closely knit tribal and family structures, Islam made little or no progress. The early spread of Islam took place in the 11th-16th centuries, when the heartlands of the Muslim world were experiencing a recoil from legalism[1]; and the new Muslim centres in Africa were very remote from the heartlands. In these circumstances, the introduction of Islam did not in general necessitate abandonment of African customs and ideas or adoption of Islamic institutions. Although rulers sometimes promoted Islamic institutions as instruments of state-building, the *sharī'ah* was observed, if at all, only in urban centres. To a large extent this is still the case today. In the 18th and 19th centuries, however, a number of militant movements, striking out equally against lax Muslims and against

[1] The trend away from legalism was linked, in the Muslim heartlands, with the popularization of Ṣūfism in the form of *darvīsh* orders. There is no evidence that Ṣūfism was important in negro Africa until the early 19th century, when the Qādirīyah, long established among the Saharan Moors, and the recently formed Tijānīyah, won large followings in both Western and Central Sudan. (The Tijānīyah was founded by Ahmad al-Tijānī (1737–1815) of Fez; the Qādirīyah by 'Abd al-Qādir al-Gīlānī (1077–1166) of Baghdād).

pagans, gave rise to the formation of some more strictly Islamic states and societies and to a considerable further spread of Islam. After the end of the period of this study, Islam made more gains, partly because the European authorities promoted urbanization and because some of them made use of Islamic institutions, which they could understand better than indigenous customs. In the modern independence movements and independent régimes, secular nationalism rather than Islam appears to have exercised most influence on the leaders.

## THE WESTERN SUDAN

In this region, the pastures of the Sāḥil (sub-Saharan steppe) supported Berber tribes, who were grouped in the Ṣanhājah confederation and were known as "veiled" Berbers from their custom of muffling the face. The oases, and the Senegal and Niger banks, supported Negro agriculturists, who warred and traded with the Berbers. Islam began to penetrate later than in the Maghrib, but by the 10th century had won a foothold among the Berbers. The definite conversion of the Ṣanhājah was brought about through the Almoravide (*Murābiṭ*) movement in the 11th century. Many of the Berbers migrated northwards in the armies of the Almoravide general Yūsuf ibn Tāshfīn (1056-1106), who conquered the Maghrib and later Muslim Spain. In the western part of the region, an Arab tribe from the Maghrib, the Maʿqil, immigrated during the 13th-14th centuries and merged with the local Berbers, who since then have spoken a form of Arabic and are known as "Moors".[1] Further east, above the northward bend of the Niger, the Berbers have kept their language and their blue veils, and are known as "Tuareg" (Ṭawāriq, sing. Ṭāriqī).

Requirements of defence and trade may explain why organized Negro states arose in the Sāḥil. By the 9th century the Berbers, having increased in numbers and cohesion, pressed upon the Negroes in the oases and either pushed them towards the Senegal river or subjugated them as tribute-paying cultivators. The Sahara had never been an insuperable obstacle to contact between the Mediterranean and Negro worlds. Berber caravans carried on an important traffic in gold, which they bartered for salt, always a precious commodity in inland Africa, and for Mediterranean goods. The Negro states obtained the gold from lands further south, while the Berbers extracted the salt from deposits in the Sahara. Arabic sources

[1] The Maʿqil were descended from the Banū Hilāl and Sulaym tribes which entered the Maghrib from Egypt and Arabia in the 11th century. The Mauritanian "Moors" are sometimes called Shanāqiṭah (sing. Shinqīṭī), after the name of a famous oasis.

show that Islam had begun to take root among the Negroes on the upper Senegal in the early 11th century. Berber merchants resided permanently in Negro towns and set up intermediary trading towns such as Awdaghost. The main caravan route led from Tafilalet (south of the Atlas) to the capital of Ghana, then the most important Negro state, where a quarter with a mosque was allotted for Muslim merchants. Special Muslim trading settlements (e.g Kugha) are also mentioned. Some of the Negro chiefs made a profession of Islam; e.g. the ruler of a place called Kawkaw (Gao?) some time before 985; a ruler of the Takrūr (Tokolor, Toucouleur) on the Niger named War Jabi (d. 1040); and the ruler of a Mande (Mandingo) state called Malel, who was converted when he saw the rain-making power of a Muslim visitor.

The state of Ghana has been described by Ibn Ḥawqal (d. c. 977) and the Andalusian Bakrī (d. 1094). Their accounts leave uncertainty as to the meaning of its name and the location of its capital (which may have moved). In the 11th century the capital appears to have been at Kumbi Saleh, 200 miles north of the modern Bamako. The state had been founded by the Soninke, a Mande-speaking tribe. Its rulers received tribute from chiefs of vassal clans, and exercised influence over a far-reaching empire, but are unlikely to have extended it to anywhere near the modern Ghana (formerly Gold Coast). In 1076 an Almoravide general, Abū Bakr, conquered the capital of Ghana, and the empire disintegrated into its constituent parts. One of these was Ghana itself, which survived under different rulers until 1230. The Almoravide conquest brought about the conversion of its people to Islam, but was not followed by any permanent Berber occupation. Islam then spread to the Soninke towns which had acknowledged Ghana, such as Dyara (near the modern Nyoro) and Galam (near the modern Bakel, on the middle Senegal); to the Takrūr settlements on the upper Senegal; and to Mande trading centres in the Masina district on the upper Niger, of which the most important was Jenné. The pattern which emerged, and which long characterized Sudanese Islam, was that Islam became the religion of certain ruling groups and of the trading class and was fostered by professional *ʿulamāʾ*, but did not touch the cultivators. As Bakrī observes with reference to the Mande chief of Malel, "he was sincerely attached to Islam, as were his offspring and entourage; but the people of his kingdom remained polytheists."

One of the Mande states was Mali, which arose at the confluence of the upper Niger and Sankarani rivers. Its rulers of the Keita dynasty used the title *Mansa.* The ruler Son Jata moved the capital to Nyani, further up the Sankarani, and by a series of conquests in 1250–1255 subdued many of the small states and built up the strongest and longest-lasting Muslim empire seen in the Western Sudan's history. Mali reached its zenith in the mid-14th century under Gongo Mūsà, who subdued Timbuktu (a trading town, founded by Berbers in 1077) and Songhay (on the Niger east of Timbuktu). He made the pilgrimage to Mecca in 1324/5 and brought Maghribī and Egyptian *ʿulamāʾ* to Nyani. Some of the other *Mansas* did likewise. They maintained security on the routes and fostered trade, introducing elements of Mediterranean Muslim civilization. These developments, which are described by Ibn Baṭṭūṭah who visited Mali in 1352–53, affected only the state hierarchy and left no imprint on Sudanese culture.[1] Ibn Baṭṭūṭah makes it clear that Islam was hardly practised outside the ruling group. Mali afterwards decayed, and some of the small Muslim states such as Songhay again made themselves independent. The authority of Mali was also challenged by the pagan Mossi tribes of the upper Volta region, who developed strong and centralized state structures, and by Berbers (Tuareg), who regained Timbuktu. Mali was finally extinguished by Songhay troops.

The Songhay tribe, with their capital at Gao, cast off the yoke of Mali and rose to greatness under their ruler Si ʿAlī Ber (1464/5–1492) of the Sonni dynasty, who conquered Timbuktu and Jenné; the chronicle of Timbuktu describes him as a cruel tyrant, and although a Muslim, ignorant of Islam. In 1493 the throne was usurped by Muḥammad Turé, founder of the Askia dynasty of Songhay. He based his authority on Islam rather than on Sudanese power-symbols, favoured *ʿulamāʾ* and imported Maghribī shaykhs, and even attempted to enforce the *sharīʿah*. In 1497 he went on pilgrimage to Mecca and received Sharīfian investiture as ruler of Takrūr (the name commonly used in Arabic writings for the whole Western Sudan). Under the Songhay domination, trade flourished, and Jenné became a particularly important commercial centre. At this time contact first began with the Portuguese, who (it has been conjectured) pronounced Jenné as "Guinea" and gave the name to West Africa as a whole. Muḥammad Turé met with no success in his efforts to introduce Islam by war and other means among the Mossi (against whom he led a *jihād*), the Bambara (a pagan Mande-speaking people), and the Fulbe (Peul or Fulani), a nomadic cattle-breeding people who then roamed between the Futa Toro district on the Senegal and the Masina district on the Niger and had mostly remained pagan. Moreover Islam almost disap-

[1] Ibn Khaldūn (1332–1406) in his History of the Berbers has left an account of the rulers of Mali extending to 1390.

peared among the Mandinka (Mandingos) of the former Mali empire, while pagan "universal" cults attained wide diffusion.

The Songhay empire was weakened by recurrent factional struggles among Muḥammad Turé's successors. In 1591 the Moroccan Sultan Aḥmad al-Manṣūr "al-Dhahabī", claiming possession of some disputed salt mines in the Sahara and coveting the wealth of Songhay, sent a force overland consisting of 3000 men, mainly Spanish Muslims, under Jawdhar Pāshā. Although they were reduced by their march to 1000, their possession of fire arms enabled them to rout the Songhay troops with ease. They captured Gao and Jenné, and made their headquarters at Timbuktu. The Moroccan Pāshās controlled only a quite small strip along the northward Niger bend; they received no reinforcements from home and became virtually independent. Their oppressive rule ended c. 1660. Timbuktu then declined under Tuareg domination, but Jenné kept some commercial importance.

For nearly two centuries after the Moroccan invasion, no strong indigenous Muslim states emerged. Islam continued to be the religion of the commercial towns, and of the Soninke and Dyula traders, whose valuable role was recognised and encouraged by leaders of pagan states and tribes. Even today, in some Sudan regions, "trader" and "Muslim" are synonymous. Otherwise the former territories of Mali and Songhay disintegrated into hundreds of pagan village-states. In the Mande country, the pagan Bambara founded more important states on the Senegal at Segu and Karta, while the pagan Mossi states continued to dominate the upper Volta region.

The nomadic Fulbe (sing. Fulo) had spread eastwards from Futa Toro through Masina and the Hausa-speaking lands to Adamawa (in the north of the modern Cameroun Republic), and southwards to Futa Jalon (in the north east of the modern Republic of Guinea). In many places they settled among the agricultural people, imposing themselves as an aristocracy and sometimes adopting the local languages. This occurred among the Tokolor (Takrūr) people on the Senegal, and in Masina and Songhay. Islam thereby spread to the Fulbe, and a class of *ʿulamāʾ* called *torodbe* (sing. *torodo*) arose among them. The so-called "red" Fulbe, who held to the nomadic cattle-rearing way of life and in some places (e.g. among the Tokolor and in Futa Jalon) constituted the ruling class, were little influenced by Islam and indeed mostly remained pagan.

The centuries-long existence of Muslim states had not brought about any basic cultural change in the Western Sudan, nor in the Central Sudan. Islam, as already said, was mainly a class cult; and the attitude of most of its followers was by no means exclusivistic. The chronicles quote many examples of rulers who, while professing Islam, did not abandon inherited pagan customs. The tolerance shown by such Muslim rulers may well have been linked with a continuing respect for spiritual forces recognised and controlled by pagan beliefs and rituals. Conversely pagan rulers, even though they might be "divine kings" or leaders of rain-making cults, were glad to have Muslims in their entourages, not merely as economically useful merchants, but also as bringers of additional spiritual strength.

In reaction against the customary accommodation between Islam and pagan cults, a new Islamic movement—legalistic, exclusivistic and militant—arose in the second half of the 18th century. Its leaders were *ʿulamāʾ*, and in particular Tokolor *ʿulamāʾ*, who probably derived their ideas from passages in lawbooks such as the *Mukhtaṣar* of Khalīl ibn Isḥāq (d. 1365), the standard compendium of the Mālikite school; they are unlikely to have been influenced by external currents, because they began to appear before the Wahhābite movement and the Tijānīyah order acquired importance. Assuming military leadership also, they waged holy war *(jihād)* against lax Muslims and pagans alike, and set up more strictly Islamic states in the whole Sudan belt from the Senegal to the Nile.

In the Western Sudan, the first *jihād* began as early as 1725 in Futa Jalon under the leadership of a *torodo*, Ibrāhīm Mūsà (d. 1751), who incited immigrant Fulbe against the pagan rulers and inhabitants. After long struggles and occasional compromises with the pagans, the *jihād* was successfully concluded by his associate Ibrāhīm Sori (d. 1784), who became the Fulbe war leader and politico-religious ruler *(almami;* Ar. *al-imām)*. The pagans were finally converted, enslaved, or expelled. In Futa Toro, another cleric, Sulaymān Bal, inspired a *jihād* against the Tokolor rulers and also carried it to a successful conclusion before his death in 1776, after which his lieutenant ʿAbd al-Qādir (d. 1806) became the first *almami*. An interesting feature in both these states was the custom whereby the rulers were chosen by conclaves of participants in the *jihād* and their descendants, who became the new aristocracies. The chosen ruler's authority was thought to derive from God, and was consecrated by a ceremony of enturbanment. His duty to God was then to rule in accordance with the divine law. Such a basis of authority was entirely new to the Sudan. In Futa Jalon for some time after Ibrāhīm Sori's death, the rulership was alternated every two years between his descendants and those of Ibrāhīm Mūsà. From 1837 to 1872, however, there was a single ruler, the capable *almami* ʿUmar; he made extensive conquests, and quelled a revolt of zealots who were led by a "marabout" *(murābiṭ;* i.e. *darvīsh* shaykh) and were called Hubbus (from their slogan *ḥubbu Rasūli-'llāh,* "love for God's Prophet). The states of Futa Toro and Futa Jalon lasted until the French conquests, in 1881 and 1896 respectively. The most important of these militant movements, namely the revolt of ʿUthmān dan-Fodio beginning in 1804, took place in the Central Sudan and is discussed in the next section. Under the inspiration of ʿUthmān dan-Fodio's success, a theologian, Shaykh Ḥamad Bari (d. 1818) launched a revolution in Masina in 1810 and set up an Islamic state as near to the ideal as is likely to be realized. Within its small and compact territory, the executive power was able to enforce the *sharīʿah* strictly. The state of Masina lasted until 1862.

In the 19th century, *darvīsh* orders began, apparently for the first time, to gain ground in the Central and Western Sudan. Prominent among them was the Tijānīyah order, which combined mysticism with resignation to God's will[1] and strict Islamic observance. Its rise was associated with the career of Ḥājj ʿUmar ibn Saʿīd Tal. Born in the "theocratic" state of Futa Toro, he spent many years at Mecca and Madīnah, where he was appointed *khalīfah* (representative) for the order in the Western Sudan.[2] His travels across Africa brought him into touch with all the theocratic states then existing, and with new ideas and the menace of European expansion. His propaganda in Futa Toro having failed through the opposition of the established Muslim leaders, he launched from 1853 onwards a series of campaigns against the pagans, particularly the Bambara. Although well versed in Tijānī theory, as his writings show, he became a military rather than a spiritual leader and used the Tijānī allegiance to bind his Tokolor followers to him as *khalīfah.* Spurred on by an insatiable lust for conquest, he subdued vast regions between the Senegal and the Niger. He clashed with the French in 1854, and overthrew the state of Masina in 1862, killing its ruler, Shaykh Ḥamad's grandson. His wars caused much destruction and bloodshed. In 1864 he lost his life before he had had time to set up a stable administrative structure. Although his son Amadu Seku of Segu was recognized as titular head of the empire, the provincial governors, who were Ḥājj ʿUmar's sons and nephews or associates, ruled independently. The most successful was a nephew, al-

---

[1] For this reason the Tijānīs in Algeria and Morocco were submissive to French authority. In Turkey, however, they have since World War II figured prominently as agitators against the secular Republic.

[2] His account of his training and appointment by Muḥammad Ghālī, Tijānī leader in the Ḥijāz, appears in his *Rimāh Ḥizb al-Rahīm,* on the margin of ʿAlī Ḥarazim, *Jawāhir al-Maʿānī,* Cairo 1348/1929, pp. 190–194.

Tijānī (d. 1887), who gained control of Masina and ruled it from a new capital. The others were often in mutual conflict, and had to suppress continual revolts of their subjects. They also had to face the penetration of the interior by the French, who finally swept away the last remnants of Ḥājj ʿUmar's empire.

Coincident with the French penetration, which began in 1878, was the rise of a Mandinka adventurer, Samori ibn Lafiya, who attempted to form a Mandinka empire in the upper Niger basin; his career was brought to an end by the French in 1898. A number of other militant leaders, some claiming to be *mahdīs*, appeared during this period of change.

## THE CENTRAL SUDAN

By "Central Sudan" is meant the belt stretching from the Songhay district on the middle Niger through Hausaland, Bornu, Kanem and Waday to Dār Fūr in the modern Republic of the Sudan. The history of Islamic diffusion in this belt differs from that of the Western Sudan. Although trade routes linked it with Tunis, Tripoli and the Nile valley, the main points of commercial interchange were situated in the Sahara, not in the bordering Sāḥil as they were in the Western Sudan. Yaʿqūbī, writing in 889, speaks of commerce in slaves by a route running from Tripoli through Zawīlah (in the Fazzān) to Kawār (now Bilma; an oasis midway between Fazzān and Lake Chad) where the Negro chiefs and traders sent slaves for sale. The Saharan people whom the Arab writers most frequently mention are the Zaghāwah (probably Hamitic nomads akin to the Berbers), whose guarantee of safe passage was necessary. In the 11th century trade slackened on account of disturbed conditions in the Sahara. Bakrī states that traders did not go south of Zawīlah into Kanem (by which he meant the whole Zaghāwah region), and that this region was pagan. In the second half of the 11th century, a Zaghāwah clan who ruled Kawār and the Tibesti mountains extended their sway to Kanem in the narrower sense, an ill-defined area north east of Lake Chad. For some three centuries the state of Kanem controlled the central Saharan trade routes and kept them safe. The ruling group, though of nomadic origin, at first adopted the Sudanese "divine kingship" system; later, doubtless as a consequence of their trans-Saharan contacts, they embraced Islam. A king named Hume at the end of the 11th century is mentioned as the first Muslim king. He and his son Dunama (c. 1100–1150) dominated wide areas extending to the Fazzān. This Dunama went three times to Mecca as a pilgrim, and was drowned near Suez on his third pilgrimage. The rulers of Kanem extended their authority over the So (Saw) tribes of Bornu, a district west of Lake Chad, and maintained relations with Tunis, Tripoli, and Egypt. The state reached its zenith under another Dunama (c. 1221–1259), who according to Ibn Khaldūn presented a giraffe to the Ḥafṣid ruler of Tunis al-Mustanṣir (1249–1277).[1] Towards the end of the 14th century, revolts and troubles with an allied clan, the Bulala, caused the ruler ʿUmar to transfer the dynasty's seat from Kanem to Bornu. For over four hundred years Bornu was the most important state in this region, reaching its zenith of power and extent under capable rulers in the 16th century, after which Tuareg invasions, famines, and finally a Fulbe *jihād*, weakened its authority. The "Sayfāwah" dynasty of Kanem and Bornu was thus one of the longest lasting in Muslim history.

The history of the region between Songhay and Bornu is confused. By the 16th century a number of town-states with their own peculiar forms of government had differentiated themselves. The peoples of the region, known collectively as the So, had developed a walled-town organization; but the dynasties ruling these states were in many cases immigrants from the north, and in one case, Wangara, from the west. Some of the dynasties gradually expanded and gained control of other small-town entities, making their home town the dominant centre and giving its name to the state. The term "Hausa" by which these states are known is a linguistic rather than an ethnic term, though at that time linguistic unity was far from having been achieved; the actual meaning of the word is "left bank" (of the Niger). The principal Hausa states were Katsina, Kano, Zanfara, Gobir, Wangara and Zazzau (Zegzeg or Zaria). The last named lay furthest to the south and was a loose collection of uncoordinated tribes. West of it on the Niger lay the Nupe state, with an organization of considerable antiquity.

In this region, Islam was not spread to any great extent by traders, except perhaps in Katsina. The Hausa states (unlike Kanem) evidently did not maintain direct trading relations across the Sahara, even though the walled towns possessed well-stocked markets, organized craft industries and wide trade connections. Places in the Sahara, such as Air (a mountainous district with small oases, some 400 miles north of Kano), were used as intermediary exchange centres, and were still partly under Hausa influence and not yet completely dominated by the Tuareg. The

[1] Although Maqrīzī (1364–1442) states that Dunama Dabalemi (1221–1259) was the first ruler of Kanem who embraced Islam, it is clear that Islam had been spreading since the 11th century. The geographer Ibn Saʿīd (d. 1274), writing in 1240, indicates that Islam was well established among the ruling class.

assimilative genius of the Hausas quickly claimed most foreign Muslims who settled among them. Islam as a legal cult was introduced from Kanem and also by immigrant clerics from the Western Sudan. The Chronicle of Kano in its record of the reign of Yaji (c. 1349–1385) mentions the clerics as "Wangara"; they may have been Dyula (Mandingo) traders from Mali, but certainly some were Tokolor or negroid Fulbe.[1] The Chronicle shows that they introduced an element of conflict into the Kano state, and that the conflict was resolved in the normal Sudanese fashion by absorbing Islamic elements into the state structure and thus neutralizing their power to effect change. A class of *ʿulamāʾ*, here called *malam*,[2] was admitted into the traditional fabric to give the state Islamic support. They were officials, appointed by the king, and formed part of his entourage on ceremonial occasions and military expeditions. Muḥammad Belo, son and successor of ʿUthman dan Fodio, wrote in justification of the *jihād* against Bornu and the Hausa states: "Whoever wished adopted the faith. Some practised it as sincerely as they could. Others mingled it with elements which nullified it; such was the case with the majority of the kings".[3]

The only Hausa attempt to form an empire had been made in the 16th century by the *Kanta* (ruler) of Kebbi, a state on the Songhay border. At first allied with the Askia ruler of Songhay Muḥammad Turé, whom he helped in a campaign to wrest Agadez (Air) from the Tuareg, the *Kanta* afterwards broke with the Askia, and as champion of Hausa resistance to Songhay aggression dominated a wide range of Hausa states. After his death in 1545, Kebbi declined under his successors. The eastern Hausa states, and even Kano, were dominated by Bornu. By the end of the 18th century the pagan kingdom of Gobir had risen to be the strongest single Hausa state.

At that time the new formalist concept of Islam began to spread from the Western to the Central Sudan. The preaching of a "forerunner", Jibrīl ibn ʿUmar, among the semi-Hausaized Tokolor *torodbe* (clerical) settlers in Gobir, inspired the revolt of Shaykh ʿUthmān dan-Fodio against the pagan ruler in 1804. ʿUthmān, born in 1754 into one of these clerical families,[4] reacted against the customary accommodation of Islamic profession and pagan practice. The *jihād* which he waged drew

[1] The Kano Chronicle also speaks of shaykhs from the west who visited Kano and Bornu in the mid-15th century, presumably on pilgrimage. Formerly pilgrims had taken the Saharan and North African route; after the establishment of Islam in formerly Christian Nubia (see pp. 165-6), they began to use the trans-Sudan route to the Red Sea ports.

[2] From Arabic *muʿallim*, i.e. religious teacher.

[3] *Infāq al-Maysur*, ed. C. E. J. Whitting, London 1951, p. 10.

[4] *dan-fodio* = *ibn al-faqih*.

in the immigrant Fulbe and Tokolor groups, including even the nomadic Fulbe, and overwhelmed Gobir and the other Hausa states but not Bornu. A vast area, extending to the Nupe and Yoruba lands with their developed state systems and to the Bauchi and Adamawa plateaux with their unorganized pagan populations, was brought under Fulbe domination. Sons and nephews, and associates, of ʿUthmān were installed in the conquered territories as governors. Islam, which had been merely a class cult in the Hausa city states, began to reach the cultivators in many areas after this *jihād*, which imposed on them a new ruling class. Before long, however, the Hausa assimilative genius brought about the absorption of the conquerors. The clerical leaders had already become Hausaized. The new aristocracy nevertheless retained a religious-historical and racial-fictional pride of origin vis-à-vis the autochthones, whom they called Habe, an uncomplimentary term taken from Fulfulde (the language of the Fulbe). Large numbers of slave villages were established, and although this was no new phenomenon, having been a feature of the state of Zaria, their existence helped the Islamizing process because Islam formed the only common link between the villagers. Even so, the indigenous Hausas changed only slowly in spirit and outlook.

ʿUthmān dan-Fodio's capital was Sokoto, a city which he founded in 1810 in former Gobir territory. He died in 1816, and although succession was not in principle hereditary, the subsequent "*imāms*" were his descendants, beginning with his son Muḥammad Belo (d. 1837). The provincial governors *(amīrs)* also tended to become hereditary and virtually independent, though they long continued to seek confirmation in office and to pay homage and sometimes tribute to Sokoto. Among the most important were ʿAbd Allāh, brother of ʿUthmān, who ruled Gando (west of Sokoto; now in the Niger Republic), and Modibbo[1] Adama, leader of the Fulbe who conquered the plateau in the north of what is now the Cameroun Republic and founded the city of Yola on the Benue river in what is now Nigeria; the plateau has since then been known as Adamawa after him. Muḥammad Belo, though frequently at war, was not an able general, but was an outstanding literary figure; he has left Arabic works in prose and verse, including a valuable history. He and his successors and the lesser *amīrs* had to contend with revolts and Tuareg incursions; and despite the piety of some rulers, the early religious ardour waned. In many of the territories where the conquerors had taken over formerly pagan

[1] Many derivations of this word have been suggested, e.g. from Arabic *mudabbir* (i.e. religious teacher; c.f. *malam*) or *muʿaddib*; but the most likely is from *modi*, the commonest Sudan term for "cleric".

states (Katagum, Bauchi, Zaria, Nupe, and the Yoruba state of Ilorin), the people did not move towards Islam, and there was consequently no unity between the rulers and their subjects. It is remarkable that such a loose conglomeration of states could maintain any measure of unity; but the rulers shared a common attachment to Islam and also a common pride of race. The amīrates of Ilorin and Nupe were overthrown in 1896 by the British under Sir George Goldie. In the early years of the 20th century, Sokoto and most of the northern amīrates, and also Bornu, entered into agreements whereby they remained in existence under British protection, in accordance with Sir Frederick Lugard's system of "indirect rule."

An important result of the *jihād* was that the Hausa language came to be used as the *lingua franca* over a vast area and began to develop a literature. Hausa and Swahili were the most important African languages which became instruments of written communication under Islamic influence; they were written in the Arabic script, which was replaced by Latin script in the colonial period.

Bornu despite its long Islamic record had been a target of the *jihād* in 1808, but had survived heavy blows through the energy of its own clerical leader, Shaykh Muḥammad al-Amīn al-Kanemī (d. 1835). With the support of the Shuwa Arabs of Kanem, he finally drove out the invaders (except from the Katagum district in the west of Bornu). He kept the *Mai* (i.e. king) of the Sayfāwah dynasty as nominal ruler, being himself content to wield the power behind the throne; but his son ʿUmar killed the last Sayfāwah *Mai* in 1846, and became titular as well as effective ruler with the title *Shaykh*. During his long reign (1835–1880) he maintained the state's cohesion against numerous external and internal threats. Under his successors there was a rapid decline. In 1893 Shaykh Hāshim was attacked and killed by the slave-trader and adventurer Rābiḥ ibn Faḍl Allāh, who came from the Nilotic Sudan (then under Mahdist rule) with a well armed force of 2000 men and gained control of much of the Chad region after causing great devastation. The French finally defeated and killed Rābiḥ in 1901. Shaykh Hāshim's nephews continued after 1902 to rule under British and German protection, at Maiduguri and Dikwa respectively.

South east of Bornu lay the state of Bagirmi, stretching east from the Shari river. Its Negro dynasty had arisen in the 16th century, and became Muslim by the middle of the 17th. After achieving some importance as a slave-trading and agricultural centre, Bagirmi in the 19th century led a precarious existence under continual attack from its north eastern neighbour Waday and from Bornu. After being overthrown by the slave-raider Rābiḥ, the dynasty resumed authority under French protection. The introduction of Islam into Waday (known also as Bargu and Dār Ṣāliḥ), a region with many Negro tribes and a large influx of nomadic Baqqārah (cattle-breeding) Arabs, dates from the foundation of the Ṣāliḥ dynasty by ʿAbd al-Karīm (d. 1655?), an immigrant from the Nile valley. Waday developed into a large state with an elaborate hierarchical structure headed by an absolute monarch, and was constantly engaged in war with its neighbours Dār Fūr and Bagirmi and in internal struggles. Abeshr (Abéché) was founded as the capital in 1850 by a vigorous ruler, Muḥammad Sharīf (1835–1858). The dynasty ended when the French deposed the last ruler in 1912. Dār Fūr (the land of the Fūr tribe) had like Waday been subject to the Tunjur, immigrants from the Nilotic Sudan, until their hegemony was overthrown (c. 1640?) by Sulaymān Solong, reputedly an Arab, whose dynasty introduced Islamic institutions and lasted until the country was annexed to the Egyptian Sudan in 1874.[1] Later Dār Fūr fell to the Mahdists, but after their defeat regained its independence under a scion of the old dynasty, ʿAlī Dīnār. The Anglo-Egyptian Condominium allowed him virtually complete independence, but failed to support his territorial claims against the French on the western border. He therefore during the first World War made contact with the Sanūsīs and the Turks, and repudiated British authority. He was killed in 1916 while resisting a British expedition. The Sultanate of Dār Fūr was then abolished.

## THE NILOTIC SUDAN

The geographical position of the Nilotic Sudan has made it a zone of interaction between Hamites, Negroes and Arabs. In the arid north and better watered centre, the population was basically Hamitic, consisting of riverain Nubians with an early Negro admixture which had strongly influenced their language; of rainland cultivators with a greater Negro admixture; and of nomadic Bejah roaming (over a much wider area than today) between the Nile, Red Sea and Abyssinian foothills. South of the Hamitic zone lived various groups of Negroes and Nilotes.

The spread of Islam was blocked by the presence of Christian states. Christianity had become the state religion of Nobatia (Nubia) in 540–45 and of Makoria (further south) in 569–70, thanks to the missionary enterprise of both the Monophysite (Coptic) and Orthodox (Melkite) Churches of Egypt, while Alodia (on the Blue Nile) had become Christian in 580

[1] The last Khedivial governor of Dār Fūr was the Austrian Slatin Pāshā.

under the influence of the Monophysite Abyssinian state of Axum (itself Christianized in 333). After the Muslim conquest of Egypt, two Christian states on the Nile above the first cataract are mentioned: Maqurrah, stretching to near the ʿAtbarā confluence, with its capital at Dongola; and south of it ʿAlwah, stretching some way up both the White and Blue Niles, with its capital at Sōbah near the modern Kharṭūm. The Arab governor of Egypt, ʿAbd Allāh ibn Saʿd ibn Abī Sarḥ, besieged Dongola in 651/2, but withdrew after concluding a commercial treaty which provided for mutual rights of transit and settlement and for annual delivery of stated amounts of merchandise (including slaves to be supplied by the Nubians). Apart from minor troubles, this pact ensured peace for many centuries until the rise of the Baḥrī Mamlūk régime in Egypt. Little is known of the history of the two Christian states. Muslim merchants were active as far south as Sōbah, where they had a special quarter, and Arabs who settled among the Bejah worked the gold mines of the Wādī al-ʿAllāqī south of Aswān. The Arab immigrants in this phase lost their Arabic but kept their religion. One Nubianized Arab clan, the Banū Kanz, played a part in the downfall of Maqurrah, which resulted mainly from internal disintegration. Egyptian military interventions during and after the reign of the Mamlūk Sultan Baybars I (1260–1277) accelerated the process, but did not lead to a permanent Egyptian presence. At the same time beduin Arab tribes were encouraged to migrate southwards from Egypt; they found the lands south of the inhospitable Nubian zone well suited to their way of life. The first king of Dongola bearing a Muslim name is mentioned in 1316, and an inscription dated 1317 records the transformation of the church at Dongola into a mosque. Two years later the throne was usurped by a chief of the Banū Kanz bearing the title Kanz al-Dawlah. After the collapse of the old political structure, Dongola lost its former governmental and commercial importance.

The immigrant beduin Arabs came, not to plunder, but in search of a suitable habitat, and needed to live in amicable symbiosis with the settled population. They made no attempt to proselytize. In this later phase they either absorbed or intermingled with the Hamitic nomads and semi-nomads, such as the Shāʾiqīyah and Jaʿalīyīn, who identified themselves with the stronger culture and became Arabic-speaking as well as Muslim. Islam and Arabic also began to spread among the cultivators in areas having close contact with the Arab or Arabized tribes; but elsewhere the process was slow. The encyclopaedist ʿUmarī (writing c. 1340) and the traveller Ibn Baṭṭūṭah (1352) regarded the Nubians as Christian, though the king of the time was Muslim; and the Ethiopian monk Taklā-Alfa, who travelled through Dongola in 1596, distinguished between Muslims and Nubians.[1] Ultimately, however, Christianity disappeared without a trace. Whole-hearted adhesion to Islam appears to have been brought about by immigrant and indigenous *ʿulamā*, such as Ghulām Allāh ibn ʿĀʾid, who settled at Dongola c. 1360–80 and founded a clerical family. The Nubians were to become fervent Muslims, while remaining strongly attached to their own language, customs and mode of life. Most of the Bejah nomads clung likewise to their Hamitic speech and social structure. But all Nubians and Bejah who changed their habitat and mode of life became Arabized.

According to traditional sources, ʿAlwah survived the downfall of Maqurrah; but nothing is known of its subsequent history. It apparently broke up into its constituent chieftaincies owing to the weakness of the central authority. Quite possibly this may have occurred even before the end of the 13th century.[2] The traditional accounts, which have been shown to be unreliable,[3] attribute the conquest of Sōbah to an alliance between ʿAbd Allāh Jammāʿ, founder of an Arabized Bejah clan called ʿAbdallāb which had grown powerful on the main Nile to the north, and ʿAmārah Dūnqas, founder of the Funj dynasty, who is reported to have built his capital Sennār (on the Blue Nile) in 1504.

The Funj, who were originally cattle-rearing nomads, inherited certain aspects of the legacy of ʿAlwah. Their organization and symbols of power were neither Arab nor Muslim. The date when the Funj rulers adopted Islam is not known, but must have been fairly soon after the foundation of Sennār, because they then entered into relations with Muslim groups over a wide area. They directly governed the Jazīrah (between the Blue and White Niles), and were recognized as overlords by the ʿAbdallābī, Jaʿalī, Shāʾiqī and other tribal states on the main Nile and by various nomadic tribes. The relatively stable conditions prevailing under the Funj régime facilitated the spread of Islam. Scholars and holy men were attracted to the territory, where they found the soil prepared by the earlier vague diffusion of Christianity among the basically Hamitic inhabitants and by the spiritual vacuum resulting from its disappearance.

[1] AL-ʿUMARĪ, *Masālik al-Abṣār*, tr. M. GAUDEFROY-DEMOMBYNES, Paris 1927, pp. 48–49. *Oriente Moderno*, xviii (1938), pp. 54–56. Scrolls recently discovered at Ibrīm record in Coptic and Arabic the consecration of a bishop of Ibrīm and Faras at Cairo in 1372 (*Illustrated London News*, July 7, 1964, pp. 50–53). (These villages in the Nile valley north of Wādī Ḥalfā belong to the "Berberene" territory of northern Nubia later annexed to Egypt by the Ottoman Turks).

[2] See two articles by P. M. HOLT, *A Sudanese historical legend; the Funj conquest of Sūba* in B.S.O.A.S. xxiii (1960), pp. 1–12, and *Funj origins; a critique and new evidence*, in Journal of African History iv (1960), pp. 48–49.

[3] HOLT, *op. cit.*

The rooting of Islam in the hearts and lives of the people was the work of definite missionaries, such as Maḥmūd al-ʿArakī in the first half of the 16th century, who after studying Mālikite law and theology in Egypt founded fifteen *khalwahs* (seminaries) in his homeland on the White Nile. Many of the early missionaries came from outside, particularly from the Ḥijāz and to a less extent Egypt. The most effective were those who introduced popular Ṣūfism, such as Tāj al-Din al-Bahārī (d. 1550). From their indigenous pupils influential clerical families were formed. At the same time groups of Nubians migrated southwards and founded settlements, bringing Islam but adopting the Arabic language. The most important aspect of the Islamic pattern which emerged was the tempering of legalism with mysticism. The religious leaders, called *"fekis"*, combined the roles of *faqīh* (lawyer-theologian) and *faqīr* (Ṣūfī ascetic and teacher). The prevalent school of law was the Mālikite, and the most influential Ṣūfī order was the Qādirīyah. Islam was thus received among the Nilotic Sudanese peoples in a way not seen in Negro Africa; and in contrast with the Central and Western Sudan, a wholly Muslim society was evolved. Moreover, since Arabic spread along with Islam, the Nilotic Sudan became culturally part of the Near East, while the other regions of the Sudan belt (except Mauritania) retained their essentially African culture. On the periphery, the tribes of Kordofān and Dār Fūr belonged culturally to the Central Sudanese region. Although Arab cattle-breeding nomads known as Baqqārah have roamed in Dār Fūr and Waday for centuries, and have assimilated Negro elements in varying degrees, their language has not spread except as a *lingua franca*.

The Funj dynasty appears to have produced some able rulers, who extended their sway across the White Nile into Kordofān and warred twice with Abyssinia; but symptoms of internal weakness were also apparent. As the dynasty declined, the vassal states and tribes repudiated its suzerainty. The rulers relied more and more upon a slave-recruited army, and lost all power when the governor of Kordofān revolted in 1762 and assumed control as hereditary regent. The remnant of the Funj state which survived until the Turco-Egyptian conquest in 1821 was very weak, and there was no other state on the Nile capable of resisting the invaders.

The Turco-Egyptian administration, contrary to the normal Sudanese pattern of authority, ruled directly through its own officials and almost obliterated indigenous political institutions. In consequence the *"fekis"* became the main custodians of Sudanese traditions and aspirations. This situation prepared the way for the Mahdist rising in 1881. The influence of the mystical orders had been revived by the work of Aḥmad ibn Idrīs

(d. 1837), a Maghribī *shaykh* settled at Mecca, who sent missionaries into Muslim Africa where they found a fruitful field for their propaganda. One of these was another Maghribī, Muḥammad ibn ʿAlī al-Sanūsī (d. 1859), who founded the Sanūsiyah order in Cyrenaica; but the most influential in the Nilotic Sudan was Muḥammad ʿUthmān al-Mirghanī (d. 1853), founder of the Khatmīyah order. The slave-trade and army recruitment also prepared the way, in that communities were broken up and the scattered individuals found a bond of faith and hope in attachment to Islam through the medium of the religious orders and their leaders.

In 1881 a "*feki*" of Dongola, Muḥammad Aḥmad ibn ʿAbd Allāh, proclaimed himself the expected Mahdī. After initial successes had demonstrated the effectiveness of his divine mission, he quickly won the allegiance of the diverse elements of the population, from the cattle-raising Baqqārah to the settled cultivators. When he died in 1885 at the summit of his success, he was succeeded by his lieutenant, the Baqqārah leader ʿAbd Allāh al-Ṭaʿā'ishī, who although unable to fulfil the Mahdī's program of conquest successfully maintained the unity of the vast state until his defeat by Anglo-Egyptian forces in 1898.

## THE NORTH EASTERN (ETHIOPIC) ZONE

This zone embraces very great contrasts, in its physical geography and in the origins, languages, cultural levels and religions of its human occupants. Its destinies have always been more closely linked with the Red Sea than with the Nile valley. Not later than the 5th century B.C. it began to receive from Arabia an imprint of Semitic languages and culture. In the first or second centuries A.D. immigrants from across the Red Sea founded the kingdom of Axum in the Tigrai district. Christianity was adopted during the 4th century (traditionally in 333 A.D.) as the royal cult, and gradually became, in its Monophysite form, the religion of the people. The establishment of Islam in Arabia and Egypt isolated Christian Ethiopia from other Christian states (except the Nubian states on the Nile), but did not prevent pilgrimage to Jerusalem and contact with the Monophysite (Coptic) Patriarch in Egypt, from whom the Ethiopian Church received its single bishop. There were also intermittent diplomatic contacts with Egyptian rulers. The journey to and from Cairo and Jerusalem was usually made on board Arab ships through the Red Sea, but sometimes along the more difficult Nile valley route – e.g. by St Ewstatewos (Eustatius) when he visited the Christian king of Maqurrah and the Coptic Patriarch Benjamin II (1327-1339). Although at times the

Christian Ethiopian state seemed like a beleaguered fortress in the midst of a flood of Islam, it showed a remarkable power of resistance, and Christianity became a "national" characteristic of its people. The Church, while dependent on Monophysite Alexandria for its basic doctrines and rituals and for its bishop, was well established by the 6th century, and the process had begun whereby its forms were to be distinctively Ethiopianized[1].

In the torrid coastlands, the heterogeneous inhabitants of the few port towns came into contact with Islam at an early date. While the Muslim empires made no effort to expand into Ethiopia, the Dahlak islands off Maṣawwā are mentioned as a place of banishment for adversaries of the Umayyad Caliphate in 714 and were probably also a trading centre.

From the ports, Islam spread to the Kushitic nomads of the lowlands, Bejah in the north, Saho and ʿAfār (Danāqil) further south towards the Gulf of Tajūrah. Well-frequented routes led through the Bejah country from Upper Egypt and Nubia to Red Sea harbours, which were used by pilgrims and Yamanī merchants because the Gulf of Suez was hazardous for sailing ships; the chief port between the 11th and 14th centuries was ʿAydhāb, which the Egyptian Mamlūks destroyed, and afterwards Sawākin. The busiest trade routes between the Ethiopian highlands and the coast led through Harar to the port of Zaylaʿ on the Gulf of Aden. The trade was conducted by Muslim merchants, who played the major part in the expansion of Islam throughout the region. The isolation of Christian Axum diverted its energies away from the Red Sea towards Hamitic Africa. Profound cultural changes ensued, and for centuries the Christian emperors' way of maintaining authority involved them in a nomadic mode of existence. While Axum expanded and consolidated its hold over the highland districts of Amhara and Gojam and western Shoa, a number of Muslim states arose along the trade routes in eastern and southern Shoa – Ifat, ʿAdal, Mora, Hobat and Jidaya. South of the Hawash (Auasc) river, among the settled Sidama and among nomadic tribes, Islam was adopted by rulers of other Kushitic states – Fatajar, Dawaro, Hadya and Bali – partly as an instrument of resistance against Semitic Christian expansion. In the south east, within the territory of Dawaro, the town of Harar developed as the only permanent (and still surviving) Muslim inland urban centre, with a unique Semitic language of its own. From the time of the Negus (emperor) ʿAmda Syon (r. 1312-1342), the Christian state engaged in a long struggle for dominance over

[1] A community of indigenous Jews, called Falasha, also arose, probably in the 5th century A.D. They played a big part in early medieval Ethiopian history, and still exist today.

the Muslim and the remaining pagan (Agao) states. Eventually the Negus was almost everywhere accepted as overlord. Although warfare continued, it had little to do with religion.

In the later middle ages Ifat (Arabic: Awfāt) in the south eastern highlands became the most important Muslim state under a dynasty of rulers, the Walasmaʿ, who seized power in 1285. They controlled the nomad state of ʿAdal, which had dominated Zaylaʾ, but were themselves subdued by the Negus in 1332 and overthrown after another defeat in 1415. The last ruler's grandson, after a spell of exile in the Yaman, re-established the state as the Kingdom of ʿAdal (called also Sultanate of Zaylaʿ). Harar later fell into the possession of this Sultanate and became its capital. In the early 16th century the Sultan had acknowledged the overlordship of the Negus and was pursuing a conciliatory policy towards the Christian kingdom. The armed forces of ʿAdal appear to have consisted mainly of Danqalī and Ṣōmālī tribesmen.

The Ṣōmālī people, who speak a Kushitic language, probably stemmed from the area south of Zaylaʿ and Berberā and east of Harar. Like other Hamitic nomads, they adopted Islam in integral groups. According to their oral traditions, the various tribes were converted by immigrant Muslim preachers, who were possibly also merchants and may well have organized some of the tribal formations; the great Ṣōmālī lineages claim descent from Arab "saints". The earliest recorded mentions of the Ṣōmālīs date from the 15th and 16th centuries, when they probably began their great southward expansion which was to carry them past Maqdishū (Mogadiscio) and across the Juba river into parts of modern Kenya. This process, in which the Ṣōmālīs absorbed the earlier Barābirah and Bantu inhabitants of the Horn of Africa, may have been connected with the great north westward migration of the Galla tribes, whose original habitat was in the south of the modern Somalia. The Gallas, also a Hamitic nomad people, were at that time all pagan. The Ṣōmālīs became fervent Muslims, while adhering to their own customary law which absorbed elements of the *sharīʿah.* Their various tribes gave allegiance to Ṣūfī orders such as the Qādiriyah and Rifāʿīyah, and venerated particular saints. Writing, when used at all, was done only by the religious leaders and solely in Arabic. Despite their numerical and territorial expansion, lack of unity among the tribes prevented the Ṣōmālīs from becoming an effective political force.

In 1527 the Walasmaʿ ruler of ʿAdal was overthrown and killed by a military leader, Aḥmad ibn Ibrāhīm, nicknamed Grañ ("the left handed") and said to have been a Ṣōmālī. Assuming the title "Imām", he led his ʿAfār and Ṣōmālī warriors on a *jihād* which in the next ten years overran the other Muslim states and almost the whole of the Christian Ethiopian state. (The parts played in this struggle by the Portuguese and the Ottoman Turks are related in chapter II, pp. 57-59). After Aḥmad Grañ's defeat and death in 1543, the movement petered out, and the Negus Galawdewos (Claudius; r. 1540-1559) recovered much of the lost ground. The Imām had been unable to garrison or administer his conquests, the nomad troops being moved mainly by lust for booty. Although both Arabic and Ethiopian chronicles state that he burnt churches and monasteries and forcibly converted the people to Islam, the invasion produced little permanent effect on the religious pattern in the highlands, where the national Christian Church had deep roots; the already existing "Jabartī" (i.e. Ethiopian Muslim) minority was only slightly strengthened.

Much more important in the long term was the irruption of the Galla tribes into the Ethiopian highlands, beginning c. 1537 and continuing into the next century. They overwhelmed and eventually settled in vast areas in the south, and at times threatened the existence of the Christian state. In the southern Sidama region, earlier under the sway of Bali and other Muslim states, Islam was virtually eliminated. It was kept alive by the ʿAfār and Ṣōmālī nomads, and by the people of Harar, who in the mid-17th century formed an independent amīrate which was to last more than two centuries.

The waves of Galla immigration contributed further to the isolation of the highland plateaux and complexity of the population pattern. The Gallas who settled in the plateaux mostly became either Christian or Muslim. In the 18th and 19th centuries, when the Christian state was weak, Islam made considerable new gains, particularly among the Galla elements. Those in the central highlands of Wallo (Dessié), Raya and Yeju found in the profession of Islam a means of remaining distinct from the dominant Amharic-speaking Christians. In the south, in the territories of the former Muslim Sidama states, a considerable part of the area which had been lost to Islam was regained by conversion of the Galla invaders, through the agency of Muslim traders who had settlements along the routes. In the Galla language, "trader" and "Muslim" are denoted by the same word (*naggādi*). Religious orders also, as elsewhere in the Ethiopic region, played a big part in the diffusion and consolidation of Islam. Trading relations, particularly with Harar, later carried Islam to more distant Galla settlers, e.g. in 1820-1870 to the Galla conquerors of Jimma and other former Sidama states in the south west. Islam also spread among other Galla tribes (but not as the state or majority religion) and among certain Gurage and Sidama groups.

The progress of Islam was halted by the triumph of the Christian state over the Egyptian invasion of 1875-76 and Mahdist invasion of 1888-89, and by the centralizing policies of the emperors Theodore, John and Menelik, who unified Abyssinia and extended its boundaries to include Harar and many other regions inhabited by Muslim and pagan peoples.

## EAST AFRICA

The East African coast has been exposed to Near Eastern influences since ancient times. Literary[1] and numismatic evidence, though scarce, shows that merchants from Egypt and sailors from Arabia Felix (the Yaman) and Persia frequented the harbours of Azania (i.e. the land of the Zanj) and married native women; but it is not known whether permanent settlements were established then, or only in Islamic times. In the 9th century A.D., Zanj formed the principal element in the slave population employed in reclaiming the marshes of southern ʿIrāq. If the Arabs had taken over this system of slave-colonies from the Sāsānian administration, we may presume that they had also inherited an organization for obtaining slaves from East Africa. The earliest definite archaeological evidence is a mosque inscription on Zanzibar island dated A.D. 1107, and even its provenance is unknown.

Much has been made of the supposed Shīʿite origins of immigrants to the East African coast on the vaguest indications from legends, whether written (e.g. in the statements of the 16th century Portuguese writer de Barros) or oral; but there is no confirmatory evidence from early Arab geographers and *adab* writers such as Masʿūdī of any migrations or refugee movements at all. On the contrary, they show that the coast was under the organized control of pagan Zanj and that Islam did not become the religion of the people of the coastal ports until the 13th century. The only reference to early Muslim settlement is Masʿūdī's mention of a group on a peninsula (Qanbalū) on the island of Pemba, which was a staging point for the trade between the Persian Gulf and the East African coast; Masʿūdī personally visited Qanbalū in 916. Since trans-ocean trade with the Zanj centres was active, the rulers might have been expected to adopt Islam quickly; but the value of belonging to it was probably not yet apparent. Only after the Barbarā (now Ṣōmālī) coastal towns became Muslim did Islam move southwards, possibly as a factor in dynastic

[1] *Periplus of the Erythraean Sea*, written at Alexandria c. A.D. 100 (or c. 300?); *Geography* of Claudius Ptolemaeus, written at Alexandria c. 150 and re-edited c. 400; *Christian Topography* of Cosmas Indicopleustes, written at Alexandria in 547.

changes. A Muslim dynasty was founded on the island of Kilwah around 1150.

Arab writers divided the coast into three zones: Barbarā[1], the land of the Eastern Barābirah ("Berbers"), also called the Banādir coast, which exported ivory and frankincense; the land of the Zanj, among whose exports were ivory, ambergris, ginger, timber and slaves; and the land of Sofālah, which exported gold. The Barābirah were clearly Kushitic nomads, kinsmen or ancestors of the Ṣōmālīs and Gallas. South of Maqdishū lay a belt of Kushite-Zanj interpenetration. Further south there were no nomads on the coast. The term "Zanj" commonly denoted Bantu-speaking Negroes, but was originally applied also to the pre-Bantu coastal population, who may have been Kushites mixed with Negroes and perhaps with an Indonesian (Malagasy) element; Masʿūdī calls the Zanj *Aḥābīsh* ("Abyssinians"), presumably meaning Kushites. He and later writers mention kings of the Zanj in the coastal towns. The Zanj in these towns engaged in trade, but possessed no ocean-going ships; they willingly did business with the Muslims. The organizers of the town-states, who (if this conjecture is correct) were Kushites, were later supplanted by Arab and Īrānian immigrants whose descendants formed Muslim dynasties. Apart from the urban ruling and commercial classes, the coastal regions were inhabited by Bantu peoples, organized only as family groups, who had been moving northwards as far as the southern Barbarā coast c. 500-800. The third zone, called Sofālah, stretched from the modern Dar es-Salaam to Moçambique. Beyond, to the land of the "Wāq-Wāq", Muslim navigators did not sail voluntarily, on account of dangerous currents and cessation of the monsoons. The gold was obtained on the coast by barter from the hinterland people. Masʿūdī describes Sofālah as the furthest limit of Zanj settlement and mentions its king's title *Mfalme* (a Bantu word). Arabo-Īrānian traders also reached and settled in the Comoro islands, which were to become Islamized, and Madagascar. Madagascar too was regarded as Wāq-Wāq country, but was later (from Idrīsī's time) called al-Qumr[2].

After Masʿūdī's account, there is a hiatus in Arabic material for two hundred years. From Idrīsī's account (c. 1154), it is clear that Islam had gained the Barbarā coastal places, but not yet the Zanj to the south except the people of the island of Anjabā (Zanzibar?); indeed he refers to Zanj pagan practices. Not until the time of Ibn Saʿīd (d. 1274) did Islam become the cult of the ruling class in the coastal towns of the Zanj zone (*Bilād al-*

[1] Later the name of a town (Berberā) on the Gulf of Aden coast.
[2] The name was afterwards confined to the Comoro islands.

*Zanj*). The Sofālah zone was still pagan; Ibn Saʿīd writes of Ṣayūnah, capital of the "Sufālīyūn, who are Zanj, worshipping idols". Ibn Baṭṭūṭah gives definite evidence that Kilwah was Muslim in 1329, and Abū'l-Maḥāsin ibn Taghribirdī that Lamu was Muslim in 1383.

The most important of the Muslim town-states were Maqdishū, Barāwah, Lamu, Pate, Malindi, Mombasa and Kilwah. They maintained commercial relations with Arabia, the Persian Gulf, India, Ceylon, and China. Like Sawākin on the Red Sea and Zaylaʿ on the Gulf of Aden, many of them were located on small off-shore islands, presumably for defence. The Muslim *Sawāḥilah* ("coast-dwellers") were preoccupied with commercial and inter-port rivalries, and did not penetrate inland; their outlook was towards the ocean. They do not appear to have contemplated spreading Islam among the Bantu of the hinterland, whose religio-social structure based on family groups was unfavourable for the reception of a monotheistic-legalistic universal religion; but they absorbed Bantu elements into the coastal Muslim community, with its distinctive, predominantly Islamic, "Shīrāzī" civilization. The use of the term "Shīrāzī" derives from local legends. There is evidence, however, that the immigrants included not only ʿOmānī and Yamanī Arabs, but also Īrānians, who must have come from or through Fārs and its capital Shīrāz; an inscription at Maqdishū records the death of a "Shīrāzī" from Nīshāpūr in 1269. This civilization probably developed on the Banādir coast and then spread southwards through migrations of families or small groups. Modern knowledge of it is derived mainly from its material remains. The ruins of mosques and palaces from the 13-15th centuries, particularly at Kilwah and at Gedi (near Malindi), display a unique architectural style, whose source and inspiration are not yet traceable. The Swahili ("coastal") language, basically Bantu with many Arabic loan-words, began in this period to evolve as the spoken idiom, but was not yet written. The Muslim town-states remained independent of external domination, and generally also of each other. The dynastic affairs of some of them are recorded in surviving chronicles; of others, such as Gedi, nothing is known. In the 14th century Maqdishū declined and Pate grew strong in the north, while further south Kilwah was the wealthiest and most powerful state, the Muslim settlements in Sofālah being its dependencies. At that time the gold was obtained from an inland empire, whose kings had a royal title recorded by the Portuguese as Monomotapa. The problems of this empire's chronology and origins are disputed and unsolved. Recent research suggests that it arose considerably later than the 9th century A.D. and that its ruling class was Bantu rather than Hamitic. The remarkable buildings, with fine unmortared stonework, at Zimbabwe and elsewhere are in all probability its monuments.

The Shirāzī civilization faded away during and after the period of Portuguese dominance. In 1598 Vasco da Gama with four ships touched at Moçambique, then a small Muslim settlement, and after missing Kilwah reached Mombasa and Malindi. He established friendly relations with the Sultan of Malindi and obtained the pilot who guided him to Calicut in India – probably Aḥmad ibn Mājid, an eminent Arab navigator and nautical writer whose works survive[1]. From 1505 onwards, under the viceroy Francisco d'Almeida and his successors, the Portuguese demanded tribute and allegiance to their king from the Muslim rulers, many of whom complied. Kilwah was occupied in 1505, but the garrison was removed in 1509, and the town then fell into decline. Mombasa, though burnt in 1505, rose in commercial importance and became the centre of Muslim opposition, while its rival Malindi became Portugal's firm ally. The Portuguese, whose main interests lay elsewhere, exercised only a loose and insecure control, and owed much to the help of Malindi and other friendly states. Their principal forts and customs houses were at Malindi, Mombasa (where they quelled a revolt in 1528) and Moçambique, and on Zanzibar and Pemba islands. Although they built churches outside the town walls, they did not in general attempt to proselytize the "Moors", and made little cultural impact. While not seeking to ruin the Muslim towns, they upset the equilibrium of coastal life and helped to bring about an economic retrogression. Their activities greatly reduced Muslim shipping from India and South Arabia. Movements of Galla and Bantu Nyika tribes in the north, and of Bantu raiding bands in the south, also aided the process. On account of the decline in trade, which was the sole urban function, and of the growing insecurity, most of the towns decayed and some (e.g. Gedi) were abandoned altogether. One of the lost resources was the old trade in gold. With a view to obtaining gold, the Portuguese took over the Muslim settlements at Sofālah in 1505 and Moçambique in 1507, and later settled on the Zambezi delta and river. They stopped the exportation of textiles and beads from Kilwah, which had formerly been bartered for gold by Muslim merchants. The flow of gold now dried up, perhaps because the workings were exhausted, but probably also because internal troubles and tribal invasions weakened the kingdom of the Monomotapa. A Portuguese missionary's attempt to convert the Monomotapa failed in 1561, and the last remnant of the kingdom vanished in the early 17th century. In the Horn of Africa, the Portuguese had little or no influence, though Barāwah,

[1] *Kitāb al-Fawā'id fī Uṣūl 'Ilm al-Baḥr wa'l-Qawā'id*, ed. G. FERRAND, Paris 1921–23.

then a republic governed by twelve religious leaders, paid tribute to them. Their and other European ships began to take more southerly routes to India, avoiding this coast. Previously (13th–15th centuries), Maqdishū had been a flourishing state under the native dynasty of Fakhr al-Dīn, builder of a surviving mosque, one of whose successors is described by Ibn Baṭṭūṭah as a "Berber" speaking the local language but knowing some Arabic. In the 16th–17th centuries, under another dynasty, the town was exposed to Ṣōmālī pressure and lost importance.

Portuguese weakness was revealed when a Turkish corsair from the Yaman, Mīr ʿAlī Bey, began raiding with help from Maqdishū, Lamu, and other towns. Mombasa fell to him in 1588, and its Shaykh proclaimed allegiance to the Ottoman Sultan. In the sequel, the Turks were captured by a Portuguese force, while Mombasa was sacked by Bantu raiders called Zimba, who had already devastated Kilwah. They had advanced northwards, apparently from the Zambezi valley, and were notorious as cannibals. They next attacked Malindi, but were defeated by a local tribe, the Segeju, and not heard of again. The Portuguese then gave Mombasa to the Sultan of Malindi, and built a strong castle (Fort Jesus) to dominate the town. Later they sent the Sultan Ḥasan's son Yūsuf to Goa, where they brought him up as a Christian with the name Dom Jeronimo, and eventually, in 1630, placed him on the throne. A year later he rebelled and reverted to Islam. The rebellion was crushed after long fighting. Yūsuf himself, who had avoided capture, died in 1637.

The declining Portuguese power was overthrown by Arabs from ʿOmān, who had freed their own country from the Portuguese in 1650 (Chapter II, p. 92). From 1660 onwards their fleets harrassed the Portuguese outposts and did increasing trade with the Muslim towns. In 1698 they captured Mombasa after a two-year siege, and put an end to the Portuguese presence north of Moçambique. Among the many places which fell to them, they chose for their headquarters Zanzibar island. Their grip, never tight, was afterwards weakened by internal troubles and an Īrānian invasion of ʿOmān, which led to a change of dynasty in 1744. They successfully disposed of a Portuguese force which reoccupied Mombasa for eight months in 1728; but the governor whom they appointed would not acknowledge the new Āl Bū Saʿīd dynasty, and Mombasa remained independent under his descendants, the Mazrūʿī family, until 1837. Maqdishū, seized by the ʿOmānīs in 1704, now fell to the Ṣōmālīs. While continuing to receive tribute from various places, the ʿOmānī Arabs only governed and settled on Zanzibar and Pemba islands. Some of the mainland towns formed "Shīrāzī" confederacies. Buildings from the 18th and early 19th centuries give evidence of revived prosperity on the coast. Important factors in this were the ivory trade and the connected slave trade, to which the ʿOmānīs imparted new impetus. Some of the slaves were sold to Arabia and the Near East, others to the French Île de France (Mauritius) and Bourbon (Réunion).

The ʿOmānī Arabs adhered to the Ibāḍite sect, but made no effort to propagate Ibāḍism. On the contrary, the 18th and 19th centuries saw a steady immigration of Arabs from Ḥaḍramawt, who reinforced or introduced their own customs and the Ḥaḍramī tradition of learning based on the Shāfiʿite code. They also began to write the Swahili language in Arabic characters with Ḥaḍramī poetic forms and traditional themes. The fusion of the various Muslim elements—residual Shīrāzī, Islamized Bantu and Ḥaḍramī—gave rise to the Swahili culture-synthesis as it exists today.

ʿOmānī influence on the coast, from Maqdishū to the Ruvuma river, was largely restored by Saʿīd ibn Sulṭān (r. 1821–1856), the greatest Āl Bū Saʿīd ruler, who resided from 1832 onwards almost always at Zanzibar. In the early part of his reign clove cultivation was introduced to the island from Mauritius and since then has been its economic mainstay. In 1837 he recovered Mombasa from the Mazrūʿīs, who had vainly appealed in 1823 for British protection. His reign marked a turning point in East African history. The great growth of the ivory trade led to an Arab-Swahili penetration of the interior which changed the hitherto seaward outlook of the coast-dwellers. The ivory trade was tied up with the slave trade, slaves being required mostly as carriers of merchandise in territory where beasts of burden could not survive. The Arab and Swahili traders penetrated deeply—across Lake Tanganyika to the Congo river, and to Lake Nyasa—and set up politically independent trading stations such as Tabora and Ujiji; but they were not propagators of Islam. Only individuals closely associated with them, such as Yao chiefs and traders, adopted an Islamic veneer.

The dynastic link with ʿOmān ended with Saʿīd's death, after which ʿOmān was inherited by one son, while Zanzibar and its dependencies passed to another son Mājid (r. 1856–1870) and then to the latter's brother Barghash (r. 1870–1888). Commerce, exploration and the anti-slavery movement sharpened European interest in East Africa and involved the Sultans in European diplomacy. Their closest links were with the British, who generally supported them but pressed for action against slavery. In 1873 Barghash was forced to decree prohibition of the slave trade. He then, with help from the British Consul Sir John Kirk, endeavoured to reform his government and to strengthen its hold on the coast; but he was unable to establish any authority over the inland Bantu tribes and Muslim traders, and the British government did not support his claim to sovereignty over the interior. First the German Dr. Karl Peters and then the Scotsman Sir William Mackinnon made agreements with Bantu and Swahili chiefs between the coast and the Great Lakes, and finally East Africa was divided into British and German spheres (1887–88), while most of Somalia went to Italy (1889). These events prompted an Arab rising in Zanzibar, which became a British protectorate in 1890 by virtue of Anglo-German and Anglo-French agreements, and subsequent anti-British and anti-German risings on the coast led by the Mazrūʿis and by a preacher named Būshīri.

Under colonial rule, however, the spread of Islam, especially in German East Africa (Tanzania), was more effective than before. Throughout the centuries of Muslim coastal settlement, no Bantu community as a whole had adopted Islam. The coastal communities had grown through absorption of Bantu individuals. In the colonial phase this process continued with considerably increased rapidity. At the same time, use of Swahili as the *lingua franca* spread, and Swahili culture together with Islam strongly influenced some of Bantu tribes near the coast and tended to unify them. The Yao tribe, having become traders in southern Tanzania and northern Moçambique, moved towards Islam in much the same way as certain groups in the Western Sudan had done, finding in it a means of maintaining their distinctness while ensuring that it changed their social institutions as little as possible. In the interior, however, Islam even when embraced by significant numbers of the population has not yet become integrated into the social structures of the Bantu peoples.

# BIBLIOGRAPHY


ANDERSON, J. N. D., *Islamic law in Africa*, London 1954.

BARTH, H., *Travels and Discoveries in North and Central Africa* (1848–1855), London 1857–59, reprinted 1965.

CHAILLEY, BOURLON, BICHON, AMON D'ABY, QUESNOT, *Notes et études sur l'Islam en Afrique Noire*, Paris 1962.

DELAFOSSE, M., *Haut Sénégal et Niger*, vol. 2, Paris 1912.

FROELICH, J. C., *Les musulmans d'Afrique Noire*, Paris 1962.

GADEN, H. (tr.), *La vie d'El Hadj Omar*, Paris 1935.

GREENBERG, J. H., *The influence of Islam on a Sudanese religion*, New York 1946.

HILL, R. L., *Egypt in the Sudan, 1820–1881*, London 1959.

HOGBEN, S. J., *The Emirates of the Northern Nigeria*, revised ed. with A. H. M. KIRK-GREENE, London 1966.

HOLT, P. M., *The Mahdist State in the Sudan*: 1881–98, Oxford 1958.

LEWIS, I. M. (ed.), *Islam in Tropical Africa*, London 1966.

MACMICHAEL, Sir H. A., *A History of the Arabs in the Sudan*, 2 vols., Cambridge 1922, reprinted 1967.

MAḤMŪD AL-KĀTĪ, *Ta'rīkh al-Fattāsh*, ed. and tr. by O. HOUDAS and M. DELAFOSSE, Paris 1913–14, reprinted 1964.

MARTY, )., *Études sur l'Islam et les Tribus du Soudan*, 4 vols., Paris, 1920; *L'Islam en Guinée, Fouta Djallon*, Paris 1921; *Études sur l'Islam en Côte d'Ivoire*, Paris 1922; *Études sur l'Islam au Sénégal*, Paris 1921.

MONTEIL, V., *L'Islam Noir*, Paris 1964.

PRINS, A. H. J., *The Swahili-speaking peoples of Zanzibar and the East African Coast*, London 1961.

AL-SA'DĪ, 'ABD AL-RAḤMĀN, *Ta'rīkh al-Sūdān*, Arabic text, ed. & tr. by O. HOUDAS, Paris 1898 and 1900.

SMITH, MARY, *Baba of Karo*, London 1954.

SMITH, M. G., *Government in Zazzau*, Oxford 1960.

*Tadhkirat al-Nisyān*, tr. by O. HOUDAS, Paris 1901.

TRIMINGHAM, J. S., *Islam in the Sudan*, London 1949, reprinted 1966 (Nilotic Sudan); *Islam in Ethiopia*, London 1952, reprinted 1966; *Islam in West Africa*, Oxford 1959; *A History of Islam in West Africa*, London 1962; *Islam in East Africa*, Oxford 1964; *The influence of Islam upon Africa*, London and Beirut 1968.

# ĪRĀN
## UNDER THE ṢAFAVIDS AND IN THE 18TH CENTURY[1]

BY

HELLMUT BRAUN

Translated from the German text in *Neuzeit*, with slight modifications and amplifications.

The Īrānian people have a long history. In antiquity they founded and maintained empires which came into close contact with contemporary Europe, both as neighbours and as enemies. Their course took a new turn with the Arab conquest in the 7th century A.D. and with the subsequent spread among them of Islām. Īrān became a part of the immense empire of the Caliphs; but within that empire Īrānian influence soon made itself strongly felt, and in the spiritual and political life of Islām illustrious sons of Īrān played leading rôles. The Persian language began to acquire new strength as a literary vehicle, and Īrānian poets composed in it works which have not only ranked ever since as the best in the national literature, but have also secured for this literature an esteemed place in the cultural heritage of all mankind. Īrānian civilization in general showed an astonishing power of assimilation, against which foreigners coming to the country, whether as conquerors, mercenaries, traders or scholars, seldom ever remained immune; and this characteristic has remained apparent, right through to modern times. On the other hand, there was never any prospect during the centuries following the Arab conquest that the national territory might be reunited into a single empire under Īrānian leadership. Īrān became the goal of successive waves of invading Turkish and Mongol peoples from Central Asia, who after making their conquests kept the kingship and the sword in their own hands. Pen-wielding professions, however, had to be left to men of Īrānian birth; and not infrequently the last word in both peace and war lay with an Īrānian secretary risen to be *wazīr*.

This state of affairs continued more or less unchanged until the beginning of the 16th century A.D. The last great conqueror, Tīmūr, had

[1] Limitations of space obliged the author to keep mainly to political history. In accordance with the indigenous custom, the country and its people are called *Īrān* and *Īrānians*, the term *Persian (Fārsī)* being reserved for the language.

died in 1405, and his heirs had not been able to keep his vast empire together. The first provinces to shake off the Tīmūrid grip had been those in the west of the empire, i.e. in the Mesopotamian plain and in the adjacent mountains to the north and east. In this region, which during the 15th century lay beyond the reach of the Mamlūk and Ottoman empires then dominating the Muslim West, independent states were established by leaders of Turkish tribal groups, two of which left their mark upon the future development of Īrān: namely the kingdoms of the Qara Qoyunlu ("Black Sheep") and Aq Qoyunlu ("White Sheep") Turkomān hordes.

At the court of the greatest Aq Qoyunlu ruler, Uzun Ḥasan (r. 1453–1478), an honoured place was held by a religious dignitary, Shaykh Junayd of Ardabīl (d. 1460). He was the grand master and spiritual head (*pīr* or *murshid*) of a religious order, whose members, like those of other mystic fraternities, were called *Ṣūfīs*. In the course of the 15th century, they also came to adopt a Shīʿite label. According to the tradition of the order, the Shaykh's family tree went back to ʿAlī, the Prophet Muḥammad's cousin and son-in-law, through Mūsà al-Kāẓim, the seventh Imām in the line recognized by the Twelver Shīʿites; though recent researches have revealed that sources dating from before the foundation of the Ṣafavid empire make no mention of this tradition and describe the family's origin as Kurdish.[1] Outstanding in the chain of ancestors was Ṣafī al-Dīn Isḥāq (1252–1334; see Table on p. 209); he was regarded as the founder of the *Ṣafavid* dynasty, which took its name from his title Ṣafī al-Dīn. The order's communal life was strictly regulated, and the grand master's power over the fanatically devoted adherents was immense. The first grand master in whom this power aroused political ambitions was the already mentioned Shaykh Junayd. His son and successor, Shaykh Ḥaydar, grew up at Uzun Ḥasan's court, but in 1470 was taken to Ardabīl for initiation into the order; he was later married to Uzun Ḥasan's daughter Martha, entitled ʿĀlamshāh Begum, by whom he had three sons: Sultan ʿAlī, Ibrāhīm and, youngest of the three, *Ismāʿīl* (b. July 17, 1487), the future founder of the Ṣafavid state. It was Shaykh Ḥaydar who organized and trained the rank and file of the adherents, turning them into combatant units adequate for the military exigencies of the time. He introduced the uniform head-dress—the Ṣafavid *tāj*—which was worn with the blue *darvīsh's* cloak and had a very distinctive look with its red-coloured design in twelve patches, said to symbolize allegiance to the

---

[1] Zeki Velidi Togan, *Sur l'origine des Safavides*, in *Mélanges Louis Massignon*, Tome 3, Damascus 1957, pp. 345–357; Ahmad Kasravi, *Shaykh Ṣafi va tabār-ash*, Tehran 1323/1944.

Twelve Imāms; before long its wearers came to be known by the Turkish term *Qizilbāsh* (*Kizilbaş*), i.e. "Red-Heads".

From these years when the *darvīsh* hordes first began to figure in organized military operations date the earliest reports concerning their structure and origins. Without exception they are described as tribes (*ṭabaqāt*) of Turkish descent. If their origins can be inferred from their names, they must have been Turkish tribes from Asia Minor and perhaps also Syria. Among them the following eight appear to have been the most important: (i) *Rūmlū*, i.e. "the Anatolians"; (ii) *Shāmlū*, i.e. "the Syrians"; (iii) *Ustājlū*; (iv) *Qājār*, from whom sprang the later dynasty; (v) *Qaramānlū*, from the district called Caramania on the north side of the Cilician Taurus; (vi) *Dhū'l-Qadr*, an arabicized form of *Dulgadir*, from the neighbourhood of Elbistān in the eastern Taurus; (vii) *Afshār*, from Āẕarbāyjān; and (viii) *Tekkelü*, from the district called Tekke in southern Anatolia.

Ḥaydar's campaigns, like those of his father, were directed northwards and in particular against the province of Shīrvān in southern Caucasia. They brought down upon him the wrath of his mistrustful cousin, the Aq Qoyunlu ruler Ya'qūb. In July 1488 Ḥaydar fell in battle, and in 1490 Ya'qūb's death plunged the Aq Qoyunlu régime into internecine strife from which it never recovered. Rival pretenders sought to use Ḥaydar's three sons as pawns in their struggles for the throne, during which Sulṭān 'Alī, the next acknowledged grand master, lost his life; but the two younger brothers were kept safely hidden in Gīlān by devoted followers. The Qizilbāsh, who had stayed their hand during the Aq Qoyunlu wars, looked upon Ismā'īl as the future grand master; and the order's highly efficient intelligence and propaganda machinery went into action on his behalf. Consequently, when Ismā'īl at the age of only 12 years emerged from hiding in the summer of 1499 and moved upon Ardabīl, supporters streamed to his side from all directions; and with each succeeding victory, the hordes following the youthful grand master grew larger.

The campaigns which in a few years were to win for Ismā'īl a great kingdom began in the spring of 1500 with an expedition through Armenia to Erzinjān, which served to rally further adherents. This was followed in the summer by an invasion of Shīrvān, where Ismā'īl's father and grandfather had warred before him. The local ruler, who held the title Shīrvānshāh and traced his ancestry back to the Sāsānids, at this time also controlled the coastal belt between Bākū and Darband (Dāghistān). Ismā'īl defeated the Shīrvānshāh's troops and made himself master of the entire territory. Members of the old princely family were left in charge under Ṣafavid suzerainty until 1535, when the territory became a province of the Ṣafavid kingdom and thus, it may be said, of Īrān; later it passed for a time into the hands of the Ottoman Sultans, and by the peace treaty of Gulistān in 1813 it was ceded by Īrān to Russia.

These successes of the Ṣūfī army alarmed the Aq Qoyunlu ruler, Alvand, to such a degree that hostilities could not be avoided. In the late summer of 1501 Ismā'īl routed the Aq Qoyunlu army at the battle of Sharūr, in the Aras valley upstream from Nakhchuvān. The way to Tabrīz having thus been opened, Ismā'īl moved quickly to take over the whole of Uzun Ḥasan's heritage. It must have been in the autumn of 1501 that the young Ṣafavid leader entered the capital and there let himself be proclaimed sovereign ruler. Among the steps taken in this connection was one of great importance: the Shī'ite profession of faith was declared obligatory in the Ṣafavid dominions. The new religious régime was certainly not welcomed at the time by all Iranians; but with the extension and consolidation of Ṣafavid rule, the Shī'ite form of Islamic belief percolated widely and deeply through the entire nation.

The origins of the *Shī'at 'Alī*, i.e. the group of Muslims supporting Muḥammad's son-in-law 'Alī, stretch back to the first century of Islām. Their principal tenet is the unquestioning belief that the Prophet was succeeded in his combined temporal and spiritual office, as worldly leader and as custodian of the divine revelation, by a line of physical descendants called *Imāms*, beginning with 'Alī and his two sons Ḥasan and Ḥusayn, and continuing with Ḥusayn's descendants in the direct line. While the origins of the movement must have been purely Arab, its basic principle of dynastic succession was manifestly compatible with the traditional Īrānian concept of hereditary and divinely illuminated monarchy. As to the forms of Shī'ite doctrine professed in Ismā'īl's time, available information is very scarce. The forms elaborated during the following centuries were those of Twelver *(Ithnā 'asharī)* or *Ja'farī* Shī'ism, so called after the number of acknowledged Imāms, or after the sixth Imām Ja'far al-Ṣādiq to whom many of the Shī'ite teachings are ascribed. This version became the distinctive religion of Īrān, and has left its imprint upon the attitudes and whole way of life of the people.

During the years 1501–1510 the Ṣafavid armies were fully occupied in conquering and consolidating a realm, similar in extent to that once ruled by the Aq Qoyunlu, in northern and western Īrān, Mesopotamia and eastern Anatolia. After the overthrow of Uzun Ḥasan's grandson Alvand, the latter's cousin Murād, who had governed central and southern Īrān, met with defeat in 1503. Greater difficulty was experienced in securing the northern provinces, where the Ṣafavid might had to be staked in full before the local potentates could be subdued. With the subjugation of the province of Diyār Bakr, original home and last stronghold of the Aq Qoyunlu Turkomāns, in 1507, Ismāʿīl concluded his Anatolian campaigns. His deepest westward thrust during that year, into the lands of the partly but not wholly Shīʿite Dhū'l-Qadr tribe of Turkomāns around Elbistān and Marʿash, had carried him close to the frontiers of territory then belonging to the Ottoman dynasty; and further advance in that direction must have been considered inadvisable. In the following year, however, the young Ṣafavid prince was able to conquer and annex the province holding the chief sacred places of the Shīʿites, namely the Arab ʿIrāq with its capital Baghdād and its shrines of the Imāms at Karbalā', al-Najaf and elsewhere. By 1510, the following territories had been brought under Ṣafavid rule: Āẕarbāyjān, the heartland of the realm, with Shīrvān to the north and the southern Caspian coastal provinces of Ṭālish, Gīlān, Māzandarān (Ṭabaristān) and Astarābād (Gurgān); the Persian ʿIrāq with Hamadān and Iṣfahān, and Yazd and Kirmān, in central Īrān; Fārs, less its coastal belt, in the south; Khūzistān and Luristān in the south west; the Arab ʿIrāq and parts of northern Mesopotamia (al-Jazīrah), together with Diyār Bakr and parts of Kurdistān and Armenia, in the west.

In the east an increasingly formidable challenge came from the Özbeg rulers of Transoxiana, who after 1505 sought to extend their power south westwards into Khurāsān. The danger became acute with the collapse of the Tīmūrid sultanate of Harāt. At the time when Ismāʿīl first embarked on his career of conquest, this state had been under the rule of Sultan Ḥusayn Bāyqara (r. 1469–1506), one of Tīmūr's descendants and a notable patron of the arts and sciences, at whose court Īrānian culture brought forth some of its greatest masterpieces. Even during his lifetime, however, his ill health and his quarrels with his sons had sapped the foundations of the state; and after his death powerful attacks by the Özbegs under their vigorous leader Muḥammad Shaybānī Khān (known also as Shāhī Beg or Shaybeg; b. 1451, d. 1510) soon brought final ruin. Shaybānī Khān had begun his career of conquest somewhat earlier than Ismāʿīl Ṣafavī; between 1495 and 1500 he had subjugated the greater part of Transoxiana, and in 1505 he invaded Ḥusayn Bāyqara's realm, which then comprised Ṭukhāristān (Bactria), Qandahār, Sīstān, and a disputed title to Gurgān and Māzandarān, in addition to the whole of Khurāsān, thus forming a predominantly Īrānian domain. In 1508 the Özbeg leader defeated Ḥusayn Bāyqara's son and successor Badīʿ al-Zamān, who took refuge at the

Ṣafavid court; with him the Tīmūrids disappeared from Īrānian, though not from Indian, history. Ismāʿīl himself came into conflict with the Özbegs when they began to penetrate into western Khurāsān. On December 1/2, 1510, the two armies met in a hard fought battle near Marv,[1] which ended thanks to a stratagem in victory for Ismāʿīl, while Shaybānī Khān was killed; the Özbegs then lost their conquests south of the Oxus (Āmū Daryā). Ismāʿīl entered Harāt in triumph, and with a view to securing his new conquests through outposts in Transoxiana, gave help to Bābur, the Tīmūrid prince of Kābul, who was attempting to recover Samarqand from the Özbegs; the combined Tīmūrid and Ṣafavid forces entered the city in 1512, but were finally defeated by the Özbegs, who forthwith re-invaded Khurāsān, obliging Ismāʿīl to conduct a new eastern campaign in 1513.

The position in the east had hardly become stable when strife arose with the Ottoman empire in the west. The throne at Constantinople had passed in 1512 to Salīm I, "the Grim", who had peremptorily decreed extreme measures to root out the Shīʿite communities in Anatolia. Not without reason, he had formed the opinion that the fusion of Shīʿite religious ideas with the now manifest political ambitions of the Ṣafavids was likely to promote seditious tendencies among his Shīʿite subjects.[2] The chronicles report cruel persecutions, which must have caused deep resentment on the Ṣafavid side. Another factor exacerbating Ottoman-Ṣafavid relations was the attitude of the Qizilbāsh, who still felt that Anatolia, the original homeland of so many "Red-Heads", should rightfully belong to their realm. The rift between the two empires rapidly deepened, until in the summer of 1514 Ottoman and Ṣafavid armies marched out to war. They met on August 23 in the broad high-lying valley of Chāldirān (Çaldiran) in Āẕarbāyjān north east of Lake Vān. Thanks to the Ottoman army's use of artillery, this great battle ended in victory for Salīm and defeat for Ismāʿīl; the only serious reverse of his career, but not a complete disaster. It was the first of a long series of engagements between Ottoman and Īrānian armies to be fought during this and the following centuries. Its main immediate effect was to compel Ismāʿīl to drop all plans which he may still have had for expansion into Anatolia; and this tended to shift the centre of Ṣafavid power towards the more purely Īrānian

[1] Sometimes called the Battle of the Murghāb (the river of Marv).

[2] See below under Central Asia, pp. 225-227, and HANNA SOHRWEIDE, *Der Sieg der Safawiden in Persien und seine Rückwirkung auf die Schiiten Anatoliens im 16. Jh.*, in "Der Islam" XLI (1965); R. M. SAVORY, *The principal officers of the Safavid state...* (1501–1524) in BSOAS XXIII/1 (1960); JEAN AUBIN, *Etudes safavides, I; Šah Ismāʿil et les notables de l'Iraq persan*, in JESHO II/1 (1959).

provinces. Another eventual result was the demarcation of the frontier between the two empires, roughly along a line which, in the north, was to prove historically durable.

With this settlement came the end of the Ṣafavid state's phase of external growth. Its hub continued to be the province of Āẕarbāyjān with the capital Tabrīz, whence the government's authority radiated in all directions regardless of ethnic aspects. To the west it did not extend very far and was to recede during Ismāʿīl's lifetime, the city and province of Diyār Bakr being lost in 1516 to the Ottomans, who with their superior and increasing military power were able to make their occupation permanent. Relations with his western neighbour formed Ismāʿīl's main anxiety and prompted him to seek connections with European powers, as Uzun Ḥasan had done; but in contrast with the active dealings between Īrān and Europe, and in particular Venice, which had taken place in the days of the Aq Qoyunlu, Ismāʿīl's endeavours did not lead to any exchanges of ambassadors. The situation looked dubious in European eyes, and the new territorial pattern in the Middle East did not favour trade. Little is known of Ismāʿīl's approaches to European rulers. The only document known to have been preserved is a letter from Ismāʿīl dated August 1523 to the Holy Roman Emperor Charles V, suggesting joint action against the Ottoman empire; it cannot have reached Charles earlier than 1524, the year of Ismāʿīl's death. Charles's reply, which was favourable, is dated August 1525, and a second letter from Charles written in 1529 shows that the news of Ismāʿīl's death only reached him during that year. Under Ismāʿīl's successors, Īrān and various European states exchanged a fair number of diplomatic missions, chiefly with a view to making common cause against the Ottoman enemy. None of these initiatives led to any effective alliance or simultaneous campaign against the Ottoman empire, probably because contemporary logistics, and means of communication generally, were inadequate when such huge distances were involved.

All this might seem to suggest that the empire founded by Ismāʿīl Ṣafavī can be looked upon as a mere continuation of the Aq Qoyunlu state; but such a view would not adequately account for its extraordinarily rapid emergence and growth. It also possessed a peculiar and distinctive quality in that its nucleus continued to be the religious order, in which had been formed from generation to generation a body of followers inflexibly devoted to the grand master. Their mystic veneration of the charismatic leader, carried in Ismāʿīl's time to the point of venerating him as a divine being, imparted a singular, and without doubt religiously based, inner strength; and their proselytizing zeal to spread the cult of

ʿAlī among all Muslims released this strength for worldy conquest in pursuit of the missionary goal. During the period of Ismāʿīl's rise to power and for some time afterwards this fanatical religious spirit prevailed. Profoundly convinced of the truth of their faith, the victorious "Ṣūfīs" propagated, and when controverted forcibly imposed, the Shīʿite doctrines. Such ruthlessness was characteristic not only of the environment but also of the age.

In its internal structure, the early Ṣafavid state was modelled on the long familiar pattern briefly mentioned at the beginning of this chapter: military commands, whose holders received the title *amīr*, went to leaders of the Turkish Qizilbāsh tribes; the civilian sector went to Īrānians; and at the stop stood the absolute ruler in the person of the Ṣafavid *shaykh*. According to his genealogy, Ismāʿīl must have had much more Turkish and Greek than Īrānian blood in his veins, and his mother tongue was an Āẕarī Turkish dialect; poems, mostly in Turkish, from his pen have been preserved, as well as poems by his Ottoman adversary, Salīm, who used Persian as the language of higher literary expression. Ismāʿīl began organizing his government immediately after the proclamation of sovereignty in 1501. The royal court accompanied the Shāh and at first had no permanent abode; but certain head offices of government departments were immobile, and the court tended increasingly to pass the winter at the chief city, Tabrīz, which may therefore be said to have been the capital. The second dignitary of the realm was the *wakīl*, i.e. regent or viceroy, who held extensive powers as deputy of the sovereign and acted also as army commander with the title *amīr al-umarāʾ*, i.e. chief *amīr*. Beneath him came the *amīrs*, who were of various grades. In return for their services on military campaigns, they received fiefs, which the Shāh was in a position to grant generously since by Shīʿite law he was the titular owner of all landed property in the realm. To the fief-holder went the right to draw the tax revenue of the assigned land, whence he had to pay prescribed sums to the royal court and provide for the contingent of troops which he was pledged to keep available. The civilian sector of the government was headed by the *wazīr*. Ismāʿīl took over his first *wazīr*, who was an Īrānian, from the preceding Aq Qoyunlu régime. This disposition of the high offices of state was afterwards modified, by Ismāʿīl himself. He separated the office of army commander from that of *wakīl*, and combined those of *wakīl* and *wazīr*. The latter combination proved durable; in subsequent times the holder of the two offices was called "grand *wazīr*" (*wazīr-i aʿẓam*). A peculiar feature of the Ṣafavid régime was the development of a religious bureaucracy headed by an official with the title *ṣadr*. Although this office was probably not invented by Ismāʿīl, prototypes being found in the Tīmūrid and other earlier régimes, the influence which it acquired in the Ṣafavid administration gave to it a new and distinctive significance. Among the functions of the *ṣadr* were supervision of pious endowments (*awqāf*) and regulation of the affairs of the *sayyids*, i.e. of the section of the population claiming descent through ʿAlī and Fāṭimah from the Prophet.

Viewed in the light of subsequent evolution, Ismāʿīl's historical achievement may be said to have been the restoration of the old Īrānian empire, or—in modern parlance—the foundation of the Īrānian national state. All the evidence indicates, however, that he did not in any way think of himself as an Īrānian national leader. His aim was to extend his own and his followers' authority as far as possible in all directions, and to secure this authority through the use of all the instruments at his disposal, including that of religion. Yet his achievement should not be underestimated. The state which he founded was to prove soundly based and durable. Being gifted with an ability to assess his own potentialities correctly, he did not let himself be tempted by ambitions of limitless conquest. Contemporary Shīʿites and European travellers alike judged Ismāʿīl very favourably. While he knew how to instill fear, he also won the most extraordinary devotion from his followers and subjects.

The legacy which Ismāʿīl left to his eldest son *Tahmāsb* I (b. 1514, r. 1524–1576) was not an easy one. Already in Ismāʿīl's own career a turning point had come with the reverse at Chāldirān; in the last ten years of his reign he had ceased to be an all-powerful ruler towering above his associates. The Qizilbāsh tribes, from whose ranks were drawn the dignitaries of the empire, had become more and more unruly, and bitter feuds had arisen. When Ismāʿīl's premature death left Tahmāsb to reign as a minor, effective power passed to these Praetorians; and when Tahmāsb attained his majority, he was faced with the problem of asserting authority over them. Nor was he spared that bane of oriental monarchies, the succession struggle; he had to defend his throne against brothers who rose with rival claims. To overcome these internal troubles alone, a strong-willed ruler would have been needed; and on top of them came grave external threats. The Ṣafavid realm lay wedged between two more powerful empires, each with a vigorous ruler at the helm. The Ottoman Sultan Sulaymān I, "the Magnificent", launched three great campaigns against his weakened eastern neighbour. In the first of these (1534–1536), Baghdād and the Arab ʿIrāq were lost by Īrān to the Ottomans; and in all three, Āẕarbāyjān was temporarily overrun. After the third campaign, a peace treaty was signed at Amasya in northern Anatolia in 1555; this brought to a close the first phase of conflict between Īrān and the Ottoman empire. The exposed position of Āẕarbāyjān in the path of Ottoman invasions must have been the reason why Shāh Tahmāsb chose Qazvīn to be his capital; the transfer of government offices to that city from Tabrīz was probably completed before 1530. Tahmāsb did not enter into any alliances or compacts with Christian powers, despite approaches by some of them; he could not bring himself to collaborate with infidels. In the east, much suffering was caused by repeated Özbeg attacks; but relations with the Great Moghols, whose rise to power in India had coincided with that of the Ṣafavids in Īrān, were generally cordial, even though the city and province of Qandahār were becoming a bone of contention between them. All considered, the accounts of Tahmāsb's long reign show that he was not fully equal to his high position. His commendable and openly expressed love of peace was offset by failure to take effective action against internal and external adversaries; while his love and patronage of learning and art, especially calligraphy, carpet-weaving and miniature-painting, were inhibited as his years advanced by an increasingly bigoted and timorous piety. Tahmāsb is one of the few Muslim monarchs who have left memoirs; written in Persian, they are much inferior to the memoirs written in Eastern (Chagatāy) Turkish by the Moghol ruler Bābur, but have some historical value.

Conditions deteriorated rapidly during the reigns of two of Tahmāsb's sons, who were enthroned one after the other. The first and younger of them, *Ismāʿīl II*, the "Bloodthirsty" (r. 1576–1577), initiated a reign of terror. This unfortunate prince, who had fought with distinction in the Ottoman wars, had later been accused of treason by his ever suspicious father and kept prisoner in a fortress for nineteen years, which left him a physical and mental wreck on his return to normal life. As Shāh, he put to death many of his brothers and other relatives before coming himself to a mysterious end after only eighteen months on the throne. In his place was set his surviving elder brother, *Muḥammad Khudābandah* (r. 1577–1588), a pleasure-loving prince who had renounced the succession after Tahmāsb's death and was victim to an eye-disease which in his later years rendered him virtually blind. Control of affairs thus passed to others, and particularly to his queen Khayr al-Nisāʾ Begum, entitled Mahd-i ʿUlyā, a woman endowed with both energy and prudence. In the long run, however, she could not maintain her position against the hostility of the Qizilbāsh, by some of whose *amīrs* she was finally murdered; it seems probable that they were alarmed by the growth of Īrānian influence at the court under the patronage of Mahd-i ʿUlyā, who came of a prominent

Īrānian family from Māzandarān. After her death, an increasingly important rôle fell to the eldest of the Shāh's and her sons, Ḥamzah, who besides holding the rank of crown prince served as his father's deputy with power to promulgate decrees under the royal seal.

The weakness of the monarchy and the factional strife among the Qizilbāsh *amīrs* left the way open for the success of a revolt which began in Khurāsān as early as 1580 and largely determined the subsequent course of events. Separated from the rest of the country by extensive deserts, this great province and its chief city, Harāt, often showed a tendency towards autonomy. Moreover, defence of its northern rim, which formed the most vulnerable frontier of the entire realm, required a considerable concentration of military forces. It was the custom to send royal princes, even when of minor age, to various provinces as representatives of the crown; in accordance therewith, Muḥammad Khubādandah's second son, 'Abbās, had resided at Harāt since the last years of Tahmāsb's reign. His presence supplied the powerful local *amīr* with a card to be played against the central government, and in 1581 he caused the ten year old 'Abbās to be proclaimed Shāh; but in the early summer of 1583 an understanding was reached whereby the Harātīs reaffirmed their loyalty to Muḥammad Khudābandah, and peace was maintained for a few years. In 1586 the same farce was repeated at Harāt; while at the capital, Qazvīn, the crown prince Ḥamzah was murdered at the instigation of some of the Qizilbāsh *amīrs*, and the Shāh was forced to proclaim his third son, Abū Ṭālib, successor in disregard of the second son, 'Abbās. These events, together with a new Özbeg invasion, impelled the Khurāsānian factions to strike against Qazvīn, which they entered in September 1588 after the old Shāh had moved to Iṣfahān; and in a speedily arranged coup d'état, Muḥammad Khudābandah was deposed and 'Abbās was proclaimed Shāh, at the age of seventeen.

*'Abbās I*, "the Great", was to reign forty years from the date of his accession, probably October 5, 1588, until his death on January 21, 1629. At first it seemed that like his predecessors he would be a puppet in the hands of a general; but it was not long before he brought about a complete change in the situation. He intervened adroitly in the quarrels of the Qizilbāsh *amīrs*, and made good use of methods customary in that age, including extreme cruelties; then he addressed an appeal to all Qizilbāsh chiefs for loyalty to his person as master of the Ṣafavid order and as Shāh. Their traditional loyalty being still alive, this evoked a good response, and the Shāh was able to bring together a body of Qizilbāsh supporters, called *Shāh-seven* ("King's Friends"), with whose aid he quickly and finally

crushed all hostile conspiracies. Besides this, ʿAbbās took other steps, which show that he well understood the danger of reliance on a Praetorian guard; their effect was to strengthen the position of the crown, while the Qizilbāsh were weakened and a new body of troops was brought into being.

Under the early Ṣafavids, the army had consisted solely of Qizilbāsh troops, who were mounted and organized in tribal groups like a militia; the only permanent nucleus was the royal bodyguard, called the *qūrchī* troops, who were also mounted and were equipped with lances, swords, battle-axes and shields. Attempts to break the Qizilbāsh monopoly had already been made in the reign of Tahmāsb, who was the first Shāh to recruit Georgians and Armenians for service in the army and at the court; but this was not done systematically and effectively until the reign of ʿAbbās. He established a corps of royal slaves, named in Turkish *qullar* and in Persian *ghulāmān* and consisting, like the Ottoman Janissary corps, of sons of the subject non-Muslim peoples, mainly Caucasians and in particular Georgians. These troops, and the military commanders picked from among them, came to form the principal counterweight against the "Red Caps". Meanwhile further reforms had become necessary in view of technological developments. Conflicts with the Ottoman army, which was equipped with excellent heavy arms of advanced types, showed clearly that the Īrānian army could no longer do without similar weapons. The change was facilitated by the availability of help from a European expert, the Englishman Robert Sherley, who in 1598 came to Īrān with a party of adventurers headed by his brother Anthony Sherley. The Shāh's efforts resulted in the formation of a corps of musketeers (*tufangchī*) about 12,000 strong and of an artillery corps (*tūpchī*) about 10,000 strong; but the Īrānian predilection for lightly armed and highly mobile cavalry forces was deep-rooted, and under ʿAbbās's successors the artillery was neglected; it never became a strong military force comparable with the Ottoman artillery. For the first time under the Ṣafavids, men of Īrānian (*Tājīk*), i.e. of non-Turkish, origin were enlisted in large numbers during ʿAbbās's reign into these new military bodies, particularly as musketeers.

ʿAbbās had to sustain long and hard wars to defend his realm against external aggression, and the facts of geography dictated that they should be waged on two fronts. As hitherto, the mightiest adversary was the Ottoman empire. Fighting on this front had already recommenced soon after Tahmāsb's death, and the years 1578–1584 had witnessed the elimination of Īrānian authority from the Caucasian territories, where Ottoman influence, already strong since the treaty of Amasya, now became temporarily paramount. In 1585 Tabrīz had fallen, and in 1588 the district of Qarabāgh was also lost. Meanwhile Khurāsān was being overrun by the Özbegs. ʿAbbās met this grim situation with statesmanlike foresight. He opened negotiations with the Sublime Porte and bought a much needed peace on humiliating terms. By the treaty of Constantinople, signed in 1590, he had to acknowledge the *status quo* by ceding to the Ottomans all the territories which their troops had occupied: all Āẕarbāyjān and most of Qarabāgh, except Ardabīl which remained Īrānian; large areas of Īrānian Kurdistān including Shahrazūr; Luristān; and Georgia, Shīrvān and Dāghistān in Caucasia. On top of this he assumed an obligation which the Shīʿites viewed with distaste, namely to ban the utterance of anti-Sunnite curses in the public prayers; and he also sent his nephew Ḥaydar to the Sultan's court as a hostage.

Having thus secured his position in the West, ʿAbbās devoted the next twelve years to reasserting the internal authority of the monarchy and to warring against his turbulent neighbours in the north east. There the Shaybānid Özbeg dynasty was at its zenith under the Khān ʿAbd Allāh II (r. 1583–1598). In 1591–1592 Özbeg invaders overwhelmed Khurāsān and thrust as far south as Sīstān, cutting off the Ṣafavid territories further to the east and in particular Qandahār, which had to be abandoned to the Moghol emperor Akbar. ʿAbd Allāh's death, however, gave rise to internal trouble among the Özbegs, and ʿAbbās judged the time propitious for an offensive against them. In the summer of 1598 he reconquered the whole of Khurāsān and made a triumphal entry into Harāt. Although further Özbeg attacks had to be faced in later years, they no longer posed a serious threat to Īrānian sovereignty. ʿAbbās's last campaign in the east took place in 1622 and resulted in the recovery of Qandahār.

Hostilities with the Ottoman empire began again in 1603. A surprise attack by the Īrānian army led to the recovery of Tabrīz in October of that year. While ʿAbbās with the main body continued the successful offensive in the north west against an Ottoman army commanded by Chighālah Pāshā, smaller Īrānian forces advanced southwards towards Baghdād and northwards into the Caucasian provinces. In 1612 a peace treaty was concluded at Constantinople, setting the frontier on the line established by Ismāʿīl I and Salīm I; this meant the retrocession of all the subsequent Ottoman conquests, in return for which the Shāh undertook to deliver 200 pack-loads of silk annually to the Sublime Porte. The fact that this silk was never delivered gave the Ottomans a pretext to resume war against Īrān in 1616, but the *status quo* was soon restored by the treaty of Sarāb. The peace only lasted until 1623, when Shāh ʿAbbās re-commenced hostilities with a view to reconquering the Shīʿite holy places in ʿIrāq. The capture of Baghdād on November 28, 1623, initiated the second of the two periods of Īrānian rule in ʿIrāq under the Ṣafavids; the first had extended from 1508 to 1534, and the second was to last until 1638. Nādir Shāh's efforts to recover ʿIrāq in his campaigns of 1733 and 1745 were to prove unsuccessful.

ʿAbbās eagerly and uninhibitedly sought diplomatic contacts with European powers. Material difficulties, however, still prevented any realization of his and their visions of joint action against the Ottoman empire. The only Western ruler involved in hostilities with the Sublime Porte during ʿAbbās's reign was the Habsburg emperor Rudolf II, against whom the Sultan Murād III declared war in 1591 following the pacification of the Īrānian frontier through the truce of 1590 with Shāh ʿAbbās. The fighting with the emperor's troops was brought to a stop in 1606 by the signature of a peace treaty in which the Ottomans made a number of concessions, having need of a free hand for action on the Īrānian frontier, where hostilities had been recommenced in 1603. ʿAbbās's negotiations with the Moghol emperor Akbar in India with a view to joint action against the Özbegs also led nowhere.

In other fields, however, Īrān's increasingly numerous and frequent contacts with the courts of Europe produced more fruitful results. The restoration of security and order had made possible a remarkable expansion in the country's economy, which also benefited from ʿAbbās's personal interest and encouragement. He was particularly concerned to free the country from economic dependence on its western neighbour. In the export trade, while textiles, wool and spices were by no means insignificant, far the most important item was silk. In every European and Near Eastern market there was an intense demand for Īrānian silk; no other commodity in contemporary trade was so highly regarded. Īrān's westward exports had long been despatched by two main routes: via Baghdād and Aleppo to the Mediterranean, and via Tabrīz to Trebizond on the Black Sea. Although Vasco da Gama's discovery of the sea passage round the Cape of Good Hope had opened a third possible route, this had hitherto been very little used for Īrānian trade on account of the political situation in the southern coastal regions.

The island of Hurmuz at the mouth of the Persian Gulf had been captured, first in 1507 and then finally in 1515, by the Portuguese under Afonso de Albuquerque. To secure their sea-route to India, they had built a fortress on the island which became one of the chief centres of their power in the east; from it they had been able to dominate the Persian Gulf and the coasts further east with little difficulty. For many years maritime trade in the Indian Ocean remained virtually a Portuguese monopoly. The decline of Portuguese strength in the later years of the 16th century coincided with successful moves by ʿAbbās to bring the southern coastlands under the control of the Īrānian central government. To compete with the Portuguese mart on Hurmuz, he approved the establishment of English, Dutch and French "factories" at a hitherto unimportant spot on the nearby mainland, which the European merchants called Gombroon, or the like; and in 1622 his forces acting in conjunction with a fleet sent by the English East India Company were able to seize Hurmuz and drive out the Portuguese. The island city was totally destroyed; but in its place the mainland settlement, now renamed Bandar ʿAbbās, attained great prosperity, rising rapidly to become one of the chief commercial centres of Asia. To this port were attracted not only a great part of Īrān's own imports and exports, but also an important transit trade, mainly in goods from India for markets in Turkey, the Levant and Caucasia; these were shipped to Bandar ʿAbbās and then sent on overland by caravan. Most of the caravansarais whose ruins can still be seen on Īrānian routes are said to have been built by Shāh ʿAbbās, and undoubtedly date from either his reign or later in the Ṣafavid period.

The European envoys who arrived during ʿAbbās reign were encouraged by the Shāh to attract merchants from their countries to Īrān; and he himself likewise sent envoys to Europe with commercial as well as diplomatic functions. The first mission of this sort was entrusted to the already mentioned Sir Anthony Sherley, who set out for Europe in 1599 with an official Īrānian delegation; he was authorized to give assurances that European merchants willing to make their domicile in Īrān would be exempt from taxes and customs-duties, and that they would not be subject to the jurisdiction of the Īrānian law-courts but would receive special protection from the Īrānian government against any risk of molestation by the religious authorities. All this led to the growth of a flourishing two-way trade between Īrān and Europe, handled on the Īrānian side by Armenians who founded settlements in Europe, and on the European side by the commercial companies of the new maritime powers, Holland and England, and presently also of France.

ʿAbbās's strong rule brought internal prosperity to Īrān. Universal security and the building of roads and caravansarais gave a great stimulus to traffic and trade, and after the Shāh had transferred the seat of government to Iṣfahān in 1598, the enlargement and embellishment of that city gave wide scope for constructive endeavour. This move from the periphery to the interior, though determined initially by strategic considerations, symbolized the tendency of the Ṣafavid régime to assume a more specifically Īrānian character. Even though the Turkish element still constitutes a substantial fraction of Īrān's population today and has continued to supply much of the country's military and political leadership right up to modern times, the various Turkish groups tended with the passage of the years to become culturally Īrānized; and this process was accelerated by Shāh ʿAbbās's reforms, which gave rise to a wider recuitment of Īrānians into the governing classes and thus to a better equilibrium between the two elements.

Concomitantly with these developments came a new upsurge of Īrānian cultural life, especially in fields of art and learning which benefited from the Shāh's interest and patronage. To his enthusiasm was due the worthy embellishment of the new capital city. The well preserved monuments of Iṣfahān bear witness to the genius of his architects, who knew how to combine grandiose planning with exquisite taste and delicacy of execution. In the traditionally Īrānian ornamental arts a peak of perfection was reached, with superlative results in some specialities such as the architectural use of glazed tiles and the weaving of carpets. Contrasting strangely with this artistic fecundity was the barrenness of the Īrānian poetical genius during ʿAbbās's reign and indeed the whole of the Ṣafavid period. This appears to have been due to lack of patronage by the Ṣafavid rulers, who had little taste for panegyrics by poets; ʿAbbās, in particular, saw his duty as being to channel the creative energies of writers into the task of broadening and deepening the fund of Shīʿite religious literature.

History's verdict on ʿAbbās the Great's rule has rightly been favourable, in view of the internal prosperity and external glory to which he led his country, not to mention the artistic triumphs achieved by the contemporary generation with his encouragement. It should not be forgotten, however, that as a true son of his epoch and environment he held and acted upon ideas which are repugnant to modern standards and were to bring disaster to his dynasty and his country. Worst of all was his attitude to his sons. He looked upon them as potentially dangerous rivals, against whom he must secure his position. No doubt he was anxious to forestall any repetition of the events which had surrounded his own childhood and accession; and in all oriental dynasties revolts of princes had been an ever-recurrent feature, arising largely from the polygamous family system. Whether or not ʿAbbās's sons presented any real threat, they were all excluded from the succession by their father's order; one of them he caused to be murdered and two to be blinded, and only one died a natural death. Not until shortly before his own death did ʿAbbās designate a successor, namely his grandson Sām Mīrzā. The lack of any agreed principle of succession was to be an important factor in the downfall of the Ṣavafids. From ʿAbbās's time onwards it was customary to give the royal princes a secluded upbringing in the ḥarem, where their life, led exclusively among women and eunuchs, offered the worst possible preparation for eventual rulership. Inexperienced and untrained, and worse still, psychologically retarded or unbalanced, they would be brought out onto a throne on which they were to sit as absolute monarchs, encompassed with a halo of sanctity and endowed with absolute command over the lives and properties of their subjects.

Contemporary accounts indicate that the people remained faithfully loyal to the Ṣafavid Shīʿite theocracy during the later period of its rule. There are no reports of opposition to senseless or pernicious edicts of any Shāh. From the time of ʿAbbās I onwards, however, the position of the ruler differed markedly from what it had been in the early Ṣafavid period. After being freed from dependence upon the Qizilbāsh, the monarchy had become much stronger, and systematic steps had been taken by ʿAbbās to underpin its strength. He set up a control mechanism of his own and financed its operation mainly with revenues from the royal domains (*khāṣṣah*), which he greatly enlarged. Under his successors this process was carried further, until whole provinces were removed from the jurisdiction of the regular governmental authorities to become domains owned and directly administered by the Shāh. This unchecked inflation of the monarch's wealth and prerogatives frequently made itself felt in the form of oppression by royal officials, and inherently tended to weaken the fabric of the state. While the power of the Qizilbāsh slowly but perceptibly declined, the rise of a new governing class was made impossible by the arbitrary despotism of the successive monarchs. The régime thus came to lack any inner supporting structure.

ʿAbbās I's grandson and successor Sām took the name of his murdered father and reigned as *Ṣafī I* (1629–1642). Under this young and unstable ruler things soon went wrong. His unquenchable bloodthirstiness wrought havoc among the notables of the kingdom and virtually liquidated the governing élite. The neighbouring empires were not slow to take advantage. Both the Ottomans and the Özbegs again made war, and the former, after temporarily occupying Hamadān and Erivan, permanently conquered Baghdād and all ʿIrāq in 1638, while the latter raided as far as Qandahār, which the Moghols later seized and held from 1634 to 1650. There was a marked recovery, however, in the reign of Ṣafī's son *ʿAbbās II* (1642–1666). Coming to the throne at the age of only nine after his father's early death, he grew up to be a moderate and prudent ruler, though without his grandfather's outstanding personality. Good ministers enabled him to maintain an equitable and for those days very liberal mode of rule, under which Christians as well as Muslims could live their lives unmolested. Buildings no less fine than those of ʿAbbās I's reign were erected, the territories of the realm were securely held, and Qandahār was recovered.

In succession to ʿAbbās II, who also died young, his eldest son Ṣafī was crowned under the name *Ṣafī II*; but since the new Shāh's health was poor and conditions in the country were rapidly deteriorating, a second coronation was fixed for a date selected as auspicious by the astrologers, namely March 20, 1668, and on this occasion he assumed the name *Sulaymān* under which he was to continue reigning until his death in 1694. Īrānian history records no similar example of a ruler's being renamed and recrowned. Superstitious, sanctimonious and idle, this Shāh had no firm grip on the reigns of government. Even less concern for state affairs was shown by Sulaymān's son and heir *Sulṭān Ḥusayn* (r. 1694–1722); he allowed himself, however, to be pushed by the fanatical *mullās* of his entourage into adopting a malevolent policy towards the religious minorities.[1] This gave offence to important groups of the population and led to the break-up of the Ṣafavid empire. The largest single block of non-Shīʿites was located in the eastern provinces and consisted mainly of Afghān tribes. The attitude of Īrānian officialdom towards them had never been particularly cordial, in view of the Shīʿite-Sunnite antagonism; and conversely they were eager to cast off Īrānian suzerainty, partly for confessional reasons in that they were Sunnites, and partly because as mountaineers and nomads they were accustomed to a life of unchecked freedom and resentful of any administrative control. Inter-tribal fighting and forced migrations of contumacious tribes during the reign of ʿAbbās I had left the fertile lands of Zamīndāvar and Qandahār (on the lower Hilmand and Arghand-Āb rivers in the south of what is now Afghānistān) open to infiltration by new tribes from the mountains. From this time come the first historical mentions of the Ghalzay tribe. Overtures by their chief, Mīr Vays, to the Moghol emperor Awrangzēb, with a view to exchanging Ṣafavid for Moghol suzerainty, impelled Shāh Sulṭān Ḥusayn to send to Qandahār a ruthless and capable governor, the Georgian prince

[1] Sunnite tribes eventually rebelled in Dāghistān (Lezghians) and Harāt (Abdālī Afghāns) as well as Qandahār, while the Christian Georgians refused to fight any more for the Shah. At Kirmān and Yazd the Zoroastrians welcomed the rough Ghalzay rebels as liberators. The government was more worried about ʿOmānī attacks on Īrānian ports and shipping (see pp. 92–93).

Giorgi of Kartli who was known by the Islāmic name Gurgīn Khān. He restored order, sent Mīr Vays as a prisoner to Iṣfahān, and continued to rule the province with an iron hand. The wily Afghān, however, made good use of his enforced sojourn at the capital. He contrived to win the confidence of the weak-willed Shāh and was allowed to return to Qandahār, where presently, through a coup d'état accomplished in 1709, he successfully did away with the Georgian governor and destroyed the Īrānian garrison, and then proclaimed himself an independent ruler. He, and after his death in 1715 his eldest son Maḥmūd, defeated all punitive forces sent by the Ṣafavid government and rejected all proposals for face-saving compromise. The Afghāns also raided into the neighbouring Īrānian provinces. One such raid, led by Maḥmūd, carried the Afghān army into the heart of Īrān. On March 8, 1722, the Afghān and Ṣafavid forces met at the village of Gulnābād, some twelve miles east of Iṣfahān. The defeat of the numerically and technically superior Ṣafavid army sealed the fate of Shāh Sulṭān Ḥusayn and the dynasty. Iṣfahān was then besieged and starved into surrender. On October 22, the city capitulated and the Shāh abdicated, and three days later the Afghān conqueror *Maḥmūd* ascended the throne of Īrān.

This event marked the effective end of the once glorious dynasty of the Ṣafavids, under whose leadership the Īrānian people had been reunited in a single state after nearly a millennium of dismemberment and had given further proof of capacity for great achievements. Twelver Shīʿism, which the Ṣafavids had established as the official religion, had taken a firm hold upon the majority of the population and was to remain a strong bond linking heterogeneous elements in a common national consciousness. Although subsequently many of the formal aspects of the state structure built by the Ṣafavids were to change character or to be discarded, the essential framework was viable. The Ṣafavid tradition remained alive, and is not dead even today.

For several decades Ṣafavid princes, who escaped a massacre of their family perpetrated at Iṣfahān by Maḥmūd, continued to figure in political life. Ḥusayn's third son Tahmāsb saw fit after his father's abdication to let himself be proclaimed Shāh at Qazvīn on November 17, 1722. *Tahmāsb II* could claim that he was his father's designated successor; Maḥmūd that the old Shāh had formally abdicated in his favour. The immediate result was a division of the country into Ṣafavid and Afghān spheres.

As on previous occasions, this collapse of authority in Īrān was a signal for aggression by neighbouring empires. The first military move, however, came from a power which had not previously appeared among Īrān's enemies, namely Russia. Under Peter the Great (r. 1689–1725) the Russian empire's sway had been extended right up to the Caucasus mountains; and in the vision of this ambitious Tsar the Caspian Sea was destined to be a Russian lake. A Russian expedition entered Īrānian territory in 1723, but did not at first advance beyond Darband, where the Caucasus mountains touch the Caspian coast. Only when the Russians received an appeal from Gīlān for help against the Afghāns did Peter send some troops by sea to Enzelī (now Bandar Pahlavī); and it was to forestall the Ottoman Turks that the main Russian force advanced beyond Darband to Bākū. In this situation the Russian and the Ṣafavid Īrānian governments negotiated a treaty, the first ever concluded between the two countries. It was signed on September 23, 1723, but never ratified by Tahmāsb. By it Russia undertook to recognize Tahmāsb as the rightful ruler of Īrān and send troops to help him against the Afghāns, in return for which Īrān was to cede not only Dāghistān (with Darband) and Shīrvān (with Bākū), where Russian forces were present in strength, but also the south Caspian provinces of Gīlān, Māzandarān and Astarābād (known also as Gurgān). This first Russian thrust into the Middle East greatly alarmed the Sublime Porte and nearly led to a war between the two empires. Already in the summer of 1723, before the arrival of the Russian force, the Sultan had sent an Ottoman governor to Shīrvān, where the population was partly Sunnite and therefore not particularly loyal to Shīʿite Īrān. To counteract the Russian move, two Ottoman armies now marched into Īrānian territory, one into the north through Armenia towards Nakhchuvān and the other from Baghdād towards Kirmānshāh. Thanks mainly to efforts of the French ambassador in Constantinople, the two great powers were brought to the conference table, and on June 24, 1724, they concluded a treaty defining the interests of each in north western Īrān. The demarcation line was drawn so as to leave Dāghistān and the eastern part of Shīrvān in Russian hands; further south, it was made to run firstly due south from the confluence of the Aras and Kur (Kura) rivers through Ardabīl to Hamadān, and then to Kirmānshāh. Territories west of this line were to become Ottoman and east of it were to be governed by Tahmāsb, who was recognized as Shāh of Īrān.

These projects were to a large extent realized, though it was not until a year later that Ottoman troops were able to capture Tabrīz, whose inhabitants bravely resisted their besiegers. The situation was nevertheless quite unstable. In the northern regions, the Russians after Peter's death abandoned their forward policy; and in southern Īrān, Shāh Maḥmūd, who had at first achieved considerable success in extending his authority but had later fallen mentally and physically sick, was murdered on April 22, 1725, and supplanted by his nephew *Ashraf*, a man of more agreable character and also of greater military ability. Ashraf offered the throne to the old Shāh Ḥusayn and only assumed it himself after the latter's refusal. He defeated Tahmāsb's forces and drove them off the plateau down to the Caspian lowland. He was in no position, however, to consolidate the Afghān rule in Īrān. While the resentful Īrānians remained antagonistic to their Sunnite Ghalzay conquerors, reinforcements ceased coming from home, where a brother of the murdered Maḥmūd set himself up at Qandahār as an independent ruler. For Tahmāsb things began to take a better turn in Māzandarān, where the chief of the Qājār tribe, Fatḥ ʿAlī Khān, rallied to his cause and urged him to subdue Khurāsān. That great province had since 1722 been in the hands of a war-lord subject to neither of the two rival central governments. The ambitious Qājār had soon, however, to face a dangerous competitor in the person of Nadr Qulī, a young soldier of the Afshār tribe from Khurāsān, who was later to wear the crown of Īrān as *Nādir Shāh*.

Nādir had risen to prominence as a troop commander in Khurāsān, and in the late summer of 1726 he rallied to Tahmāsb. Having sized up this prince's weak-kneed character, he saw clearly that to fulfil his own ambitions he must act with speed and resolution. During the same autumn he contrived to do away with his rival Fatḥ ʿAlī Khān and obtain the position of commander of the royal bodyguard with the honorific name Tahmāsb Qulī Khān. Having thus won unrestricted military authority, he embarked on a career of conquest. First Khurāsān, then Iṣfahān fell before his onslaught; the decisive battle against the Afghāns was fought near Damghān in the autumn of 1729. Their defeat enabled Tahmāsb to ascend the throne of his ancestors. Ashraf planned a further stand at Shīrāz, but was driven out by Nādir and afterwards, while fleeing to Afghānistān in the summer or autumn of 1730, was killed by a Balūchī bandit.

The old frontiers, however, had yet to be restored; and this task required a settlement of accounts with the Ottoman empire which held the provinces lost by Īrān since 1723, namely part of Shīrvān, Georgia, Āẕarbāyjān, part of the Īrānian ʿIrāq including Hamadān, and Īrānian Kurdistān including Kirmānshāh. They were reconquered in two stages. In 1730 Nādir recovered the central and western territories as far as Tabrīz, but was prevented from advancing further by a revolt of the Abdālī Afghāns in eastern Khurāsān, which he crushed in 1731. During Nādir's absence, Tahmāsb ventured forth from Iṣfahān on a campaign of his own against the Ottomans, which fared so ill that most of the recently recovered Īrānian territories fell once more into Ottoman hands. In January 1732 he signed a formal peace treaty, which let him off lightly as it fixed the frontier on the line of the Aras, making the lands north of that river Ottoman but leaving those south of it to Īrān. Nādir, however, ignored these proceedings. Immediately after his return, he not only re-declared war against the Porte but also, on August 31, 1732, deposed Tahmāsb and sent him with his ḥarem into confinement near Mashhad; on September 7, 1732, he installed an eight months old son of Tahmāsb as Shāh *ʿAbbās III*, and himself assumed the office of regent. In his second campaign against the Ottomans, which he launched forthwith, Nādir's immediate objective was Baghdād; after heavy fighting he failed to take it. He therefore entered into negotiations with the Ottoman governor of Baghdād, who held plenary powers, and on December 19, 1733, they agreed to a peace settlement on the basis of a return to the frontier of 1639, i.e. the retrocession of all Īrānian provinces seized by the Ottomans after 1723. The government in Constantinople, however, was unwilling to ratify this agreement, and fighting recommenced. In Russia these developments were watched with interest. In general the Russians favoured the Īrānian cause. They had already withdrawn from Gīlān in 1732, and they evacuated Dāghistān and eastern Shīrvān in 1735 after receiving an assurance from Nādir that these provinces would never be ceded to the Ottoman empire and that his struggle against that empire would be pursued with all the means at his disposal. Thus ended the first Russian occupation of Īrān's northern provinces.

In the resumed fighting with the Ottomans, which took place mainly in Caucasia, Nādir won important victories, and the Sublime Porte in 1736 accepted terms for an armistice similar to those agreed at Baghdād in 1733. Meanwhile Nādir had taken steps to convoke an assembly (*quriltāy*) of officers, officials, *ʿulamāʾ* and notables, who foregathered in January 1736 at his camp on the Mughān steppe near the confluence of the Aras and Kur rivers. In a veiled way he signified to them that he might now be willing to accept the monarchy. The ceremony of his coronation took place at the camp on March 8, 1736. Before consenting to be Shāh, Nādir imposed certain conditions, of which the most important was that Sunnism should replace Shīʿism as the state religion; and through his envoys at the peace talks in Constantinople he unsuccessfully sought Ottoman recognition of the Jaʿfarite, i.e. Twelver Shīʿite, system of law as a school (*madhhab*) of equal standing with the four schools long acknowledged as orthodox in Sunnite Islām. Nādir's reasons for making this move, which earned him the bitter hostility of large sections of the Īrānian people, cannot be precisely determined. Since he came from a Shīʿite environment, the Afshārs having been one of the Qizilbāsh tribes, and since his conduct and what is known of his outlook suggest that he was not a religious man, it may be surmised that his primary motive was political. The Shīʿah was too closely associated with the old royal house, whose continuing prestige in the popular memory could only hinder his plans. Moreover there were Sunnite Afghān and Turkomān contingents in his army. Various indications also suggest that he had notions of emulating the conqueror Tīmūr; although it now suited his purpose to seek an understanding with the other great Muslim state, the Ottoman empire, his ultimate ambition may well have been to unite the entire Muslim world under his sceptre. The strategy of his later campaigns gives reason to believe that this was so.

These campaigns were not planned merely with a view to restoring the Īrānian empire within its old frontiers. Nādir's next offensive, though initially aimed at the reconquest of Qandahār, was carried beyond Afghānistān into India, where after two centuries of rule the Moghol dynasty was now on the wane. Nādir defeated the Moghol army at Karnāl, north of Delhi, on February 24, 1738, made a triumphal entry into the capital, and took possession of fabulous booty including the celebrated "Peacock Throne". [The throne called by this name in later times and still to be seen at Tehrān is not the one taken by Nādir from Delhi; the latter was robbed and destroyed by Kurds after Nādir's death, and the former is the throne of the Qājār Fatḥ ʿAlī Shāh, which was first known as the "Sun Throne" but later renamed "Peacock Throne" after the Shāh's marriage to a wife called Tāʾūs Khānum, i.e. "Madame Peacock".] Nādir's policy in India was moderate and cautious. He annexed the Afghān territories up to the Indus, and left the Moghol emperor Muḥammad Shāh in office under his suzerainty. During the Īrānian army's stay in Delhi, however, false rumours gave rise to rioting in which a number of Nādir's soldiers lost their lives; he retaliated with a massacre of thousands of the townsfolk.

In his next campaign Nādir pushed beyond the Ṣafavid frontiers in another direction, namely to the north of Afghānistān. In 1740 he made war against the Özbegs, crossed the Oxus and conquered the Khānate of Bukhārā. The Khān was left in possession of his territories north of the Oxus under Nādir's suzerainty, but the territories between the Oxus and the Hindū Kush mountains were annexed to Īrān. Later in the year Khwārizm (Khīvah) was also subdued. All these conquests shifted the centre of gravity of the empire to Khurāsān; and the city of Mashhad, which thanks to its more westerly and somewhat better protected location had already in Ṣafavid times begun to overshadow the old regional metropolis Harāt, now became for a few years the capital of the whole empire.

No further successes of comparable importance emerged from Nādir's later campaigns, which were in the west. Moreover a change came over his character in his later years, and arbitrary despotism got the better of him. Investigations into an unsuccessful attempt on his life in 1741 cast incriminatory but even then not uncontested suspicions on his eldest son Riẓā Qulī, who by his father's afterwards bitterly regretted decision was blinded and thus disqualified from the succession. With restless energy, and despite worsening health, Nādir continued to organize expedition after expedition. A long campaign against the stubbornly unsubmissive mountaineers of Dāghistān cost him heavy losses and nearly embroiled him with the Russians, who feared an Īrānian encroachment into the North Caucasus. His favourite project of an accord with the Ottomans came to nothing, because the Sunnite religious authorities at Constantinople persisted in opposing any recognition of the Twelver Shīʿah as a fifth orthodox "school". Hostilities were consequently resumed, and although they took a course generally favourable to Īrān, Nādir finally made peace with the Sublime Porte in 1746 on the old basis of a return to the 1639 frontiers; the cities and provinces of Baghdād and Mosul thus remained Ottoman, while Georgia, Shīrvān, and the city and province of Erivan were left under Īrānian sovereignty.

Nādir's ambitions envisioned not only territorial empire but also dominion over the adjacent seas. Under his impulsion a vigorous but costly effort was made to create Īrānian navies in the Persian Gulf and in the Caspian Sea. After failing in 1735 to capture Baṣrah, an Īrānian naval expedition was able in 1736 to regain control of the Baḥrayn islands, which had been under Ṣafavid suzerainty. Taking advantage of civil strife in ʿOmān, then an important maritime state with East African possessions including Zanzibar, Nādir sent Īrānian forces which maintained themselves in the country from 1737 until 1744, when they were expelled by a local Arab leader, Aḥmad ibn Saʿīd, founder of the subsequent ruling dynasty of Masqaṭ. Preoccupation elsewhere deflected Nādir's attention from the Gulf in his later years, and the removal of his guiding hand put an end to Īrān's naval enterprises.

The oppressive taxation and heavy casualties resulting from Nādir's excursions beyond the Ṣafavid frontiers caused much discontent among the Īrānian and Shīʿite elements of the population and the army; and in the last years of his life numerous revolts broke out. At the same time Nādir himself became even more suspicious, rapacious and bloodthirsty.

On June 19, 1747, while encamped in Khurāsān, he was murdered by some officers who feared for their lives.

Nādir has been compared with Tīmūr, Napoleon, and his younger contemporary Frederick the Great of Prussia. He was certainly a conqueror in the grand style—the last of the kind to appear in the east. As a military leader and organizer he towered above his adversaries. Far from being a reckless adventurer, he planned his campaigns and trained his troops with meticulous care and precision. In war and diplomacy alike he showed awareness of the limits of his military strength. In the conduct of internal affairs of state, however, he was less competent. The entire administrative system was centred upon him; he personally appointed officials even in the lower grades and maintained a network of spies to report upon them. For the public welfare he showed, in general, little concern. While the people suffered impoverishment, he hoarded enormous sums in the treasury. Efforts were indeed made to promote commerce and industry; in view of the royal monopoly of the silk trade, Nādir was eager that business should flow freely. The European merchants thus received generally helpful treatment from the Īrānian authorites. During Nādir's reign the long established connections with the Western maritime nations, England, Holland and France, began to be matched by new links with Russia, which was actually the first European state to establish regular diplomatic representation in Īrān, through an ambassador at the Shāh's court and a consul at Rasht. Attempts were made by English merchants to organize transit trade through Russia to Īrān; but a first scheme authorized by Peter the Great came to nothing, and a second venture launched in Nādir's reign was soon banned by the Russian government. In general, however, military activity left little scope for other interests. Literature, art and science could not flourish in such conditions, and Nādir himself took no interest in such fields of human endeavour. Only architecture enjoyed his patronage; Mashhad in particular, and a few other cities (though not Iṣfahān) were adorned with monumental buildings. In the gallery of Īrān's monarchs Nādir presents a tragic figure. Lasting credit is nevertheless due to him for having saved the Īrānian state from disintegration after the fall of the Ṣafavids.

Many more years were to elapse before stable conditions reappeared in Īrān towards the end of the 18th century. The tribulations of this period were interrupted, however, by two decades of relatively peaceful development under *Muḥammad Karīm Khān Zand* (r. 1750–1779), who is described as the best-natured ruler Īrān has known. He had not been one of Nādir's generals like Āzād Khān Afghān, who seized power in Āẕarbāyjān after

Nādir's death, nor a great tribal leader like Muḥammad Ḥasan Khān Qājār, the master of Māzandarān and other northern parts, who was a son of the Fatḥ ʿAlī Khān murdered at Nādir's instigation and father of the future Qājār Shāh, Āqā Muḥammad Khān. Karīm Khān's clan, the Zand, were of Īrānian stock from the neighbourhood of Nihāvand. In Iṣfahān power had been seized by a Bakhtiārī tribal chief, ʿAlī Mardān Khān, who had enthroned a puppet Ṣafavid prince, *Ismāʿīl III*. Karīm Khān rallied to ʿAlī Mardān and was put in charge of the administration as *wakīl*, i.e. regent; and when the Bakhtiārī was killed in 1750, he became sole actual ruler, though he never assumed the title Shāh. By 1759 he had eliminated the other claimants to power in Īrān: Āzād Khān was defeated and eventually gave allegiance; the Qājārs were driven back to Māzandarān, where Muḥammad Ḥasan Khān met his death. Karīm Khān was content to let Khurāsān remain under the authority of Nādir's heirs. Shīrāz became the capital of his realm, and at his court learning and the arts were fostered. His government was notable for its concern for the people's welfare and for its successful restoration of the national finances through prudent husbandry. As a military leader also, Karīm Khān won a good name. It was said of him that in the heat of battle he would always be found in the front line. Aside from internal campaigns undertaken to assert his authority and establish security, he sanctioned only one military venture beyond the frontiers; this was into southern Mesopotamia, where in 1775 an Īrānian force captured Baṣrah. The real motive for this move was probably a desire not so much to challenge the Ottoman supremacy in ʿIrāq as to counteract the then commercial supremacy of Baṣrah. The insecurity prevalent in Īrān during the 18th century had caused the maritime trade to shift increasingly to the Ottoman port. The Dutch East India Company for some years carried on its trade from Khārg island in the Persian Gulf, and the English Company had maintained a "factory" at Baṣrah since 1727. Karīm Khān wished to attract the companies back to an Īrānian port, and with this end in view he did much to develop Bushire (Būshahr), which had already come to the fore under Nādir as the base for his incipient navy. The capture of Baṣrah placed one of the main arteries of Middle Eastern trade under Īrānian control; but after Karīm Khān's death in 1779, the Īrānian garrison quit the city to join in the struggle for power at home.

During these decades Khurāsān was under a separate régime. Following Nādir's death his nephew ʿAlī Qulī, who had rebelled against him, seized power at Mashhad and put most of Nādir's kinsmen to death; he took the name *ʿĀdil Shāh* and reigned less than two years until his brother *Ibrāhīm* eliminated him. The latter after a brief spell on the throne was deposed and killed by supporters of Nādir's direct descendant *Shāhrukh*, a son of the already mentioned Riẕā Qulī by a daughter of Shāh Sulṭān Ḥusayn Ṣafavī. This worthy prince was blinded in 1749 by rebels, but was reinstated through the intervention of Aḥmad Shāh Durrānī, the founder of the new Afghān realm, whose suzerainty he acknowledged. Harāt was already under Afghān rule. His weak government lasted until 1796, when Āqā Muḥammad Qājār, after eliminating the Zands, reunited Western Khurāsān with Īrān. Shāhrukh was then forced, under torture from which he died, to hand over what remained of Nādir's hoard of jewels.

## THE IMĀMS

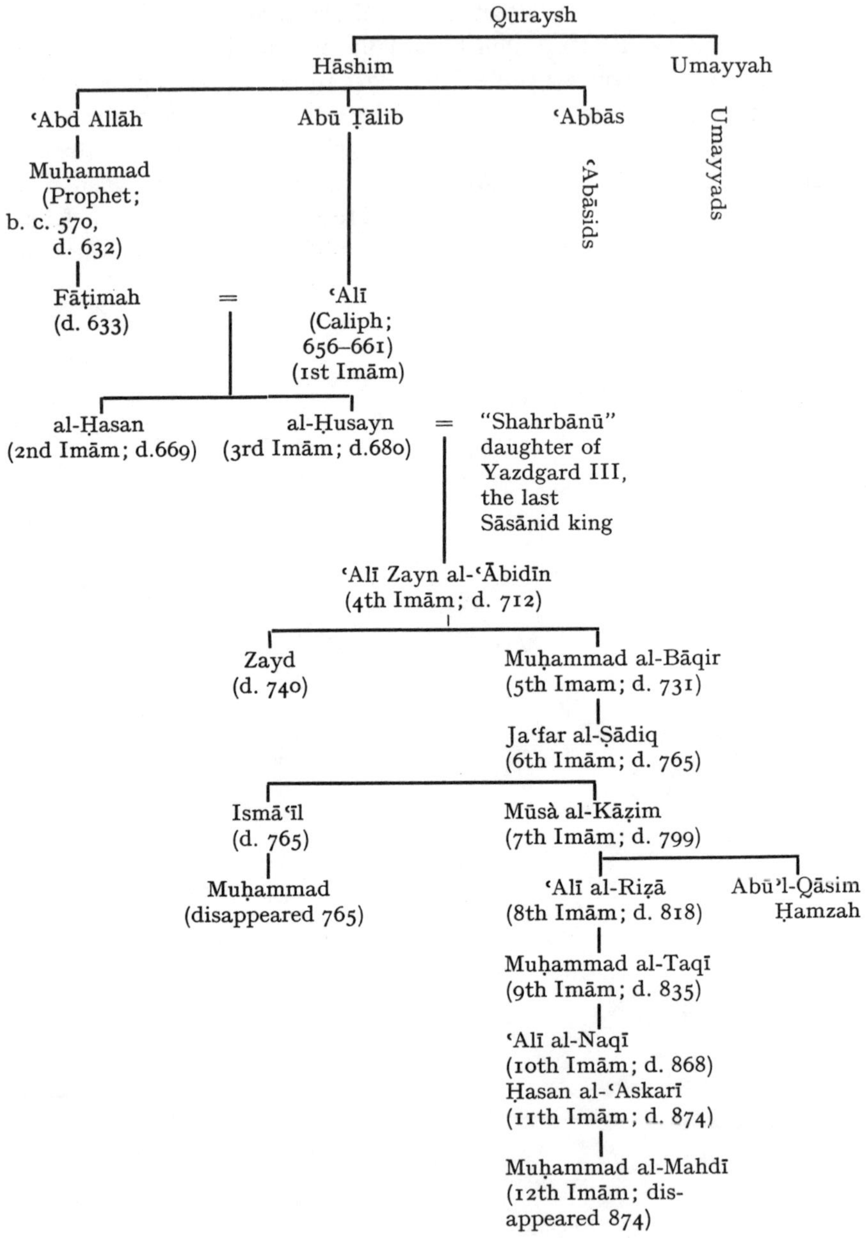
Quraysh
Hāshim
Umayyah
ʿAbd Allāh
Abū Ṭālib
ʿAbbās
Umayyads
ʿAbāsids
Muḥammad (Prophet; b. c. 570, d. 632)
Fāṭimah (d. 633)
=
ʿAlī (Caliph; 656–661) (1st Imām)
al-Ḥasan (2nd Imām; d.669)
al-Ḥusayn (3rd Imām; d.680)
=
"Shahrbānū" daughter of Yazdgard III, the last Sāsānid king
ʿAlī Zayn al-ʿĀbidīn (4th Imām; d. 712)
Zayd (d. 740)
Muḥammad al-Bāqir (5th Imam; d. 731)
Jaʿfar al-Ṣādiq (6th Imām; d. 765)
Ismāʿīl (d. 765)
Muḥammad (disappeared 765)
Mūsà al-Kāẓim (7th Imām; d. 799)
ʿAlī al-Riẓā (8th Imām; d. 818)
Abū'l-Qāsim Ḥamzah
Muḥammad al-Taqī (9th Imām; d. 835)
ʿAlī al-Naqī (10th Imām; d. 868)
Ḥasan al-ʿAskarī (11th Imām; d. 874)
Muḥammad al-Mahdī (12th Imām; disappeared 874)

## THE MASTERS OF THE ṢAFAVID ORDER

- Mūsà al-Kāẓim (7th Imām; d. 799)
  - Abū'l-Qāsim Ḥamzah
    - Fīrūz Shāh Zarrīn-kulāh (13th generation) (migrated from the Yaman to Iran, 12th cent.?)
- (Fīrūz al-Kurdī al-Zanjānī?) (11th/12th cent.?)
  - Ṣafī al-Dīn Isḥāq (6th generation) (founder; b. 1525, d. 12 Sept. 1334)
    - Ṣadr al-Dīn (master, 1334–1391)
      - Khwājah 'Alī (master, 1392–1429)
        - Ibrāhīm (master, 1429–1447)
          - Junayd = Khadījah (master, 1447–1460)
            - Ḥaydar (master, 1460–1488) = Martha
              - Ismā'īl I = Tājlū Khātūn (b. 17 July 1487) (r. 1501–23 May 1524)

- 'Alī Beg Aq Qoyunlu
  - Khadījah
  - Uzun Ḥasan (r. 1453–1478) = Despina
    - Martha
    - Ya'qūb
      - Tājlū Khātūn
- Kalo Yoannis (Emperor of Trebizond)
  - Despina

## THE ṢAFAVID SHĀHS

- 1. ISMĀ'ĪL I (b. 17 July 1487) (r. 1501–23 May 1524)
  - 2. TAHMĀSB I (b. 22 Feb. 1514) (r. 23 May 1524–14 May 1576)
    - 4. MUḤAMMAD KHUDĀBANDAH (b. 1532)(r. 24 Nov. 1577–Sept. 9, 1588) (d. 1595) (= Khayr al-Nisā Begum)
    - 3. ISMĀ'ĪL II (b. c. 1535) (r. 14 May 1576 –24 Nov. 1577)
    - Ḥaydar
    - Parī Khān Khānum
  - Alqāṣ (b. 1516, d.c. 1575)
  - Bahrām (b. 1517, d. 1550)
  - Sām (Mīrzā) (author) (b. 1517, d. 1549)

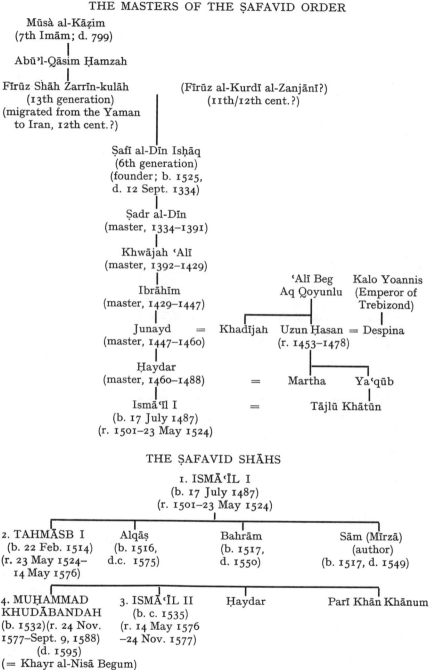

## THE ṢAFAVID SHĀHS (continued)

Ḥamzah (b. 1566, (d. 4 Dec. 1586)

5. ʻABBĀS I, the Great (b. 27 Jan. 1571)(r. Sept. 9, 1588–21 Jan. 1629)

Abū Ṭālib

Tahmāsb

Children of ʻAbbās I:

Tahmāsb

Ṣafī

Riẓā Khudābandah

Amānullāh

Zubaydah

Son of Ṣafī:

6. Sām, reigned as ṢAFĪ I (r. 21 Jan., 1629–11 May 1642)

7. ʻABBĀS II (b. 20 Dec. 1633) (r. 11 May 1642–26 Oct. 1666)

8. Ṣafī (reigned as ṢAFĪ II, 26 Oct. 1666–20 March 1668, then as SULAYMĀN; d. 29 July 1694)

Children of Sulaymān:

9. SULṬĀN ḤUSAYN (b. 1688) (r. 29 July 1694 –23 Oct. 1722) (d. 1726)

Shahrbānū = Mīrzā Dā'ūd Ḥusaynī

Children of Sulṭān Ḥusayn:

10. TAHMĀSB II (b. 1704) (r. 1729–1732) (d. Feb. 1749)

Maryam Begum or Khān Āqā Begum = Sayyid Murtaẓà

Fāṭimah Sulṭān Begum = Riẓā Qulī Afshār, son of Nādir Shāh

11. ʻABBĀS III (b. Jan. 1732) (r. 1732–1736) (d. Feb. 1740)

12. ISMĀʻĪL III (r. in 1750 and 1752–56)

Sayyid Muḥammad Ḥusaynī (at Mashhad, Dec. 1749–Jan. 1750)

Muḥammad Khalīl (historian)

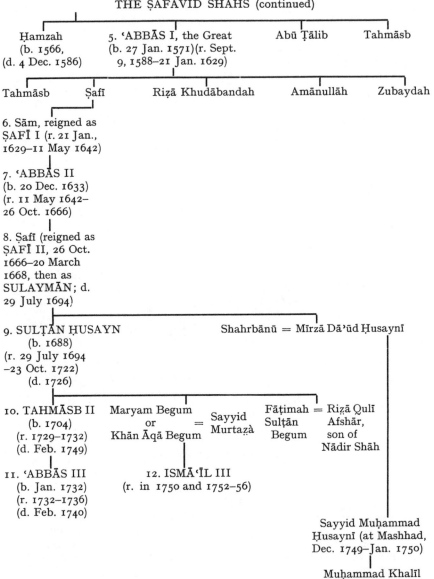

## THE AFSHĀRS

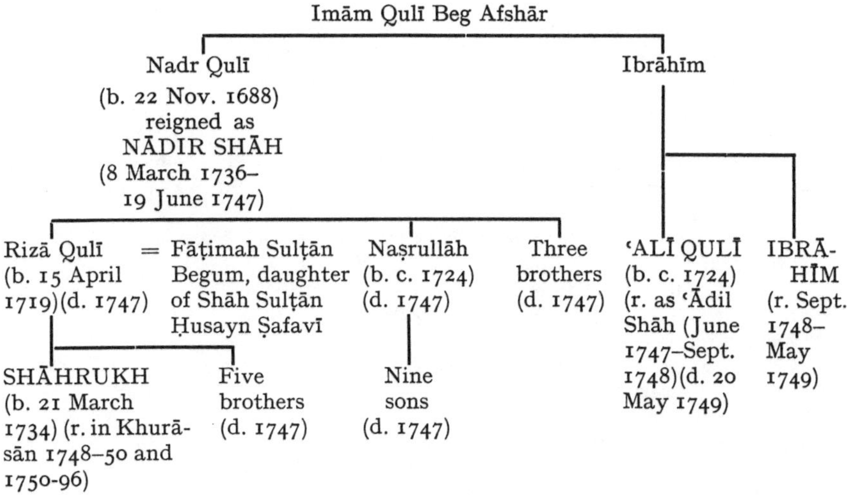
Imām Qulī Beg Afshār
Nadr Qulī
(b. 22 Nov. 1688)
reigned as
NĀDIR SHĀH
(8 March 1736–
19 June 1747)
Ibrāhīm
Rizā Qulī
(b. 15 April
1719)(d. 1747)
= Fāṭimah Sulṭān
Begum, daughter
of Shāh Sulṭān
Ḥusayn Ṣafavī
Naṣrullāh
(b. c. 1724)
(d. 1747)
Three
brothers
(d. 1747)
'ALĪ QULĪ
(b. c. 1724)
(r. as 'Ādil
Shāh (June
1747–Sept.
1748)(d. 20
May 1749)
IBRĀ-
HĪM
(r. Sept.
1748–
May
1749)
SHĀHRUKH
(b. 21 March
1734) (r. in Khurā-
sān 1748–50 and
1750-96)
Five
brothers
(d. 1747)
Nine
sons
(d. 1747)

## THE ZANDS

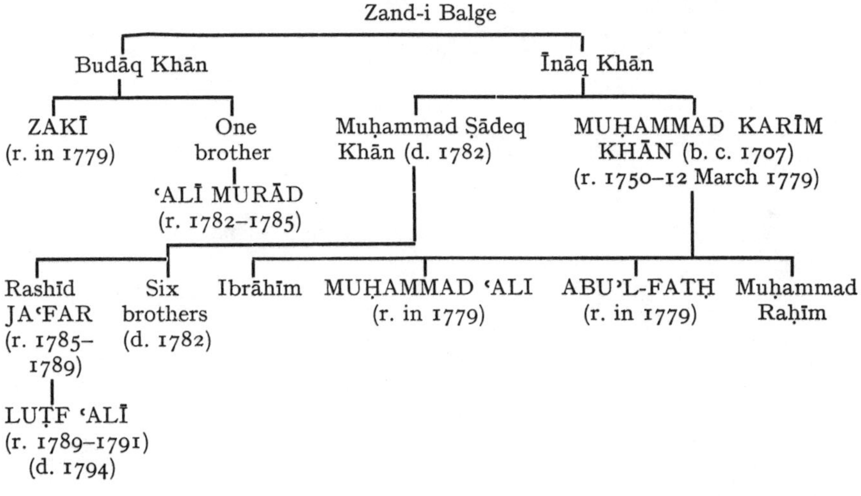
Zand-i Balge
Budāq Khān
Īnāq Khān
ZAKĪ
(r. in 1779)
One
brother
'ALĪ MURĀD
(r. 1782–1785)
Muḥammad Ṣādeq
Khān (d. 1782)
MUḤAMMAD KARĪM
KHĀN (b. c. 1707)
(r. 1750–12 March 1779)
Rashīd
JA'FAR
(r. 1785–
1789)
Six
brothers
(d. 1782)
Ibrāhīm
MUḤAMMAD 'ALI
(r. in 1779)
ABU'L-FATḤ
(r. in 1779)
Muḥammad
Raḥīm
LUṬF 'ALĪ
(r. 1789–1791)
(d. 1794)

# BIBLIOGRAPHY

(selected from the Bibliography by H. Braun in *Neuzeit*, with a few additions, by F. R. C. Bagley)

## BIBLIOGRAPHICAL

AFSHĀR, ĪRAJ, *Kitābshinasī-yi fihristhā-yi khaṭṭī-yi fārsī dar kitābkhānahhā-yi dunyā* (Bibliographie des catalogues de manuscrits persans), Tehran 1337/1958 (Publications de l'Université de Tehran, 485).

AFSHĀR, ĪRAJ, *Index Iranicus: fihrist-i maqālāt-i fārsī kih dar majallahhā-yi chāpī-yi Irān tā pāyān-i sāl-i 1338 chāp shudeh ast*, Tehran 1340/1961 (Pub. de l'Université de Tehran, 697). Articles published in Iranian periodicals up to 1959.

ELWELL-SUTTON, LAURENCE PAUL, *A guide to Iranian area study*, Ann Arbor (Michigan), 1952.

FARMAN (FARMAYAN), HAFEZ, *Iran: A selected and annotated bibliography*, Washington 1951 (Library of Congress, General Reference and Bibliography Division). Holdings of the Library of Congress.

MINORSKY, VLADIMIR, *Les études historiques sur la Perse depuis 1900;–1930; 1931–35; 1935–50*. In *Acta Orientalia* (Copenhagen), 10, 1932; 16, 1937; 21, 1951.

SABA, MOHSEN, *Bibliographie française de l'Iran ... des ouvrages français parus depuis 1560 jusqu'à nos jours*, Paris 1936, 2nd ed., revised and augmented, Tehran 1951. Books and articles.

STOREY, CHARLES AMBROSE, *Persian literature; a bio-bibliographical survey*, vol. 1, part 1, London 1927; vol. 1, part 2, London 1953; vol. 2, part 1, London 1958.

WICKENS, G. M., SAVORY, R. M., and WATSON, W. J., *Persia in Islamic times, a practical bibliography of its history, language and culture*, Montreal, McGill University, 1964.

WILSON, Sir ARNOLD TALBOT, *A bibliography of Persia*, Oxford 1930.

## GEOGRAPHICAL

BRICE, WILLIAM C., *South-West Asia*, London 1966 (A Systematic Regional Geography, VIII).

*Farhang-i Jughrāfyā-yi Irān*, 10 vols., Tehran 1328/1949–1332/1953. Ed. by General ḤUSAYN 'ALĪ RAZMĀRĀ and Brigadier NAWTĀSH (vol. X). Geographical encyclopaedia, published by the Geography Section of the Army General Staff.

GABRIEL, ALFONS, *Die Erforschung Persiens. Die Entwicklung der abendländischen Kenntnis der Geographie Persiens*, Vienna 1952.

KAYHĀN, MAS'ŪD, *Jughrāfyā-yi mufaṣṣal-i Īrān*, 3 vols., Tehran 1311/1932. Physical, political and economic.

LOCKHART, LAWRENCE, *Persian Cities*, London 1960 (revised ed. of *Famous cities of Iran*, London 1939).

PETROV, MIKHAIL PLATONOVICH, *Bibliografiya po geografii Irana. Ukazatel' literatury na russkom yazyke 1720–1954*, Ashkabad 1955.

WILBER, DONALD NEWTON, *Recent Persian contributions to the historical geography of Iran*, in *Archaeologica Orientalia in memoriam Ernst Herzfeld*, Locust Valley, N.Y., 1952, pp. 267–278.

## NUMISMATICS

POOLE, REGINALD STUART, *The coins of the Shahs of Persia in the British Museum* (Safavis, Efsharis, Zands, and Kajars), London 1887.

RABINO (DI BORGOMALE), HYACINTHE-LOUIS, *Coins, medals and seals of the Shâhs of Irân, 1500–1941*, Hertford (Eng.) 1945.

## GENERAL

ARBERRY, ARTHUR JOHN, ed., *The legacy of Persia*, Oxford 1953.

AYMARD, A., et al., *La civilisation iranienne (Perse, Afghanistan, Iran extérieur)*, Paris 1952.

BARTOL'D, VASILII VLADIMIROVICH, *Iran. Istoricheskii obzor*, Tashkent 1926; Eng. tr. in NARIMAN, GUSHTASP KAIKHOSRO, *Posthumous works*, Bombay 1935.

BARTOL'D, VASILII VLADIMIROVICH, *Istoriko-geograficheskii obzor Irana*, St. Petersburg 1903.

BROWNE, EDWARD GRANVILLE, *A literary history of Persia*, vol. IV, *A history of Persian literature in modern times (A.D. 1500–1924)*, Cambridge 1924, reprinted London 1953. (With important historical material.)

DONALDSON, DWIGHT M., *The Shi'ite religion: a history of Islam in Persia and Irak*, London 1933.

DUNLOP, H., *Perzië voorheen en thans*, Haarlem 1912.

EDWARDS, A. C., *The Persian carpet*, London 1953, 2nd ed. 1960.

GODARD, ANDRÉ, *L'art de l'Iran*, Paris 1962; Eng. tr., *The art of Iran*, London 1965.

HINZ, WALTHER, *Iran. Politik und Kultur von Kyros biz Reza Schah*, Leipzig 1938.

HUNARFARR, LUṬFULLĀH, *Ganjīnah-yi ās̱ār-i tārīkhī-yi Iṣfahān*, Tehran 1344/1965. Historical monuments of Isfahan.

IQBĀL, 'ABBĀS, *Az ibtidā-yi Safavīyah tā ākhir-e Qājārīyah pādshāhān-i Īrān kujā madfūn-and?* In Yādgār, 3, 1325/1946, No. 2, pp. 9–22. Burial places of Iranian rulers since Isma'īl I.

*Irānshahr*, 2 vols., Tehran 1342/1963–1343/1964. Pub. by the National UNESCO Committee of Iran.

IVANOV, M. S., *Ocherk istorii Irana*, Moscow 1952.

LAMBTON, ANN KATHARINE SWYNFORD, *Landlord and tenant in Persia*, London 1953 (with valuable historical chapters). *The spiritual influence of Islam in Persia*, in A. J. ARBERRY ed., *Islam today*, London 1943. *Islamic society in Persia*, London 1954. 32 pp.

MALCOLM, Sir JOHN, *The history of Persia from the most early period to the present time*, 2 vols., London 1815. Another ed., London 1829.

MU'IZZĪ, NAJAFQULĪ, *Tārīkh-i ravābiṭ-i Irān bā dunyā*, Tehran 1325/1946. History of Iranian diplomatic relations.

RYPKA, JAN, et. al., *Dejiny Perské a Tádžicke literatur*, Prague 1956; revised tr. from the Czech. *Iranische Literaturgeschichte*. Leipzig 1959. Eng. tr., *History of Iranian Literature*, Dordrecht 1968.

SPULER, BERTOLD, *Iran und der Islam*, in *Die Welt als Geschichte*, 12, 1952; Eng. tr. in G. E. VON GRUNEBAUM, ed., *Studies in Islamic cultural history*, 1954 (*The American Anthropologist*, 56, 2).

SPULER, BERTOLD, *Persien (Iran): Staatsoberhäupter, Regierungsmitglieder*. (From 1500 to 1952). In *Regenten und Regierungen der Welt*, ed. by B. SPULER, Bielefeld 1953, Part 2.

SYKES, Sir PERCY MOLESWORTH, *A history of Persia*, 2 vols., London 1915, 3rd ed. with supplementary essays, London 1930, reprinted 1951.

TAQĪZĀDAH, SAYYID ḤASAN, *Ba'zī az 'ilal-i taraqqī u inḥiṭāt-i tārīkhī-yi Irān*, in Yādgār (Tehran), 5, 1327/1948, No. 10.

UPHAM POPE, ARTHUR, ed., *A survey of Persian art from prehistoric times to the present*, 6 vols., London and New York, 1938–1939.

UPHAM POPE, ARTHUR, *An introduction to Persian art since the 7th century A.D.*, London 1938.
WILBER, DONALD NEWTON, *Iran, past and present*, Princeton 1948, and many subsequent revised editions.
WILSON, Sir ARNOLD TALBOT, *The Persian Gulf; an historical sketch from the earliest times to the beginning of the 20th century*, Oxford 1928, 2nd ed. 1954.
WILSON, Sir ARNOLD TALBOT, *Persia*, London 1932 (The Modern World series).

## THE ṢAFAVID PERIOD

AUBIN, JEAN, *Etudes Ṣafavides, I: Šāh Ismā'īl et les notables de l''Irāq persan*, in Journal of the Economic and Social History of the Orient, 2, Leiden 1959, pp. 37–81.
BAYANI, K., *Les relations de l'Iran avec l'Europe occidentale a l'époque safavide*, (Portugal, Espagne, Angleterre, Hollande, France), Paris 1937.
BELLAN, LUCIEN-LOUIS, *Chah Abbas I; sa vie, son histoire*, Paris 1923.
BERCHET, GUGLIELMO, *La repubblica di Venezia e la Persia*, Turin 1865.
DANVERS, FREDERICK CHARLES, *The Portuguese in India, being a history of the rise and decline of their empire*, 2 vols., London 1894.
FALSAFĪ, NAṢRULLĀH, *Zindagānī-yi Shāh 'Abbās-i Avval*, 3 vols., Tehran 1332/1953, 1334/1955, 1339/1960. (Publications de l'Université de Tehran).
FALSAFĪ, NAṢRULLĀH, *Tārīkh-i ravābiṭ-i Īrān va Urūpā dar dawrah-yi Ṣafavīyah*, Tehran 1316/1937.
GILANENTZ, PETROS DI SARKIS, *The chronicle of ... concerning the Afghan invasion of Persia in 1722*, tr. from the original Armenian and annotated by CARO OWEN MINASIAN, Lisbon 1959. (C. Gulbenkian Foundation Memorial Library).
HAZHĪR, 'ABD UL-ḤUSAYN, *Bā Petersburg yā Qustantīnīyah?* Tehran 1322/1943. Irano-Russian and Irano-Ottoman relations; vol. I treats of the Ṣafavid period.
HERBETTE, MAURICE, *Une ambassade persane sous Louis XIV*, Paris 1907.
HINZ, WALTHER, *Irans Aufstieg zum Nationalstaat im 16. Jahrhundert*, Berlin and Leipzig 1936. Important for the early history of the Ṣafavid order.
HINZ, WALTHER, *Schāh Esmā'īl II: ein Beitrag zur Geschichte der Ṣafaviden*. In Mitteilungen des Seminars für orientalische Sprachen in Berlin, 36, 1933, Abteilung 2, Westasiatische Studien, pp. 19–100.
KASRAVĪ, AḤMAD, *Tārīkh-i Musha'sha'īyān yā pānsad-sāleh-yi Khūzistān*, Tehran 1312/1923.
KASRAVĪ, AḤMAD, *Shaykh Ṣafī va tabārash*, Tehran 1333/1944. Argues that Shaykh Ṣafī was a Sunnite and not a Sayyid.
LAMBTON, ANN KATHARINE SWYNFORD, *The office of kalântar under the Safawids and Afshars*, in *Mélanges Massé*, Tehran 1963.
LANG, DAVID MARSHALL, *Georgia and the fall of the Safavid dynasty*, in Bulletin of the School of Oriental and African Studies (London), 14, 1952, pp. 523–529.
LOCKHART, LAWRENCE, *The fall of the Safavi dynasty and the Afghan occupation of Persia*, London 1958. (With extensive bibliography).
LOCKHART, LAWRENCE, *The Persian army in the Safavid period*, in Der Islam, (Hamburg), XXXIV, 1959.
LYSKOV, V. P., *Persidskii pokhod Petra I, 1722–23*, Moscow 1951.
MINORSKY, VLADIMIR, *La Perse au XVe. siècle*, in *Orientalia Romana*, I, 1958, pp. 99–117.
ROEMER, HANS ROBERT, *Der Niedergang Irans nach dem Tode Ismails des Grausamen*, Wurzburg 1939.
ṢAFAVĪ, RAḤĪMZĀDEH, *Zindagānī-yi Shāh Ismā'īl Ṣafavī*, Tehran 1341/1962.

SARWAR, GHULAM, *History of Shah Ismail Safavi*, Aligarh 1939.

SAVORY, R. M., *The principal offices of the Ṣafawid state during the reign of Ismā'īl I*, in Bulletin of the S.O.A.S. (London), 23, 1960, pp. 91–105.

SOHRWEIDE, HANNA, *Der Sieg der Ṣafawiden in Persien und seine Rückwirkung auf die Schī'iten Anatoliens im 16. Jh.*, in Der Islam (Hamburg), XLI, 1965.

TOGAN, ZEKI VALIDI, *Sur l'origine des Safavides*, in *Mélanges Louis Massignon*, vol. 3, Damascus 1957, pp. 345–357.

VESELOVSKII, N. I., *Pamyatniki diplomaticheskikh i torgovykh snoshenii moskovskoi Rusi s Persiei*, St. Petersburg 1890.

## PERSIAN SOURCES

See C. A. STOREY, Persian Literature, Vol. 1, Part 1.
The following important works have been printed:

ḤASAN RŪMLŪ, *Aḥsan ul-Tawārīkh*, ed. by C. N. SEDDON, Baroda 1931, tr. by C. N. SEDDON, *A chronicle of the early Ṣafawīs*, Baroda 1934. (Gaekwad's Oriental Series, Nos. 57 and 69). Extends to 1577.

ISKANDAR MUNSHĪ (ISKANDAR BEG TURKMĀN), *Tārīkh-i 'Ālam-ārā-yi 'Abbāsī*, ed. by ĪRAJ AFSHĀR, 2 vols., Isfahan 1334/1955–1335/1956. Extends to 1629. Supplement, also by ISKANDAR MUNSHI, *Ẕayl-i Tārīkh-i 'Ālam-ārā-yi 'Abbāsī*, ed. by SUHAYLĪ KHWĀNSĀRĪ, Tehran 1317/1939, covers the years 1629–1634.

KHWĀNDAMĪR' GHIYĀS UL-DĪN MUḤAMMAD, *Habīb al-siyar fī akhbār al-bashar*, ed. by JALĀL UL-DĪN HUMĀ'Ī, 4 vols. Tehran 1333/1954. Extends to 1524.

ṬĀHIR VAḤĪD QAZVĪNĪ, *'Abbāsnāmeh ...*, ed. by IBRĀHĪM DIHQĀN, Arak, 1329/1950. On the reign of Shāh 'Abbās II; extends to 1667.

TAHMĀSB I, *Tazkireh*, ed. by PAUL HORN, in Zeitschrift der Deutschen Morgenländigen Gesellschaft, 44 (1890), pp. 563–649, and 45 (1891), pp. 245–291; tr. by PAUL HORN, *Die Denkwürdigkeiten Schāh Tahmāsps des Ersten von Persien*, Strasbourg 1891. C.f. WALTHER HINZ, *Über die Denkwürdigkeiten des Schāh Tahmāsps*, in ZDMG, N.F. 13, 1 (1934), pp. 46–52.

*Tadhkirat ul-Mulūk*, a manual of Ṣafavid administration (circa 1137/1725). Persian text in facsimile (B.M. Or. 9496), tr. and explained by VLADIMIR MINORSKY, London 1943. (E. J. W. Gibb Memorial Series, N.S. 16). Valuable also for Minorsky's studies of the Ṣafavid state structure in his introduction and appendix.

## TRAVEL NARRATIVES

ALBUQUERQUE, AFONSO DE, *Comentarios*, Lisbon 1576; latest modern ed. Coimbra 1922–1923. Eng. tr. by W. DE G. BIRCH, *The commentaries*, 4 vols., London 1875–1884 (Hakluyt Society, Series 1, Nos. 53, 55, 62, 69).

DE BRUYN, CORNELIS, *Reizen over Moskovie, door Persie en Indie*, Amsterdam 1714. Translations in French, and in English (2 vols., London 1737), under name C. LE BRUN.

CARMELITES. *A chronicle of the Carmelites in Persia and the Papal Mission of the XVIIth and XVIIIth centuries*, tr. from the Latin, ed. by H. CHICK, 2 vols., London 1939.

CHARDIN, JEAN, *Voyages du Chevalier Chardin en Perse, et en autres lieux de l'Orient*. Nouvelle éd., soigneusement conférée sur les 3 éd. originales. 10 vols., and atlas, Paris 1811. Extracts in Sir JOHN CHARDIN, *Travels in Persia*, ed. by N. M. PENZER, introd. by Sir PERCY SYKES, London 1927. (Lived in Iran 1664–1670 and 1671–1677).

DE GOUVEA, ANTONIO, *Relaçam en que se tratam as guerras e grandes victorias que alconçou o grande rey da Persia Xa Abbas* ... Lisbon 1611; French tr., *Relation des grandes guerres et victoires obtenues par le Roy de Perse Cha Abbas contre les empereurs de Turquie* ..., Rouen 1646.

HERBERT, Sir THOMAS, *Some yeares travel into Africa and Asia the great, especially describing the famous empires of Persia and Industan*, London 1634; *Travels in Persia*, abridged and ed. by Sir WILLIAM FOSTER, London 1928 (The Broadway Travellers).

VON DER JABEL, TECTANDER, *Iter Persicum, kurzte doch aussführliche und wahrhaftige Beschreibung der persianischen Reise*, Altenburg in Meissen 1609; French tr. 1877. (In Iran around 1605).

JENKINSON, Sir ANTHONY, *A compendious ... declaration of the journey ... from London into the land of Persia ... anno 1561*. In RICHARD HAKLUYT, *The Principal Navigations, Voyages, and Discoveries of the English Nation*, London 1598–1600; *Early voyages and travels to Russia and Persia*, London 1886 (Hakluyt Society, 72).

Don JUAN DE PERSIA (ḤUSAYN 'ALĪ BEG BAYĀT), *Relaciones* ... Valladolid 1604; modern ed., Madrid 1946 (Real Academia Española. Biblioteca selecta de clásicos españoles). Tr. and ed. by GUY LE STRANGE, *Don Juan de Persia, a Shi'ah Catholic*, London 1926 (The Broadway Travellers).

KÄMPFER, ENGELBERT, *Amoenitatum exoticarum politico-physico-medicarum, fasc. 5*, Lemgoviae 1712; partial tr. with introd. by WALTHER HINZ, *Am Hofe des persischen Grosskönigs (1684–85). Das 1. Buch der Amoenitatis* ... Leipzig 1940 (all that concerns Iran); selections tr. by KARL MEIER-LEMGO, *Seltsames Asien*, Detmold 1933.

OLEARIUS, ADAM, *Vermehrte neue Beschreibung der muscovitischen und persischen Reyse* ... Schlesswig 1656. French tr., *Voyage très curieux* ..., Amsterdam 1727. Modern ed., abridged by H. VON STADEN, *Die erste deutsche Expedition nach Persien 1635–39*, Leipzig 1927.

RAPHAEL DU MANS, *Estat de la Perse en 1660, par le Père Raphaël du Mans, Supérieur de la Mission des Capucins d'Isfahan*, ed. by CHARLES SCHEFER, Paris 1890. (Pub. de l'Ecole des Langues Orientales Vivantes, 2e. S., 20). Valuable survey of European travels in Iran in the 16th and 17th centuries in Schefer's introduction.

SANSON, N. (Père), *Voyage ou Relation de l'Etat présent du Royaume de Perse*, Paris 1695.

SHERLEY, Sir ANTHONY, *Relation of his travels into Persia* ..., London 1613. Also: PARRY, WILLIAM, *A new and large discourse of the travels of Sir Anthony Shirley ... by sea and overland to the Persian empire* ..., London 1601; Ross, Sir E. DENISON, *Sir Anthony Sherley and his Persian adventure*, London 1933.

TAVERNIER, JEAN-BAPTISTE, *Les six voyages ... qu'il a fait en Turquie, en Perse et aux Indes*, 2 vols., Paris 1676. German tr.,*Beschreybung der sechs Reisen*, Geneva 1681. Italian tr., Rome 1682. Modern partial ed., *Voyages en Perse et description de ce royaume*, pub. par PASCAL PIA, Paris 1930.

TEIXEIRA, PEDRO, *Relaciones del origen, descendencia y succession de los reyes de Persia y de Hormuz* ..., Amberes 1610. French tr., *Voyages* ..., Paris 1681. Modern Eng. tr., *The travels ..., with his "Kings of Hormuz" and extracts from his "Kings of Persia"*, tr. and ed. by W. F. SINCLAIR, London 1902 (Hakluyt Society, Series 2, No. 9).

DE THÉVENOT, JEAN, *Relation d'un voyage fait au Levant. Suite ..., dans laquelle il est traité de la Perse*, 3 parts, Paris 1664–1684. Various modern editions and translations.

DELLA VALLE, PIETRO, *Viaggi in lettere familiari al suo amico Mario Schipano, divisi in tre parti, cioè la Turchia, la Persia e l'India,* Rome 1650. Various modern editions and translations. (In Iran 1617–1627).

## THE EIGHTEENTH CENTURY

AFSHAR, MAHMOUD, *La politique europeenne en Perse; quelques pages de l'histoire diplomatique,* Berlin 1921.

ALLEN, W. E. D., *A history of the Georgian people from the beginning down to the Russian conquest,* London 1932.

DE CLAIRAC, LOUIS-ANDRÉ DE LA MAMIE, *Histoire de la Perse depuis le commencement de ce siècle,* 3 vols., Paris 1750.

FERRIER, JOSEPH PIERRE, *History of the Afghans,* tr. from the original unpublished manuscript by Captain WILLIAM JESSE, London 1858.

FRASER, JAMES, *The History of Nadir Shah ...,* 2nd ed., London 1742.

HEKMAT, MOHAMMED ALI, *Essai sur l'histoire politique irano-ottomane de 1722 à 1747,* Paris 1937.

JAMĀLZĀDAH, Sayyid MUḤAMMAD 'ALI, *Tārīkh-i ravābiṭ-i Rūs va Īrān,* in the periodical Kāvah, Dawreh-yi Jadīd, Berlin 1920–1921.

LĀRŪDĪ, NŪRULLĀH, *Zindagānī-yi Nādir Shāh,* Tehran 1319/1940.

LOCKHART, LAWRENCE, *Nadir Shah: a critical study based mainly upon contemporary sources,* London 1938. Very thorough presentation, with comprehensive bibliography.

MINORSKY, VLADIMIR, *Esquisse d'une histoire de Nader-Chah,* Paris 1934 (Pub. de la Société des Etudes Iraniennes ..., No. 10).

QŪZĀNLŪ, JAMĪL, *Tārīkh-i Niẓāmī-yi Īrān,* Tehran 1315/1936, vol. 1.

PETROV, G. M., *Kratkii ocherk razvitiya russko-iranskikh ekonomicheskikh i politicheskikh otnoshenii v 18 v.* In *Sovetskoe Vostokovedenie* 6, 1949, pp. 327–335.

SYKES, Sir PERCY MOLESWORTH, *A history of Afghanistan,* 2 vols., London 1940, vol. 1.

---

HANWAY, JONAS, *An Historical Account of the British Trade over the Caspian Sea ... to which are added, The Revolutions of Persia during the present century, with the particular history of the great usurper Nadir Kouli,* 4 vols., London 1753.

OTTER, JEAN, *Voyage en Turquie et en Perse,* 2 vols., Paris 1748.

PICAULT, CHARLES, *Histoire des révolutions de Perse pendant la durée du XVIIIe. siècle,* 2 vols., Paris 1810.

SOYMONOV, FEDOR IVANOVICH, *Opisanie Kaspiiskago Morya i chinennykh na onom Rossiiskikh zavoevanii,* ed. by G. F. MILLER, St. Petersburg 1763. (Russian clashes with the Afghans).

---

ARUTIN TANBURÎ, *Tahmas Kulu Han'in tevarihi.* Türk harflerine çeviren ESAT URAS, Ankara 1942. (Pub. de la Société d'Histoire Turque, S. 2, No. 7) (History of Nādir Shāh until his coronation).

DURRI EFENDI, AHMED, *Prodromus ad tragicam vertentis belli Persici historiam seu legationis a Fulgida Porta ad Sophorum regem Szah Sultan a. 1720 expeditae authentica relatio, quam redux e Perside Legatus Durri Effendi Turcarum Imperatori Achmet III in scripto consignavit.* Tr. from the Turkish by P. THADDAEUS KRUSINSKI. Leopolis (Lwow). 1733. French tr., *Relation de Dourry Effendi,* Paris 1810. Eng. tr., *The chronicles of a traveller, or the history of the Afghan wars with Persia,* London 1840.

GULISTĀNA, ABŪ'L-ḤASAN IBN MUḤAMMAD AMĪN, *Das mujmil et-Târikh-i Ba'dnâdirîje*, (incomplete text) ed. by OSKAR MANN, Leiden 1891; partial tr. by Sir JADUNATH SARKAR in *Modern Review* (Calcutta), XLV, 1929.

HAZĪN, Shaykh MUḤAMMAD 'ALĪ, *Tażkirat ul-Ahvāl*, ed. by F. C. BELFOUR. London 1831; tr. by F. C. BELFOUR, *The Life of Shaikh Mohammed Ali Hazin*, London 1830.

KAWKABĪ ASTARĀBĀDĪ, MUḤAMMAD MAHDĪ, *Tārīkh-i Nādirī*, French. tr. by Sir WILLIAM JONES, *Histoire de Nader-Chah*, Paris 1770; abridged Eng. tr. by Sir WILLIAM JONES, *The History of the Life of Nadir Shah*, London 1773.

*Vaṣīqeh-yi ittiḥād-i Islām-i Nādirī*. In Yādgār, 4, Tehran 1326–7/1947–8, No. 6, pp. 43–55. Complete text of Nādir's manifesto on religion.

N.B. L. LOCKHART gives particulars of many more Persian and other sources, and also critical assessments, in his *Fall of the Safavi Dynasty* and *Nadir Shah*.

# CENTRAL ASIA: THE LAST CENTURIES OF INDEPENDENCE

BY

BERTOLD SPULER

Translated from parts of the author's *Geschichte Mittelasiens seit dem Auftreten der Türken*, in *Handbuch der Orientalistik*, 5. Band, 5. Abschnitt, with slight modifications.

## ÖZBEGS AND SHAYBĀNIDS

One of the great historical events of the early 16th century was the Özbeg conquest of western Central Asia. In the previous century this region had been linked politically with eastern Īrān under the rule of Tīmūrid princes and exposed to the strong influence of Persian culture, of which Transoxiana again became a major centre, as it had been before the Mongol invasion. The severance of these links by the Özbeg conquest was to have far-reaching consequences in Muslim and world history. Who then were the Özbegs, and what was their previous record?

When the Golden Horde empire was established around the year 1242, a territory stretching roughly from the south end of the Ural mountains and the upper Tobol' river eastwards to the upper Irtîsh river was assigned to two brothers of the reigning khān Batu, namely *Orda* and *Shîban* (pronounced in Arabic fashion *Shaybān*). Two political entities, reflecting the nature of the terrain, then emerged in this expanse of steppe: Shaybān and his descendants led the nomads roaming in the western part, Orda and his led those in the eastern part. Between them no definite boundary existed; but their southern limits were the Üst Yurt plateau (Russian: Ust Urt', i.e. "highland"), the Jaxartes river (Sîr Daryā), and the southern mountain fringe of Semirechia ("Seven Rivers Land"). The terms "White" and "Blue" were used to distinguish the "Hordes" then in occupation of this territory, but their meaning is obscure and sometimes comprised the "Golden Horde" also. A 15th-century writer thinks that the Blue Horde did not split off from the White Horde until around 1300.

Practically no information has come down about men and events in this vaguely outlined tract, apart from names of a few chiefs and reports of occasional raids into the Īlkhānid empire. Scholars cannot even say why the followers of the Shaybānid khāns began in the 14th century to call themselves Özbegs (Russian: Uzbeks), thereby adopting the name of the famous Golden Horde ruler *Özbeg* (r. 1313–1341) as their folk-label. The seizure of the Golden Horde throne in 1380 by *Tokhtamïsh*, who was a descendant of Orda, appears to have induced a migration of the "White Horde" clans (as they were thereafter always named) into Golden Horde territory. The Özbegs and their ruling family were then able to win gradual mastery of the steppe region up to the north bank of the Sïr Daryā, and afterwards to carry their power further afield. Their principal habitat, however, was still in the far north west, with a centre some way east of the middle Urals and a commercial orientation towards the Volga basin rather than Central Asia.

The Özbegs made their first thrusts in the direction of Bukhārā, Khwārizm and Astarābād (Gurgān) in the winter of 1405–1406. From 1415 onwards they fought for possession of the Sïr Daryā estuary against the troops of Ulugh Beg, who then controlled it from Samarqand as viceroy for his father, the Tīmūrid ruler Shāhrukh. After inflicting a severe defeat on Ulugh Beg at Sighnāq in 1426/27, the 17-year old Özbeg commander *Abū'l-Khayr* finally captured the district in a swift advance in 1428. He was then chosen by the clans to be their khān, and as such became head of the Özbeg aristocracy, whose members, as always among nomadic peoples, knew how to defend their liberties. He conquered Khwārizm in 1430/31, and after eliminating successive rivals, overran the entire north bank of the Sïr Daryā up to the gates of Farghānā in or about 1445. Sighnāq on the river was probably his capital.

From this point, Abū'l-Khayr, like many earlier rulers of the bordering steppe, began to fix his gaze on Transoxiana and the Īrānian plateau; and in 1451, using a well tried technique of infiltration, he offered his services to the Tīmūrid prince Abū Saʿīd. It seems, however, that Abū'l-Khayr must have over-estimated his strength; for in 1456/57 he failed to halt an incursion of the Mongol Oirats up to the middle Sïr Daryā, and made no move when some of the chiefs and tribes who were his subjects transferred their allegiance to the powerful ruler of Mogholistān, Esen Bogha II, thereby acquiring the name Qazāqs (Russian: Kazakhs), i.e. "deserters" or "emigrants". They formed a community which was long to maintain a nomadic way of life and tribal structure, together with many ancient beliefs under an Islāmic veneer, even after the absorption of older established tribes and clans of the region such as the Dūghlāt (later called Dūlāt) of Semirechia. The "desertion" of the Kazakhs continued the process whereby the Central Asian Turks split into a number of distinct ethnic groups; dispersion and disunity have throughout the centuries characterized the life of the Turkish nation in Central Asia. During a campaign to subdue the Kazakhs, Abū'l-Khayr lost his life in 1468.

### MOGHOLISTĀN IN THE 15TH CENTURY

This event at first seemed to have eliminated all danger to the Tīmūrid Abū Saʿīd's control of western Central Asia; but other enemies also looked with covetous eyes on the renewed wealth and glory of the Transoxianan cities and planned aggression against them. The first serious challenge came from Mogholistān, where the Jagatāyid rulers had successfully defended their independence against all Tīmūr's onslaughts. The territory of Mogholistān ("land of the Moghols", i.e. Mongols) was then reckoned to comprise the Tarim basin (where the capital Aq Ṣu was located), a north eastward lying area around the Ṭurfān oasis, and a northward mountain zone stretching to the Ala Tau range and including the Narîn (upper Sîr Daryā) valley, the Issîq Köl basin, the valley of the Ili and its tributaries, and the Ebi Noor basin. In view of the lack of sources, practically nothing can be said about the contemporary population pattern, except that sections of the turkicized Dūghlāt tribes (whose principal seat was in Semirechia) dwelt around Kāshghar. The Moghols (Mongols) in this territory had, as in other regions, adopted Turkish speech and the Islāmic faith during the 14th century; they were later to become assimilated with the Kazakhs.

Relief from political pressure on the western flank after Tīmūr's death permitted a redeployment of forces in Mogholistān. The khān *Uways* (or *Vays*; r.c. 1418–1429) embarked on campaigns to spread Islām among the "pagan" Oirats on the Ili river, or Kalmüks as they are called in the Muslim sources; his efforts must have been costly, as he was twice taken prisoner by his enemies. He then turned his attention to internal development and laid the foundations for an advance of agriculture in the Ṭurfān oasis. The western frontier apparently remained quiet in his reign. His death was followed by a succession struggle between numerous rivals in which the victor was *Esen Bogha II* (r.c. 1429–1462). This ruler set his sights on Transoxiana, and launched a series of attacks which for a time looked like a dangerous threat to Abū Saʿīd. In 1451–53 he plundered Sayrām (formerly Isfījāb), Tashkent and Yasî (later the town of Turkistān); but after a setback on the Ṭalās (Ṭarāz) river, he was obliged to withdraw hurriedly to the east, where the Oirats had in the meantime begun an offensive. They raided far and wide, sometimes almost to the Oxus (Āmū Daryā), under the vigorous direction of their ruler Esen Tayji. After the latter's death in 1455, however, Abū Saʿīd successfully kept the forces of Mogholistān in check and later neutralized them completely. He acquired Harāt, always a strategic keypoint, in 1457, and afterwards set up Esen Bogha's elder brother *Yūnus* as a pretender to the throne of Mogholistān. Yūnus did not in fact make much headway until after his brother's death in 1462. Meanwhile a phase of collaboration between the Oirats and Abū Saʿīd had been started in 1459 by an Oirat embassy to Harāt. By these devices the goal of Tīmūrid policy, namely to ward off pressure from Transoxiana's vulnerable north eastern flank, was for the time being achieved.

Ten more years were needed before Yūnus, after repelling a new Oirat invasion of Semirechia in 1472, firmly established himself as heir to his brother's heritage. He was in no position, however, to curtail the power of the Turkish chiefs (*begs*) and their clans, who since Esen Bogha's early years had held all real authority in large tracts of Mogholistān, such as Kāshghar, the upper Sīr Daryā valley, the Issīq Köl and Atbash districts, etc. Yūnus was obliged to cede the south western part of the Tarim basin, including Kāshghar, Yārkand and Khotan, to the Dūghlāt clan as a sort of vassal principality. The Dūghlāts won much esteem for their services to the economic welfare of the district, in spite of fratricidal strife within their clan which lasted until 1479/80.

Having come to a provisional understanding with the Dūghlāts, Yūnus was free to try his hand in the west, where he made extensive conquests at the expense of his erstwhile protectors, the Tīmūrids. He spent his last years at Tashkent,[1] happy to be again living in a civilized urban environment, and died there in 1486/87 at the age of about 70. His death was followed by a division of Mogholistān into two parts under two of his sons. The western part went to *Maḥmūd*, who made Tashkent his capital and fended off a few attacks by the now enfeebled Tīmūrids. Eastern Mogholistān was governed by *Aḥmad*, who held fast to the nomadic way of life and persevered in a war begun by his father against China for possession of the oasis of Komul (Chinese: Ha-mi). The Chinese with the help of a commercial blockade finally prevailed over Aḥmad and kept the place. Aḥmad also claimed Kāshghar and Yengi Ḥiṣār from the Dughlāts and warred against them until around 1499 without any lasting success.

## THE FALL OF THE TĪMŪRIDS

Such were the adversaries who threatened Tīmūr's descendants from the north and the east. Before the Shaybānid and Jagatāyid fortunes are

[1] Tāshkand, the former Shāsh or Chāch.

traced further, something must be said about the last phase of Tīmūrid rule in Central Asia. As has been seen, *Abū Sa'īd* (r. 1452–1469) overcame his enemies in several different wars. His days, however, were numbered. Changes in the political conjuncture in western Īrān brought him into conflict with the Aq Qoyunlu, who took him prisoner after defeating his army and then executed him in 1469. This blow buried all hopes that Īrān might remain united under Tīmūrid hegemony and that its war-stricken economy might be restored.

Moreover, it soon became doubtful whether Tīmūr's descendants, despite the many services which till the end they rendered to Persian culture, could retain any sovereign authority at all. In Transoxiana the new Tīmūrid ruler *Aḥmad Sulṭān* (r. 1469–1494) engaged in endless wars with his brothers and in particular with *'Umar Shaykh*, who ruled Farghānā. This strife enticed Yūnus, the ruler of Mogholistān, to intervene, and 'Umar Shaykh became virtually his vassal. For Aḥmad Sulṭān, the loss of Tashkent and Sayrām to Yūnus in 1484 was a bitter blow; but his attempt after Yūnus's death to recover the two towns came to nothing. He lost his life in July 1494 while invading Farghānā, where his brother 'Umar Shaykh had died in the previous month. In the ensuing succession struggles, Samarqand fell to 'Umar Shaykh's son and heir Bābur for a few months in 1497. Neither he, nor his cousin 'Ali, son of Aḥmad Sulṭān, were able to hold the city. In 1500 Tīmūr's capital was captured by the Özbeg ruler Muḥammad Shaybānī.

Events in the preceding decades had shown that the Shaybānids after the loss of Abū'l-Khayr in 1468 were by no means a spent force. His grandson *Muḥammad Shaybānī* (known also as *Shāhbakht* and *Shaybaq*) was able in the course of an adventurous career to build up a strong army. He had spent much of his youth at Ástrakhan, and was afterwards protected by Maḥmūd, the ruler of western Mogholistān, who in or about 1490 gave him the town of Yasī[1] as a fief. From this base he drove the Tīmūrids out of Transoxiana during the years 1495 to 1500. After securing his position in that territory against other rivals, he cast off the suzerainty of the Jagatāyids in 1503. He had already seized Tashkent and Sayrām.

In Harāt and Balkh, however, the most distinguished contemporary Tīmūrid prince, *Ḥusayn Bāyqara* (r. 1469–1506), remained in possession of his heritage. At his court the renowned *wazīr* 'Alī Shīr Navā'ī (1440–1502) endeavoured to raise his mother tongue Chaghatāy (Jagatāy) Turkish

[1] Later called the Town of Turkistān (Shahr-i Turkistān) because it contains the tomb of the 12th century "Saint of Turkistān", Aḥmad Yasavī. His mystic aphorisms are among the earliest relics of written Turkish.

to a level of literary equality with Persian.[1] Thanks to this master's work and also to Bābur's Memoirs, this branch of Turkish became a well established written language. Persian, however, remained in favour under Ḥusayn Bāyqara, as under all Tīmūr's descendants; far from being neglected, Persian literature and art received their keen encouragement. Particularly valuable were the labours of Ḥusayn Bāyqara himself and of the scholars around him to collect and preserve the text of Firdawsī's *Shāhnāmah*. Jāmī (1414–1492), the last of the seven foremost classical poets of Īrān, and Mīrkhwānd (1433–1498), the well known historian, lived in this prince's reign and were in close touch with his court. His death on May 4, 1506, was followed by a rapid collapse. Only a year later, on May 14, 1507, his son *Badīʿal-Zamān* was driven out of Harāt by the Özbegs under Muḥammad Shaybānī. Harāt and Balkh, and also in the same year Khwārizm, were annexed to the Shaybānid realm.

The Özbeg conqueror, while quite unscrupulous in his methods and ready to commit many cruel acts, was regarded by his new subjects as a benevolent ruler. Theologians, scholars and poets enjoyed his special favour. In regard to Persian culture he showed no less receptivity than the Tīmūrids whom he had supplanted.[2]

Other prey were also targets of Muḥammad Shaybānī's warlike ambition. After 1500 he turned against Mogholistān, then weakened by the conflict between the rival brothers Aḥmad and Maḥmud which had continued since 1487, and was able to take both brothers prisoner. Aḥmad died soon afterwards, but Maḥmud after being released resumed the struggle until Muḥammad recaptured him and had him executed in 1508 at Khojent. The Jagatāyids then lost the western part of Mogholistān for good; only the lands east of the Ili river and south of the Tien-shan mountains remained in their hands.

---

1 *ʿAli Shir Navāʾi*, special volume of the "Izvestiya Akademii Nauk SSSR, otd. literatury i yazyka" VI/6 (1947); EVGENII EDUARDOVICH BERTEL'S, *Navoi*, Moscow/Leningrad 1948; WILHELM BARTHOLD, *Herat unter Ḥusein Baiqara, dem Timuriden*, German tr. by WALTER HINZ, Leipzig 1938 (Abhandlungen für die Kunde des Morgenlandes, XXII/8), Eng. tr. by V. MINORSKY in V. V. BARTHOLD, *Four studies on the History of Central Asia*, Leiden, 1956–1962.

2 PAVEL PETROVICH IVANOV, *Ocherki po istorii Srednei Azii (XVI seredina XIX v.)* (Sketches of the history of Central Asia, 16th–mid–19th cents.), Moscow 1958, pp. 21–53; Sir HENRY HOYLE HOWORTH, *History of the Mongols*, 4 vols. and appendix, London 1876–88, II, pp. 619–713; RENE GROUSSET, *L'Empire des Steppes*, Paris 1939, pp. 559–564; HERMANN VAMBERY, *Geschichte Bukharas oder Transoxaniens*, 2 vols., Stuttgart 1872, II, pp. 619–713; LUCIEN BOUVAT in *Encyclopaedia of Islam*, 1st ed., IV, pp. 292–294. Letters exchanged with Shāh Ismāʿīl Ṣafavī, in Yādgār (Tehrān) II/3 (1945–46), pp. 21–32.

## CENTRAL ASIA'S NEW ROLE AFTER 1500

Muḥammad Shaybānī's victorious advance at first seemed likely to bring forth a new empire embracing the former Tīmūrid and Jagatāyid domains; but events did not turn out in this way. Their actual course was largely determined by the momentous changes which were transforming the whole pattern of political power and religious alignment in Western Asia during these years. Central Asia was for centuries to feel the after-effects of these changes, which must now be briefly considered.

The Ottoman empire, after its painful but not mortal defeat by Tīmūr at Ankara in 1402, had rapidly regained strength under exceptionally capable rulers. The many other Turkish states of Asia Minor were eliminated or defeated in a succession of struggles spread over a hundred years. The conquest of Constantinople in 1453 fulfilled a long-standing Muslim ambition and heightened Ottoman prestige just at the time when Tīmūrid strength was entering, after the murder of Ulugh Beg in 1447, into its phase of decline. In the early 16th century, the Ottoman Turkish sultans added Syria, Egypt and Mesopotamia to their realm. The concentration of such vast authority in their hands required a broader legitimation than could be given by the ideology of frontier warfare, which had in former times, even after the fall of Constantinople, formed the moral basis of the Ottoman state. In its place was put a new ideology, projecting the Ottoman sultans as defenders of the Sunnite faith. This did not meet with unanimous assent, because the old spirit, which was linked with a veneration for the Imām ʿAlī often far exceeding the limits allowed by Sunnite orthodoxy, still remained alive. The official shift to strict Sunnism in the reign of Selīm I (1512–1530) consequently drove many of his subjects, when faced with the choice, into the Shīʿite camp. A considerable number actually migrated to Īrān, where the Shīʿite faith was being carried to supremacy, from 1501/2 onwards, by a dynasty of Turkish (Āẕarbāyjānī) origin, namely the Ṣafavids.[1] This influx from Asia Minor must have strengthened the Ṣafavid ranks very considerably and probably helps to explain why neither Selīm I, despite his victory at Chāldīrān in 1514, nor his successors, were able to make permanent conquests on the Īrānian plateau. The Ṣafavid state proved to be solidly based, and capable of resisting not only Ottoman armies but also Özbeg and other Central Asian Turkish invaders. Having set out to conquer Khurāsān, Muḥammad Shaybānī was defeated and killed in a battle near Marv, probably on December 2, 1510; he was then 59 years old.

[1] See under Īrān, pp. 183–7 above.

This victory left the Ṣafavids in control of Khurāsān and temporarily also of Khwārizm. They failed, however, in an attempt to secure Transoxiana, which would if successful have made that country once again, as so often in its long past, a frontier bastion of Īrān. With this aim in view, they gave support to the already mentioned Tīmūrid prince, *Bābur* son of 'Umar Shaykh, who at first scored a number of successes, including the temporary capture of Samarqand and Bukhārā; but in 1512 he was defeated north of Bukhārā and had to retreat south eastwards to Kābul. His presence there was by no means welcome to the inhabitants, any more than it had been in Transoxiana, because he persisted in collaborating with the Ṣafavids and with Shī'ite refugees from Shaybānid rule; and eventually he and his men had to quit Kābul also. After further long campaigns he was to win a brilliant recompense in another land. The once fearsome name of the Mongols was carried by this cultured prince, who saw himself as their heir, to India. In Central Asia, apart from the small principality of Badakhshān, Bābur was the last Tīmūrid ruler; in India he became the first of the Great Moghol ("Mongol") emperors. He died in 1530.

The limits set to both Ottoman and Özbeg expansion by these events in the early 16th century were to prove historically durable. Apart from temporary vicissitudes, Īrān's western frontier continued till the end of the Ṣafavid period to follow the lines determined by the battle of Chāldirān and by the Ottoman conquest of Mesopotamia in 1534; with slight modifications it is still the same today. The north eastern limits of Īrānian influence, as fixed by the failure of Bābur's efforts in Transoxiana, have for the most part also remained stable. The belt stretching along and south of the Āmū Daryā westwards to the Caspian Sea has since that time formed a boundary between states, and also between religious communions. Transoxiana and most of the eastern Persian-speaking lands (now included in Afghānistān and in Soviet Tājīkistān) remained predominantly Sunnite, while Īrān became almost wholly Shī'ite. Although the spread of Persian culture into Central Asia did not come to a stop in the subsequent period, the sectarian rift seriously impeded its advance. In Transoxiana, as in India, literary expression in Persian began to evolve on more or less independent lines shaped by indigenous Sunnite influences. Despite som- emigration of Īrānian poets and artists, reciprocal contacts with the culture of the Īrānian plateau were rare. While the great Persian classice retained their popularity and influence in these countries, the contempos rary literary products of Īrān, even when quite untheological, ceased to be studied and used as models. This situation, besides depriving both sides of the possible fruits of cultural intercourse, undoubtedly lay in large measure at the root of the marked retrogression of Persian in Transoxiana (except in the mountains of Tājīkistān). During this period, Turkish as the "Sunnite language" became the normal instrument of expression throughout Central Asia. This change in the language position, together with the weakening of the cultural links with Īrān, caused a gradual drop from the high level which had been attained under the influence of the common cultural development prevailing in medieval times.

The events of the early 16th century thus tended to sever Transoxiana's ancient links with the south, and at the same time to involve the country in strife on its southern flank. On the other hand, it was no longer threatened by attacks from the north east, which in the 15th century had caused frequent alarm, especially when the non-Muslim Oirats penetrated almost to the Āmū Daryā. Since Sunnite Islām had gradually spread further eastwards into Semirechia and in the Tarim basin, there was no more need for "holy wars" against the inhabitants of those parts. Contemporary sources, of which the principal is the *Tārīkh-i Rashīdī* of Muḥammad Ḥaydar Dūghlāt,[1] have almost nothing to say about these important environmental changes, and give only sparse information about political events, in 16th century Central Asia.

The north eastward limits of Islām before the Turks began to embrace it around the year 960 lay in the Samarqand district and the Farghānā valley and in the Afghān mountains. The conversion of the Transoxianan Turks was not followed by any further expansion as long as the Qara Khitāy and the Mongols clung to other religions. The Muslim Turks themselves in the period c. 960–1220 fixed their gaze almost exclusively on Īrān and the Near East and streamed forth in that direction; thoughts of extending their territory and spreading their religion into eastern Central Asia evidently did not occur to their minds. It was not until the 14th century, when the Mongols of the Jagatāy "horde" went over to Islām and Tīmūr set himself up as its far from chivalrous defender, that Qur'ānic doctrine began to permeate the whole Tarim basin and the rest of Mogholistān. Some of the local rulers then assumed the role of champions of Islām against their eastern neighbours. In the following centuries, wide stretches of eastern Central Asia were won over in this way, and in China also the number of Muslims, known as Dungans, began to rise. The only firm check on Islām came with the switch of the Mongol tribes of Mongolia to lamaistic

---

[1] English translation by N. Elias and E. D. Ross, *A history of the Moghuls of Central Asia, being the Tārīkh-i Rashīdī of Mīrzā Muḥammad Dūghlāt*, London 1898. This history goes up to 1541.

Buddhism towards the end of the 16th century. Up to that barrier, the Turkish-speaking nations and tribes rallied almost without exception to the banner of the Qur'ān.

The general situation in the early 16th century may accordingly be summarized as follows. In Īrān and Asia Minor, the Ṣafavid and Ottoman empires had replaced the former medley of unstable petty states. In India likewise the Moghol empire was soon to arise where small states had stood before, thus bringing the number of strong and well established Muslim governments up to three. The peoples and states of Central Asia now faced barriers, which proved insuperable, to any southward expansion. Only in the east, in the direction of Mogholistān, Mongolia and China, had no solidly based state come into being, with the result that frontier changes and power shifts, still merely local and intra-Muslim in scope, occurred frequently in these decades. Meanwhile in the west, a formidable rival—one whose future importance Jingiz Khān and Tīmūr would never have dreamt of—had arisen to confront the Central Asian states, namely Russia. At this time the Tsar Ivan "the Terrible" made the first Russian approach to Ṣafavid Īrān for an alliance against Ottoman Turkey and also against Bukhārā.[1] Barred by these strong neighbours from outward expansion, the Central Asian states no longer possessed sufficient strength for empire-building nor sufficient internal resources for noteworthy cultural archievement. The centuries ahead were consequently a period of stagnation and decay.

## THE ECLIPSE OF CENTRAL ASIA

The defeat and death of Muḥammad Shaybānī in 1510 and the subsequent course of events showed that the Īrānian plateau would not again be conquered by Central Asian Turks, as it so often had been in previous centuries. For long to come raiders from Transoxiana and Khwārizm persisted in harrying the Īrānian provinces of Khurāsān and Māzandarān, in much the same way that the Crim Tatars harried Lithuania and Poland in this period. Nevertheless the Ṣafavids (also Turks by origin) held their ground and welded Īrān into a strong and independent state with a distinctive character of its own. In the past, states formed in Central Asia had never attained more than merely local importance unless they were

[1] Details in A. Ya. Shpakovskii, *Torgovlya Moskovskoi Rusi s Persiei v XVI–XVII st.* (Muscovite Russia's trade with Persia in the 16th–17th centuries), Kiev 1915; A. P. Novosel'tsev, *Russko-iranskie politicheskie otnosheniya vo vtoroi polovine XVI v.* (Russo-Iranian relations in the second half of the 16th century), in *Mezhdunarodnye svyazi Rossịi do XVII v.* (The international relations of Russia up to the 17th century), Moscow 1961.

able to expand into Īrān and the Muslim heartlands. The careers of the Saljūqs and Khwārizmians, and of the Mongol Īlkhāns and Tīmūr, form a record of Central Asian thrusts towards the centres of Muslim civilization. In the 16th century, the Shaybānids, despite their very considerable strength, failed to break out of Central Asia. They consequently led an isolated existence, on the margin of high politics and "world" history. Central Asia as it entered the modern age sank to the level of an outlying Muslim province; its subsequent history as such does not require more than a brief summary here.

The successful struggle against the Ṣafavid intervention in Central Asia during the years 1510–1512 gave rise to disruption. Khwārizm fell after 1512 into the hands of a chieftain of Shaybānid descent named *Īlbars*, who organized the territory as a Sunnite outpost against the Shīʿites and as a base for constant raiding into the adjacent Īrānian provinces. He and his descendants stood firm through the 16th and 17th centuries against all attempts to subdue their realm, including invasions by the Buddhist Kalmüks in 1613 and 1632. Khwārizm came to be designated more and more commonly by the name of its capital city Khīvah, until at last the old name passed out of use. The khānate of Khīvah maintained its independent statehood for three and a half centuries.

The khānate of Sibir, in the far north west, also secured independence. After long struggles, lasting from 1563 to 1569, the reigning khāns were supplanted by a rival from a collateral branch, named *Quchum*. In 1579 he came into conflict with Russians advancing from beyond the Urals, and in 1581 he was routed and driven from his territory. Although he came back and won a victory in 1584 over the Cossack leader Yermak, who was drowned while escaping, he did not succeed in halting the Russian influx. Russian settlements were founded at Tümen (Russian: Tyumen) in 1586 and at Tobol'sk in 1587. After a severe defeat on the Ob' river in 1598, Quchum was obliged to take refuge with the Noghāy Tatars, and in 1600 he was murdered. His son *Ishim* kept up a long resistance, and collaborated in this with the Kalmüks, but could not ultimately weather the storm. The conquest of the khānate of Sibir opened the way for the future spread of Russian rule, not only to the Pacific Ocean, but also into Central Asia. Moreover, trade between East Europe and East Asia began in the ensuing decades to flow through Russian territory, and this switch to the Siberian route greatly diminished the economic importance of Transoxiana.

Apart form Khīvah and the East Uralic plain, the other territories in Central Asia where the Özbegs had settled were reunited in the second half of the 16th century by a Shaybānid ruler, *ʿAbd Allāh II*. After vigorously defending his clan's patrimony on the Zarafshān river, he got the better of his adversaries, among whom the most important was the reigning khān *Aḥmad* (1552–1556). From then on ʿAbd Allāh steadily extended his sway. He seized Bukhārā, which he made his capital, in 1557, and subdued Balkh, Samarqand, Tashkent and Farghānā during the years 1573/74–1583. He also quelled revolts against his authority. He assumed the title *khān* in 1583, after the death of his feeble-minded father Iskandar, whom he had placed on the Özbeg throne in 1561 but who had never actually governed. ʿAbd Allāh in his conduct of affairs showed consistent respect for the Sunnite *ʿulam'ā*,[1] on whom he lavished gifts. He also never wavered from a policy of strict centralization, designed to curb the influence of the *biys* (*begs*), though he left them in possession of their lucrative feudal tenures. He reorganized the administration, reformed the coinage, and sponsored the construction of public buildings, bridges, etc., the work being mostly done by purchased slaves. At the same time he embarked on a series of campaigns which enabled him to seize Kulāb, Badakhshān (where a Tīmūrid dynasty had until then kept control), and also Gīlān. On the other hand, he failed to occupy Khīvah, Mashhad and Kāshghar, and merely devastated those places. The Özbegs were driven out of their conquests in Khurāsān, notably Harāt, and out of Astarābād and Gīlān, by the Ṣafavid Shāh ʿAbbās I in 1598.

This great Īrānian ruler was ʿAbd Allāh's chief adversary in the later years of his reign. ʿAbd Allāh sought to outflank him by suggesting alliances to the Ottoman sultan Murād III and the Indian Moghol ruler Akbar, with whom he exchanged embassies in 1585. ʿAbbās in like manner made approaches to the Habsburgs, in the hope of synchronizing their respective campaigns against the Ottoman Turks in western Īrān and in Hungary. Diplomatic missions from the Özbeg khāns are also reported to have arrived from time to time at Kāshghar and Khotan and in the Crimea.

Around the year 1590, it seemed highly probable that Central Asia would gain and keep a new unity under the strong hand of ʿAbd Allāh II. At that time, however, he came into conflict with his only son ʿAbd al-

---

[1] The Jūybār Khōjahs, a group of *ʿulamā'* who held the guardianship of a shrine at Bukhārā, form the subject of a monograph based on a collection of documents which has survived from this time. The documents contain valuable information about contemporary religious, economic and social conditions, and have been studied by PAVEL PETROVICH IVANOV, *Khozyaistvo Dzhuibarskikh Sheikhov. K istorii feodal'nogo zemlevladeniya v Srednei Azii v XVI i XVII vv.* (The economy of the Jūybār Shaykhs. A contribution to the history of feudal land tenure in Central Asia in the 16th and 17th cents.), Moscow and Leningrad 1954. (The original texts cannot be verified as only Russian translations are given.) On general developments, c.f. V. V. BARTHOLD, *Four Studies*, III, pp. 135–145.

Mu'min, who after receiving the governorship of Balkh aspired to hold supreme power in his father's lifetime as his father had done in his grandfather's lifetime. The protracted struggle between father and son enabled the Kazakhs to invade Transoxiana up to the gates of Tashkent and Samarqand; it only ceased with ʿAbd Allāh's death in 1598 on a punitive expedition against the Kazakhs. ʿAbd al-Mu'min was not then able to win the succession, and two months later he was murdered. ʿAbd Allāh's empire thereupon fell to pieces, and his line expired.

The last attempt to unite Central Asia came thus to an end just at the time when Shāh ʿAbbās the Great of Īrān was rising to the height of his power. Although raids by Central Asian Turkish nomads, particularly Turkomāns, continued to afflict north eastern Īrān in the following centuries, these were only pin-pricks. The Īrānian plateau was never again threatened by large-scale invasion from the north east.[1] The blows which smote Īrān in the early 18th century when the Ṣafavid empire collapsed came from different directions: from Qandahār, from Ottoman Turkey and from Russia.

## THE TARIM BASIN UNDER THE LAST JAGATĀYIDS

Before the destinies of Transoxiana are traced further, a glance may be cast at the south eastern region of Central Asia, inhabited by peoples now wholly Turcophone and ruled by the successor states of the khānate of Mogholistān. In the eastern half of this region, the old dynasty descended through Jagatāy from Jingiz Khān was still strong in the early part of the 16th century. The khān *Manṣūr* (r. 1503–1545), son of the earlier mentioned khān Aḥmad, was able with help from his brother *Saʿid* to break the power of the Dūghlāt clan. The two brothers then apportioned the territory, leaving the former Dūghlāt domains in the south west of the Tarim basin under Saʿīd's control, while Semirechia, Yulduz and the Ṭurfān oasis were governed by Manṣūr. Their mutual understanding and support enabled them to repulse Shaybānid attacks and give the country a long period of internal peace. Both brothers were convinced Muslims and followers of the urban way of life. They further reduced the influence of the nomad elements, and opened the Tarim basin to penetration by the revived culture of Samarqand and Bukhārā. Probably by this time "Chaghatāy" Turkish had completely displaced the earlier Indo-European languages of this region, although Muḥammad Ḥaydar Dūghlāt (c. 1500–

[1] On the "geopolitics" of Iran, c.f. BERTOLD SPULER, *Iran im Spiel der Weltmächte im 20. Jh.*, in Die Welt als Geschichte, 1954/II, pp. 119–131.

1551) wrote his well known *Tārīkh-i Rashīdī* (to which reference has already been made) in Persian. There is no evidence of any Chinese influence in this region during the 16th century.

The two princely brothers also apportioned their military responsibilities. Manṣūr concentrated on the east, where there were still possibilities of spreading Islām by conquest. In 1513 he obtained the submission of the oasis of Komul (Ha-mi), long an objective of Muslim rulers in this area, and in 1517 he made it his capital and base for further inroads into China. His eastward thrusts carried him at times as far as Tun-huang, Su-chow and Kan-chow in the Chinese province of Kan-su. Mention of his activities consequently appears in Chinese as well as native chronicles. Although the Muslims of Eastern Turkistān were not destined to hold these places for long, the spread of Islām in China's western provinces was probably accelerated by conversions which then took place.

During this time, Saʿīd Khān invaded the province of Ladākh, till then a dependency of Tibet. In 1531 the historian Muḥammad Ḥaydar Dūghlāt was governor of the district—an indication that the powerful Dūghlāt clan must then have been on good terms with the khān. The ending of this cordial relationship was to do the country much harm. *ʿAbd al-Rashīd Khān*, who succeeded his father Saʿīd in 1533, sought greater freedom of action and would no longer concur in the former balanced distribution of authority. Ḥaydar accordingly quit Rashīd's service and established himself in Kashmīr, in 1541.

These events led to a complete change in the situation. While the two Jagatāyid brothers and their successors were pinned down by military commitments in the east and south, the Kazakhs were left free to infiltrate into northern Mogholistān. The entire Ili and Kunges valleys were lost to them. ʿAbd al-Rashīd saw his authority confined to the Kāshghar area, which lay beyond the range of the Kazakhs across the impenetrable Hindū Kush mountains. New internal forces also made their presence increasingly felt after Saʿīd Khān's death. In this territory, as in other Muslim lands, descendants of the Prophet and his Companions enjoyed special respect. Their standing was particularly high in the strongly orthodox Tarim basin, where the zealous spirit of the *ghāzīs* (frontier warriors) remained alive. The real, and probably also many purported, descendants of Muḥammad and ʿAlī and of the three "Rightly Guided" Caliphs were grouped in clans, whose leading members received the name *Khōjah* ("Master").

The Khōjahs themselves split into two factions, those "of the White Mountain" (*Aqtaghlîq*) and those "of the Black Mountain" (*Qarataghlîq*), with Kāshghar and Yārkand as their respective centres of influence. Their prestige grew after Manṣūr Khān's death in 1545, as his sons were at cross purposes. The period of peaceful development in the Tarim basin had ended. According to Chinese sources, *Shāh Khān* (r. 1545–c. 1570) was opposed by his brother Muḥammad, who succeeded with help from the Oirats in capturing part of the Komul oasis, and was finally killed in battle against a third brother some time after 1570. Details of these affairs are lacking, because the Chinese sources have nothing to report after the cessation of the threat to China from Komul. The next information they give concerns the appearances of a Turkish khān from Ṭurfān at Peking in 1647 and 1657, i.e. after the Manchu dynasty's triumph in China.

In the western part of the region, ʿAbd al-Rashīd's death in 1565 (or 1570?) was followed by the accession of his son *ʿAbd al-Karīm* (or *ʿAbd al-Laṭīf*?), who reigned at Kāshghar until 1593 and gave Yārkand in fief to his brother Muḥammad. The latter was evidently still in office when the Portuguese Jesuit missionary Benedict Goes passed through Kāshghar in 1603.[1] The grant of this apanage doubtless averted strife within the dynasty, but also enhanced the fragmentation of the country and contributed to the shift of effective authority into the hands of the Khōjah families. The dispersion of human settlement in the Tarim basin favoured this trend, which led to the emergence of a growing number of small city states in different oases. Not only Kāshghar and Yārkand, but also Aq Ṣu and Khotan, became strongholds of Khōjah clans. The "White Mountaineers" at first maintained close links with the Kazakhs, who were then divided into three hordes (*jüz*), the Great or Elder, the Middle, and the Little or Younger; they roamed over the steppe expanse north of the Aral and Caspian Seas as far as the Irtish and Tobol' rivers, and had recently (as mentioned above) taken possession of the Ili valley. The "Black Mountaineers", on the other hand, looked for help to the Kirghiz (or Qarakirghiz) tribes living on the southern slopes of the Tien-shan mountains. Meanwhile the presence of Jagatāyid khāns was tolerated because they lacked real power. When a khān named *Ismāʿīl* attempted to redress this situation and to overthrow the "White Mountaineers", the latter brought in a Mongol tribe, the Dzungars, who had broken away from the Oirats in 1620 and had inflicted heavy losses on the Kazakhs with whom they clashed in 1635 and again in 1643. Thanks to their Dzungarian allies, the "White Mountaineers" in 1678 simultaneously defeated the khān

[1] He travelled in 1602–1607 under the name ʿAbd Allāh from India via Kābul, Badakhshān, the Pamīrs, Yārkand and Aq Ṣu to Su-chow, where he stayed from the end of 1605 till his death in 1607. An Armenian named Isaac who travelled with him reached China safely. The story is told in N. TRIGAUTII, *De expeditione Christiana apud Sinas, suscepta a Societate Jesu*, Leiden 1616.

Ismāʿīl and the "Black Mountaineers" of Yārkand. The head of the "White Mountain" faction then set himself up at Yārkand as "khān". The last of Jingiz Khān's heirs in Muslim Eastern Turkistān was thereby eliminated. At Bukhārā, however, and in the Crimea under the Girāy dynasty, descendants of the "World Conqueror" continued to reign for another century. The Tarim basin entered a new phase under the "Holy State" of the Khōjahs.[1]

## THE TARIM BASIN UNDER DZUNGARIAN AND CHINESE HEGEMONIES

The sanctity of the Khōjah state does not appear to have been impaired by its utter dependence on a power which was by no means Islāmic; for the Dzungars ("men of the army's left wing") were lamaistic Buddhists. During the upheaval of 1678 they moved into the Kāshghar district, and thereafter they installed nominees of their own choice from either of the two Khōjah factions as khāns of the Tarim basin. From Kāshghar, the lamaist Dzungar ruler *Galdan* (r. 1671–1697), with moral support from the Tibetan Dalai Lama, invaded and occupied Semirechia, and also Ṭurfān and Komul: the two oases had apparently remained in the hands of Jagatāyid princes, who were then driven out. Galdan also made a series of attacks, beginning in 1688, on other Mongol tribes, especially the Khalkhas. He was obliged to discontinue them when Chinese forces intervened against him. After a long campaign led by the Manchu emperor K'ang-hsi in person, Galdan was finally defeated and forced to commit suicide in 1697.

The next Dzungarian ruler *Tsevang Rabdan* (r. 1697–1727), who was Galdan's nephew, fought with the Kazakhs, from whom he captured Tashkent and the town of Turkistān in 1723, and with the Chinese for possession of the oases of Ṭurfān and Komul, both of which he occupied after nine years of fighting (1715–1724). He had in his service a Swedish military adviser, formerly a sergeant in King Charles XII's army, who had been taken prisoner in Russia. Though foiled by the Chinese in an invasion of Tibet, he kept intact the Oirat hegemony over Eastern Turkistān. His son and successor *Galdang Tsereng* (r. 1727–1745) finally divided the Tarim basin into four separate states: Kāshghar, Aq Ṣu Yārkand and Khotan. While able to extend his sway westwards over the Kazakhs, he lost territory in the far north east to the Chinese in 1732.

[1] Described by Martin Hartmann, *Ein heiliger Staat im Islam*, in *Der islamische Orient*, I (1899), p. 195 ff.

After his death, a rebellion of the native Turkish inhabitants broke out in the Tarim basin, and the governments of the four city states were overthrown. The Dzungars were weakened by a civil war in 1753–54, and the Turks were able to cast off the last traces of their suzerainty in 1757. This deliverance mattered little; for the Chinese, who had subdued the Dzungars of Dzungaria in campaigns lasting from 1755 to 1758, sent a strong army into the former Dzungarian dominion of the Tarim basin, which had several times in earlier centuries been subject to China. They conquered the country in an eventful and hard-fought campaign lasting from 1757 to 1759, and annexed it to the Manchu empire under the name Sin-kiang ("New March").

The collapse of the Dzungarian empire—the last nomad empire in Central Asia—removed the curbs formerly imposed on the Kazakhs and Kirghiz by the Dzungars, who had restricted their movements and tried to confine them to the oases. They now reoccupied Semirechia and the northern margins of the Tien-shan. The Kazakh magnates of the "Great Horde" (*Kishi Jüz*) and "Middle Horde" (*Orta Jüz*) were well disposed towards the Chinese empire and paid tribute right up to the mid-19th century, thereby securing rights to exchange their horses and cattle for Chinese silk. This trade grew significantly in the following decades, to the satisfaction of both parties. Chinese trading posts were set up at various places in the Kazakh lands, while Kazakh caravans made their way to the Tarim basin and Outer Mongolia.

At the same time Russian influence gained ground, following the establishment of the fortress of Orenburg near the southern Urals in 1735. The "Great" and "Middle" Kazakh hordes finally submitted to Russian suzerainty in 1854, after which date their trade with China gradually ceased; and a new area began in the history of northern Central Asia. Events in the western part of this vast region now call for attention.

## COMMON FACTORS IN THE EVOLUTION OF WESTERN CENTRAL ASIA SINCE 1600

The Chinese conquest of the south eastern part of the Turkish-speaking zone was a portent of the fate in store for the entire Turkish-speaking population of the Central Asian and East European land-mass. Already, in the 16th century, the Tatars of the Volga basin had been subjugated by a foreign power. The history of every single territory records sooner or later a similar subjugation, and in almost all cases apart from Eastern Turkistān the conquering power was Russia.

Since Transoxiana and Western Turkistān in the period between the 16th and 19th centuries no longer shared a common political destiny, the history of each state in the region must be examined separately, just as the study of the Mongol empire has to be replaced after the mid-13th century by studies of the smaller empires into which it split. Attention may nevertheless be given to the many shared characteristics and close mutual contacts which existed between these states, despite the frontiers separating them. Above all there was a common attachment to strict Sunnism, strongly felt by all inhabitants of the region, whether Turks or Īrānians (Tājīks), peasants or nomads, courtiers and officials or rulers. This left an imprint on the country still discernible today, and (as said earlier) caused its cultural development to diverge more markedly than before from that of Īran, where Shīʿism had taken firm root. The religious mood of Central Asia in these centuries, while neither responsive to changing circumstances nor conducive to new theological insights, gave the people a moral strength which restored their peace of mind after the grim experiences of the 13th to 16th centuries, and instilled in them a sense of common identity. Islāmic charity—always a feature of this religion—with its organized institutions, such as the *darvīsh* monasteries and their kitchens where the poor were fed, and the *madrasahs* and mosque schools where workmen's sons received education, contributed on the material side to the maintenance of social harmony.

In such a society, where religion permeated all public life and all classes and tribes, there could be no effective challenge to the influence of the religious authorities (*ʿulamāʾ* and *fuqahāʾ*) and of the *darvīsh* orders, among whom the Naqshbandīs and Kubrawīs were the most important. A ruler who agreed and worked with them could count on their weighty support; and in their roles as judges (*qāḍīs*) and auxiliaries in the law courts, as officials in many administrative functions, and as *imāms* among the nomads, they stood in very close contact with the people. Attempts to limit their prerogatives were always hazardous, even when prompted by justifiable motives. Certain khāns of the period lost their thrones in this way. The Central Asian historians, in their portrayals of such events and in their judgements on leading personalities, reflect orthodox Sunnite viewpoints, as they were bound to do in the social context of the time.[1]

Historiography, as the years advanced, could no longer be limited to repetition or rearrangement of already known data, even though this was

---

[1] The religious and social preconceptions of contemporary Indian Muslim historiography are perceptively studied in P. Hardy, *Historians of Medieval India: Studies in Indo-Muslim historical writing*, London 1960.

still the practice in theology, which emanated from Sunnite tradition (*taqlīd*) and was supervised in these countries by boards of censors under a *ra'īs* (comparable with the *ṣadr* in Shīʿite Īrān) to ensure doctrinal purity. The historians, while not changing their inherited preconceptions, had to make ideological assessments of new events and situations. Only a small amount of research has as yet been done into the Central Asian chronicles of this period, because their subject matter (unlike that of earlier compilations) lacks world significance; closer study may perhaps bring to light details hitherto overlooked. The manuscripts being generally located in Central Asia, and the few printed editions being virtually unobtainable, foreign scholars are for the time being dependent on works by Russian authors, whose statements of fact cannot always be verified.[1] Although the Central Asian chronicles are with few exceptions written in Persian (as are the contemporary Indian chronicles), sectarian bias against Īrān pervades them (and likewise the Sunnite Indian chronicles) to an extent which imposes caution in their use. In both Central Asia and India, pressures for emphatic expression of religious animosities and for self-justificatory portrayal of past events swelled the volume of historical writing.

In other fields besides theology and historiography, a similar uniformity prevailed in these centuries. Such a state of affairs accorded with Muslim tradition, and had been fostered in the middle ages by the freedom (far greater than in medieval Europe) with which artists, scholars and merchants travelled from one Muslim land to another. They still travelled to and from Transoxiana, but in declining numbers. The Shīʿite victory in Īrān impelled many Sunnite scholars and poets who were staunch in their faith to migrate into the Shaybānid territories: among them were members of Sultan Ḥusayn Bāyqara's entourage, who kept alive among the Özbegs a heritage from the Sunnite Īrānian culture of Harāt. The 16th and 17th centuries were fairly rich in poets who wrote in Persian, using the traditional lyric and panegyric forms;[2] only thus could poets hope for royal patronage. In the 18th and 19th centuries, the mystic-pessimistic Persian verses of *Bīdil* (1644–1730), of ʿAẓīmābād in north west India, were admired and often imitated, not only in India and Afghānistān, but also in Transoxiana; in Īrān, however, they were ignored.

---

[1] On account of the inaccessibility of the sources, the author in writing the next three sections (on Bukhārā, Khōqand and Khīvah) had to depend for many details on works of IVANOV, GAFUROV, etc., as well as those of BARTOL'D (BARTHOLD), and to eliminate bias attributable to the "Marxist" theory of history. As regards the sources, see PAVEL PETROVICH IVANOV, *Arkhiv Khivinskikh Khanov* (The archives of the Khāns of Khīvah), in ZIVAN, VII (1939), pp. 5–26.

[2] e.g. Mushfiqī, at the court of ʿAbd Allāh II; Mīr ʿĀbid Sayyidā (d. between 1707 and 1711), at the Jānid court.

Neither the Persian nor the Turkish literature of Central Asia in these centuries has yet been closely and objectively examined by scholars. Among the Turkish legacies are several epics. Literary activity in Turkish was particularly vigorous at the court of Khōqand. The best known Turkomān poet of the period, Makhdūm Qulī (c. 1735–c. 1780), lived mainly at Khīvah; his lyric, philosophic and didactic religious poems are still very popular and have been printed in several editions in recent years. A 17th century ruler of Khīvah, Abū'l-Ghāzī Bahādur Khān, composed in Chaghatāy Turkish a valuable history of the line of Jochi, which is also one of the chief sources for the history of his own khānate.[1] Besides original work, a considerable amount of translation and adaptation from Persian was accomplished: e.g. of legends and folk tales, and also of chronicles—notably that of Mīrkhwānd (d. 1498). Vocal and instrumental music, and the related art of poetic declamation, remained popular but were still tradition-bound.

In the conditions then prevailing in Central Asia, education could not advance beyond the state already reached in the middle ages.[2] As in all other Muslim lands, it was almost exclusively reserved for boys. At the primary school (*maktab*), pupils aged anything between six and fifteen years learnt to read mechanically from the Qur'ān and from Arabic and Persian religious texts, with little or no comprehension of their meaning. The teachers, whose pay consisted of fees from parents, were often *imāms* of adjacent mosques. Corporal punishment was normal. For the nomads, similar instruction was supplied on a less ample scale through "*yurt* schools"; quite large numbers of Tatar teachers worked in them among the Kazakhs. Above the *maktab* stood the *madrasah*, which in Central Asia as elsewhere was essentially a theological college; a thorough grounding in Arabic was of course also provided, and elementary mathematics were studied when competent staff was available. In general, these colleges were supported by income from pious foundations (*waqfs*) and were to be found only in places inhabited by sedentary Özbegs and Tājīks. Students began to attend them as early as the age of eight, and not infrequently stayed fifteen or twenty years; they generally finished their studies with the acquisition of certificates of competence to teach, granted without formal examinations by prominent *khōjahs*. Judges and court auxiliaries,

[1] Text and French translation by Baron J. J. P. Desmaisons, *Histoire des Mogols et des Tatars*, St. Petersburg, 1871. See also A. N. Kononov, *Rodoslovnaya Turkmen*, Moscow 1958.

[2] c.f. A. S. Tritton, *Materials on Muslim Education in the Middle Ages*, London 1957 (with bibliography on pp. ix–xii); B. Spuler, *Die Minderheitenschulen der europäischen Türkei...*, Breslau 1936, and in "*Idel-Ural*", Berlin 1942.

*imāms*, and also (especially at Bukhārā) government officials, received their training at these institutions. The best known were at Bukhārā, and there were many at Khīvah also. Students from India, Kashmīr, Eastern Turkistān and Russia flocked to Bukhārā, where the number of theology candidates in 1790 is said to have totalled nearly 30,000.

The common destiny of the Central Asian states was shaped in part by geographic factors. With the gradual sedentarization of formerly nomadic elements in Transoxiana, and the contemporary resurgence of urban elements in Eastern Turkistān, virtually the entire zone lying north and east of the region of Īrānian and Afghān settlement came to be occupied by a sedentary population of town-dwellers and peasants thoroughly imbued with Islāmic civilization. Although the nomads were still numerous, and capable on occasions, particularly at Khōqand, of playing important or decisive parts right up to the 19th century, in general their influence was on the wane. The governments of the three khānates tended increasingly to look upon them as trouble-makers and to promote, or welcome, their sedentarization; the government of Khīvah was the most active in this respect. Another method in widespread use for control of the nomads was indirect rule; tribes which submitted to the ruler were kept quiet through the instrumentality of their own chiefs acting as intermediaries. The Turkomāns, and also the Kazakhs and Kirghiz pressing down from the north, were usually handled in this way. Tribal revolts were nevertheless frequent, but could in most cases be put down quickly. For this the nomads had only themselves to blame, as they were normally disunited and mutually antagonistic. Only at Khōqand, and then only for a short time, were the reins of government ever seized by local nomads.

These developments invested the Central Asian states with a new function as barriers against invading nomads, whether Kazakhs and Kirghiz from the north, or Mongol tribes from the east such as the Dzungars (whose initial impact fell on the Kazakhs and Kirghiz). Despite extensive territorial losses in the north, the khānates with such strength as they could muster blocked the path of any new nomad avalanche; and in so doing they acted as involuntary protectors of the Īrānian region. Any invader seeking to reach it would have first had to overrun their territories on the Sīr Daryā and Amu Daryā. As for the Turkomāns, although they were long to be a thorn in the flesh of nearby Īrānian provinces and sometimes of Khīvah and Bukhārā also, they never threatened the independence of Īrān, least of all while the Ṣafavid régime remained strong.

The role of the Central Asian khānates cannot be appreciated without reference to their northern neighbours, the Kazakhs and Kirghiz (then known in Europe as Kirghiz and Qarakirghiz respectively).[1] During most of the 16th century, these two nomadic peoples were in firm possession of Semirechia; but they did not either then or in the 17th century combine to form an organized state. From 1533 onwards the Kazakhs met with increasingly heavy pressure from the Oirats, who had begun to push south westwards. By about 1570 the zone between the Ili basin and the upper Yenisei was in the hands of the Oirats. The Kazakhs afterwards suffered much distress from famines. The ensuing movements of the northern nomads were bound to have an impact on the settled region between the Sîr Daryā and Amu Daryā, and were among the factors which contributed to its fragmentation into separate states at the end of the 16th century.

The Kirghiz are thought to have migrated southwestwards from the upper Yenisei in the 16th century.[2] They occupied the northern half of the modern republic of Kirghizia, where they held their ground against encroachments by the Kazakhs and from Mogholistān; and in 1586, probably under Oirat pressure, they made their first attempts to break into the Tarim basin and Farghānā.

The Qaraqalpaqs first appeared under this name in the 16th century. They settled on the lower Sîr Daryā around 1590; before then they are thought to have lived a nomadic life along with the Noghāy Tatars.[3]

In holding back the nomads, the Central Asian khānates not only shielded the Īrānian plateau, but also preserved the long standing social order of their own territories. This placed the ruling dynasties in positions of acknowledged leadership but not of autocratic power. The principal clans, with their chiefs (*biys*, i.e. *begs*) who acted as the officers of the always numerous armed forces, and the religious classes with their influential dignitaries, formed such powerful groups that not even vigorous and despotically inclined rulers could afford to disregard them. Attempts to override one or the other of these groups brought many a khān to a bad end.

This dual aristocracy of clan chiefs and theologians maintained its patriarchal sway right up to the Russian occupation. At the base of the

[1] ANNEMARIE VON GABAIN has attempted an appreciation of the nomad incursions from the nomad point of view in her article *Kazakentum, eine soziologisch-philologische Studie*, in *Acta Orientalia Hungarica*, XI/1–3, 1950, pp. 161–167.

[2] This is the opinion of A. N. BERNSTAMM, *Istoricheskoe proshloe kirgizskogo naroda* ("The past history of the Kirghiz people"), Frunze 1942; it is contested by K. T. PETROV, *K istorii dvizheniya kirgizov na Tyan- shan' i ikh vzaimootnosheniy s oirotami* (On the history of the Kirghiz immigration into the T'ien-shan and their relations with the Oirats), Frunze 1961, and *Ocherki feodal'nykh otnoshenii v XV–XVIII vv.* (Sketches of feudal relationships in the 15th–18th centuries), Frunze 1961.

[3] On 17th and 18th century population movements in Khwārizm and Türkmenistan, see *Central Asian Review*, VIII/3 (London, 1960), pp. 264–272 (with map); also TOLSTOV and others in Nar. S.A. II, pp. 11–15 (on the Turkomāns, with map of their present distribution), and pp. 160–168 (on the Kirghiz).

social structure stood the peasants and with them manumitted slaves, who were employed on a large scale in agriculture. The peasants were free men, not legally bound to the soil. In the event of drought or other disaster, they could expect help from the great landowners, who would make loans of livestock to them; repayment was not normally demanded unless the donors themselves met with adversity. If the peasants were then unable to pay, they might be placed in bondage for debt and would not for the time be able to leave the land; but they did not even so lose all their rights. For tasks such as road building, maintenance of irrigation works (always performed with great care), and the not infrequent construction of new canals, cooperative effort by all the local inhabitants (other than nomads) was required; they worked under the supervision of a water-controller called the *mīrāb* or sometimes the "white-beard" (*aqsaqal*). The irrigation economy also necessitated agreements on water distribution, choice of crops, allocation of costs of irrigation works, etc. When land hunger appeared in consequence of population growth, portions of state land (*amlāk-i pādshāhī*) or royal domain (*amlāk-i sulṭānī*) were regularly made available. The area in private possession grew in this way, and not only large proprietors but also small cultivators benefited. Moreover, land ownership could be made inalienable by the foundation of a *waqf*, with provision for the future subsistence of the administrator (*mutawallī*). Since *waqf* properties were not exempt from taxation and were normally rented, peasants as far as possible avoided working on them.

The agricultural land tax (then called *māl va jihāt*, as in Ṣafavid Īrān) was levied as a rule in kind, but increasingly in cash; it should legally have been ten per cent of the crop, but higher rates were in practice often charged, probably around twenty per cent, though details are not known. Besides the land tax there were various dues, some of ancient origin and some of unknown scope (e.g. *tawajjuhāt, ikhrājāt*). The *zakāt* (capital levy), charged in accordance with Islamic law on flocks and herds and on commercial stocks, should correctly have been 2½ per cent but was likewise often higher in practice. Horticulture and caravan traffic were also taxed. From time to time the khāns demanded special contributions for their own or their armies' needs.

Collection of the taxes was often farmed out to contractors, who usually overcharged the taxpayers by demanding prescribed "gifts" for the ruler and gratuities such as an extra sheep. In addition to taxes, conscript labour was demanded for road and canal maintenance and construction, and for military service of indeterminate length in the numerous wars waged by the khāns against each other and against the nomads and the

Īrānians. These wars took a heavy toll of blood and stranded many a peasant lad far from his home.

Large landed properties were held by the khāns and their families and the *biys*,[1] and by religious personalities and institutions such as the *madrasahs* and the *darvīsh* monasteries. Members of the two leading classes also invested in handicraft workshops, caravansarais, stud farms, and other profit-yielding enterprises. Common concern for the protection of their property was one of the motives underlying the generally close cooperation between them. Influential families were able to extend their holdings of agricultural and pastoral land, since new fiefs (*suyurghāl* or *tuyūl*) were often granted by the rulers and new *waqfs* were often established. Estates acquired in either of these ways could in practice often be sold, especially if they were tax-exempt (*mulk-i ḥurr*, or *khāliṣah*).

Cultivation of the large estates was entrusted to sharecroppers, who were required to cede up to half of the crops, and also to prisoners taken in the frequent wars. A generally well stocked slave market operated at Bukhārā throughout this period. In the 19th century demands for the ransoming or unconditional release of slaves were raised from time to time in Īrānian and Russian negotiations with the khānates. The demands of the then politically weak government of Īrān were rejected out of hand, on the ground that the slaves were indispensable in agriculture.[2]

Together with agriculture, and with stockbreeding which provided the main livelihood of the nomads, industry and trade were essential components of the economy of the Central Asian states. Glazed tiles, carpets, silk fabrics, metal wares, and miniatures in the style of Behzād, stood out among the products of the artisans. Gold for the metal workers was imported mainly from Īrān and Russia, silver from China through Farghānā. On the other hand, production techniques in basic crafts such as pottery making and gun founding remained at a quite primitive level. In general, artistic creativity declined as time moved on; at Khīvah, however, some noteworthy tile work in mosques and *madrasahs* was done in the 19th century. The old skill in carpet weaving outlived the 19th century and the Russian conquest, though not without adaptation to changing fashions; Özbeg carpets even today vie with those of Īrān and

[1] Called *manap* by the Kirghiz in the north.

[2] c.f. Ivanov, *Khozyaistvo Dzhuibarskikh sheikhov* (see note on p. 230 above), and "*Udel'nye zemli*" *Seiid-Mukhammed-Khana khivinskogo* (The feudal estates of the Khān Sayyid Muḥammad of Khīvah) in ZIVAN, VI (1937), pp. 27–59; Central Asian Review, II/2 (1954), pp. 134–138; also A. Mukhtarov, *Materialy po istorii Ura-Tyube. Sbornik aktov XVII–XIX veka* (Materials for the [agrarian and irrigation] history of Ura-Tübe; a collection of documents from the 17th–19th cents.), Moscow 1963 (44 documents with transcriptions and translations, giving a good view of everyday problems in this field).

Turkey, and like them have influenced European and American tastes besides being influenced thereby. The Central Asian technique of irrigation, which came to be known as the "Farghānā method", has served as a model in the entire Soviet Union.

The old-established and far-flung trade of Central Asia was conducted mainly by a class of merchants called the Sarts, Īrānian and in part Soghdian by origin but Turkicized in speech, though generally bilingual. Bukhārā and Samarqand were the chief centres, Marv also took a share, and Tashkent after 1790 rapidly gained commercial importance. During the 17th and 18th centuries the volume of goods exchanged with foreign countries, including Russia, remained considerable. As in earlier times, the route from Kazan' via Ufa and Bashkiria was the most frequented. A route from Orenburg or Ástrakhan via Mangīshlaq also came into use. Other important outlets were Īrān and the Tarim basin (reached through Farghānā). A limited amount of trade was done with India, where Russian merchants did not then have direct access, even though a Russian envoy was received by the Moghol emperor Awrangzēb in 1696.

Through this trade, the northern steppes, and beyond them Russia, were supplied with Central Asian products such as cotton and silk fabrics, karakul pelts, carpets, and sometimes also precious stones and ornamented weapons. In exchange, Central Asia and the countries further south received woollen fabrics, satins, hides and skins, silver (which was also imported from China), hunting falcons, and wooden articles such as needles, nails, buttons, dishes and bludgeons. Metal goods, axes and fire-arms were obtained mainly for the khāns and their courts, and often through exchanges of gifts. The renewed minting of gold coins in the 18th century for the first time since the Mongol period is thought to have depended on imports of gold from Europe via Orenburg. Imports from the Tarim basin consisted of goods in transit from China and also India, principally tea, porcelain and silver.

Nevertheless, the growth of traffic on the new maritime route to the Far East by way of South Africa reduced the importance of the old silk highway through Central Asia. The khānates consequently did not increase their trade much above the medieval level and did not share in the world economic upsurge of this period.

## THE KHĀNATE OF BUKHĀRĀ

At Bukhārā, which had been the seat of Shaybānid rule, the old dynasty did not absolutely expire, but in a sense lived on through a female member of the line. In 1599 *Bāqī Muḥammad,* whose mother was a Shaybānid princess and whose father *Jān* was a prince of the former ruling family of Astrakhan, gained possession of the Transoxianan part of his maternal grandfather's legacy. Certain parts, notably Tashkent and the town of Turkistān, were lost to the Kazakhs: they consequently lay for many years to come beyond the pale of urban Muslim civilization. The dynasty founded by Bāqī Muḥammad is called either Jānid after his father or Ashtarkhānid from the Tatar name for Astrakhan. Jānid rule was long maintained south of the Oxus in the district of Balkh, where the heirs apparent (though seldom the rulers) resided from time to time. No lasting territorial gains could be made on any of the northern flanks at the expense of the southward thrusting Kazakhs. Khurāsān had been permanently lost to the Ṣafavids after ʿAbd Allāh II's death in 1598. The khān *Imām Qulī* (r. 1611–1643) warred with the Kazakhs and reached the Sīr Daryā estuary; in 1612/3 he temporarily occupied Tashkent, where he perpetrated a frightful massacre. His long reign was followed by that of a capable ruler, *ʿAbd al-ʿAzīz* (r. 1645–1680), in which the country enjoyed stability. An Indian army sent by the Moghol emperor Shāh Jahān, who aspired to restore Tīmūrid rule in Central Asia, invaded the Balkh district in 1645 but withdrew two years later on account of the climate. After the death of ʿAbd al-ʿAzīz, a rebellion in the Zarafshān valley initiated a phase of disintegration. Around the year 1710, the people of the Farghānā valley seceded and set up the new state of Khōqand. Details of the political history of these years have yet to be exhumed from unpublished and mostly still unexamined manuscripts in Central Asian libraries, but are not likely to be of absorbing interest. Constant internal struggles between the Jānid khāns (whose dates of accession are in some cases not known) and the leading Özbeg *biys* and clans precluded external adventure and weakened the central government's hold on the provinces. The clan chiefs gained more and more independence, just as the *derebeys* did in the Ottoman empire during the 18th and early 19th centuries. Despite these and other difficulties, indicated by a debasement of the currency in 1709, the economy appears to have been prosperous. Agriculture benefited from new irrigation works, and trade remained active. Bukhārā had the most important grain market in Central Asia. Bukhāran merchants possessed trading posts in the Tarim basin and in the depths of Siberia, where they worked hand in hand with Tatar dealers.

In neighbouring Īrān, the Ṣafavid régime was overthrown in 1722, and much blood was shed as the country fell to pieces and was forcibly reunited by Nādir Shāh. During all this time, the Bukhārān throne was occupied by a feeble khān, *Abū'l-Fayẕ* (r. 1711–1747). He submitted to Nādir Shāh, who entered Bukhārā in 1740, and was left on his throne. Balkh had already been lost in 1737. The numerous wars, internal disorders and famines of this period stimulated emigration from Bukhārā and Samarqand, which had been going on for many years, mainly to Farghānā, and now became quite massive. During and after these troubles, the Jānid court came to be dominated by hereditary "mayors of the palace" (*ataliqs*) from the Mangit clan, who got the better of rivals from the Keneges clan and steadily tightened their grip. From 1747 onward all real power lay with the atalīq *Muḥammad Raḥīm Biy* (d. 1758) and his heirs; but the last puppet Jānid Khān was not deposed until 1785. The long reign of Jingiz Khān's descendants at Bukhārā thereby came to an end. The founder of the new Mangit dynasty, which lasted until 1920, was *Murād Ma'ṣūm Shāh* (r. 1785–1800), who married a princess of Jingizid lineage. Although Muḥammad Raḥīm had assumed the title *khān* in 1753, the later Mangit rulers used the title *amīr*.

The pre-existing social structure and pattern of land ownership underwent no change when the Mangits assumed power, except that the influence of the religious dignitaries rose even further. As has been said, Bukhārā then swarmed with theology students.

At the same time, internecine wars with the other khānates recommenced. The amīr *Ḥaydar* (r. 1800–1826) began his reign by butchering a large number of his relatives, and through this ruthless precaution largely averted internal strife. He repelled an attack from Khīvah in 1804, and then became involved in a long and obstinate struggle with the khān of Khōqand. He ran into a dangerous situation in 1821, when an incursion of Khīvan troops up to the gates of Bukhārā coincided with a revolt of the Khitāy Qïpchāqs, an Özbeg tribe living between Samarqand and Bukhārā who had been driven to defiance by the burden of taxation and conscription. Fighting went on until the revolt was quelled in 1825. A second revolt of this tribe and a rising at Samarqand took place in 1826, but came to nothing.

In the meantime Ḥaydar had died, leaving the treasury depleted by his lavish expenditure not only on warfare but also on his ḥarem. His successor *Naṣr Allāh* (r. 1826–1860), who secured the throne by the same brutal method, is described by contemporary travellers as a cruelty-loving tyrant surrounded by like-minded sycophants of mostly unknown origin. He did not, however, lack energy. He sponsored new irrigation works, strengthened the armed forces, and built up the artillery. Fighting with the other khānates and with dissidents continued in his reign. His successive campaigns against Khōqand from 1839 onwards all ended in failure. He was at war with Khīvah from 1842 to 1846. His perennial objective was Shahr-i Sabz ("Green City", south of Samarqand), which his forces did not capture until the year of his death. The constant fighting exhausted the country's strength. Shahr-i Sabz was one of many towns and districts in Bukhāran territory which made themselves practically independent of the central government. Another was the Balkh district (now Afghān Turkistān), which the Bukhārans had recovered in 1826; it was finally lost in 1849 to the Afghāns. While the Central Asian khānates grew weaker, Afghānistān came to the fore as a middle-ranking power.

Central Asia, like Afghānistān, was now closely watched by the Russians and the British, who both sent envoys to the court of the amīr of Bukhārā. Naṣr Allāh's son and successor *Muẓaffar al-Dīn* (r. 1860–1885) did not modify his father's policy in the light of this obviously not disinterested attention from the two great European powers. He persevered in internecine local struggles and remained at war with Khōqand until 1866. His troops failed in 1865 to gain possession of Tashkent, in circumstances mentioned below. Shahr-i Sabz had again been lost early in his reign.

During all this time, the Russian empire's boundaries were drawing near to Bukhārā, with the submission of one Central Asian Turkish tribe after another to Russian authority. In some cases they submitted voluntarily, as did the Kazakhs, whose chiefs had first entered into relations with the Tsars as early as 1594. The Bashkirs living in the Urals north west of the Kazakhs had already submitted to Ivan IV in 1554. The Kazakh khān *Tyavka* (or *Tevke*) strengthened his people's westward links when he received an envoy from Moscow in 1694, and another in 1698 from the Kalmüks, a Buddhist Oirat tribe whose migrations carried them to the lower Volga. Although the Kazakhs were defeated in the east by the Dzungars in the same year 1698, Tyavka was able to retain the leadership, probably with Russian support; he became the lawgiver of his people, and died in 1718. When the Dzungars renewed their attacks and took Tashkent, Sayrām and the town of Turkistān from the Kazakhs in 1723, large sections of the Kazakh people grouped in the "Great" and "Middle Hordes" submitted to Dzungarian rule. The Kirghiz on the Yenisei did likewise. At that time the nearest Russian outpost was the newly founded fort of Ust'-Kamenogorsk on the upper Yenisei. In this critical situation, the khān of the "Lesser" Horde, *Abū'l-Khayr,* whom all the Kazakhs had earlier acknowledged as their overlord, turned to Russia in 1730 and offered allegiance to the Tsars. The treaty then concluded was renewed several times in the subsequent decades. One result was that the Russians, when they began to advance up the Sīr Daryā in 1847, could count on a good deal of sympathy from the Kazakhs. They moreover appeared in Kazakh eyes as allies against the khānates of Khīvah and Bukhārā, which held sections of the Kazakh nation in subjection. At the same time, Russian moves to restrict the authority of the Kazakh nobles (called the "White Knees") provoked a rebellion which broke out in 1842 and was not finally suppressed until 1873; its leaders were the "sultan" Kenesarī (d. 1847) and his son Ṣiddīq. The Kazakhs were placed under the Russian administrative system by regulations of 1822 and 1867–1869.[1]

By the mid-19th century, the Russian empire was thus a near though not yet contiguous neighbour of Bukhārā. The khānate's population at the beginning of the century had been estimated by travellers at two and a half to three millions, half peasants and town-dwellers, and half stock-breeders. The city of Bukhārā had about 70,000 inhabitants (three quarters of whom could speak Persian as well as Turkish), while Samarqand had about 30,000. The khānate then stretched from what is now Afghān Turkistān and from Ḥiṣār in what is now Soviet Tājīkistān to the town of Turkistān and the western entrance to the Farghānā valley, where Ura-Tübe and beyond it Khojent were disputed with the khānate of Khōqand in interminable wars. Marv had been lost to Khīvah in 1825.

From 1861 onwards, the Russians resumed their gradual southward advance. They clashed with Bukhāran troops in 1866 and again in 1868, and were victorious. In July 1868 the amīr Muẓaffar al-Dīn was obliged to accept a Russian protectorate and cede large portions of his territory, including Samarqand which had been occupied by General Konstantin Petrovich von Kauffmann on May 14, 1868. With Russian help, the amīr was able to secure some territorial compensation in the south east. Russian suzerainty deprived Bukhārā of freedom to conduct external relations, but did not disturb the country's internal administration or religious life.

## KHŌQAND

The town of Khōqand and surrounding district of Farghānā in the middle Sīr Daryā valley began to slip out of the grasp of the Jānid khāns at the end of the 17th century, when Bukhārā was convulsed by rebellion and disorder. Being protected by mountains on nearly all sides, Farghānā

---

[1] S. P. Tolstov, T. A. Zhdankc, S. A. Abramson and N. A. Kislyakov, *Narody Srednei Azii i Kazakhstana* (The Peoples of Central Asia and Kazakhstan), II, Moscow, 1963, pp. 322–337 and 702–704.

was less vulnerable than the areas north and west of it to penetration by the Dzungars, and consequently became a land of refuge for peoples exposed to their attacks. The immigrants brought with them new skills and wealth, and radically altered the ethnic pattern. In the 15th century, Farghānā had been inhabited by Turks and by "Sarts" (i.e. Īrānians; also called "Tājīks"); the latter dwelt around Marghalān and Sokha, the former mainly around Andījān. In the early 16th century Özbegs were superimposed upon them. The next immigrants were Kirghiz, who began to arrive in the late 16th century, and gradually installed themselves during the 18th century in the foothills of the Alai range south of the valley and then in the ranges to the east and north east. Another group of some importance was the Qïpchāq tribe, Özbeg in speech but similar to the Kirghiz in social structure. To all these more or less clearly defined ethnic groups were added, during the 18th century, further immigrants from several quarters: "Sarts" from Samarqand and Bukhārā, Özbegs driven from their homes by the Dzungars and also members of the Qaraqalpaq and other Turkish tribes, and Turkish and so-called "Arab" refugees from the Tarim basin after the Chinese conquest.

Since most of these immigrants had no ties with the khānate of Bukhārā, the secession of Farghānā took place without commotion under the leadership of a chief named *Shāhrukh* (d. 1722/3), whose ancestry went back to the Shaybānid Abū'l-Khayr according to some sources or to the Tīmūrid Bābur according to others. The new dynasty, sprung from a clan named Ming which for many years provided its main support, proved vigorous, and did much to develop the towns, extend irrigation, and promote agriculture and silk-worm rearing. Particular attention was given to the important transit trade, which was conducted mainly with and through Eastern Turkistān. In Farghānā, as in the Tarim basin, *khōjah* families were influential but their pretensions were gradually cut short. Even so, the authority of the ruling family long remained slender, and small in territorial extent. After the Chinese conquest of Eastern Turkistān in 1759, Khōqand was shaken by internal disorders, and its khāns saw fit during the subsequent decades to acknowledge Chinese suzerainty. Besides Khōqand, there were several small states in and around Farghānā, reflecting the multiplicity of ethnic groups which had not then begun to assimilate with one another. Not until the 19th century did a tendency to fusion, even between Özbegs and Tājīks, become apparent. Certain groups preserved their tribal organization through the 19th century, and with it a political influence of their own; among these were the Qïpchāqs, who remained distinct from their speech-kin the Özbegs and were listed as a separate community of 40,000 souls in 1920. Khojent (now renamed Leninābād, at the entrance to the Farghānā basin), and the valleys in the mountains south west of Khōqand, continued to be peopled by Īrānians, mainly Mountain Tājīks with the local name Ghālcha (from *ghārcheh*, i.e. "cave-dweller").

The unification of the Farghānā valley into a single state under the khāns of Khōqand was a task undertaken in the 19th century, initially by the khān *ʿAlīm* (r. 1799–1809; according to Nalivkin, 1808–1816).[1] After securing his throne against several rivals, he went to war against Bukhārā, and seized and held Ura Tübe and Jīzaq (west of Khojent). This was the starting point of Khōqand's rise to importance, and of the simultaneous decline of Bukhārā, which unlike Khōqand and Khīvah, suffered many territorial losses and made few gains in the 19th century.

The *biys* of Khōqand, foreseeing that an increase in their khān's strength might diminish their own influence, viewed his successes less with pleasure than with dismay. They therefore often refused to join in his military ventures, and he was consequently obliged to recruit a new army consisting of Tājīks. Having thereby curbed the nobles and freed himself from anxiety on their account, he embarked on further campaigns of conquest, beginning with a northward expedition which in 1808 gave him possession of Tashkent. This city then had about 70,000 inhabitants and was an important commercial centre, especially for trade with Orenburg; it had belonged nominally to Bukhārā, but was actually governed by an aristocracy of *khōjahs*. The Kazakhs around Tashkent, being in no mood to acknowledge any superior authority, attempted to rebel, but were crushed by ʿAlīm Khān in the cold winter of 1808–1809. In 1809 (or perhaps 1816) ʿAlīm Khān, whose career is related by native historians with an antipathy perhaps reflecting Özbeg resentment of his Tājīk army, was assassinated—allegedly on account of his "cruelty and tyranny".

His brother and successor *ʿUmar* (r. 1809 [or 1816?]–1822) is depicted by the historians in approving terms. He adopted the old caliphal title *Amīr al-Muʾminīn* ("Prince of the Believers"), and relied on the country's traditional aristocracy of *biys* and *ʿulamāʾ*. He patronized Turkish poets, presumably court poets, and himself composed verses.

In renewed fighting with Bukhārā, Ura Tübe and Jīzaq changed hands frequently while Samarqand remained in Bukhāran possession, even though the dissidents of Shahr-i Sabz threw in their weight on the Khōqandian

---

[1] VLADIMIR PETROVICH NALIVKIN, *Histoire du khanat de Khokand*, tr. A. DOZON, Paris 1889 (Pub. de l'Ecole des Langues Or. Vivantes, III/4). The Russian original *Kratkaya istoriya Kokandskago khanstva* appeared at Kazan in 1886.

side. In 1814, however, the town of Turkistān and surrounding district, hitherto governed independently by a Kazakh "sultan" nominally subject to Bukhārā, were captured and held, whereupon the Kazakh chiefs from the Sīr Daryā to Semirechia gave allegiance to the khān of Khōqand. The khān left them free to manage their own affairs under his suzerainty, but began in 1817 to strengthen his rather weak position by building a string of forts: first at the mouth of the Sīr Daryā, then at Awliyā-Ata (since 1938 Jambol), Pishpek (or Pishkek; since 1926 officially Frunze), and Toqmaq (an ancient settlement east of Pishpek). Towns with mosques and *madrasahs* soon sprang up around these forts, which served their purpose in 1821 when a Kazakh revolt in the Chimkent and Sayrām districts north of Tashkent had to be suppressed.

ʿUmar's son and successor *Muḥammad ʿAlī* or (in abbreviated form) *Madalī* (r. 1822–1842) came to the throne at the age of twelve. In 1831 he added to his father's conquests the mountain tract south of the Farghānā valley, which was inhabited by Tājīk shepherds and gold-panners living under the patriarchal rule of their own chiefs. It had long been their custom to send men down to the valley in summer as seasonal workers. The district was left under the administration of indigenous governors. As Madalī grew older, he reportedly became addicted to wine and ḥarem pleasures, and also more and more tyrannical. At the same time he exhausted the country's strength in vain attacks on the former frontier fortresses of Jīzaq and Ura-Tübe, which had seceded. Finally the people under the leadership of the *ʿulamāʾ* appealed to the Bukhārans, who in 1839 took Khojent and forced Madalī to acknowledge Bukhāran suzerainty. In a second advance in April 1842 they entered Khōqand city. The detested khān was then torn to pieces.

Although in the following years the Bukhāran garrison was expelled with Kirghiz and Kazakh help, and both Khojent and Tashkent were recovered, the khānate of Khōqand never again achieved internal stability. The noble clans had been weakened by the frequent wars, and nomadic elements, principally the Qīpchāqs and also the Kirghiz, now gained the upper land. In 1845 they thrust aside the new khān of the Khōqandian dynasty, and entrusted the practical conduct of affairs to the Qīpchāq chief *Muslimān Qul*. Under his rule, arable lands, already in short supply, were taken by nomads and turned into common pastures, while peasants who still received irrigation water were required to pay dearly for it, and were also forced to give daughters in marriage to nomads without receiving the customary bride price (*kalīm*) for them. These injustices prompted a revolt which overthrew the nomad régime and eliminated its leader in October 1851. The lands taken by the nomads for grazing were then reallotted to the sedentary people for cultivation. The khān *Khudāyār* now gained real authority, but failed to hold it against the rivalry of his brother *Mallā Beg*, who deposed him in 1858. This led to a Qîpchāq resurgence, accompanied by new seizures of arable lands for use as pastures and new clashes between the sedentary people and the nomads. The drama at Khōqand was now being played in full view of the advancing Russians. An expedition under General Perovskii had captured Aq Mechet on the Sîr Daryā in 1853; and Fort Perovsk (so named after him; now Qîzîl Orda) had been built on its site. Soon afterwards Russian troops coming from the north east occupied Toqmaq and temporarily also Pishpek.

The Khōqandian troops based on fortresses in the principal towns were still strong enough in these years to quell successive revolts; of Kirghiz at Ōsh in the east of the Farghānā basin in 1845; of inhabitants of Khōqand city in 1856; and of Kirghiz and Kazakhs in the belt between Pishpek and Turkistān town in 1857–58. Hostilities were also resumed against Bukhārā, again for possession of Ura Tübe and Jīzaq and again without any decisive result. Early in 1862, however, when Mallā Beg ordered his army numbering perhaps 40,000 men and comprising infantry, cavalry and artillery, to assemble for war with Russia, they refused to obey; and in March of that year, at his capital, he met a violent death.

Khōqand never recovered from this disaster. Bukhāran troops marched into the capital in 1862, and again in 1865 when they compelled the new khān *Sayyid Sulṭān* to retrocede Tashkent; but that city was captured on June 28, 1865, after two days of bloody street fighting, by the Russian troops of General Mikhail Grigor'evich Chernaev. The loss of Khojent in 1866 limited Sayyid Sulṭān's authority to the Farghānā basin. The Russians recognized the khānate's autonomy within that territory by a treaty of 1868, and respected it until 1875, when Khudāyār Khān, who had regained the throne in 1871, was ejected by a rebellion; they then sent in troops, and finally compelled his son *Nāṣir al-Dīn* to renounce all sovereign rights on March 2, 1876. Khōqand, unlike Bukhārā and Khīvah, was thus annexed outright to the Russian empire. The territory became the province (*oblast*) of Farghānā, and the seat of government was moved to New Marghalān (now renamed Farghānā like the province). Khōqand city continued to be the valley's biggest urban and commercial centre. Neither the administrative system nor the population pattern underwent much change in the following decades; only at New Marghalān did Russians settle in any number.

The Russian occupation did not have adverse after-effects on the economy of Farghānā as it did on that of Khīvah, which was by-passed by a new road and later also railway laid north of Lake Aral. Farghānā had already made great economic advances during its independent life in the 19th century. The centuries-old irrigation system[1] was carefully maintained, and supplemented by several new canals. Distribution of water to peasants and nomads was regulated by state officials and tribal elders respectively, and prescribed rates for it, payable in cash, were charged. Although cultivators could under these arrangements sometimes be oppressed, or even totally deprived of regular water supply, the revenue was normally used for canal construction and maintenance, which could otherwise only be done by the use of locally conscripted labour. At times when normal conditions prevailed, as they did on the whole up to 1842, the nomads showed a growing tendency to settle on the land as cultivators. The arable area, despite large extensions, was insufficient for the country's needs. Farghānā was densely populated and for those days quite highly urbanized; the city of Khōqand had approximately 8000 houses, 360 mosques, 12 *madrasahs* and numerous caravansarais. In these circumstances, market gardening was very important in the agriculture of Farghānā. As long as the established native administration, in which clan chiefs and religious dignitaries held leading posts, was allowed to go on functioning, conditions in this province favoured a continuance of its economic advance after 1876.

## KHĪVAH

The khānate of Khwārizm or Khīvah south of Lake Aral was not directly affected by the downfall of the Shaybānids of Bukhārā in 1598–99, as it had been able to keep out of their clutches; but it benefited indirectly through the relaxation of pressure from that quarter. Its forces proved strong enough to beat off a long series of Kazakh attacks between 1613 and 1632. During that time, probably in 1615, the capital was moved from Urgench to Khīvah because the branch of the Oxus on which Urgench lay dried up. Further attacks by Kazakhs in 1648 and 1652/53 were successfully repulsed by *Abū'l-Ghāzi Bahādur Khān* (r. 1644–1663), an able ruler and at the same time (as mentioned on p. 238) an eminent historian. He also defended the country against the Bukhārans and reached the gates of their capital in 1661. His son and successor *Anūsha* (r. 1663–1687) not

[1] Details in V. V. Bartol'd, *K istorii orosheniya Turkestana* (History of irrigation in Turkestān), Leningrad 1927. Also P. P. Ivanov, *Kazakhi i kokandskoe khanstvo* (The Kazakhs and the khānate of Khoqand), in Zivan, VII (1939), pp. 92–128.

only beat off attacks by neighbours, but also led his Özbeg and Turkomān squadrons in hard-hitting raids against them; Khurāsān, no longer strongly defended after the death of ʿAbbās the Great, suffered most from his pillaging and slave-raiding.

In the subsequent decades, Khīvah sank into provincial insignificance. Authority slipped out of the hands of the khāns, nine of whom reigned between 1687 and 1716, and from the late 17th century onwards passed gradually into those of a clan named Qungrat. A Russian expedition, ordered by Peter the Great to march to Khīvah, was forced by cold weather and heavy losses in 1717 to turn back without reaching its goal. After Nādir Shāh's invasion of Khīvah in 1740, the territory was under Īrānian suzerainty until his death in 1747; but the Qungrats were able to maintain their grip. Irruptions of Turkomān nomads into the settled country, especially around 1770, were stubbornly beaten back. The real ruler of the country was the Qungrat "army commander" (*inaq*) *Muḥammad Amīn* (d. 1790), and after him his successor *Uways* (1790–1804). Only after the latter's death, however, did the Qungrat rulers assume the title *khān*; their dynasty was to last until 1920. As to the level of civilization, Khīvah stood far below Bukhārā. Military influence predominated, on account of the frequent wars with nomadic intruders; neither the *ʿulamāʾ* nor the civilian officials ever played leading parts. Canal maintenance was neglected, and formerly cultivated tracts reverted to steppe in this period.

Land hunger may therefore have been one of the motives underlying the expansionist policy adopted in the early 19th century by the Khīvan government, which before then had only controlled a quite small territory in the upper part of the Āmū Daryā delta. The Aral district, i.e. the northern part of the delta with Qungrad as its chief town, had long ago made itself independent; its inhabitants were mainly Qaraqalpaq peasants and fishermen who had immigrated in the 17th century.

In the Khīvah district, the principal population groups were the Özbegs and the so-called Sarts, descendants of the ancient Khwārizmians who had probably begun to become Turkicized in the 13th or 14th century. The Sarts were mostly town-dwelling merchants and were particularly numerous at Hazār Asb on the Āmū Daryā.

Sections of the surrounding tribes, Kazakhs and above all Turkomāns, had long been in close contact with the Khīvans, often on the battlefield, but more frequently in the market place, their products being complementary. This contact encouraged some of the Turkomāns to switch from stockbreeding to agriculture. *Mullās* trained at Khīvah had considerable influence among the Turkomāns, especially among those of the senior

Yomut tribe, and generally used it in ways favourable to the Khīvan government.

In these circumstances, the khān *Muḥammad Raḥīm* (r. 1806–1825) could count on widespread support when he set out deliberately to enlarge the Khīvan frontiers by conquest. He first occupied the Aral district and subdued some other Qaraqalpaq tribes, in 1811. Then, from 1812 onwards, he conquered a Kazakh-populated area east of Lake Aral up to the Sîr Daryā estuary, and subdued the Turkomāns of the Tekke tribe who ranged up to the frontier of Khurāsān. During this time, an intermittent war was going on between Khīvah and Bukhārā (as already mentioned above, p. 245); and in the course of it Muḥammad Raḥīm Khān captured Marv in 1822. Two years later he founded in the same neighbourhood the town of New Marv (pronounced Mary in vulgar Turkish and today officially so named). This long series of wars further increased the influence of the armed forces, and the khān was obliged to reward their commanders with lands confiscated from certain noble clans. A number of religious leaders and other persons who worked for him received similar rewards. Many large estates were thereby brought into being, whereas previously small properties had been normal in Khīvah. After Muḥammad Raḥīm's death, the khānate passed through a phase of internal trouble. The Qaraqalpaqs rebelled in 1827 and again in 1855–1856, the Kazakhs in 1842, and the people of Marv in 1827, 1842 and 1854. From 1856 to 1864 a stubborn struggle was waged against a combination of Turkomān and Qaraqalpaq rebels led by Sayyid Muḥammad. Heavy taxation, excessive use of forced labour for canal digging, and conscription for the army, lay at the root of most of these rebellions. Though all were suppressed, they obviously weakened the fabric of this small state. Some years earlier, in 1819, its population had been estimated at 300,000; its capital city was then reported to have 3,000 houses, but in 1842 to have only 4,000 inhabitants.

The rebellions failed on account of disunity among the rebels and absence of external support for them; neither Īrān, nor Afghānistān, nor Bukhārā, intervened on their behalf. After the middle of the 19th century, the situation changed. Renewed fighting with the Qaraqalpaqs around Qungrad in 1858–59 was stopped by the Russians. In the preceding years, Russia had advanced closer to Khīvah, with the occupation of the Mangîshlaq peninsula in 1834 and foundation of Fort Raimskoe (from Raḥīm?) at the mouth of the Sîr Daryā in 1842. From 1869 onwards a Russian garrison of steadily increasing strength sat on the east coast of the Caspian Sea at Krasnovodsk ("Red Water"; in Turkomān, Qîzîl Suv). Already in 1840 the Russian slaves in Khīvah had been released at the demand of a

Russian diplomatic mission, nothwithstanding the failure of a second Russian military expedition against Khīvah sent by the Tsar Nicholas I in 1839. A similar demand by the Īrānian envoy Riżā Qulī "Hidāyat"[1] in 1851 was turned down. British emissaries also arrived, but did not establish close or lasting links.

In spite of these threatening developments, the small states of Central Asia did not draw together for common defence, but continued to fight with one another. Khīvah was also in the thick of internal conflicts with the Yomut Turkomāns during all this time. Meanwhile the Russians had imposed a protectorate on Bukhārā and fastened their grip on the territories north and east of Khīvah. In such circumstances, this small khānate, already much weakened by wars, rebellions and frequent throne-changes, could only fight delaying actions in the face of a combined offensive mounted in 1873 by the Russians. Khīvah was invaded from the west, north west and east, and after a short struggle surrendered to the Russian General von Kauffmann on June 2, 1873. The Qungrat dynasty was confirmed in its sovereignty over a much reduced territory on the south bank of the Āmū Daryā, but was not permitted to have relations with foreign states or the other khānates, or to enter into any commitments without Russia's consent.

In the same year, part of the Turkomān country, from Krasnovodsk to the Khīvan border and the Atrek river, was annexed to the Russian empire. Further east, the Turkomāns of the Tekke tribe fought bravely for their freedom from 1879 to 1881; but they were completely isolated, as Īrān did not help them, and could not possibly have withstood the well prepared Russian advance. Their principal stronghold Gök Tepe ("Blue Hill") fell, after a hard-fought siege of forty days, to General Mikhail Dmitrievich Skobelev on January 24, 1881.

Finally, Russian rule was extended to Marv and the lower Murghāb valley when the people were induced to submit on January 31, 1884, and to the districts of TashKöprü and Panjdeh further south when Russian troops checked an Afghān advance down the Kushk river in March 1885. The line then reached is still the frontier of the Russian empire today.

The khānate of Khīvah was thus completely surrounded by territories governed, or in the case of Bukhārā, protected by Russia. Although the Qungrat dynasty remained formally sovereign until 1920, Khīvah lost practically all freedom of action in 1873.[2]

---

[1] His account of his mission, *Safāratnāmah-yi Khwārizm*, was translated by C. Schefer, *Ambassade au Kharezm*, Paris, 1876-9 (Pub. de l'Ecole des Langues Orientales Vivantes, 1, 3).

[2] Details in V. V. Barthold, *Four studies on the history of Central Asia*, ed. and tr. by

## THE TARIM BASIN AFTER THE CHINESE CONQUEST

In contrast with Russian rule in Central Asia, which represented the first intrusion of a European power into that region, Chinese hegemony was not a new phenomenon in the history of Eastern Turkistān. Moreover, the Manchu and Chinese rulers of the Tarim basin at first did little to change the existing internal order. From the start of their victorious campaign in 1757-1759, they benefited from the collaboration of leading native clan-chiefs intent on scoring advantages in mutual feuds. Recalcitrant members of the clans were deported to China, unless they were able to escape to neighbouring territories still under Muslim rule. Most of the refugees went to Farghānā, where their presence might have posed a threat to the foreign régime in the Tarim basin if the khāns of Khōqand had concurred. These Muslim rulers, however, preferred the benefits of tributary vassaldom to the Chinese emperor, and restrained their fugitive co-religionists from anti-Chinese action. The grateful Chinese repaid them by granting privileges in Eastern Turkistān to Khōqandian merchants. One of these was the right to set up trading posts, where business could be done on more or less duty-free terms arranged in frequent negotiations between the Khōqandian and Chinese authorities. The khāns of Khōqand for their part exacted ever higher taxes from the merchants, and supervised them through officials (*khudāidāds*) somewhat similar to consuls; there was one in residence at Kāshghar. The principal Khōqandian and also Kazakh exports were horses and cattle, while China supplied Khōqand with silk. Khōqandian merchants also handled transit trade between China and Russia.

The Turkish inhabitants of the Tarim basin, being thus virtually deprived of external support, were obliged to stay quiet, and the Chinese made this easier for them by leaving their social institutions virtually intact. The former *amīrs* continued to perform their functions in the role of imperially nominated *begs*, and as such were required from time to time to present themselves submissively in Peking. Among their responsibilities were administration of justice, water distribution, and tax collection. The mass of the population consisted of peasant proprietors, who had to pay a land tax (*kharāj*). Tenant farmers and large landowners were also to be found. A census taken in or about 1770 recorded some 260,000 Turks in the country, and listed first wheat, then barley, rice and beans, among their crops.

---

V. Minorsky, Leiden 1956–1962, III, pp.146–170; also P. P. Ivanov, *Ocherki po istorii srednei Azii (XVI seredina´ XIX v)* (Sketches on Central Asian history, 16th to mid-19th centuries), Moscow 1958.

The Chinese authorities were eager that waste lands should be opened up, and generally willing that they should be assigned to the natives; this was indeed what happened in a land settlement operation in 1842–44. Already in 1822, however, a considerable number of Chinese families had been settled in the Kāshghar district. All considered, the country's life evolved smoothly. A revolt in 1826–27 led by *Jahāngīr*, a member of one of the old *khōjah* clans, was put down quite quickly. The close political and commercial ties with Khōqand, which had aided Jahāngīr, were finally broken in 1832. Thereafter the rulers of Khōqand showed restraint until 1845, when their troops began to infiltrate into the Tarim basin; they reached Kāshghar in 1857 and held it for a few months. From 1860 onwards Khōqand was pinned down by Russian moves. The Khōqandian tribute to China was last paid in 1862.

The armed infiltration from Khōqand, and a rebellion of the Dungans (Muslim Chinese) which began in 1861, kindled hopes of independence in the Tarim basin. They were to be briefly realized through the energy of *Ya'qūb Beg*, a native nobleman whose real name was *Muḥammad Bā Dawlat*. He revolted against the Celestial Empire in 1865 and soon freed the greater part of Eastern Turkistān from Chinese tutelage. In 1870 he assumed the title *Ataliq Ghāzī* (roughly "father-hero"), and in 1870 he declared himself a vassal of the Sultan of Turkey. He received a certain amount of British support.[1] His realm, which he named *Jiti Shahar* ("Seven Cities"), for a time embraced the Ṭurfān oasis and even Urumchi, which he captured in 1872. Four years later, however, he was put to flight by a Chinese counter-offensive, and on May 31, 1877, he died a probably not natural death. His realm broke up, and after the collapse of the Dungan rebellion in 1878, was again brought under Chinese sovereignty. In practice the Chinese grip remained tenuous. During most of the first half of the 20th century, Russian influence carried more weight. In Eastern Turkistān, however, the phase of Russian ascendancy was to be only transient.

---

[1] T. Saguchi, *The social history of Eastern Turkestān in the 18th–19th centuries* (in Japanese with Eng. summary), Tokio 1963; Yuan Tsing, *Yakub Beg (1820–1877) and the Moslem rebellion in Chinese Turkestān*, in Central Asian Journal VI/2 (The Hague, 1961), pp. 134–167 (with list of sources); also C.A.R. VII/4 (1959), pp. 403–408.

# BIBLIOGRAPHY

A very extensive bibliography of Russian and other works, prepared by B. Spuler, appears at the end of his *Geschichte Mittelasiens seit dem Auftreten der Türken* in JETTMAR, K., HAUSSIG, H. W., SPULER, B., and PETECH, L., *Geschichte Mittelasiens*, Leiden 1966 (*Handbuch der Orientalistik*, 5. Band, 5. Abschnitt). C. A. STOREY gives details of Persian chronicles in *Persian Literature*, Vol. 1, Part 1. Works in Western languages are few, and not easily obtainable except perhaps in microfilm. The list below has been prepared by F. R. C. Bagley.

BARTHOLD, VASILII VLADIMIROVICH, *Zwölf Vorlesungen uber die Geschichte Mittelasiens*. Deutsche Bearbeitung von THEODOR MENZEL, Berlin 1935. Tr. by Mme. M. DONSKIS, *Histoire des Turcs d'Asie Centrale*, Paris 1945. Tr. by VLADIMIR MINORSKY, *Four studies on the history of Central Asia*, 3 vols., Leiden 1956–1962 (I, A short history of Turkestan; History of the Semirechye. II, Ulugh Beg and his times. III, Mīr 'Alī Shīr; A history of the Turkman people).

CZAPLICKA, MARIE ANTOINETTE, *The Turks of Central Asia in history and at the present day*, Oxford 1918.

GROUSSET, RENÉ, *L'empire des Steppes*, Paris 1939.

PELLIOT, PAUL, *Haute Asie*, Paris 1931.

SHABAD, THEODORE, *Geography of the U.S.S.R.: a regional survey*, New York 1951 (useful also for Central Asia).

LEIMBACH, WERNER, *Die Sowjetunion*, Stuttgart 1950 (Geography, with extensive sections on Central Asia).

KRADER, LAWRENCE, *Social organization of the Mongol-Turkic pastoral nomads*, The Hague 1963.

SKRINE, F. H., and ROSS, Sir E. DENISON, *The heart of Asia; a history of Russian Turkestan and the Great Asian Khanates*, London 1899.

SARKISYANZ, EMANUEL, *Geschichte der orientalischen Völker Russlands bis 1917*, Munich 1961 (Central Asia, pp. 160–233 and 310–361).

HOWORTH, Sir HENRY HOYLE, *History of the Mongols, from the 9th to the 19th century*, 4 vols., London 1876–1888, supplement and indices, London 1927 (based on European materials).

ḤAIDAR MĪRZĀ DUGHLĀT, MUḤAMMAD, *The Ta'rīkh-i Rashīdī*, tr. by Sir E. DENISON ROSS, ed. with notes by N. ELIAS, London 1895.

ABŪ'L-GHĀZĪ BAHĀDUR KHĀN, *Shajarah-yi Turk*, tr. from the Chaghatāy by Baron J. J. P. DESMAISONS, *Histoire des Mogols et des Tatars*, 2 vols., St. Petersburg 1871–1874.

MĪR 'ABD UL-KĀRĪM BUKHARĪ, called NADĪM, *Histoire de l'Asie centrale (Afghanistan, Boukhara, Khiva, Khoqand) depuis les dernières années du règne de Nadir Chah (1153) jusqu'en 1233 de l'Hégire (1740–1818)*, tr. by CHARLES SCHEFER, Paris 1876. Persian text, Bulāq (Cairo) 1873.

DE LEVCHINE, ALEXIS, *Description des Hordes et Steppes des Kirghiz-Kazaks*, tr. from the Russian, Paris 1840.

MAJERCZAK, R., *Renseignements sur les Kazaks ou Kirghizes-Kazaks depuis la formation de la Horde Kazak jusqu'a* RN *du XIXe. siécle*, in Revue du Monde Musulman, 43 (1921), pp. 54–220.

VAMBÉRY, ARMINIUS (HERMANN WEINBERGER), *Geschichte Bucharas oder Transoaniens*, 2 vols., Stuttgart 1872, Eng. tr., *History of Bokhara*, London 1873.

LERCH, PETER, *Khiva oder Kharezm, seine historischen und geographischen Verhältnisse*, St. Petersburg 1873.

NALIVKINE, VLADIMIR PETROVITCH, *Histoire du Khanat de Khokand*, tr. by AUGUSTE DOZON, Paris 1889 (Pub. de l'Ecole des Langues Orientales Vivantes III/4). (Russian original, Kazan 1886.)

DE KHANIKOFF, NICOLAS, *Boukhara, its Emir and its people* (Eng. tr.), London 1845.
RIẒĀ QULĪ KHĀN HIDĀYAT, *Ambassade au Khorezm*, tr. by CHARLES SCHEFER, Paris 1876 (Pub. de l'École des Langues Orientales Vivantes, S. 1, 4).
HOLDSWORTH, MARY, *Turkestan in the nineteenth century: a brief history of the Khanates of Bukhara, Khokand and Khiva*, Oxford 1959.
HARTMANN, MARTIN, *Chinesisch-Turkestan. Geschichte, Verwaltung, Geistesleben und Wirtschaft*, Halle an der Saale 1908.
HARTMANN, MARTIN, *Der Islamische Orient, Berichte und Forschungen VI–X: Ein Heiligenstaat im Islam, Das Ende der Čaghataiden und die Herrschaft der Choğas in Kašgarien*, Berlin 1905.
SAGUCHI, TORU, *The social history of Eastern Turkestan in the 18th–18th centuries*, Tokyo 1963 (in Japanese, with English summary).

# INDIA UNDER THE MOGHOL EMPIRE

BY

HERBERT HÄRTEL

Translated from the German text in *Neuzeit*,
with slight modifications

At the beginning of the 16th century A.D., India was politically fragmented to a degree which had not been seen even in comparable periods of decadence recorded earlier in her history. Half a millennium ago, a foreign invasion surpassing any since the arrival of the Aryans had established Muslim Turkish conquerors on Indian soil. They had founded the Sultanate of Delhi, which in a chequered and bellicose career had built up a Muslim empire in the subcontinent. The inability of its rulers to devise intelligent policies for holding it together had led to its rapid collapse and disintegration into small states. Incessant struggles between sultans, governors and vassals thenceforward filled the scene. The grimmest act of the drama came when Tīmūr, the "scourge of Asia", took note of India's hopeless weakness and swept down upon Delhi in the winter of 1398–1399, spreading fire and rapine in his path, but only to depart booty-laden just as quickly as he had arrived. The bloodshed which he caused in north India, and the famine and anarchy which he left behind him, were so destructive that political chaos ensued. Only south India drew any benefit from these events. The Hindu state of Vijayanagar, which had arisen earlier in the 14th century in opposition to the short-lived Muslim Sultanate of Madura, was able to keep control over the whole region south of the Kistna and Tungabhadra rivers for two hundred years. While this anti-Muslim kingdom in the south survived and grew, the Muslims failed to reestablish a unitary state in the rest of the country. In the Deccan the Bahmanī Sultanate broke up during the late 15th and early 16th centuries into the "Five Sultanates of the Deccan", while in the north the Lōdī sultans warred with independent Muslim and Hindu princes in an attempt to reassert the authority of the Sultanate of Delhi. Among the other states, the Sultanate of Gujarāt and the Hindu principality of Mewār in Rājpūtāna were relatively strong. Europeans were acquiring their first footholds on Indian soil at this time. The Portuguese captured Goa from the Deccan Sultanate of Bījāpūr in 1510.

The fragmentation of India came to an end with the rise of the Moghol empire, founded in 1526 by Bābur. For the next two hundred years a Muslim ruling group was to hold power in the predominantly Hindu subcontinent.

The Turco-Afghān sultans of the Lōdī dynasty achieved only limited success in their efforts to build up a new north Indian empire comparable with the old Sultanate of Delhi in the days of its might. *Iskandar Lōdī* (r. 1489–1517), the most notable of these sultans, was a skilful diplomatist and military tactician besides being a fanatical Muslim; he was able to expand his initially diminutive realm, and his son *Ibrāhīm* (r. 1517–1526) gained some further successes. Ibrāhīm, however, lacked the power to impose obedience on the naturally turbulent Afghān noblemen. His excessive severities only enhanced their recalcitrance and finally drove his mightiest vassal, Dawlat Khān Lōdī, governor of the Panjāb, to conspire against him with the Tīmūrid ruler of Kābul, Muḥammad Ẓahīr al-Dīn Bābur, whose intervention made short work of Ibrāhīm's life and throne.

In the person of *Bābur*, a new and remarkable figure appeared on the Indian scene: an exceptionally able general and ruler, with a romantic cast of mind and outstanding literary talent. At the age of eleven he had in 1494 inherited his father's principality of Farghānā and taken in hand the task of defending it. At fourteen he had occupied Samarqand, but later had been driven out by invading Özbegs, and finally had fled with such troops as he could muster to Kābul, which he secured in 1504. In his Memoirs, written in Chaghatāy Turkish, which are a most valuable historical source, he speaks of the longing for India which came over him at Kābul. He may therefore have already formed an intention to strike when Dawlat Khān's approach offered him an occasion.

In November 1525, Bābur set out with 12,000 troops on his historic march into India, and on April 21, 1526, he reached the plain of Pānīpat on the northern approach to Delhi. There he met the far larger army of Ibrāhīm Lōdī, and with great tactical skill routed it at the first engagement. Among the dead strewn on the field was Ibrāhīm himself. Delhi and Āgra lay open to the victorious army, and in the following months Jaunpur, Gwālior and other places gave allegiance to Bābur, who assumed the title *Pādshāh*. He had not yet come to grips, however, with an adversary whom he judged to be much more formidable than Ibrāhīm Lōdī. This was Rānā Sangrām Singh of Mēwār, leader of a powerful league of Rājpūt princes bent upon establishing Hindu supremacy. They met at the battle of Khānwa, west of Āgra, on March 16, 1527, and Bābur again won a complete victory. He was then able to extend his authority into

Oudh (Awadh) and southern Bihār. After these successes, he held sway over a domain stretching from the Oxus to the border of Bengāl and from the Himalaya to Gwālior. This was the nucleus of the Moghol[1] empire built up by later rulers of the dynasty which he founded. He died of a disease in 1530, at the age of 47.

The task of conserving, let alone expanding, Bābur's heritage called for a strong and steady hand. His son Muḥammad *Humāyūn*, who came to the throne at the age of 23, was brave and highly cultured, but lacked the energy, foresight and decisiveness requisite in the head of so new a dynasty. In 1535 he became involved in war with the Sultan of Gujarāt, Bahādur, who was then at the height of his power, having in the previous year captured an important Rājpūt fortress, Chitor. In a bold campaign, Humāyūn defeated and overthrew Bahādur and conquered most of Gujarāt, but neglected to consolidate Moghol authority in the territory. Moreover he had left his rear uncovered against the growing danger posed by a rebellious Afghān chief in Bihār, Shēr Khān. As soon as Humāyūn moved off to the east, Gujarāt was lost. His hesitant operations against the rebels resulted in an overwhelming victory for Shēr Khān, who had meanwhile assumed royal rank, at the battle of Chausa in 1539. Further weakened by rebellion and desertion on the part of his brothers, Humāyūn suffered another defeat in the following year and had to abandon his throne and country. He fled with a small following first to Lahore, then to Sind, and finally, after being refused admission to Kābul by his own brothers, to Īrān, where Shāh Tahmāsb gave him refuge. His life in exile abroad did not pass without humiliations.

Shēr Khān, now *Shēr Shāh*, of the house of Sūr, was not only the founder of the second short-lived Afghān empire in north India (1540–1545), but also, notwithstanding unfavourable representations by Moghol historians, a ruler of remarkable ability, in statecraft and administrative skill no less than in military leadership. In five years, as many as Bābur had needed to conquer his empire, Shēr Shāh not only took over that empire but also built up a highly efficient administrative machine and introduced a revenue system which was to remain the prototype for later times. He also reformed the judiciary, and greatly expedited postal and commercial traffic by installing rest houses and relay stables along the roads. He was fated, however, to reign only five years. In 1545 he was accidentally killed while besieging the fortress of Kālinjar in north India. After his death

[1] *Moghol (Mughal)* is the Perso-Arabic form of the word Mongol. Besides meaning Mongol in race or language, it is applied to Muslim descendants of the conquering Mongol armies, generally Turkish-speaking and largely of Turkish stock.

the Sūrī empire soon fell to pieces under unworthy successors. Humāyūn, who in 1547 had taken Kābul from his brother Kāmrān with Īrānian help, marched into India and after defeating the Sūrī forces reentered Delhi in July 1555. In January 1556 he accidentally fell from a step and died.

Humāyūn's son Jalāl al-Dīn Muḥammad *Akbar* (r. 1556–1605) had been born and brought up in disturbed surroundings and was only thirteen years old when his father died. He was then in the Panjāb, under the care of a Turkomān army commander, Bayram Khān, who had enthroned him and taken charge of affairs as regent. The Moghol sovereignty was precarious in the extreme. Within a short time, Āgra and Delhi were lost on account of the cowardice of their Moghol governor. The most important leader of the opposing forces was a Hindu general, Himu, who served as minister to the Sūrī Afghān pretender, ʿĀdil Shāh, but probably aimed at a restoration of Hindu rule. In 1556, at the decisive second battle of Pānīpat, Bayram Khān defeated Himu's numerically much superior army, after Himu himself had fallen. In the following year, another Sūrī prince, Sikandar Shāh, who had been holding out in the Panjāb, surrendered to the Moghol army. Akbar chose Āgra for his capital. In 1561 he was able to throw off the tutelage of Bayram Khān, which had become burdensome to him, and in 1562 he surmounted a dangerous conspiracy in his ḥarem. As soon as he stood on his own feet, Akbar set out to enlarge his kingdom. He succeeded in building up an empire more extensive, solid and durable than any yet seen in Indian history. The long series of his conquering campaigns began with the annexation of Gwālior in 1559, carried out by Bayram Khān before his fall. Mālwa was conquered in 1561, but in 1563 Akbar's attention was distracted by a revolt of Özbeg officers in his army. In the following year the old Hindu kingdom of Gondwāna was overthrown, and the empire was thus brought into direct contact with two of the Deccan sultanates, Berār and Golconda. Shortly afterwards, four of them—Aḥmadnagar, Bīdar, Bījāpūr and Golconda—finally joined forces against the Hindu kingdom of Vijayanagar and won an overwhelming victory at Talikota in January 1565. The Hindu king was killed, and the once flourishing capital city was laid waste. The territory then fell apart under a number of petty states. The destruction of Vijayanagar, which had been an important centre of medieval Hindu culture, was a severe blow to the Hindus of south India. It also had consequences affecting Europe; for the valuable trade between Goa and Vijayanagar was ruined, and the power of the Portuguese was thereby seriously weakened. The boundaries of Muslim rule were not pushed southwards at this time, as the

Deccan sultanates after their combined victory quickly resumed their internecine strife.

In Akbar's opinion, the Deccan was then a particularly desirable field for conquest; but the territories north of it had first to be subdued. In 1568 Akbar captured Chitor, and in 1569 two other important Rājpūt strongholds, Ranthambor and Kālinjar, voluntarily surrendered to him. Three years later he conquered and annexed Gujarāt. After three years of campaigning, Bengāl also was annexed, in 1576; and the Sultan of Khāndesh acknowledged Moghol suzerainty in 1577. The worst crisis which Akbar had to face arose in 1580–81, when a revolt against his religious policies broke out in the eastern provinces and his younger brother, Muḥammad Ḥākim, whom the rebels hoped to place on the throne, marched from Kābul where he was viceroy into the Panjāb. Akbar himself led an army to Kābul and reestablished imperial authority, while another army went to Bengāl and successfully crushed the rebels. The emperor soon resumed his policy of conquest with undiminished zeal. Kashmīr in 1585–86, Sind in 1591, Orissa in 1592, Balūchistān in 1594 and Qandahār in 1595 were successively incorporated into the Moghol empire. Akbar then had his hands free to act in the Deccan. He achieved initial successes with the conquest of Berār in 1596 and reconquest of Khāndesh, which had seceded in 1601; but these were his last acquisitions.

Akbar's later years were darkened by grief and anxiety. Two of his sons died of drink, and the third, Salīm, openly schemed to seize the throne during his lifetime. Notwithstanding this disloyalty, Akbar had no choice but to designate Salīm as successor. Assuming the name Jahāngīr ("world conqueror"), he took the crown on October 24, 1605, after a week's mourning for his father, who had died, according to one account, "surrounded by friends, with the faith of the Prophet in his ears and the name of God on his lips".

Akbar's military achievements, summarized above, present only one, admittedly important, facet of his historical image. His greatness sprang from an accompanying statesmanship which enabled him to fuse the conquered parts into a solid political whole. Earlier Muslim rulers had mostly seen fit to govern in disregard or defiance of the interests of their Hindu subjects. Akbar's policies were marked from the outset by a willingness to tolerate Hinduism and let Hindus play a real even if modest part in the government. The abolition of the hated poll tax (*jizyah*) on non-Muslims in 1564, and the consideration with which he treated the vanquished, gave evidence that he had set his course towards a comprehensively Indian rather than a specifically Muslim empire. He showed particular concern to win the loyal collaboration of the Rājpūt military nobility. Their alliance, cemented by Akbar's marriages to Rājpūt princesses, meant that the most important Hindu force in north India became a bulwark of the Moghol régime.

Another element in Akbar's policy of toleration was his personal interest in religious matters. He summoned to his court priests and scholars of all the faiths represented in India so that he might learn about their doctrines and discover truth by comparing them. After losing faith in Islām, he patronized all the religions and in 1582 propounded a monotheistic creed of his own, called the *Dīn-i Ilāhī*, through which he hoped to transcend Islām and Hinduism and bring about a religious unification of India. Such hopes went beyond the realm of possibility, and his new religion, which he never attempted to force upon his subjects, died with him.

Noteworthy among Akbar's internal policies were his attempts to curb further growth of the deeply rooted feudal system and to put the economy on a sound footing. For these purposes, an elaborate bureaucracy was built up, and a taxation system based upon Shēr Khān's reforms was put into effect by the Hindu finance minister, Todar Mall. In order that just assessments might be fixed, agricultural lands were carefully surveyed, classified and valued, account being taken of past crop records as well as current prices. The detested tax-farmers were eliminated, and to a considerable extent payment in kind was replaced by cash payment. Although oppression and corruption by officials were by no means wholly swept away, Akbar tried his utmost to suppress such evils.

During Akbar's reign much attention was paid to the arts. In earlier times, some of the Sultans of Delhi and other Muslim rulers had been connoisseurs of Persian culture and had patronized the arts, especially architecture, leaving a fine legacy of mosques and other buildings in which Persian and Indian styles are happily combined. Akbar and his son and grandson erected a vast number of edifices, which in their wonderful grace and charm continue to be the glory of India. The exquisite city of Fatḥpūr Sīkrī, completed for Akbar in 1576 and used for a time as his capital, contains the greatest architectural masterpieces of his reign. Among the other arts, poetry and historiography in Persian, and music and miniature painting in which Akbar took particular interest, received ample encouragement and flourished. Akbar was the real founder of the celebrated Moghol school of miniature painting.

In the light of all these achievements, Akbar is classed with Asoka as one of the greatest rulers in Indian history.

Nūr al-Dīn *Jahāngīr* (r. 1605–1627), the son of Akbar and a Hindu princess, was a man of capricious temperament, with a bent to religion and art, but without his father's military and statesmanlike qualities. In general he carried on Akbar's policies, particularly toleration at home and conquest outside. In dealing with the religious problem he showed considerable shrewdness. Orthodox Muslims had been scandalized by the indifference which Akbar, as his ideas matured, had shown towards the various organized religions. Jahāngīr, while maintaining toleration, conciliated the Muslim ruling class by showing consideration for the welfare of Islām. The empire thus enjoyed religious and political peace, and the emperor could devote much of his time to the arts. He was himself an accomplished painter and man of letters. He was afflicted, however, by a curse which lay on the Tīmūrid family. Like his brothers he was addicted to drink, and he was also an opium addict. While he thus undermined his health, his very intelligent and beautiful Īrānian consort Nūr Jahān gained influence and power. The reins of government fell almost entirely into her hands, so much so that she signed imperial decrees and had her name imprinted on coins. In these circumstances, military activity was not a prominent feature of Jahāngīr's reign, though he did in fact institute several campaigns. In 1614 the Rājpūts of Mēwār, who had moved their headquarters from Chitor to Udaipūr, were finally defeated; their prince, Rānā Amar Singh, acknowledged Moghol suzerainty. Another success came in 1620 with the capture of Kāngra, a fortress in the Himalayan foothills which had resisted Akbar's troops. These were Jahāngīr's only territorial acquisitions. In the Deccan, a long war was waged with a view to the conquest of Aḥmadnagar; but although the city fell to Jahāngīr's son Khurram in 1616, the stubborn sultanate continued to defy the Moghols under its capable general, the Ethiopian eunuch Malik ʿAnbar, until his death in 1626. In another quarter, Shāh ʿAbbās of Īrān, who had laid claim to Qandahār, besieged and captured that city in 1622.

An event which in retrospect seems momentous, but in the contemporary Moghol empire attracted scant attention, was the first appearance of English merchants. In 1613 they obtained a charter from Jahāngīr to found their first "factory" (i.e. trading post) at the then important harbour of Sūrat on the west coast; and from 1615 to 1618 an ambassador from the king of England, Sir Thomas Roe, resided at Jahāngīr's court.

The danger to Muslim dynasties inherent in the lack of a definite rule of succession in Islāmic law is well illustrated by the events of Jahāngīr's later years. He suffered the same unhappiness which he had caused to his own father. Among his four sons Khusraw, Parvīz, Khurram and Shahriyār, the most capable was Khurram, who had subdued the Rānā of

Udaipūr and then, in the war with Aḥmadnagar, won a passing success for which he was rewarded with the title Shāh Jahān ("world-king"). The empress Nūr Jahān, however, aspired to keep her political influence under her husband's eventual successor, and although she had at first favoured Khurram, she gradually came to look upon him as too formidable a partner and transferred her favour to the insignificant Shahriyār. Khurram then rebelled, and the ensuing civil war lasted several years, incidentally preventing any move to reconquer Qandahār. He was repeatedly outmatched, and in 1625 sought and obtained his father's pardon. When Jahāngīr died in October 1627, Khurram was absent in the Deccan. He won the throne with the help of a brother of Nūr Jahān, Āṣaf Khān, who on his orders put to death Shahriyār and other potential pretenders. His accession, under the name Shāh Jahān, was proclaimed at Āgra in February 1628.

*Shāh Jahān* (r. 1628–1658) was more warlike than Jahāngīr, and the empire certainly needed vigorous military leadership at this juncture. The Moghol position in the Deccan had become so precarious that Shāh Jahān was obliged during the early years of his reign to commit most of his troops to that sector. His efforts, unlike his father's, finally met with success. Of the five sultanates formed in the Deccan after the break-up of the Bahmanī empire, the two smallest, Berār and Bīdar, had been absorbed by their neighbours, so that three remained—Aḥmadnagar, Bījāpūr and Golconda. Part of Aḥmadnagar had been annexed by Akbar. Shāh Jahān invaded Bījāpūr in 1632, and annexed Aḥmadnagar in 1633 after the surrender of the historic fortress of Dawlatābād. In 1636 he made peace with Bījāpūr and Golconda, which became vassal states under Moghol suzerainty.

Shāh Jahān is remembered, however, not for military campaigns but for his brilliant court and for his superb buildings; above all, for the Tāj Maḥall, the wonderful mausoleum which he caused to be built at Āgra over the tomb of his beloved consort Mumtāz Maḥall, who died in 1631 and was a niece of Nūr Jahān. Internally the empire already showed symptoms of the maladies which contributed to its subsequent decline. Reports by European travellers show that the emperor's mania for building bore heavily on the country, and that arbitrary and corrupt exactions by officials were bleeding the people dry. The government itself suffered accordingly. Shāh Jahān's attitude towards non-Muslims, though induced by a deep personal faith in Islām, contravened the rule of toleration which since Akbar's time had so largely ensured the stability of the realm. His order that certain Hindu temples which were under construction should be demolished conformed with strict Islāmic law but not with the empire's interests. In the years 1645–47 he attempted to realize the old ambition of the Moghols to add their Transoxianan fatherland to their Indian empire; but although the districts of Balkh and Badakhshān were conquered, the whole costly enterprise had soon to be abandoned because the Moghol troops, being accustomed to the climate and comforts of India, could not stand the harsh conditions of life in Central Asia. An equally expensive failure to recapture Qandahār, in campaigns which went on from 1649 to 1652, gave further evidence of the inferiority of the Moghol forces compared with non-Indian armies, which were making more and more use of European weapons and methods.

The fact that the empire nevertheless stood unshaken must, after due allowance for Shāh Jahān's share of military successes, be attributed mainly to the sound foundations on which it had been placed by Akbar.

Shāh Jahān desired that the succession should go to his eldest son Dārā Shikōh, a prince of liberal outlook with outstanding intellectual gifts but relatively little military experience. Unfortunately for the emperor, his other sons could not be left out of the reckoning. There was little likelihood that the paternal decision would be respected by Murād, the youngest, a foolhardy youth then governor of Gujarāt; by the irresolute Shujāʿ, governor of Bengāl; least of all by Awrangzēb, the most energetic and experienced of the four brothers.

Muḥyi'l-Dīn Muḥammad Awrangzēb, born in 1618, had been viceroy of the Deccan from 1636 to 1644, and after holding various other commands, notably at Balkh and Qandahār, had returned to his former post in the Deccan in 1652. He possessed considerable military talent, together with strong ambition and a high degree of cunning. His private life was impeccable, and his inviolable rule was to keep his given word. Such was the man who not only got the better of his brothers, but also defied and humbled his own father. He was leading a successful campaign against Bījāpūr, which since 1636 had grown through conquests to be an important power in southern India, when the inevitable civil war was sparked off by news that Shāh Jahān had fallen seriously ill. Fluctuating warfare between the armies of the different brothers ended in victory for Awrangzēb, who incarcerated his convalescent father in the fort of Āgra and in July 1658 assumed royal authority. The name which he took at his enthronement in June 1659 was ʿĀlamgīr ("world-conqueror"). Shāh Jahān remained a prisoner at Āgra, where he died in June 1666.

In the development of the Moghol empire from Akbar's time onwards, certain trends can be identified. The policy of toleration instituted by Akbar had been the main factor conducing to internal stability, and his understanding with the Rājpūts had added much to the empire's military strength. Although the unwarlike Jahāngīr ceased to win military victories, the empire's stability had been maintained during his reign thanks to continued toleration at home and untroubled relations with neighbouring foreign powers. Under Shāh Jahān, the empire was enlarged territorially through successful wars, but was weakened internally through prodigal state expenditure and partial abandonment of the policy of toleration.

In this context, the future trend was bound to depend very largely on the attitude towards toleration shown by the new ruler, *Awrangzēb* (r. 1658–1707). Since he was not only earnest in his own Islāmic faith, but also intensely antagonistic to followers of all other faiths, grave consequences ensued for the cosmopolitan Moghol empire. With narrow-minded obstinacy, Awrangzēb fanned flames by which he and the empire were to be consumed. He trampled on the feelings of his Hindu subjects in ill-judged zeal to enforce Islāmic law and bring about conversions. The most important Hindu temples in north India were destroyed at his command, with irreparable loss to Indian art; and vexatious discriminatory edicts were issued in the hope that Islām might be spread by economic pressure. After the destruction of the temple at Mathura (Muttra) in 1669, the Jāt inhabitants of the district rose in a rebellion which could not be wholly suppressed and did not subside until after Awrangzēb's death. The Sikhs of the Panjāb, adherents of a reforming religious sect founded by Guru Nānak (1469–1539), likewise became enemies of the Moghol régime after Awrangzēb had caused their ninth *guru*, Teg Bahādur, to die a martyr's death in 1675. His son Govind Singh, who became the next *guru*, later organized the Sikhs into a military brotherhood, the Khālsa ("pure"), pledged to resist the forces of Islām. The most fatal move of all was Awrangzēb's decision in 1679 to reimpose the poll-tax (*jizyah*) on all non-Muslims, including the feudal nobility and in particular the Rājpūt princes, who legally had a right to exemption. At the same time he installed a Moghol administration at Jōdhpūr, capital of the Rājpūt state of Mārwār. The Rājpūt clans, formerly the empire's trustiest vassals, then rose with few exceptions in revolt against Awrangzēb. The Moghol forces were severely strained by the Rājpūt war of 1680–81, which came after a long series of other large scale operations, notably the campaign against Assam in 1661–63 led by Mīr Jumlah, a native of Iṣfahān who was Awrangzēb's governor of Bengāl; the capture of Chittagong in 1666; and campaigns against rebellious Afghān tribes on the north west frontier from 1667 to 1675. During the Rājpūt war, Awrangzēb's son Akbar went over to the insurgents. An ingenious stratagem contrived by his father frustrated Akbar's plans; but he escaped and took refuge with the Marātha king Shambujī in the Deccan. This prompted Awrangzēb to march with his troops to the Deccan, where events were to detain him for the rest of his life.

The situation in the Deccan had changed greatly since the days of Awrangzēb's viceroyalty. A new power had appeared on the scene with the rise of the Marāthas (Mahrattas), a Hindu nation, who had acquired a leader of very high calibre by name *Shīvājī* (1627–1680). The Marātha peasants of the Western Ghāts were doughty warriors, and with their help Shīvājī had been able from about 1646 onwards to capture mountain strongholds and carve out a domain of his own around Poona. During the struggles between Awrangzēb, then viceroy, and the Sultans of Bījāpūr and Golconda, he extended his sway into the Konkan district on the west coast, which he used as a base for further campaigns and plundering raids. His power grew steadily and only suffered a temporary setback when he agreed in 1666 to visit the emperor and was interned at Āgra; for after a romantic escape he contrived to make his way back to the Deccan, less willing than ever to think of conciliation. In 1674 Shīvājī, the champion of Hinduism against Awrangzēb's oppressive policy, had himself crowned with Vedic rites as an independent monarch, with a council of eight ministers to conduct his government in accordance with ancient Hindu tradition. His treasury was replenished mainly with plunder taken in winter raiding and also, from 1670 onwards, with protection money, called *chauth* ("one quarter"), levied on districts not under Marātha rule in return for suspension of raiding.

When Shīvājī died in 1680, he left a Hindu realm spreading from the Konkan to the Carnatic and an army second to none in contemporary India for efficiency and valour. The freedom-urge stirring the Marātha people remained formidable, even though Shīvājī's son and successor *Shambujī* was a much less able leader. As already mentioned, Shambujī received the fugitive prince Akbar, son of Awrangzēb, whereupon the emperor himself went to the Deccan early in 1682.

The two sultanates of Bījāpūr and Golconda, which quarter of a century earlier had only escaped conquest by Awrangzēb thanks to the Moghol succession struggle, were not in any better position than then to offer him effective resistance. After a long siege Bījāpūr was annexed in 1686, and the city with its splendid buildings[1] fell into decay, partly as the result of plagues and famines. Golconda withstood an even longer siege, until it fell through treachery and was annexed in 1687. The fact that several years

[1] One of these, the Gul Gunbadh, has the world's largest dome. *E.I. (2)*, article *Bidjāpūr*.

were needed to reduce these two weak adversaries throws a revealing light on the efficiency of the Moghol army. In 1689, however, a Moghol force captured the feeble Shambujī, whom Awrangzēb put to death; and the Marātha capital, Rājgarh, was later taken by storm. In the following years Awrangzēb advanced far into the south and imposed Moghol suzerainty on the Hindu states of Tanjore and Trichinopoly.

By one of the ironies of history, the Moghol empire reached its greatest territorial extent at a time when its internal collapse was near. Awrangzēb had not won complete victory over the Marāthas; and the war in the Deccan continued, exhausting the empire's financial and military strength. Neither the Deccan nor the rest of India had been pacified when Awrangzēb died in March 1707, at the age of 89. For a quarter of a century he had been absent from north India and had directed all available resources into the war in the Deccan. The Rājpūts and Sikhs, however, had not given up their obstinate resistance. Awrangzēb left the empire not only weak and disorganized, but also in danger from forces which he himself had rendered hostile.

The usual succession struggle was fought, and ended in victory for Awrangzēb's eldest son Bahādur Shāh, who reigned as *Shāh ʿĀlam I* (1707–1712). His death in 1712 gave rise to further struggles. The emperors then placed on the throne in rapid succession were powerless figures whose fortunes need not be detailed here.[1] *Muḥammad Shāh* (r. 1719–1748) kept his throne during a long reign in which the Moghol empire gradually fell to pieces under the strains of factional intrigue, civil war and foreign invasion. The continued presence of Moghol emperors at Delhi for more than a century after his death was due solely to the fact that the new actors on the scene saw fit for various reasons to preserve the shadow of imperial suzerainty.

The main forces at work in eighteenth century India were as follows: (i) the Marāṭhas; (ii) the new Muslim state and dynasty of Hyderabad (Ḥaydarābād) founded in 1724 by *Niẓām al-Mulk*, formerly an officer and *wazīr* in the Moghol service; (iii) Īrānian and Afghān armies pushing in from the north west; and (iv) the British East India Company, as it grew in strength and got the better of its European rivals.

After the decline of the early Marātha kingdom under the inept Shambujī, Marātha power was restored through the efforts of the *Pēshwā*, *Balajī*

[1] *Jahāndār Shāh* (r. 1712–13) was deposed and put to death by his nephew *Farrukhsiyar* (r. 1713–19). The latter was deposed and put to death by the two *Sayyids of Bārhā*, *Ḥusayn ʿAlī* and *ʿAbd Allāh*, who had brought him to the throne and become his *wazīr* and commander in chief. The two Sayyids then enthroned three princes in one year. The last of these, *Muḥammad Shāh*, survived the overthrow of the Sayyids by Niẓām ul-Mulk.

*Vishvanāth* (r. 1714–1720), and his son *Bajī Rao* (r. 1720–1740). Their office was nominally that of second minister to the Marātha king *Shahu,* grandson of Shīvājī; but it amounted to virtual rulership and became hereditary in their line. These capable leaders aimed to establish Hindu supremacy. By 1719 they were levying the *chauth* in all parts of the Deccan and in much of south India. Bajī Rao invaded Gujarāt in 1723, occupied Mālwa in 1734–36, and marched in 1737 to the vicinity of Delhi. The Niẓām of Hyderabad then intervened on the emperor's behalf; but in 1738 he suffered a partial defeat and came to terms with the Marāthas, who were then able to carry their raids into Orissa and Bengāl. In most of the territories which they conquered, the Marāthas did not set up their own system of state administration, but instead maintained a complicated system of financial imposts, or rather extortions. Everywhere they exacted the notorious *chauth,* i.e. one quarter of the annual revenue, together with the *sardeshmukhī,* an additional contribution amounting to one tenth of the annual assessment. They thus implicitly recognized the existing governmental institutions derived from the Moghol régime.

Not only the Marāthas, but also other virtually independent rulers in India, still acknowledged the formal suzerainty of the Moghol emperor, whose actual authority did not extend beyond the Delhi district, the Panjāb and Kābul. The Marātha march on Delhi was undertaken primarily with the object of making the emperor pay a large financial contribution. Two years later, however, Delhi was visited by a mightier invader, comparable with the frightful Tīmūr. This was *Nādir Shāh* of Īrān, who after capturing Kābul and crossing the Khyber (Khaybar) pass routed the Moghol army at Karnāl in February 1739 and entered the city. When a mob set upon some of the Īrānian troops, Nādir ordered a massacre in the city. Having obtained the formal cession of the lands west of the Indus, together with a huge indemnity, Nādir Shāh hurried back to his own country, taking with him the treasure of the Moghol emperors and leaving behind him a scene of desolation.

Another and more persistent invader appeared before long in the person of *Aḥmad Shāh Durrānī,* the founder of modern Afghānistān, who took over the eastern part of Nādir Shāh's empire. Between 1748 and 1761 he invaded north India seven times. He annexed the Panjāb in 1752 and sacked Delhi and Mathura in 1757. The Afghāns soon came into conflict with the Marāthas, who overran the Panjāb in 1758 when they reached the zenith of their power. A year later Aḥmad Shāh Durrānī recovered the province from them. The Marāthas then assembled their forces and marched north to reassert their authority. On January 14, 1761, the

Marātha army met Aḥmad Shāh's Muslim army on the historic field of Pānīpat. The Marāthas suffered an overwhelming defeat. They nevertheless continued for a long time to be the strongest indigenous military power in India, because Aḥmad Shāh was not in a position to follow up his victory. There could no longer, however, be any question of a great Marāṭha empire. During the subsequent years, a number of rival Marātha principalities came into being, notably those of the *Pēshwā* of Poona, *Sindhia* of Gwalior, *Holkar* of Indore, *Gaekwar* of Baroda, and *Bhonsla* of Nāgpūr. They were to be the toughest opponents of the new power which was arising in India, namely the British.

Four years before the destiny of the Marāthas was sealed at Pānīpat, another decisive military encounter had taken place. This was the battle of Plassey, in Bengāl, which gave the British East India Company mastery over that province and paved the way for future British rule over the entire sub-continent.

Two and a half centuries had elapsed since the Portuguese established the first European bases on the coasts of India, and many years had passed since the English, Dutch and later French East India companies founded their "factories" in the 17th century. Until the mid-18th century the Europeans had in general confined themselves to trade and to occasional fighting among themselves, mainly at sea. The disintegration of the Moghol empire happened to coincide with a period of Anglo-French warfare—the War of the Austrian Succession (1740–48) and the Seven Years War (1756–63). These wars were fought not only in Europe and America, but also in India, where native troops were recruited and local potentates entered the fray.

The course of European settlement in India, and the rise of British power, are outlined in the next volume.

## THE MOGHOL EMPERORS OF INDIA 1526–1858, AND THE SŪRĪ DYNASTY 1540–1555

Tīmūr Lang (d. 1405)
|
Mīrān-Shāh (d. 1408)
|
Muḥammad
|
Abū Saʿīd (d. 1469)
|
ʿUmar Shaykh (d. 1493/4)
|
Ẓahīr al-Dīn Muḥammad BĀBUR
(b. 14 Feb. 1483)
(r. in India April 1526–26 Dec. 1530)
|
Hindāl (d. 1551) — ʿAskarī (d. 1554) — Nāṣir al-Dīn Muḥammad HUMĀYŪN (b. 6 March 1508) (first reign: 26 Dec. 1530–18 May 1540) — Kāmrān (d. 1557)

---

SHER SHĀH Sūrī
(r. 18 May 1540–22 May 1545)
|
ISLĀM SHĀH
(r. 22 May 1545– Nov. 1553)
|
ĀDIL SHĀH
(r. Nov. 1553–May 1554)
|
IBRĀHĪM
(r. in 1554)
|
ISKANDAR
(r. 1554–24 July 1555)

---

Nāṣir al-Dīn Muḥammad HUMĀYŪN
(second reign: 24 July 1555–24 Jan. 1556)

Jalāl al-Dīn Muḥammad AKBAR
(b. 15 Oct. 1542)
(r. 24 Jan. 1556–16 Oct. 1605)

(Salīm )Nūr al-Dīn Muḥammad JAHĀNGĪR
(b. 31 Aug. 1569)
(r. 16 Oct. 1605–28 Oct. 1627)

Shahriyār
(d. 1627)

(Khurram) Shihāb al-Dīn Muḥammad SHĀH JAHĀN
(b. 15 Jan. 1592)
(r. 25 Feb. 1628–19 June 1658)
(d. 2 Feb. 1666)

Khusraw
(d. 1622)

Dāvar Bakhsh
(d. 1627)

Dārā Shikōh
(d. 10 Sept. 1659)

Shujā'
(d. 1659)

Murād Bakhsh
(d. 1661)

Muḥyi'l-Dīn Muḥammad AWRANGZĒB,
'ĀLAMGĪR I (b. 3 Nov. 1618)
(r. 21 July 1658–2 March 1707)

A'ẓam Shāh
(d. June 1707)

(Mu'aẓẓam) Quṭb al-Dīn Muḥammad SHĀH 'ĀLAM I, BAHĀDUR SHĀH I
(b. 14 Oct. 1643)
(r. 26 March 1707–27 Feb. 1712)

Akbar
(d. 1705)

Kāmbakhsh
(d. Jan. 1709)

'Aẓīm al-Sha'n
(d. March 1712)

Mu'īn al-Dīn FARRUKHSIYAR
(b. 1683)
(r. 10 Jan. 1713–28 Feb. 1719)
(d. 28 April 1719)

Rafī' al-Sha'n
(d. March 1712)

Mu'izz al-Dīn JAHĀNDĀR
(b. 1661)
(r. 29 March 1712–10 Jan. 1713)
(d. 11 Feb. 1713)

Jahānshāh
(d. March 1712)

Shams al-Dīn RAFĪʻ AL-DARAJĀT
(r. 2 March 1719–9 June 1719)
(d. 12 June 1719)

Rafīʻ al-Dawlah SHĀH JAHĀN II
(r. 9 June 1719–8 Sept. 1719)

Nāṣir al-Dīn MUḤAMMAD SHĀH Rōshan Akhtar
(b. 1701)
(r. 30 Sept. 1719–24 April 1748)

Mujāhid al-Dīn AḤMAD SHĀH Bahādur
(b. 1726)
(r. 1 May 1748–4 June 1754)
(d. 2 Jan. 1775)

Bīdār Bakht
(pretender, 30 Aug. 1788–10 Oct. 1788)

ʻAzīz al-Dīn ʻĀLAMGĪR II
(b. 1688)
(r. 4 June 1754–30 Nov. 1759)

(ʻAlī Gōhar) Jalāl al-Dīn SHĀH ʻĀLAM II
(b. 1728)
(r. 26 Dec. 1759–19 Nov. 1806)

Muʻīn al-Dīn Muḥammad AKBAR II
(b. 1759)
(r. 19 Nov. 1806–30 Sept. 1837)

Sirāj al-Dīn BAHĀDUR SHĀH II
(b. 1775)
(r. 30 Sept. 1837–30 March 1858)
(d. 7 Nov. 1862)

SHĀH JAHĀN II
(grandson of Kāmbakhsh
son of Awrangzēb)
(r. 12 Dec. 1759–11 Oct. 1760)

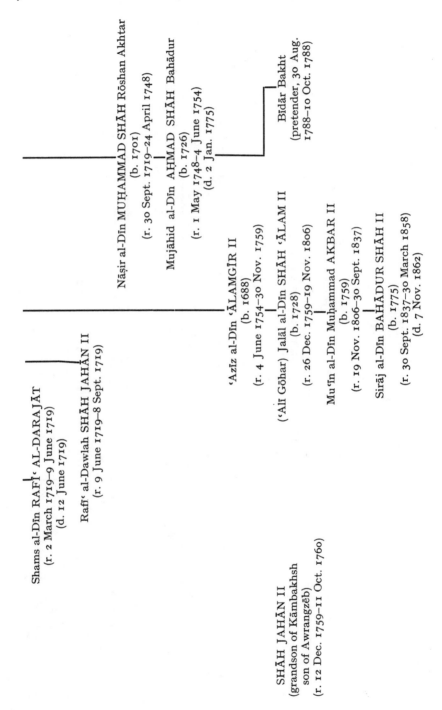

# BIBLIOGRAPHY

(based on the bibliography by Herbert Härtel
in *Neuzeit*, with additions by F. R. C. Bagley)

## GENERAL


*The Cambridge History of India*, Cambridge 1922–1937, vols. III and IV.
*The Cambridge Shorter History of India*, Cambridge 1934.
POWELL PRICE, J. C., *A History of India*, London 1955.
MAJUMDAR, R. C., RAYCHAUDURI, H. C., and WATTA, K., *An Advanced History of India*, London 1948.
SINHA, N. K., and BANERJEE, A. C., *History of India*, Calcutta, 1947.
DUNBAR, Sir G., *A History of India from the earliest times to the present day*, London 1936; German tr., *Geschichte Indiens*, Munich 1937.
MORELAND, W. H., and CHATTERJEE, Sir A. C., *A Short History of India*, London 1936.
KEITH, A. B., *A Constitutional History of India 1600–1935*, London 1936.
SMITH, VINCENT A., *The Oxford History of India*, Oxford 1919, 2nd ed. 1923.
FERNANDES, B. A., *Bibliography of Indian History and oriental research*, Bombay 1938–1942.
HUNTER, Sir W. W., *A Brief History of the Indian Peoples*, London 1907.
HUNTER, Sir W. W., *The Indian Musulmans*, London 1876, reprinted Calcutta 1945.
ALSDORF, LUDWIG, *Indien von der Mohammedanischen Eroberung bis zur Gegenwart*. In *Bruckmans Weltgeschichte in Einzeldarstellungen*; *Geschichte Asiens*, Munich 1950.
ALSDORF, LUDWIG, *Vorderindien. Bharat – Pakistan – Ceylon. Eine Landes- und Kulturkunde*, Braunschweig 1955.
*Oldenbourgs Abriss der Weltgeschichte*, Teil II, B: *Indien, Indonesien, Tibet*. By H. B. KOHLER, with advice from E. WALDSCHMIDT. Tibet by H. HOFFMANN. Munich 1954.
DE LA VALLÉE-POUSSIN, L., *Histoire du monde*, vol. 3, 6(1–2), Paris 1930–1936.
AHMAD, AZIZ, *Studies in Islamic culture in the Indian environment*, Oxford 1964.
ABID HUSAIN, *Indian culture*, Bombay 1963.
QURESHI, ISHTIAQ HUSAIN, *The Muslim community in the Indo-Pakistan subcontinent (610–1947)*, The Hague 1962.
IKRAM, S. M., and SPEAR, PERCIVAL, ed. *The cultural heritage of Pakistan*, Karachi 1955.
IKRAM, S. M., *Muslim civilization in India*, ed. by A. T. EMBREE, New York 1964.
HOLLISTER, J. N., *The Shi'a of India*, London 1953.
SHARMA, S. R., *The crescent in India*, Bombay 1954.
VACCA, VIRGINIA, *L'India musulmana*, Milan 1941.
TARA CHAND, *The influence of Islam on Indian culture*, Allahabad 1936.
TITUS, MURRAY T., *Indian Islam*, London 1930.
GARRETT, G. T., ed., *The legacy of India*, Oxford 1937.
RAWLINSON, H. G., *India, a short cultural history*, London 1952.
GOETZ, H., *The genesis of Indo-Muslim civilization*, Calcutta 1938.
SARKAR, Sir JADUNATH, *India through the ages: a survey of the growth of Indian life and thought*, Calcutta 1928.
BAUSANI, ALESSANDRO, *Storia delle letterature del Pakistan*, Milan 1958.
KRAMRISCH, S., *The art of India*, London 1954.
SMITH, VINCENT A., *A history of fine art in India and Ceylon*, Oxford 1911.
BROWN, PERCY, *Indian architecture (Islamic period)*, Bombay 1943.

## THE MOGHOL PERIOD

STOREY, C. A., *Persian Literature*, Vol. I, Part I, London 1927. (For particulars of chronicles etc. in Persian.)

HARDY, P., *Historians of medieval India: studies in Indo-Muslim writing*, London 1960.

SHARMA, S. R., *A bibliography of Mughal India (1526–1707 A.D.)*, Bombay 1939.

SHARMA, S. R., *The Mughal empire in India*, 3 vols., Bombay 1940–1941.

EDWARDES, S. M., and GARRETT, H. L. O., *Mughal rule in India*, London 1930.

KENNEDY, P., *History of the Great Moghuls*, 2 vols., Calcutta 1905–1911.

LANE-POOLE, STANLEY, *Medieval India under Mohammedan rule, 712–1764*, London 1903.

JAFFAR, S. M., *The Mughal empire from Babur to Aurangzeb*, Peshawar 1936.

PRASAD, ISHWARI, *A short history of Muslim rule in India, from the conquest of Islam to the death of Aurangzeb*, Allahabad 1939.

YUSUF ALI, *Medieval India: social and economic conditions*, London 1932.

ASHRAF, KUNWAR MUHAMMAD, *The life and conditions of the people of Hindustan (1200–1550 A.D.)*, Calcutta 1935.

MORELAND, W. H., *India at the death of Akbar, an economic study*, London 1920. *From Akbar to Aurangzeb, an economic study*, London 1923. *The agrarian system of Moslem India*, Cambridge 1929.

ELLIOTT, Sir HENRY M., ed. and tr., *The history of India as told by its own historians. The Muhammadan period*. Ed. by JOHN DOWSON. 8 vols., London 1867–1877.

BĀBUR, *Bābar-nāma*, Chaghatāy Turkish text ed. by ANNETTE S. BEVERIDGE, Leiden 1905 (E. J. W. Gibb Memorial Series); tr. by ANNETTE S. BEVERIDGE, 2 vols., London. Persian tr. put into Eng. by J. LEYDEN and W. ERSKINE, London 1826, new ed. revised by ANNETTE S. BEVERIDGE, London 1912; put into French by PAVET DE COURTEILLE, Paris 1871.

LANE-POOLE, STANLEY, *Babar*, Oxford 1899.

EDWARDES, S. M., *Babar, diarist and despot*, London 1926.

ERSKINE, W., *A history of India under Baber and Humayun*, London 1854.

GULBADAN BEGUM, *The Humāyūn-nāma: a history of Humāyūn*, tr. by ANNETTE S. BEVERIDGE, London 1902.

QANUNGO, K. R., *Sher Shah*, Calcutta 1921.

ABŪ'L-FAZL 'ALLĀMĪ, *Ā'īn-i Akbarī*, Persian text ed. by H. BLOCHMANN, 2 vols., Calcutta 1872–1877 (Asiatic Society of Gengal, Bibliotheca Indica); tr. by H. BLOCHMANN and H. S. JARRETT, 2nd ed. revised by D. C. PHILLOTT and Sir JADUNATH SARKAR, 3 vols., Calcutta 1939 (Asiatic Society of Bengal, Bibliotheca Indica).

ABŪ'L-FAZL 'ALLĀMĪ, *Akbar-nāma*, Persian text ed. by MAULAVI ABDUL RAHIM, 2 vols., Calcutta 1877–1879 (Asiatic Society of Bengal, Bibliotheca Indica); tr. by H. BEVERIDGE, 3 vols., Calcutta 1907–1939 (Asiatic Society of Bengal, Bibliotheca Indica).

BADĀ'ŪNĪ, 'ABD AL-QĀDIR, *Muntakhab al-Tawārīkh*, Persian text ed. W. N. LEE and MAULAVI AHMAD ALI, 3 vols., Calcutta 1865–1869 (Asiatic Society of Bengal, Bibliotheca Indica); tr. by G. S. A. RANKING, W. H. LOWE and Sir T. WOLSELEY HAIG, 3 vols., Calcutta 1898–1925 (Asiatic Society of Bengal, Bibliotheca Indica).

SMITH, VINCENT A., *Akbar, the Great Mogul*, Oxford 1917.

BINYON, LAURENCE, *Akbar*, London 1922.

VON NOER, Graf F. C. K. A., *L'empereur Akbar*, tr. by G. BONET MAURY, 2 vols., Paris 1883–1887.

JAHĀNGĪR, *Tuzuk* (*Memoirs*), tr. from the Persian by A. ROGERS, ed. by H. BEVER-

IDGE, 2 vols., London 1909–1914 (Oriental Translation Fund, N.S., 19 and 22).
PRASAD, B., *History of Jahangir*, Allahabad 1930.
SAKSENA, B. P., *History of Shah Jahan of Delhi*, London 1932.
SĀQĪ MUSTA'IDD KHĀN, *Ma'āthir-i 'Ālamgīrī*, tr. from the Persian by Sir JADUNATH SARKAR, *A history of the emperor Aurangzeb*, Calcutta 1947 (Asiatic Societt of Bengal, Bibliotheca Indica).
SARKAR, Sir JADUNATH, *A history of Aurangzib*, 5 vols., Calcutta 1912–1925.
SARKAR, Sir JADUNATH, *A short history of Aurangzib*, London 1930.
LANE-POOLE, STANLEY, *Aurangzeb*, London 1892.
FARUKI, Z., *Aurangzeb and his times*, Bombay 1935.
IRVINE, W., *The later Mughals*, continued by Sir JADUNATH SARKAR, 2 vols., Calcutta 1921–1922.
SARKAR, Sir JADUNATH, *The fall of the Moghul empire*, 4 vols., Calcutta 1932–1950.
SPEAR, PERCIVAL, *Twilight of the Mughuls: studies in late Mughul Delhi*, Cambridge 1951.
OWEN, S. J., *The fall of the Moghul empire*, London 1912.
KEENE, H. G., *The Moghul empire from the death of Aurangzeb to the overthrow of the Mahratta power*, London 1866.
SEWELL, ROBERT, *A forgotten empire, Vijayanagar*, London 1900, reprinted 1924.
SALATORE, B. A., *Social and political life in the Vijayanagar empire*, 2 vols., Madras 1934.
HAIG, Sir T. WOLSELEY, *Historic landmarks of the Deccan*, Allahabad 1907.
SCOTT, JONATHAN, *History of the Deccan*, 2 vols., London 1794.
DUFF, JAMES GRANT, *A history of the Mahrattas*, 3 vols., London 1826, reprinted 1921.
SARKAR, Sir JADUNATH, *Shivaji and his times*, Calcutta 1929.
SARKAR, Sir JADUNATH, *History of Shivaji*, Calcutta 1948.
SARDESAI, G. S., *A new history of the Marathas*, 3 vols., Bombay 1946–1948.
CUNNINGHAM, JOSEPH DAVEY, *A history of the Sikhs, from the origins of the nation to the battles of the Sutlej*, ed. by H. L. O. GARRETT, London 1918, reprinted Delhi 1956.
TRUMPP, E., *Die religion der Sikh*, Munich 1881.
KHUSHWANT SINGH, *The Sikhs*, London 1953.
SARKAR, Sir JADUNATH, *Mughal administration*, London 1935.
HUSAINI, S. A. Q., *Administration under the Moghuls*, Dacca 1952.
SHARMA, S. R., *Mughal administration*, Calcutta 1952.
SHARMA, S. R., *The religious policy of the Mughal emperors*, London 1940.
AKBAR, MUHAMMAD, *The administration of justice iunder the Moghuls*, Lahore 1948.
ABDUL AZIZ, *The mansabdari system and the army*, Lahore 1945.
ABDUL AZIZ, *The imperial treasury of the Indian Moghuls*, Lahore 1942.
PANT, DEVIDATT, *The commercial policy of the Moguls*, Bombay 1930.
IRVINE, W., *The army of the Indian Moguls*, London 1903.
ABDUL GHANI, *A history of the Persian language and literature at the Mughul court, with a brief survey of the Urdu language*, 3 vols., Allahabad 1929–1930.
BAILEY, T. GRAHAME, *History of Urdu literature*, London 1932.
SAKSENA, R. B., *History of Urdu literature*, Allahabad 1940.
BINYON, LAURENCE, *The court painters of the Grand Moguls*, London 1911.
FOSTER, Sir WILLIAM, ed., *Early travels in India*, London 1921.
DE ALBUQUERQUE, AFONSO, *Comentarios*, Lisbon 1576, reprinted Coimbra 1922–1923; Eng. tr. by W. DE GRAY BIRCH, *The commentaries*, 4 vols., London 1875–1884.
BARBOSA, DUARTE, *The book of Duarte*, tr. from the Portuguese by M. LONGWORTH DAMES, 2 vols., London 1918–1921.

MONSERRATE, ANTONIO, *The commentary on his journey to the court of Akbar*, tr. by J. S. HOYLAND with notes by S. W. BANERJEE, London 1922.

DU JARRIC, PIERRE, *Akbar and the Jesuits, an account of the Jesuit missions to the court of Akbar*, tr. with introd. and notes by C. H. PAYNE, London 1926.

GUERREIRO, F., *Jahangir and the Jesuits*, tr. by C. H. PAYNE, London 1930.

PELSAERT, F., *Jahangir's India*, tr. from the Dutch by W. H. MORELAND and P. GEYL, Cambridge 1925.

ROE, Sir THOMAS, *The embassy of Sir Thomas Roe to the court of the Great Mogul, 1615–1619*, ed. by Sir W. FOSTER, London 1899.

DELLA VALLE, PIETRO, *Viaggi ... divisi in tre parti, cioè La Turchia, la Persia, e l'India*, Rome 1658–1663; Eng. tr. of Part III by GEORGE HAVERS, London 1665, new ed. revised by E. GRAY, London 1892. (French tr. 1745).

TAVERNIER, JEAN BAPTISTE, *Les six voyages ...*, Paris 1676. Eng. tr., London 1678. Partial Eng. tr. by V. BALL, *Travels in India*, 2 vols., London 1889.

BERNIER, FRANÇOIS, *Voyages*, tr. by IRVING BROCK and annotated by A. CONSTABLE, London 1891; 2nd ed., revised by VINCENT A. SMITH, London 1916.

MANUCCI, NICCOLO, *Storia do Mogor*; tr. with introd. and notes by W. IRVINE, *A Pepys of Mogul India*, 1653–1708, 4 vols., London 1907–1908. (French tr. 1713.)

# INDICES

## prepared by URSULA STEIER, Hamburg

(some of the identifications and alternative names and spellings were supplied by F. R. C. Bagley)

N.B. – before a name shows that in Arabic the definite article *al* is used.

### INDEX A

Names of Persons
(including dynasties)

Ẓāhir al-'Umar, Shaykh, governor of 'Akkā 65 f., 74 f.
Zand dynasty 93, 205-207
Zápolya, John (Szápolyai János), Prince of Transylvania 30-32
Zaydān, Sultan of Morocco 106
Zayyānid dynasty 97, 103, 115, 117
Zrinyi, Count, Hungarian officer 32

## INDEX B

Names of places, nations and tribes

Abeshr (Abéché), town 165
'Abdallāb, tribe 167
Abyssinia (Ethiopia) 52, 57-59, 62 f., 68, 166, 168-179, 266
'Adal, territory 170 f.
Adamawa territory 157, 163
Adana, town 70
Aden ('Adan), town 57-63, 90, 153
Adrianople *see* Edirne
Adriatic Sea 20, 23, 143
Aegean Sea 15 f., 22, 45
'Afār (Danāqil), nation 170, 172
Afghān, Afghānistān 43, 198-207, 226 f., 237, 239, 246, 254 f., 261-263, 272
Afshār, tribe 183, 203
Ağa Çayiri, battle 27
Agadez, town 162
Agadir, town 97 f., 102
Āgra, city 261, 263, 267 f., 270
Ahlat (Akhlāṭ), town 1
Aḥmadābād, city 59
Aḥmadnagar, town 263, 266 f.
- Aḥsā, territory 80 f., 83 f., 86, 88 f.
Ainos *see* Enez
Air, district 161 f.
'Ajlūn (Gilead), district 71
Ak Kerman (Cetatea Alba, Belgorod), town 26
'Akkā (Acre), town 54, 65 f., 74-77
'Akkār, district 69
Alaşehir (Philadelphic), town 11
Ala Tau, range 221
Alai, range 248
Albania, Albanian (Arnavut) 10, 17, 20, 23-25, 27, 37, 41
Alcazarquivir (Wādī Makhāzin), battle 98, 104
Aleppo (Ḥalab), city 35, 50-55, 68-77, 81 f., 85, 194
Alexandria (al-Iskandarīyah), city 55, 67, 114, 170
Algarve, district (in Portugal) 97
Algeciras, town 112
Algiers (al-Jazā'ir), Algeria 30 f., 39, 91[1], 100 f., 103-147
Alodia, territory 165
'Alwah, territory 166 f.
'Amādīyah, town 85
Amasya, town 11, 13, 25, 32, 189, 192
Amhara, district, Amharic, language 170, 171
Āmū Daryā (Oxus), river 186, 203, 221, 226 f., 239 f., 244, 252 f., 262
Anatolia (Anadolu) = Asia Minor 8, 10-16, 27, 35-46, 51, 53 f., 119, 121, 141, 183-186
'Anazah, tribes 72, 81
Andījān, town 248
Anjabā, island 174
Ankara (Ancyra, Angora), city 14
Ankara (Çubukabad), battle 13, 225
Antalya (Adalia), town 10
Aq Ṣu, town and river 221, 233 f.
Arab(s) 18, 51-94, 97-147, 153-179, 204, 248
Arabic language 33, 51 f., 72, 158, 163, 166-168
Aragón, territory 98, 122
Aral, lake 252-255
Aras, river 200, 202
Ardabīl, town 182 f., 193, 200
Ardalān, district 78, 82
Argeş, town and river 11
Argos, town 42
Armenia, Armenian 12, 37, 43, 76, 78, 86, 183, 185, 192, 195, 200
Arzila (Aṣīlah), town 97, 104
Asia Minor *see* Anatolia
Assam, province 269
Astarābād (Gurgān), town 185, 200, 220, 230
Astrakhan (Ashtarkhān), town 223, 243 f.
Aswān, town 55, 67, 166
Asyūṭ, town 56, 65
'Atbarā, river 166
Atbash, town (on R. Narin) 222
Athens, city 40
Atlas, mountains 97, 102, 104, 107, 109-111, 155
Aures (Awrās), mountains 97
Austria 27, 32-46, 67 f., 110
Awdaghost, former town 155
Awfāt *see* Ifat
Awliyā-Ata (Jambol), town 250
Axum (Aksum), town 166, 169 f.
Ayasoluk (Ephesus), town 11
'Aydhāb, former town 170
Aydin, town 11, 15
Aytos, town 9
Āẕarbāyjān, province 28, 31, 35, 85, 185-187, 189 f., 193, 201, 205
Āẕarī Turkish language 188

Buda(pest), city 12, 30 f., 40

## INDEX C

Technical Terms
(including names of religious communities)

# ERRATA

| *page* | *line* | *instead of* | *read* |
|---|---|---|---|
| 16 | 14 | Sinob | Sinop |
| 35 | 39 | (Iasi) | (Iaşi) |
| 35 | 40 | (Choczim) | (Chocim) |
| 39 | 34 | (Kamieniecz) | (Kamieniec) |
| 39 | 35 | (Choczim) | (Chocim) |
| 40 | 2 | Zurawno | Żurawno |
| 42 | 5 | Kamieniecz | Kamieniec |
| 52 | 31 | companies | Companies |
| 56 | 14 | Asyūt | Asyūṭ |
| 58 | 5 and 15 | Maṣawwā | Maṣawwa‘ |
| 58 | 30 and 40 | Sidi ‘Alī Reis | Sidi Ali Reis |
| 61 | 34 | Pontaniak | Pontianak |
| 62 | 16 and 33 | Maṣṣawā | Masawwa‘ |
| 65 | 7 | Asyūt | Asyūṭ |
| 68 | 22 | Kisrāwan | Kisrawān |
| 70 | 1 and 9 | Jānbulāt | Jānbulāṭ |
| 77 | 34 | Kaẓimayn | Kāẓimayn |
| 77 | 36 | Kirkuk | Kirkūk |
| 77 | 36 | Khanaqīn | Khānaqīn |
| 80 | 37 | Kirkuk | Kirkūk |
| 85 | 36 | Sīvās | Sivas |
| 85 | 38 | ‘Amadīyah | ‘Amādīyah |
| 91 | note 1 | Ābd Allāh | ‘Abd Allāh |
| 93 | 4 | Ghalzā’ī | Ghalzay |
| 93 | 9 | Julfar | Julfā |
| 98 | 3 | (Asfi) | (Aṣfī) |
| 103 | 29 | east | west |
| 106 | 32 | 1628 | 1627 |
| 110 | 27 | Bougeaud | Bugeaud |
| 115 | 15 | Djidjelli | Jijelli |
| 118 | note 1 | "al-Ilj" | "al-‘Ilj" |
| 124 | 34 | *Ṭā’ifah* | Ṭā’ifah |
| 157 | 23 | on the Senegal at Segu and | at Karta on the Senegal and |
| 157 | 24 | Karta | Segu |
| 159 | note 2 | Ḥarazim | Ḥarāzim |
| 160 | 19 and 20 | Fazzān | Fezzan |
| 163 | 28 | now in the Niger Republic), | also written as Gwandu), |
| 170 | 11 | Maṣawwā’ | Maṣawwa‘ |
| 175 | 5 | Barāwah | Barawah |
| 176 | 39 | Barāwah | Barawah |
| 179 | 11 | Mazrū‘is | Mazrū‘īs |
| 179 | 11 | Būshīri | Būshīrī |
| 182 | 19 | recognized | recognised |
| 182 | 32 | Sultan ‘Alī | Sulṭān ‘Alī |
| 182 | note 1 | Ahmad | Aḥmad |
| 190 | 20 | (Chagatāy) | (Chaghatāy) |